Reinventing the University

Managing and Financing Institutions of Higher Education

D1306807

NONPROFIT LAW, FINANCE, AND MANAGEMENT SERIES

Charity, Advocacy, and the Law, by Bruce R. Hopkins

The Complete Guide to Nonprofit Management, by Smith, Bucklin &
Associates

*Developing Affordable Housing: A Practical Guide for Nonprofit
Organizations*, by Bennett L. Hecht

Financial and Accounting Guide for Non-for-Profit Organizations, 5th ed.,
by Malvern J. Gross, Jr., and Richard F. Larkin

Fund-Raising: Evaluating and Managing the Fund Development Process, by
James M. Greenfield

Fund-Raising Regulation Report, by Bruce R. Hopkins

The Law of Fund-Raising, by Bruce R. Hopkins

The Law of Tax-Exempt Healthcare Organizations, by Thomas K. Hyatt
and Bruce R. Hopkins

The Law of Tax-Exempt Organizations, 6th ed., by Bruce R. Hopkins

A Legal Guide to Starting and Managing a Nonprofit Organization, 2nd ed.,
by Bruce R. Hopkins

Modern American Philanthropy: A Personal Account, by John J. Schwartz

The Nonprofit Counsel, by Bruce R. Hopkins

The Nonprofit Law Dictionary, by Bruce R. Hopkins

Nonprofit Litigation: A Practical Guide with Forms and Checklists, by Steve
Bachmann

The Nonprofit Management Handbook: Operating Policies and Procedures,
by Tracy Daniel Connors

Nonprofit Organizations' Business Forms: Disk Edition, by John Wiley &
Sons, Inc.

Partnerships and Joint Ventures Involving Tax-Exempt Organizations,
by Michael I. Sanders

Planned Giving: Management, Marketing, and Law, by Ronald R. Jordan
and Katelyn L. Quynn

*Reinventing the University: Managing and Financing Institutions of Higher
Education*, by Sandra L. Johnson and Sean Rush

Streetsmart Financial Basics for Nonprofit Managers, by Thomas A.
McLaughlin

Successful Marketing Strategies for Nonprofit Organizations, by Barry J.
McLeish

The Tax Law of Charitable Giving, by Bruce R. Hopkins

*Tax Planning and Compliance for Tax-Exempt Organizations: Forms,
Checklists, Procedures, 2nd ed.*, by Jody Blazek

*The United Way Scandal: An Insider's Account of What Went Wrong
and Why*, by John S. Glaser

Reinventing the University

Managing and Financing Institutions of Higher Education

Edited by
Sandra L. Johnson
Sean C. Rush
Coopers & Lybrand L.L.P.

John Wiley & Sons, Inc.

New York • Chichester • Brisbane • Toronto • Singapore

Copyright © 1995 by Coopers & Lybrand L.L.P.
Published by John Wiley & Sons, Inc.

Library of Congress Cataloging in Publ
Reinventing the university
    higher education / [edited and compiled by] Sandra L. Johnson, Sean C.
    Rush.
        p.   cm. — (Nonprofit law, finance, and management series)
    Includes bibliographical references and index.
    ISBN 0-471-10452-3 (cloth : acid-free paper)
    1. Universities and colleges—United States—Administration.
    2. Universities and colleges—United States—Finance   I. Johnson,
    Sandra L. II. Rush, Sean C.   III. Series.
    LB2341.R42   1995
    378.73—dc20   94-45421

SUBSCRIPTION NOTICE

This Wiley product is updated on a periodic basis with supplements to reflect important changes in the subject matter. If you purchased this product directly from John Wiley & Sons, Inc., we have recently recorded your subscription for this update service.

If, however, you purchased this product from a bookstore and wish to receive (1) the current update at no additional charge, and (2) future updates and revised or related volumes billed separately with a 30-day examination review, please send your name, company name (if applicable), address, and the title of the product to:

Supplement Department
John Wiley & Sons, Inc.
One Wiley Drive
Somerset, NJ 08875
1-800-225-5945

For customers outside the United States, please contact the Wiley office nearest you:

Professional & Reference Division
John Wiley & Sons Canada, Ltd.
22 Worcester Road
Rexdale, Ontario M9W 1L1
CANADA
(416) 675-3580
1-800-567-4797
FAX (416) 675-6599

John Wiley & Sons, Ltd.
Baffins Lane
Chichester
West Sussex, PO19 1UD
UNITED KINGDOM
(44) (243)779777

Jacaranda Wiley Ltd.
PRT Division
P.O. Box 174
North Ryde, NSW 2113
AUSTRALIA
(02) 805-1100
FAX (02) 805-1597

John Wiley & Sons (SEA) Pte. Ltd.
37 Jalan Pemimpin
Block B# 05-04
Union Industrial Building
SINGAPORE 2057
(65) 258-1157

ABOUT THE EDITORS

Sandra L. Johnson, MBA, CPA, is a director in Coopers & Lybrand L.L.P.'s National Education Group, which coordinates the firm's services to colleges and universities and informs these clients of current developments in management, finance, taxation, legislation, accounting and reporting.

Ms. Johnson's publications include *Understanding College and University Financial Statements*, *Financial Reporting and Contributions: A Decision Making Guide to FASB Nos. 116 & 117*, in collaboration with other authors from Coopers & Lybrand and Robert Turner from Babson College, and *The Audit Committee: A Key to Financial Accountability in Nonprofit Organizations*. She also has written a chapter in *Measuring Institutional Performance in Higher Education* with Joel Myerson from Coopers & Lybrand. With Sean C. Rush, Ms. Johnson co-authored *The Decaying American Campus*. She also writes the annual *Agenda Priorities* column in the Association of Governing Boards of Universities and Colleges publication, (AGB) *Trusteeship* and articles for the NACUBO *Business Officer* and is the editor of Coopers & Lybrand's quarterly *Higher Education Management Newsletter* and *Nonprofit Management Newsletter*.

Ms. Johnson has conducted workshops on enhancing financial performance for AGB. She is a member of the National Association of College and University Business Officers (NACUBO), the Eastern Association of College and University Business Officers, and the National Center for Nonprofit Boards.

Sean C. Rush, MS, MBA, is the partner-in-charge of Coopers & Lybrand L.L.P.'s National Education Consulting practice. Mr. Rush has over 20 years of administrative, consulting and policy-level experience with colleges and universities, state government, health care institutions and service sector companies. Over his career, he has worked with approximately 100 institutions of higher learning in such areas as administrative restructuring, business process reengineering, stratgeic planning, and financing.

In addition to *The Decaying American Campus*, co-authored with Sandra L. Johnson, Mr. Rush has written numerous articles for NACUBO, and has contributed chapters to *Measuring Institutional Perfor-*

mance in Higher Education and *Productivity in Higher Education*. He has also co-authored, primarily with professionals from Coopers & Lybrand, such publications as *Managing the Facilities Portfolio, Organizational Structure and Responsiveness, Business Process Redesign for Higher Education, Contract Management or Self-Operation,* as well as numerous others. He is a frequent speaker at professional seminars and meetings for the National Association of College and University Business Officers (NACUBO), the Southern Association of College and University Business Officers, the National Association of College Auxiliary Services, and the Association of Physical Plant Administrators of Colleges and Universities.

Mr. Rush is one of eight gubernatorially appointed members of the *Massachusetts Public Health Council.* In this capacity, he is responsible for the development and promulgation of state public health policy and regulations as well as the review and approval of all Determination of Need (DON) application within the commonwealth.

ABOUT THE CONTRIBUTORS

Janet M. Buehler, JD, is a manager for Coopers & Lybrand L.L.P.'s National Tax Services Group located in Washington, DC. She is a facilitator and advisor for client matters, which are referred to the IRS National Office. Ms. Buehler also provides tax consulting and review to complex business transactions for tax-exempt clients.

John A. Fry, AB, MBA, is a partner at Coopers & Lybrand L.L.P. and serves as the firm's National Director for Consulting Services to Higher Education. For over 10 years, he has worked with distinguished colleges and universities in the areas of strategic planning, organizational restructuring and productivity improvement. Mr. Fry has served as an instructor in management at both New York University's Stern School of Business and the Graduate Program at Hunter College of the City University of New York.

David J. Ernst is a managing associate in the San Francisco office of Coopers & Lybrand L.L.P's Higher Education Consulting practice. His specialties are information technology management, strategic planning, and business process reengineering. Mr. Ernst joined the practice after twenty years as a senior administrator and chief information officer at the San Diego and San Francisco campuses of the University of California and at Stanford University. He served on the CAUSE Board of Directors and is a charter faculty member of both the Director and Manager programs of the CAUSE Management Institute.

Kaye B. Ferriter has nearly 20 years of tax consulting experience with Coopers & Lybrand L.L.P. She is currently the tax director for the Healthcare, Higher Education and Not-for-Profit Group in Coopers & Lybrand's National Tax Services, and has primary responsibility for tax services to the firm's tax-exempt clients. She is a frequent speaker at industry meetings of healthcare and educational groups and is co-author of "Taxation" in *Colleges and University Business Administration, Fifth Edition*, NACUBO, 1992. Ms. Ferriter is a member of the AICPA, the Massachusetts Society of CPAs and the American Bar Association (Tax Section), and is a board member of Accountants for Public Interest and the Jane Doe Safety Fund, an organization supporting battered women's shelters.

Janet Fuersich is a partner in Coopers & Lybrand L.L.P.'s Human Resource Advisory Group with primary responsibility for the Human Resource and Compensation Consulting Practice in the New York Metro Region. Currently, she also is working with several organizations to design alternative reward programs that support new organization systems and is involved in designing prototypes for team-based and quality initiatives. Ms. Fuersich is a member of the Society for Human Resource Management, the New York Compensation Association, and the American Compensation Association, for which she also is an instructor in the Certified Compensation Professional Program.

Patrick J. Hennigan, a vice president at Morgan Stanley Group, Inc., manages the firm's Higher Education Group and serves as senior banker to major public and private universities and colleges. He has been a higher education finance specialist for the past twelve years. Mr. Hennigan has served actively with the National Association of College and University Business Officers and the Eastern Association in serving on conference panels and in co-authoring *NACUBO Guide to Issuing and Managing Debt* (1994). He was a professor in the School of International and Public Affairs, Columbia University, and in the Woodrow Wilson Department of Government and Foreign Affairs at the University of Virginia.

Peter Howlett, MA, is a consultant specializing in education management, including the governance of institutions of higher education. An education advisor to Coopers & Lybrand L.L.P. since 1992, he was formerly Deputy Director of the Inner London Education Authority.

Weldon E. Ihrig, BEE, MBA, has been vice chancellor for Finance and Administration of the Oregon State System of Higher Education since 1990. Mr. Ihrig had been Vice President for Finance at Ohio State University for 10 years prior, where he had previously held positions in business, student affairs and computing.

Harvey H. Kaiser, M.Arch., PhD, is currently a senior president at Syracuse University. A graduate architect with degrees from Renesselaer Polytechnic Institute and Syracuse University, he is the recipient of five fellowships for advanced study. Dr. Kaiser is the author of eleven books on architectural historic preservation and higher education administration.

Richard N. Katz is executive director, Business Planning and Practices, at the University of California Office of the President, where he is responsible for directing and supporting the implementation of strategic business and financial management initiatives in the nine-campus UC system. He is a frequent conference presenter, keynote speaker, and contributor to academic and professional journals on management and information technology subjects. He is co-author of CAUSE Professional Paper #8, "Sustaining Excellence in the 21st Century: A Vision and Strategies for College and University Administration."

George Keller, PhD, is a leading scholar of higher education, a noted strategic planner, and an award-winning writer and editor. He served as a faculty member and college dean at Columbia, a presidential assistant at SUNY and the University of Maryland system, and chair of the Higher Education Management Program at the University of Pennsylvania. Dr. Keller is the editor of *Planning for Higher Education*, the journal of the Society for College and University Planning and the author of *Academic Strategies*, an influential book for educators and has written over 100 articles. He is now an education consultant residing in Baltimore.

Jillinda J. Kidwell is a director in Coopers & Lybrand L.L.P.'s Higher Education Consulting Practice responsible for directing the firm's West Coast and Midwest college and university consulting engagements. At Coopers & Lybrand L.L.P., she pioneered the application of reengineering methods to university settings through collaborative projects based on client teams. Ms. Kidwell previously held key administrative positions in admissions at New York University and Tulane University. She is co-author of *Measurement Systems in Higher Education*, a NACUBO Effective Management Series Publication and *Business Process Redesign in Higher Education*, a NACUBO monograph which describes the adaptation of Coopers & Lybrand L.L.P.'s Breakpoint Business Process Redesign^{SM} methodology to the non-profit sector.

William Massy, PhD, is currently a professor of Education and Director of the Stanford Institute for Higher Education Research as well as professor at the Stanford Graduate School of Business. A renowned expert in the field of higher education, he also serves as Principal Investigator, Higher Education section of the U.S. Department of Education's National Center for Educational Finance and Productivity; and as Senior Research Fellow, The Finance Center, Consortium for Policy Research in Education. In addition to his prize-winning book, *Planning Models for Colleges and Universities*, co-authored with David S.P. Hopkins, Dr. Massy's numerous publications include articles such as *"Productivity in Post-Secondary Education: A New Approach"* in *Educational Evaluation and Policy Analysis*, and *"Faculty Discretionary Time: Departments and the Academic Ratchet"* in the *Journal of Higher Education*, and *Endowment: Perspectives, Policies, and Management*, published by the Association of Governing Boards of Universities and Colleges.

Marilyn McCoy, MPP, is vice president for Administration and Planning at Northwestern University, a position she has held since July 1985. She was Director of Planning and Policy Development at the University of Colorado System Office form 1980–1985. Prior to that, she served as Director of the Information for Management Program at the National Center for Higher Education Management Systems (NCHEMS). Ms. McCoy is a past president of both the Society for College and University Planning (SCUP) and the Association for Institutional Research (AIR).

Barry Munitz, PhD, is Chancellor of the California State University System, the nation's largest system of senior public higher education. He began his academic career as a faculty member of the University of California at Berkeley and has served as assistant to Clark Kerr at the Carnegie Commission on the Future of Higher Education, Academic Vice President of the University of Illinois System, and Chancellor of the University of Houston main campus. From 1982–1991, Dr. Munitz served in the private sector as president and vice Chairman of Federated Development Company, a Fortune 200 company.

Richard M. Norman, MBA, is vice president for Administration and Associate Treasurer at Rutgers, the State University of New Jersey. He is responsible for all personnel functions including the overseeing of nine union contracts. He has responsibilities in the financial and operations areas of the University including financial systems, purchasing, auxiliaries, public safety and facilities operations. Prior to his service at Rutgers, Mr. Norman spent 15 years in various positions with the Ohio Board of Regents and Central State University.

David J. O'Brien is the director of the Office of Planning Services at the Stanford University School of Medicine. He received his Masters degree in Health Administration from the University of Washington and has been at the Stanford University Medical Center since 1981. Since early 1994 he has lead a project team studying the Medical School's administrative costs and alternative models for its administrative organization.

William S. Reed, MPA, is currently vice president for Finance and Administration at Wellesley College. He has previously held senior level administration positions at Williams College, Princeton University, and the Ford Foundation. Mr. Reed has served as Chair of the Massachusetts SPRE Standards Development Advisory Group.

ABOUT THE CONTRIBUTORS

John R. Sack, as director of the Stanford Data Center, is responsible for support and operation of institutional information systems at Stanford University, including administrative and library information systems. A major goal for his organization is the implementation of accessible, university-wide systems and services that deliver information in an open, client/server environment, migrating from the current terminal-to-host mainframe architecture.

Norman R. Smith, EdD, MBA, is in his seventh year as president of Wagner College. He has been a college administrator for nearly 25 years. Before Wagner, he was assistant dean of the Harvard Graduate School of Education and assistant dean of the Harvard John F. Kennedy School of Government. Currently, Dr. Smith is on the Executive Committee of the Board of Trustees for the New York State Coalition of Independent Colleges and Universities and is also a member of the Board of Directors of Anchor/Dime Savings Bank.

James F. Sullivan, MS, PhD, was vice chancellor of Administration at the Davis and Riverside campuses of the University of California for 18 years. He had also been an associate professor in the Graduate School of Management at U.C. Riverside and Dean of University Extension for 10 years at U.C. Davis. Retired in 1991, Dr. Sullivan currently does occasional consulting, teaching and writing.

Quentin Thompson, MSc, has headed the education consulting practice of Coopers & Lybrand, UK for the past decade. He has led many national studies covering policy and management of higher education and has worked with over fifty institutions of higher education. A former advisor on education to the United Kingdom government, Mr. Thompson has also worked directly in the education sector.

Robert M. Turner, MS, MBA, DBA, is an assistant professor of accounting and holds the Lowell Schulman term chair at Babson College in Wellesley, Massachusetts. Previously, he has taught at Boston College, Boston University, and LeMoyne College in Syracuse, New York. He had also been director of Financial Aid at Boston College and associate dean of Admissions and Financial Aid. The author of numerous articles on financial reporting, primarily on the nonprofit sector, Dr. Turner has recently written a monograph for Coopers & Lybrand L.L.P. entitled *Financial Reporting and Contributions: A Decision-Making Guide to FASB Nos. 116 & 117*.

Julia Tyler is currently administrative director of the MBA program at London Business School. Previously, she was a senior consultant in the

Education and Training Group at Coopers & Lybrand, UK, providing consulting services to the higher education section.

Kenneth D. Williams, CPA, is a higher education partner at Coopers & Lybrand and is the associate chairman of Coopers & Lybrand L.L.P.'s National Higher Education and Not-for-Profit Group. His responsibilities have encompassed accounting, auditing and consulting services to a broad range of public and private clientele, with primary emphasis on higher education. Mr. Williams is currently the chairman of the AICPA's Not-for-Profit Organization Committee and has also served on the AICPA Practice Review Committee.

Acknowledgements

The Editors wish to very sincerely thank the contributors of this book. We owe them our deepest gratitude. They are dedicated professionals who gave willingly of their time and experience in the hopes that their work might assist others in higher education. Without their important contributions, *Reinventing the University* would not have been possible.

Each of the contributors spent countless hours researching and writing their chapters. Many of them asked others to review their work. We owe these numerous individuals a special debt as well.

The Editors want to particularly thank our assistants, Kim Johnson and Tina O'Rourke, at Coopers & Lybrand L.L.P. Their indomitable spirits and dedication to their work contributed greatly not only to this book but to every project they undertake.

We also wish to thank Clark L. Bernard, the Chairman of Coopers & Lybrand's National Higher Education Group, for his invaluable help during this project. His support was especially important to the completion of this book.

Finally, we owe a special thanks to our editor at John Wiley & Sons, Inc., Marla Bobowick, and her able assistant, Victoria Hofstad, and associate managing editor, Maggie Kennedy, for guidance and encouragement at each step towards the publication of *Reinventing the University*.

Foreword

America's system of higher education, with its 3600 institutions, is the most valued in the world. Yet the academy has never been more criticized and more vulnerable, both in terms of its financial health and its public image. Higher education must confront its detractors directly, recognizing that some of their criticism is valid. Colleges and universities are expensive; many of our institutions could be better managed; they can—and must—adapt to new ways of thinking and behaving.

College and university presidents play key roles in helping our institutions change. We set the tone, establish the priorities, and are ultimately responsible for the results. It is no easy task, but there are few more important ones if America's higher education system is to continue to live up to its reputation. Our administrations need to be open to new ways of doing "business." There are new revenue opportunities to explore, "best practices" to implement in managing institutional assets, and tools to help restructure our administrative operations.

Reinventing the University: Managing and Financing Institutions of Higher Education is an important book for leaders of academic institutions. It addresses the reinvention of our institutions to become more service-oriented, less costly, and better positioned for the future. This book provides valuable information on how to accomplish these objectives. The authors who contributed to this book are recognized authorities in their respective fields; we can learn much from them.

At the University of Pennsylvania, we are confronting these issues. Although the University of Pennsylvania is one of the oldest institutions in America, with good financial security, we believe that no organization today, especially universities, can afford to be complacent. Continuous re-evaluation and improvement is a necessity in our fast-paced world. I recommend this book to college and university presidents, senior administrators, business officers, trustees, and to those professionals who serve higher education. It explains the latest financial and management tools for higher education in clear language; it is well researched, well presented, and thought-provoking.

Higher education is one of America's most important assets. We

■ xvii ■

must do everything we can to continue to improve it and to preserve it for this generation and for those generations to follow.

Dr. Judith Rodin
President
University of Pennsylvania

Preface

Change has dramatically confronted higher education in the last decade, challenging it to its very roots. Colleges and universities have been rocked by a volatile economy, changing demographic trends, weakening public opinion, lagging state and federal support, and other forces. Some institutions are directly confronting the changing environment; others are more reluctantly considering adaptation. Although they struggle with how best to do it, most institutions perceive that changing the way they have traditionally financed and managed their activities is critical to their survival. *Reinventing the University* has become a necessity as well as a "buzzword" in the industry. Minor changes, tinkering around the margin, are no longer adequate.

In many circles, change—and *reinventing* the university involves the most fundamental change—has been given a bad name, and it truly is not easy for us to cope with either as individuals or as institutions. But the more we cling to the notion of permanence and the more we resist change, the less likely we are to see the creative opportunities it presents. A firestorm raging through a forest seemingly destroys everything in its path. But out of the debris, new, stronger growth emerges. Not everything was destroyed; the seeds of life survived, and in fact, the forest was cleansed and revitalized by the fire.

We need to think of reinventing higher education in a similar way. Change is good, cleansing, and revitalizing; it presents new opportunities we either could not see or that did not previously exist. Who would have imagined twenty years ago that colleges and universities would be embracing business process reengineering and other forms of restructuring? Who would have imagined the new revenue opportunities some institutions are discovering? Who would have imagined their focus on such tools for adaptation as establishing mission statements, engaging in strategic planning, and linking planning efforts to budgeting?

Not only can change be revitalizing, it is an inevitable fact of life. As a philosopher once said, "Nothing is permanent but change." It is to higher education's benefit to accept change and to embrace reinventing the enterprise before change—in the form of even more government regulation and accountability to a myriad of agencies and society in general—is forced upon our institutions. Here, higher education might learn from health care—reinvent, adapt to society's needs and expectations, listen to your "clients" and "customers"—before the government further intrudes.

However necessary reinventing higher education is and however positively we frame the notion of change, it shakes us to our roots as individuals and as institutions. Like the fire raging through the forest, the idea of reinventing higher education can be terrifying. Once change is embraced, new ways of doing things eventually emerge, but there is a period of great upheaval and turmoil before the transformation begins. This is where higher education is today—in the midst of the turmoil before the new institution takes shape. Such a critical period in higher education's evolution calls for strong, visionary leadership to point the way to the future and to set the tone for continuous change. As Peter Drucker has noted, "the modern organization . . . must be organized for the systematic abandonment of whatever is established, customary, familiar, and comfortable, whether that is a product, service, or process; a set of skills; human and social relationships; or the organization itself. In short, it must be organized for constant change."[1]

Although we may no longer be able to escape from change as a given in life, there are tools to help institutions use change positively, as the cleansing, revitalizing force it is meant to be. A key tool for a college or university is its "core values," the most critical values under which an institution operates, its core philosophy. Widely known and accepted core values are unifying and grounding for an institution around which its leaders can proclaim to the internal community and external customers and clients: *This is who we are.* The institution that knows its core values is better able to understand the shifts and demands of its environment; it is better equipped to reinvent itself and to make continual improvement an accepted way of institutional life.

There are other necessary tools for reinventing the university, and the objective of this book is to present "best practices," the most innovative thinking by recognized authorities, and critical tools for managing and financing higher education *now* to best position it for the *future*. The underlying premise of *Reinventing the University* is that as our world changes so too must higher education if it is to position itself successfully for the new millennium. We believe a sea change is in the making, demanding a new vision for America's 3,600 institutions of higher learning. Each chapter in this book presents historical and current trends, the most practical and cutting-edge guidance available, and thought-provoking, insightful ideas about what the future trends are likely to be.

---

[1] Peter F. Drucker, "The New Society of Organizations," *Harvard Business Review*, September–October 1992, p. 96.

Reinventing the University is presented in six sections:

Part I: Introduction

This chapter, "Searching for Solid Ground," establishes the context for the book. It presents its theme: external market forces as well as internal institutional issues call for reinventing the enterprise and for a new vision for managing America's institutions of higher learning in a financially viable fashion.

Part II: The Challenges of Institutional Change

The four chapters in Part II focus on meeting the challenges of change at a college or university. Change management requires several ingredients: understanding the current climate, having a vision of the future, leading the enterprise towards the future, and learning the tools for change. Each of these ingredients is discussed in this section of the book.

The first chapter, "Managing Transformation in an Age of Social Triage," compares the hard-nosed reallocation of resources and politically sophisticated priority setting that colleges and universities need to employ today to the health care environment. In a medical emergency, a key individual sets the priorities for care in an environment where total needs far outstrip available assistance. The second chapter, "Governing Change," discusses the role of governing boards, presidents, and senior administrators in the change process. The third and fourth chapters, "Leading Transition" and "Rethinking the Academy's Administrative Structure," present an overview of administrative restructuring, tools for the restructuring or reengineering process, and a case study of restructuring at the Stanford University School of Medicine.

Part III: Funding the Enterprise

Higher education's revenue streams are increasingly constrained while its costs continue to rise. These facts have been widely reported and are not new. However, some institutions are broadening their revenue streams by exploring creative, new sources. Others, particularly smaller private institutions, are reviewing their current revenue sources, and coming to some difficult necessary conclusions: tuition is by far the major source of revenue and for this reason, tuition policy must be carefully reviewed and continually monitored.

The two chapters in Part III discuss institutional revenue streams, the first from the public university system perspective and the second from the tuition-dependent, private institution perspective.

Part IV: Managing Institutional Capital

This section of the book addresses five major areas of institutional capital: endowment, debt, human resources, facilities and information technology. Like the chapters in Part III, these chapters present practical guidance for trustees, presidents, senior administrators, and other institutional managers on how best to manage institutional capital. In short, increasing demands are being placed on an institution's endowment (for those fortunate enough to have this resource), debt (for which there are a greater number of increasingly complex tax-exempt and taxable vehicles), employees (who are being asked to do more, often in fewer numbers), and facilities (which have been neglected in the last few decades and for which a major capital infusion is now needed), and information technology (which is critical to the process). Strategic choices must be made about how best to use and manage endowment, debt, people, and facilities and information technology. These five chapters present the necessary tools and information.

Part V: The Trend Toward Greater Accountability

There are growing demands for accountability from our institutions of higher learning. The government and its agencies, the public to whom the government responds (and answers), and technical standard-setting bodies are initiating these demands. Why is there a trend towards greater accountability? The short, and most obvious answer, is that colleges and universities receive funding from many sources, and especially in financially constrained times, resource providers want to make sure their monies are being used wisely and responsibly. As the public sees tuition rising and accessibility to higher education becoming more limited, more and more questions are raised.

The longer answer is that all of America's institutions, leaders, and even its values are facing greater societal skepticism. The 1990s is not a time of heros. No sooner does a "hero" appear than we learn some dark, tainting secret. America's colleges and universities are no longer the organizational heros of our culture. Once highly praised, they are increasingly viewed with skepticism.

Part V presents four chapters, the first, "Transformation of Education in the United Kingdom," discusses the changes to higher education in the United Kingdom, mostly involving growing demands for accountability, and compares that system of higher education in the United Kingdom to that of the U.S. The second, "Assessing Outcomes: The SPRE Initiative," talks about the recent State Postsecondary Review Entities more commonly known as SPREs, the latest form of accountability American colleges and universities may face. Standard-setting bodies, the Financial Accounting Standards Board and others, are also focusing greater attention on higher education and other types of not-for-profit organizations and the underlying reasons and some concrete examples of their demands for accountability are presented in Chapter 15. The last chapter in this section, "The Question of Tax Exemption," discusses why colleges and universities were granted tax-exempt status (with its substantial benefits) and possible threats to that status.

Part VI: Epilogue

Reinventing the University concludes with a chapter by George Keller on "Creating a Vision for the Future." Dr. Keller argues that a strategic plan with vision provides a great incentive to action. Colleges and universities need a vision to respond to the new environment and to prepare for the future, to bind together the separate elements of many campuses, and to circumvent fierce discussions about the details of immediate reallocation of resources.

Our contributors represent a wide variety of professional backgrounds. Many presidents, chancellors, or very senior administrators at public or private institutions; a few specialize in serving colleges and universities at Coopers & Lybrand L.L.P.; one is a professor at Babson College whose research specialty is accounting and reporting issues for higher education; one is an investment banker specializing in structuring debt for colleges and universities, and several are widely recognized and prolific authors on higher education management issues. All are "thought leaders" in their respective fields. Although the editors have worked closely with the contributing authors, each chapter represents the viewpoint of the contributors.

American higher education stands at a crossroad, poised to enter the new millennium in just a few short years. While it is the most highly respected educational system in the world, it is being challenged on many fronts both from within the academy and externally in the eyes of the public and society at large. How will American higher education confront its challenges? Will it emerge from the firestorm weakened or revitalized? We believe the latter. Too much is at stake for colleges and universities to simple drift forward towards the year 2000. The time has come for higher education to change, confronting directly and boldly its management and financial challenges. We hope this book contributes to a better understanding of the issues at hand and some of the tools needed to reinvent the university from a managerial and financial perspective.

Sandra L. Johnson
Director, National Higher
Education Group of
Coopers & Lybrand L.L.P.

Clark L. Bernard
Chairman, National Higher
Education Group of
Coopers & Lybrand L.L.P.

Contents

PART I: INTRODUCTION   1

Chapter One   Searching for Solid Ground   3

Sean C. Rush
Coopers & Lybrand L.L.P.

**PART II: THE CHALLENGES OF
          INSTITUTIONAL CHANGE**   19

Chapter Two   Managing Transformation in an Age of   21
Social Triage

Barry Munitz
California State University System

Chapter Three   Governing and Administering Change   49

Marilyn McCoy
Northwestern University

Chapter Four   Leading Transition   79

John A. Fry
Coopers & Lybrand L.L.P.

Chapter Five   Rethinking the Academy's   101
Administrative Structure

Jillinda J. Kidwell
Coopers & Lybrand L.L.P.

David J. O'Brien
Stanford University School of Medicine

CONTENTS

PART III: FUNDING THE ENTERPRISE   127

**Chapter Six   Revenue Opportunities for the   129
Public Institution**

Weldon E. Ihrig
Oregon State System of Higher Education

James Sullivan
University of California Riverside (Retired)

**Chapter Seven   Strategies for Optimizing Revenues   147
in the Tuition-Dependent Institution**

Norman R. Smith
Wagner College

PART IV: MANAGING INSTITUTIONAL CAPITAL   167

**Chapter Eight   Endowment Management in a   169
Global Economy**

William F. Massy
Stanford Institute for Higher Education Research

**Chapter Nine   Managing Debt in Changing   185
Financial Markets**

Patrick J. Hennigan
Morgan Stanley Group, Inc.

**Chapter Ten   Developing, Not Controlling,   209
Human Resources**

Janet Fuersich
Coopers & Lybrand L.L.P.

Richard Norman
Rutgers University

**Chapter Eleven   Facilities Management: 229
Preserving the Past, Building the Future**

Harvey H. Kaiser
Syracuse University

CONTENTS

**Chapter Twelve   Organizational and Technological   251
Strategies for Higher Education in the Information Age**

David J. Ernst
Coopers & Lybrand L.L.P.

Richard N. Katz
University of California

John R. Sack
Stanford University

**PART V: THE TREND TOWARD GREATER   277
ACCOUNTABILITY**

**Chapter Thirteen   Transformation of Education   279
in the United Kingdom**

Quentin Thompson
Coopers & Lybrand, U.K.

Julia Tyler
London Business School

Peter Howlett
Coopers & Lybrand, U.K.

**Chapter Fourteen   Assessing Outcomes: 303
The SPRE Initiative**

William S. Reed
Wellesley College

**Chapter Fifteen   Greater Accountability in   333
Financial Reporting**

Robert M. Turner
Babson College

Kenneth D. Williams
Coopers & Lybrand L.L.P.

Chapter Sixteen   The Question of Tax Exemption   363

Kaye B. Ferriter
Coopers & Lybrand L.L.P.

Janet M. Buehler
Coopers & Lybrand L.L.P.

CONTENTS

PART VI: EPILOGUE 379

Chapter Seventeen Creating a Vision for the Future 381
George Keller
Former Chair of the Higher Education Management Program
University of Pennsylvania

Introduction

Chapter One
Searching for Solid Ground

Searching for Solid Ground

SEAN C. RUSH

Coopers & Lybrand L.L.P.

1.1 Introduction   1.3 Today's Challenge
1.2 Some Historical Perspective 1.4 The Challenge of Change

- *Murphy's Law*: If anything can go wrong, it will. And at the worst possible time.

- *O'Toole's Corollary to Murphy's Law*: Murphy was an optimist.

1.1 INTRODUCTION

If American higher education in the 1990s were the judge, old Murphy would, indeed, be considered an optimist. Although there is much right about higher education in the United States, much has also gone wrong (or at least become more visibly wrong) during the past several years. After 40 years of phenomenal post–World War II growth in enrollments, programs, facilities, and public esteem, colleges and universities have become mired in a sargasso sea of unprecedented challenges. Demographics, funding cuts at the state and federal levels, tuition price pressure, government investigations, athletic scandals, and souring public opinion have all combined at one time to place enormous stress on our nation's thirteenth largest industry.

The challenges facing higher education are neither transitory nor benign. The front burner issues—accountability, access, affordability, efficiency, outcomes, quality—question the very nature of the enterprise. Much of that questioning is coming from outside the academy. Pundits, politicians, parents, students, employers, the media, and others have joined an ever-growing chorus of educational critics and commentators.

Many *within* the academy would argue that the critics do not understand how a college or university works. Those *outside* the academy would offer the counterpoint that *the academy* does not know how the "real world" works. Therein lies the crux of the problem . . . a basic and growing mismatch between public expectations and higher education's response to those expectations.

It is all too easy to jump on the bandwagon and join the critics in lamenting the decline of American colleges and universities. Our society has become quite adept at challenging its institutions, icons, and heros, systematically tearing them down but not rebuilding and replacing them. Higher education is no exception to this societal cynicism and has joined the growing ranks of the pilloried. However, athletic and research scandals, large tuition increases, high costs, and numerous other issues all provide wonderful grist for the public opinion mill and fuel for the growing criticism.

This is not to say that higher education should be immune from criticism—far from it. Like many organizations, colleges and universities have much in need of change. For families and students who are incurring considerable debt to finance an education, concern not only about the cost but also about the relevance and quality of the educational experience is justified. For a society seeking an educated, skilled, and employable populace, questions about the effectiveness and efficiency of higher education are germane. And for federal and state taxpayers, who directly and indirectly fund many aspects of higher education, scrutiny of the return on that investment is appropriate. However, will the efforts to cure the real and perceived problems kill the patient?

In many respects, higher education is at a watershed. On one side are centuries of deep tradition and inertia framed by high public esteem, and a tight historical linkage between higher education and society. On the other side are significant challenges to that history, tradition, and inertia brought to the fore by dramatically changing social demands and growing public uneasiness. In between, on increasingly muddy ground, stand our colleges and universities attempting to change to meet new and rising expectations. To succumb to tradition and inertia may, as E. Gordon Gee, president of Ohio State University, points out, cause institutions to "become dinosaurs in an academic Jurassic Park."[1] To change will require enormous acts of potentially career limiting leadership. To stand still means sinking only deeper into the mud. How and when colleges and

---

[1] E. Gordon Gee, "Universities must be the architects, not the victims, of change," *Springfield (Ohio) News Sun*, August 21, 1994, p.2.

universities search out more solid ground will largely determine the future of higher education in the United States.

1.2 SOME HISTORICAL PERSPECTIVE[2]

The linkages between American society and its colleges and universities run long and deep. The nine colonial colleges—Harvard, William and Mary, Yale, New Jersey (Princeton), King's (Columbia), Philadelphia (University of Pennsylvania), Rhode Island (Brown), Queen's (Rutgers), and Dartmouth—all evolved from a society in which religion, the state, and commerce were deeply intertwined. The two earliest colleges, Harvard and Yale, emerged from the strong assumption by Massachusetts Puritans and their sectarian counterparts in Connecticut that the church and the state shared common interests. Similar assumptions would prevail in the founding of the seven other pre-Revolutionary colleges, albeit with different religious orientations. Baptists, Quakers, Presbyterians, Congregationalists, and Dutch Reformed all founded colleges in a wave of denominational rivalries.

Religion, however, was not the only reason behind the founding of these early institutions. Underlying the creation of these colleges was a need for social order. In his history of the U.S. college and university, Frederick Rudolph writes about the mission of Harvard: "[A] religious commonwealth required an educated clergy, but it also needed leaders disciplined by knowledge and learning, it needed followers disciplined by leaders, it needed order. For these purposes Harvard was absolutely essential."[3] It was through education, the collegiate founders believed, that civilization in the New World would prosper. Rudolph continues:

A college develops a sense of unity where, in a society created from many of the nations of Europe, there might otherwise be aimlessness and uncontrolled diversity. A college advances learning; it combats ignorance and barbarism. A college is a support of the state; it is an instructor in loyalty, in citizenship, in the dictates of conscience and faith. A college is useful: it

---

[2] This historical perspective is drawn from three excellent books: *The American College and University: A History*, by Frederick Rudolph (Athens, Ga.: The University of Georgia Press, 1962); *The Soul of the American University*, by George M. Marsden (Oxford: Oxford University Press, 1994); and *Academic Strategy*, by George Keller (Baltimore: The Johns Hopkins University Press, 1983).
[3] Rudolph, *The American College and University*, p. 7.

helps men to learn the things they must know in order to manage the temporal affairs of the world; it trains a legion of teachers. All these things a college was. All these purposes a college served.[4]

The ties among church, state, and college were extremely strong. The Massachusetts General Court used the Charlestown Ferry rents to support Harvard. William and Mary benefited from a Virginia tobacco tax. Yale students were absolved from taxes and military service. Despite this financial support, however, the colonial colleges still maintained a degree of independence, be it by the composition of their boards or through their curricula.

Yet for most colonial Americans, a college education was not essential. As Rudolph points out: "The college had long been a necessity for society, but it had not become a necessity for the people. The college was clearly a source of political leaders, but not everyone aspired to be a leader. The college sustained a literate . . . ministry, but many Americans could get along without any ministry at all. For most colonial Americans, college was something that could wait."[5] Indeed, by 1776, one hundred and forty-six years after the founding of the first college, there were only 3000 living graduates of American colleges.

The Revolutionary War and its democratic ideals significantly changed the link between college and state. Religious tolerance, individual freedoms, and a rising tide of democracy spawned hundreds of new colleges in the late eighteenth and nineteenth centuries. Like their predecessors, some of these colleges were religious in origin. Others were founded by local citizens in such places as Maine, Pennsylvania, South Carolina, Ohio, Tennessee, and Indiana. In the former case, the religious institutions were the product of a missionary movement that sought to bring Christianity to "the West." In the latter case, religious sectarianism was replaced by local provincialism. Each state and territory wanted its own college and university so that its citizens would not have to go elsewhere to receive an education. Whatever the reasons, a college-founding mania enveloped the United States. Higher education had become an important social investment.

With increasing frequency, higher education also came to be recognized as an important personal investment. As America began to shift from an agrarian to an industrial society during the nineteenth century, the traditional notion of collegiate education came to be challenged. Historically, colleges had decided what was important for their students

[4] Ibid., p. 13.
[5] Ibid., p. 22.

to learn. The classical curriculum based on ancient truths became profoundly influenced by the emergence of the natural and physical sciences and, ultimately, technical and scientific education. The convergence of a growing industrialized society, and technical and scientific education, proved to be a boon to the personal fortunes of students as well as to the country. A raft of specialized colleges and institutes were founded by people such as Ezra Cornell, Johns Hopkins, Stephen Van Rensselaer, and others. Engineering, biology, geology, botany, and chemistry became, in addition to the humanities, subjects worthy of study. The Morrill Land Grant Act also provided support for state and territorial institutions with a practical, career-oriented curriculum. Now higher education served not only society but individuals as well. Higher education was not only socially necessary but, with increasing frequency, personally and economically necessary as well.

The history of American higher education is rich and deep. In chronicling it briefly in these pages, our intent is to point out the historically strong connection between institutions of higher learning and the nation's changing and growing social needs. Ironically, though, it is apparent that change has not come easily to colleges and universities. Over the past 300 years, much of the growth and innovation in higher education has come about through the *addition* of new institutions, not through the *adaption* of existing institutions. This should not be construed as a blanket statement that established institutions cannot and have not changed. All of them have transitioned from their historical roots and will continue to do so. However, change has historically come about quite slowly to U.S. colleges and universities.

The early religiously oriented colleges were created by various Protestant sects, often in reaction to the theological or pedagogical activities of other institutions. Specialized scientific and technical institutes were created because established institutions were slow to embrace the rapidly evolving natural and physical sciences in their humanities-focused curricula. Catholic institutions such as Notre Dame and Boston College were founded because growing numbers of immigrants did not have access to a college education. Women's colleges were founded in response to the fact that women could not matriculate at virtually all colleges and universities in the nineteenth century. Historically black institutions were founded for similar reasons. Community colleges were founded to expand the availability of collegiate experience to new groups and growing numbers of people.

In each of these cases, the higher education *industry* as a whole has demonstrated remarkable responsiveness and adaptability. However, within the industry, *individual institutions* have proven themselves to be less prone to significant changes. As Rudolph points out:

Resistance to fundamental reform was ingrained in the American collegiate and university tradition, as over three hundred years of history demonstrated. A historian of the University of Rochester described the traditional policy of his institution as one of "wise conservatism modified by a spirit of liberal progressivism when warranted by circumstances." This was also, except on rare occasions, the historic policy of the American college and university: drift, reluctant accommodation, belated recognition that while no one was looking, change had in fact taken place.[6]

Historically, much of the change in American higher education has occurred incrementally and at the margins. In most cases, the industry's response to changing social needs has been to add a new institution (scientific, women's, Catholic, black, etc.). At the institutional level, a dogged adherence to traditional beliefs and approaches has resulted in a "hunker down" response. "Experimentation," says Rudolph, "which was the life of the university, and innovation, which was its gift to society, were seldom tried upon the colleges and universities themselves. Their timidity prevailed."[7]

1.3 TODAY'S CHALLENGE

America's present 3600 colleges and universities are a far cry from the nine original colonial colleges. All nine continue to operate in a much larger and dramatically more complex fashion. Two (Rutgers, and William and Mary) are now publicly supported institutions. The other seven colleges, along with Cornell, comprise the Ivy League. These original institutions, and the several thousand other institutions founded during the past 200 years, form a higher education system unparalleled in the world. As noted earlier, higher education is the nation's thirteenth largest industry, enrolling 14 million students, spending $160 billion annually, and employing several million faculty and support staff. By virtually all measures, it is both a big business and a social necessity.

Yet, despite all the dazzling research, the vast public service initiatives, and the millions of students, numerous cracks and fissures can be found in higher education's foundation. Moreover, the ground it stands on is shaky at best. Public opinion about higher education has become increasingly negative as questions are raised about its costs and the quality of both its education and graduates. One need only read *U.S.*

---

[6] Ibid., p. 491.
[7] Ibid., pp. 492–493.

News & World Report's "1995 Annual Guide to America's Best Colleges" to understand how such public opinion is being shaped. Referring to institutions as "pedagogical Luddites," the article states:

> Like it or not, colleges and universities are, in fact, labor-intensive enterprises that operate in high-cost environments and produce a human product that promises to remain in heavy oversupply for the foreseeable future. Moreover, without the charity of alumni donors or taxpayer subsidies, many of these enterprises would be forced to shut their doors. Given the fundamentals, no amount of downsizing, restructuring, or tinkering at the economic edges will alter the disheartening outlook.
>
> Indeed, nothing short of an entirely new vision of the educational process will enable the large majority of schools to control costs, thereby easing the growing tuition strain on students.[8]

In the same article, the magazine calculates a "Tuition Freedom Day," the number of days in a calendar year a middle-class wage earner needs to work to pay for a year's tuition, room, and board at an average private or public institution. For a private college in 1974, tuition freedom day was March 14. By 1994, it was May 2. The "freedom days" for a public institution were February 4 in 1974 and February 14 in 1994. With such "wonderful" press, it is not surprising that public opinion may be running against colleges and universities.

Compounding the problem of public opinion, colleges and universities are beseiged by a number of internal stresses that are equally harsh and threatening—and just as difficult to address. Budget deficits and downsizing are becoming the norm as institutions contend with tuition price pressure, financial aid demands, cutbacks in research funding and reductions in state appropriations. Capital needs are enormous. The industry as a whole has a nearly *$70 billion* backlog of deferred maintenance on its physical plant and a significant need for investment in technology. Faculty productivity is being called into question, with many among the public believing that senior faculty research too much and teach too little.

Adding to the dilemma is a rapidly changing external environment. The globalization and volatility of our economy, the aging of the American population, the growing ethnic and racial diversification of our society (one-third of all Americans will be members of minority groups by the early part of the twenty-first century), family incomes that have not kept pace with inflation, and the continuing technological revolution all add to

[8] Mel Elfin with Andrea R. Wright, "America's best colleges," *U.S. News & World Report*, September 26, 1994, p. 88.

the melange of issues facing higher education in the 1990s. The combination of internal challenges and external change provide the seeds, if not the full-grown trees, of potentially significant problems for higher education.

In the midst of all the tumult, one key question must be asked: What does society need from higher education? That is precisely the question several leading private foundations asked a working group of educators, policymakers, and business leaders to examine. In early 1993, the Wingspread Group (named after the Johnson Foundation's facilities) invited 32 essayists from diverse social, professional, and economic perspectives to consider the question. Those essays and the conclusions of the group contained some stark advice for higher education. Several excerpts from the Wingspread report quickly give one the gist of its findings:

> A disturbing and dangerous mismatch exists between what American society needs of higher education and what it is receiving. Nowhere is the mismatch more dangerous than in the quality of undergraduate preparation provided on many campuses. The American imperative for the 21st century is that society must hold higher education to much higher expectations or risk national decline. . . .
>
> These conclusions point to the possibilities for institutional decline given that an increasingly skeptical public expresses the same sense of sticker shock about college costs that is now driving health care reform. The withdrawal of public support for higher education can only accelerate as students, parents, and taxpayers come to understand that they paid for an expensive education without receiving fair value in return. . . .
>
> The 3,400 institutions of higher learning in America come in all shapes and sizes, public and private. They include small liberal arts institutions, two-year community colleges, and technical institutions, state colleges and universities, and flagship research universities. In each of these categories, models of both excellence and mediocrity exist. Despite this diversity, most operate as though their focus were still the traditional student of days gone by: a white, male, recent high school graduate, who attended classes full-time at a four-year institution and lived on campus. Yesterday's traditional student is, in fact, today's exception.[9]

This is tough stuff, no doubt about it. The report's criticism is harsh, attacking the very foundation of the academy. Although new concerns are not raised, those that are—the quality of undergraduate preparation,

[9] *An American Imperative: Higher Expectations for Higher Education*, Report of the Wingspread Group on Higher Education (The Johnson Foundation, Inc., 1993), pp. 1–3.

sticker shock about college costs, and an enterprise organized to serve traditional students—have been echoed by others. Higher education has not found a way to counter them successfully. But, can it?

In this regard, one excerpt from the Wingspread Group report is particularly intriguing. That is:

> What does our society *need* from higher education? It needs stronger, more vital forms of community. It needs an informed and involved citizenry. It needs graduates able to assume leadership roles in American Life. It needs a competent and adaptable workforce. It needs very high quality undergraduate education producing graduates who can sustain each of these goals. It needs more first-rate research pushing back the important boundaries of human knowledge and less research designed to lengthen academic resumes. It needs an affordable, cost-effective educational enterprise offering lifelong learning. Above all, it needs a commitment to the American promise—the idea that all Americans have the opportunity to develop their talents to the fullest. Higher education is not meeting these imperatives.[10]

This comment seems remarkably similar to the philosophical underpinnings of the earliest colonial colleges: "A college develops a sense of unity . . . is a support of the state . . . an instructor in loyalty, in citizenship. . . . " Have colleges and universities truly wandered so far afield from their founding missions? Or has society changed so much that higher education can no longer deliver as much as it once did? And why has America's system of postsecondary education, once the subject of so much praise, now come under so much criticism?

The Wingspread Group report raises other, related questions. One of its writers, journalist John Gallagher, discusses the age-old question of how practical an education should be:

> That question is one of the fault lines running beneath higher education, with two great traditions pushing up against each other. One tradition argues that the pursuit of knowledge for its own sake creates fully-rounded men and women with sharp enough minds to succeed at anything they attempt. The other tradition contends that pursuit of practical knowledge, particularly the scientific, sharpens minds as effectively as the study of Greek and Latin, and addresses the broad needs of the people.[11]

Sound familiar? Remember those nineteenth-century institutions that were founded because the natural sciences had not been embraced by

---

[10] Ibid., p. 2.
[11] Ibid., p. 77.

the established institutions? After 350 years and the creation of 3600 institutions, the same basic questions are being asked about the role and purpose of higher education, raising the concern posed earlier from a slightly different point of view: Can higher education really be expected to "create fully-rounded men and women with sharp enough minds to succeed at everything they attempt"? And given the challenges and complexities of today's world, can higher education—or any organization—truly address "the broad needs of the people"?

Another Wingspread writer, Robert M. Rosenzweig, former president of the Association of American Universities, with his tongue firmly in his cheek, responded to the question of what society wants from higher education as follows:

- Broad access to some kind of postsecondary education for any student who wishes to try.

- Some degree—here the expectations vary widely—of acculturation and preparation for citizenship.

- A credential that is useful for occupational purposes and the training that the credential implies. The former is sometimes more important than the latter, but the credential should be available for a large and ever-growing menu of occupations.

- New knowledge, especially in science and technology, with the expectation that some, though perhaps not all, will have useful economic or other social benefits.

- Advanced training for those professionals—doctors, lawyers, scholars, for example—whose services are essential and whose training had better be all that is implied by the license they receive.

- Service to the community through outreach programs that may take a variety of forms, such as continuing and postprofessional education, agricultural extension, and its contemporary cousin, technical extension.

- Mass entertainment on a large scale, primarily through programs of intercollegiate athletics, made available to the public not merely through the opportunity to buy a ticket and attend an event, but through the opportunity to stay home and watch the games on television for nothing.

- All of the above at a low price, whether measured in tuition charges or taxes.[12]

[12] Ibid., pp. 132–133.

Throw in the delivery of a world championship to beleaguered Chicago Cubs and Boston Red Sox fans and, it would seem, you have the complete institution. Is there anything society does *not* want from higher education?

Lost in the current debate about what society *needs* from higher education is an equally important question: *What is the appropriate role of a college or university in our society today?* As we have suggested, not all that is needed and wanted by society can realistically be provided by higher education. Although higher education can play an important role in societal change, responsibility for the dissolution of families, the erosion of K-12 education, the growing gap between rich and poor, and the loss of shared values must be borne by a number of social institutions, including organized religion, government, and business. However, until the growing mismatch between societal expectations and higher education's performance is reconciled, neither will prosper.

The key to that reconciliation is something that colleges and universities have not historically done well: *change*. Higher education must learn to listen and communicate well. Where appropriate, it must adapt and change in response to its surroundings. In other instances, it must hold the line on challenges that would imperil freedom of inquiry and thought. However, in all cases, it must be ready to *change* while remaining both a part of and apart from the ebb and flow of social tides.

1.4 THE CHALLENGE OF CHANGE

Thus far, change in higher education has been an evolutionary, not a revolutionary process. It has been achieved in increments and, often, at the margins. Fundamental alteration to the status quo has been viewed with all the anticipatory pleasure of a root canal. However, even with a bad tooth, the pain eventually becomes great enough that the procedure is performed. Dispite the discomfort of the drilling, the patient is better for having done it.

Some would argue that the pain is not great enough to bring about the fundamental change that many believe is necessary in higher education. Unless a "crisis" is at hand, colleges and universities, like all organizations, will resist the call to change. Until then, stasis and incrementalism will prevail. Others would point out that the radical change espoused by many critics is unnecessary. Yes, the academy has some warts, but overall, the system works quite well. Shifting gears on a continual basis will cause institutions to be whipsawed by the mercurial nature of public opinion. Both arguments have their flaws. To wait until there is great pain before changing places institutions in a perpetually reactive mode. To ignore public opinion and expectations would be a tragic mistake.

The public (tuition payers, taxpayers, grant makers, gift givers) makes an enormous investment in higher education. And like it or not, the public is a customer of higher education. The consumer lexicon is filled with such words as *value* and *quality*, which are now applied to all organizations, including higher education. Until a better connection is made between what colleges and universities actually do (not just what they say they do), and what society needs (not just what it wants), higher education will continue to stand on shaky ground.

Unlike the past, when new institutions were established to meet unmet social needs, America can no longer afford to create new colleges at the margin. In many respects, higher education is at overcapacity or, at least, suboptimally distributed throughout the country. Adding more capacity will only exacerbate the problem. If new institutions cannot be added at the margin, the spotlight shines ever so brightly on *existing* institutions and their ability to examine and change themselves accordingly. If they cannot, in all likelihood, it will be done for them. As E. Gordon Gee, Ohio State's president, points out: "Ideally, universities should initiate this process of self-examination. But that is not always the case. Nonetheless, we are realizing that we must be architects of change, rather than victims. We must shape our own destinies aggressively, or policy makers will do it for us. And that would be to the detriment of the future and the quality of higher education."[13]

Not much time may remain for fundamental change to occur in higher education. Our society, and thus its needs and expectations, are changing at an ever-quickening pace. As Peter Drucker notes in *Managing for the Future: The 1990s and Beyond*, "In a crafts society, which ours essentially was until late in the nineteenth century, major changes occurred perhaps every 80 years. . . . Today . . . it is probably every 60 days."[14] Given this, it would seem that institutions would be well advised to begin the change process now—and to find ways to integrate the idea of change into the institutional culture. Continuous change is likely to be an increasingly important part of institutional life in the future. As Drucker notes, "the modern organization . . . must be organized for the systematic abandonment of whatever is established, customary, familiar, and comfortable, whether that is a product, service, or process; a set of

---

[13] Gee, "Universities must be the architects," p. 22.
[14] Peter F. Drucker, *Managing for the Future: The 1990s and Beyond* (New York: Truman Talley Books/Dutton, 1992), p. 339.

skills; human and social relationships; or the organization itself. In short, it must be organized for constant change."[15]

In the absence of self-initiated change, higher education does not have to look very far to gain an appreciation of what a governmentally regulated world might look like. The U.S. health care system has undergone a radical transformation during the past 25 years, all in the interest of controlling costs, achieving greater access, and improving accountability. Efforts are still under way to provide universal coverage for all citizens. Any physician will tell you that the practice of medicine has changed dramatically during that period. Checks and balances on the performance of tests and procedures abound. Insurance companies and government agencies have significant clout in the medical decision-making process. Review boards, preferred provider organizations, health maintenance organizations, and numerous other entities have transformed the way in which health care is delivered. Whether it is better or worse is the subject of another discussion. What is noteworthy is that the health care system and the industry have changed, albeit reluctantly. Activities and choices that had once been the almost exclusive province of physicians are now shared among government regulators, insurance companies, doctors, and to some extent, the consumer.

Looking a bit further, the United Kingdom offers another view of government regulation. Although a different country and a different culture, it provides an insight into some of the characteristics of higher education with large-scale government involvement (see Chapter 13 of this book). Tenure has been eliminated for all new academics. Performance-based compensation is encouraged. Funding incentives are provided to universities to make them responsive to the needs of industry and commerce. Undergraduate tuitions are paid by the government. Research activities are assessed with funding directly linked to the quality of work. Not all of this is applicable in the United States. But some of it could be.

Can American higher education examine and change itself? If history is any guide, change will come about reluctantly and slowly. Higher education's culture and governance mechanisms are simply not predisposed to change. In Chapter 2 Barry Munitz, chancellor of the California State University System, makes the following observation:

> [Some] scholars seriously question whether it is even possible to lead a contemporary university in the traditional collegial fashion when building

---

[15] Peter F. Drucker, "The new society of organizations," *Harvard Business Review*, September–October 1992, p. 96.

consensus around people and programs to be eliminated is virtually un-avoidable. The cynical observation of greatest concern is that our current governance structure allows faculty groups to stop others from bringing change, but they cannot derive and put forward proposals that eliminate colleagues and their classes. On this delicate matter, time will actually tell, but the clock is ticking ever louder.

One school of thought within the academy maintains that institutional priorities emerge from individual and departmental initiatives not from presidential vision and leadership (see Chapter 17, in which George Keller offers this and alternative ideas). Under this model, presidents focus more on management of the "business" than on obtrusive visions imposed on the academy. This "custodial" approach flies in the face of the change being demanded and, in some ways, is the cause of those demands. It is precisely this form of perceived institutional unresponsiveness that has created much of the clamor about higher education.

It also brings to the fore the complaint that many universities have become academic condominiums where individual faculty members pursue their disciplines to enhance their professional standing without regard to the institution in which they work. As William Massy and Robert Zemsky have pointed out: "At work over these more than four (past) decades is an academic ratchet that has loosened the faculty members connection to their institution. Each turn of the rachet has drawn the norm of faculty activity away from institutionally defined goals and toward the more specialized concerns of faculty research, publication, professional service, and personal pursuits."[16]

Massy and Zemsky's comment raises a thorny issue. If colleges and universities are perceived to be disconnected from the society they serve, and if faculty members are disconnected from the institution they serve, is it any wonder that higher education has a problem? On the one hand, numerous critics are challenging higher education to change and improve on several fronts. On the other, some faculty would contend that "It ain't broke, don't fix it." Let us continue our work and, in the long run, it will all work out. In between stands institutional leadership, namely the president, trying to play Solomon.

Somehow, through divine intervention or otherwise, strong, visionary leadership must emerge from within higher education. This leadership (at both the industry and the institutional levels) must achieve a number of goals:

---

[16] "The lattice and the ratchet," *Policy Perspectives*, The University of Pennsylvania, Vol. 2, No. 4, June 1990, p. 5.

- *Communicating* the uncountable tangible and intangible benefits already provided by colleges and universities to our society in a credible and accountable manner;

- *Listening* to public opinion and criticism, correcting it when it is misinformed and pleading *mea culpa* when it is on the mark;

- *Acting* on the problems and concerns by bringing about appropriate, constructive institutional change;

- *Leading*, to the extent possible, their institution by crafting a vision that links the institution and its faculty to current and future social needs.

Accomplishing any of the foregoing goals would be cause for euphoria. Achieving all of them may, in fact, require an act of God. Leading an institution and its faculty is a bit like trying to herd highly intelligent cats. It might be accomplished but not without some clawing, scratching, and hissing along the way. Yet the circumstances demand exactly this kind of leadership, action, listening, and communication.

A great football coach once said: "The best defense is a good offense," meaning that if you have the ball, the other team cannot score (unless, of course, you fumble it). Higher education is on the defensive on many fronts. *But it still has the ball*. Mounting a solid, credible, and responsive offense is the only feasible alternative. To turn the ball over to external policymakers and pundits would be an abdication of responsibility, and more important, an abandonment of higher education's vital role in society.

Higher education, indeed any organization, is unlikely to find truly solid ground in the future. The notion of solid ground probably was always a myth in organizational life. Change is occurring so rapidly now that if solid ground ever existed, higher education is not likely to reach it again. Perhaps that is where the real lesson lies: Strong, visionary leadership is needed to ready the academy for change and to institutionalize continuous change.

Despite all that is visibly wrong with higher education today, we must also not forget all that is right. With a little bit of luck, Murphy's Law will not prevail. With even more luck, we may find out that Murphy never passed the bar.

PART TWO

The Challenges of Institutional Change

Chapter Two
Managing Transformation in an Age of Social Triage

Chapter Three
Governing and Administering Change

Chapter Four
Preparing for Administrative Restructuring:
   A Strategic Approach

Chapter Five
Rethinking the Academy's Administrative Structure

Managing Transformation in an Age of Social Triage

BARRY MUNITZ

California State University System

2.1 The Challenge of Change

2.2 Historical Context

Expanding Access

The Challenge We Face Now

The Age of Triage

2.3 Where We Are Now

Public Expectations and Attitudes

Restricted General Revenue

Price Versus Access

Public–Private Partnerships and Fund-Raising

A Look at Expenditures

2.4 What Must We Examine?

Value and Reward System

2.4 Leverage and Constraint Mechanisms

Aid and Affordability

Public Accountability

Use of Technology

2.5 Leadership–Management Questions

Finding and Rewarding the New Executive

Executive Evaluation and Accountability

Unmentionables on the Table

2.6 Conclusion: We Are Still a University

Ignorance is not a lack of knowledge but the map of our condition, the tragic field we are concentrated in. Lack of understanding is the territory of an illness, a consumption that can't be cured by feeding it the facts.[1]

[1] Kent Gramm, *Gettysburg: A Meditation on War and Values* (Bloomington, Ind.: Indiana University Press, 1993).

2.1 THE CHALLENGE OF CHANGE

In talking about the State Department, Dean Acheson once commented that they were wonderful at crisis management but uneven day to day, so he hoped that all troubles were sudden and unexpected. As he said, "God help us if they are given time to think."

For those who are managing the twists and turns that are confronting American higher education, there is (whether for worse or, as Acheson might argue, better!) little time left for thinking, planning, or collegial consultation. Radical changes are occurring that will fundamentally alter the nature of the university and the governance model we have followed for the past three centuries. Not only are we testing the basic assumptions, we are also transforming traditional concepts of leadership expectations and management processes.

Adjustments in how universities are administered, how faculty teach and students learn, and how higher education is financed require a dramatically different vision and perspective from college presidents and their board members, deans, and faculty. Those leaders who look solely to the past for answers, embracing nostalgia, possibly inertia, hunkering down, or creative public relations, will be at extreme risk, along with their institutions.

New patterns in the economy, demographics, government spending policies, the use of technology, and the expectations of students and their families assure that higher education will never be the same. Political and corporate America have already responded by fundamentally restructuring the way they operate. We in higher education are only now beginning to face this momentous challenge. To be sure, we have been tested before, but the combinations and intensity of pressure, in a context of shrinking resources and fading public confidence, constitute a genuine crisis. Indeed, one of our problems is that business and elected leaders believe ever more strongly that the pace and intensity of their remodeling dramatically outstrips ours.

Much of the public problem is summed up succinctly and painfully by Thomas Kean, the president of Drew University, former governor of New Jersey, and co-chair of a new panel to study the national investment in higher education. Says Kean: "Here is the reality, plain and simple. Our ivory tower is under siege. People are questioning our mission and questioning who we are. They claim we cost too much, spend carelessly, teach poorly, plan myopically, and when we are questioned, we act defensively."[2]

[2] *Stresses on Research and Education at Colleges and Universities: Institutional and Sponsoring Agency Responses*, Report of Collaborative Inquiry Conducted Jointly by the National Science Board and the Government–University–Industry Research Roundtable, July 1994.

Responding to these public concerns in a productive fashion does not mean that we need merely tell our story more effectively, or that all will be well again if state and federal economies improve. The reality is that the layperson's understanding of higher education—and their corresponding willingness to support it—have changed dramatically, and quite cynically.

2.2   HISTORICAL CONTEXT

Resources available for higher education have traditionally varied with business and political cycles, just as public support and expectations have altered significantly with national and international crises. Government and private-sector funding have generally been linked to significant societal needs. Over the past several hundred years, however, those basic shifts have been relatively few in number, and the transformations associated with them have occurred either with a substantial infusion of dollars or at an almost leisurely pace when compared to current circumstances.

In the earliest stages of American higher education, the focus was on a limited number of small schools that were fundamentally training people for the ministry and the gentlemanly life, in that order. Eight of the original nine colleges founded in the United States were started by churches, and the one that was not—the University of Pennsylvania—later came under Episcopal control. In 1800, Harvard University had a president, three professors, and four tutors.[3]

Expanding Access

The first significant alteration in the structure of higher education occurred during the Civil War with the passage of the Morrill Act and the establishment of land grant colleges. Putting land aside and giving special franchise and license to universities in order to develop the contemporary practices needed for an agrarian society, each state expanded its commitment to study beyond high school. While we commonly (and rightly) think of the Morrill Act as the first effort to expand access to higher education beyond the traditional elite, it also initiated the process of technology transfer from universities to the public, establishing the service mission and bringing advanced lessons into the home. The outreach priority for farmers seeking advice regarding innovative land development and food production led to America's dramatically new concepts of cooperative outreach and extension services.

---

[3] Clark Kerr, *Troubled Times for American Higher Education: The 1990s and Beyond* (Albany, N.Y.: State University of New York Press, 1994).

The next basic transition came at the turn of the twentieth century as Johns Hopkins and a few other postbaccalaureate institutions modified the Germanic model and began to build a graduate research program. These advanced training and application functions reshaped the U.S. role in World War II (most notably in the Manhattan Project and its applications). Not surprisingly, the end of that war brought the next metamorphosis—the passage of the GI Bill, which marked the beginning of a dramatic increase in federal aid to students and further expanded access to higher education by establishing America's universities as the primary vehicle for socioeconomic mobility and professional advancement.

The GI Bill is of special significance because it shifted our view of education from what had been basically, until then, a privilege for relatively few, and turned it into a vested right for very many—an entitlement to go beyond high school, at low cost. For the first time in world history, a college education was available as a dramatic experience to comprehensive cross sections of all social levels. The positive effect of massive access to higher education on the ability of the country to raise productivity and improve its standard of living cannot be overstated, nor can the implications of reimbursement for educational cost in exchange for previous military employment. This monumental government commitment to financial aid—originally as a response to national service—greatly expanded the enrollment of colleges and ensured that the United States had the best educated workforce on earth. Remarkably, this massive increment in support was viewed (accurately!) as an investment, with a profound return to the public sector, not as a charitable commitment.

In her new book on the Roosevelts' domestic political agenda during World War II, Doris Goodwin Kearns notes:

> In 1940, when the average worker earned less than $1,000 a year and when tuition, room, and board ranged from $453 at state colleges to $979 at private universities, a college education was the preserve of the privileged few. By providing an allowance of what amounted to $1,400 a year, the GI Bill would carry more than two million veterans into colleges and graduate schools at a total cost of $14 billion. In the late forties, veterans would constitute almost 50 percent of the male students in all institutions of higher learning. To accommodate the new students, colleges and universities would vastly expand their physical plants. Scores of new urban campuses would be created. Moreover, under the same provision, another three million veterans would receive educational training below college, and two million would receive on-the-job training. Through this single piece of legislation, the educational horizons of an entire generation would be lifted.[4]

[4] Doris Kearns Goodwin, *No Ordinary Time: Franklin and Eleanor Roosevelt: The Home Front in World War II* (New York: Simon & Schuster, 1994).

The president himself emphasized: "Lack of money should not prevent any veteran of this war from equipping himself for the most useful employment for which his aptitudes and willingness qualify him, . . . I believe this nation is morally obligated to provide this training and education."[5]

Shortly after the passage of the GI Bill came the huge research effort driven by a response to *Sputnik*; during the Cold War, our fear of falling behind our adversaries in science drove a massive investment in (and expansion of) research universities. Basic research became a national priority. The essential strategy for according prestige and reward at post-secondary institutions was through faculty research activities, and that constituted a healthy link between society's needs and professional values. Status was endowed by peer assessment, and in most instances, undergraduate quality was a reflection of postbaccalaureate accomplishments. Thus the federal government's objectives in research and what it was willing to fund once again had a fundamental effect on the culture and scope of higher education, without a gap between faculty status and society's expectations and without any perception that sacrifice would be required elsewhere to advance research as a priority.

The Challenge We Face Now

The Morrill Act, the GI Bill, and the research orientation may be the great events that shaped the American university as we now know it, and at first glance the collection of recent events constitutes one additional component of a basically comparable pattern. Particularly in California, the major significance of recent history, however, lies in its fundamental distinction to each of the earlier transformations, which were accompanied by massive infusions of public money and comprehensive public confidence. Now we are threatened by a triage pressure between competing social requirements whose call upon the tax dollar is just as persuasive and with an overall shrinking pool of general revenue resources and political reinforcement. Every other leap—Morrill Act, Germanic model, GI Bill, and post-*Sputnik*—was accompanied by substantial inflows of investment and essential citizen support for that resource priority.

Funding and planning strategies have historically focused on growth, whether it be in quality, functions, or numbers. Even the Great Depression, or earlier dips in state budgets, were viewed as temporary aberrations in an essential upward spiral. Now, faced with a profound challenge to core rationale—driven by changes in demographics, politics, the economy, and technology—universities find themselves in a constrained resource environment that cannot be considered short-term or

[5] Ibid.

shallow. Leadership and management responses, therefore, must focus on selective excellence, expansion by substitution, specialization, radical sharing of expertise and equipment, resource reallocation, and program elimination. The "outside world" wonders why this is so new and strange and difficult, since they are well into confronting the same confluence of events. While academic executives try to explain the unique values and social mores of their world, they must also recognize that without an essential shift in the way we do business, political and corporate confidence will continue to erode.

Pop philosopher George Carlin refers to this type of situation as "vuja de"—one that we have never seen before and hope never to see again!

The Age of Triage

Managing in this restricted environment presents very different challenges for higher education administrators, and therefore also requires different skills and experiences. Presidents and provosts, deans, and department heads ask themselves if they can simultaneously reform and cut back, but in fact they have no choice. One could call this our Age of Triage because it mandates politically sophisticated priority setting and hard-nosed reallocation of resources in a social environment where competing public needs have comparable emotional pulls. Triage at a health center, confronting an emergency where total needs far outstrip available assistance, establishes a sequence for care as one key individual orchestrates the application of harsh priorities. Following that analogy, universities are literally going to face problems as would patients entering a hospital after a catastrophe, examining choices and saying "Well, this is a very serious problem to you, but in fact, you are clearly going to live. I am not so sure this other client will survive though, so I am going to have to take her problem first and then move over to you." Indeed, in this instance, as in war, some will slip away because the wounds are too serious, others will be left to survive on sheer luck, and some will disappear from neglect.

Kenneth Boulding, writing in *AGB Reports*, has noted that "the skills of managing a declining institution are not only different from, but are probably in some sense greater than those required to manage institutional growth. . . . The manager of a declining institution is required to think of more things that haven't been thought of. In a growing institution, the stakes are easily corrected; in a declining institution they are not."[6] Other scholars seriously question whether it is even possible to lead

[6] Kenneth E. Boulding, "The management of decline," *AGB Reports*, September–October 1975.

a contemporary university in the traditional collegial fashion when building consensus around people and programs to be eliminated is virtually unavoidable. The cynical observation of greatest concern is that our current governance structure allows faculty groups to stop others from bringing change, but they cannot derive and put forward proposals that eliminate colleagues and their classes. On this delicate matter, time eventually will tell, but the clock is ticking ever louder.

Frankly, higher education has never been very good at setting priorities in this context, because until now institutions have always been able to assume that "if this is so critical to society, society will invest in its fruition." Even during the Great Depression of the 1930s, although overall budgets were severely limited, the expectation was that short-term constriction would surely be followed by recovery and expansion. Never before have higher education's leaders been told that "to do this, you have to give up that," or "meet this additional objective but prove to us that the traditional services are still necessary." New leadership will be required to manage in this very different environment—these people will come to the table not just equipped with different skills, but protected by different allies and strengthened by different psychological and political alliances.

2.3 WHERE WE ARE NOW

Exhibit 2–1 shows very clearly the spending priorities in California during the 1990s and the drain of funding away from higher education. This trend is not unique to America's largest state. Between 1990 and 1993, public spending on higher education in the United States declined by $7.76 billion (including budget cuts and inflationary loss).[7] Federal spending on education is seriously constrained by the growing pressure of entitlements. (The Bipartisan Commission on Entitlement and Tax Reform reported in August 1994 that by the year 2012, such entitlements as social security, Medicare, Medicaid, and civil service pensions will consume the entire federal budget, leaving no tax money for any other program.[8]) Expenditures in many states have been similarly crippled.

The California State University (CSU) is a prime example of the trauma and challenge faced by many universities. After four years of deep cuts, the CSU would need $950 million in additional funding to return to the same level of enrollment and service that it provided in 1990. That money will not be forthcoming, in part because the share of the state budget spent on higher education has declined by more than 20 percent

[7] *Report of the States* (Washington DC: American Association of State Colleges and Universities, 1994).
[8] Reported in *Los Angeles Times*, August 9, 1994.

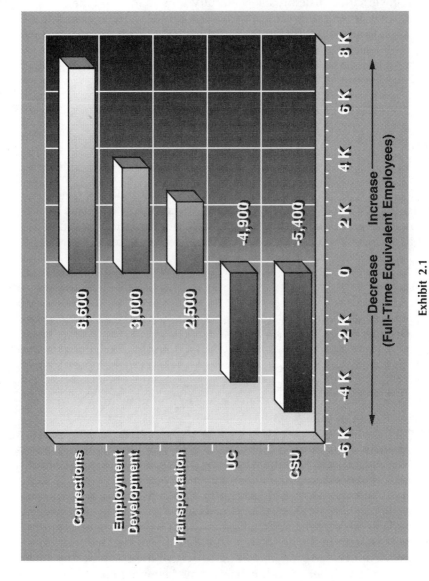

Exhibit 2.1
Change in employment of California State Agencies, 1989–1993

and the state budget itself is now smaller in real dollars than it was four years ago. As a result, 65,000 students who should be on our campuses are not being served, and deferred maintenance and other concerns continue to mount. Legislators and voters have rejected attempts to finance capital improvements. Despite the budget reductions, the institution must begin by protecting quality. That simple but essential commitment requires drastic restructuring, particularly with the recognition that in the very near future we face a huge surge of new students (the children of the baby boomers, whom Clark Kerr[9] refers to as "Tidal Wave II") heading to our campuses and requiring excellent service with fewer dollars.

Public Expectations and Attitudes

According to a collaborative report from the National Science Board and the Government–University–Industry Research Roundtable (GUIRR), higher education faces "an increasingly diverse array of constituents demanding satisfaction for their investment in the nation's colleges and universities." It should be no surprise that the principal forces driving fundamental reconsideration in higher education are external to the university. Clark Kerr, in *Higher Education Cannot Escape History*, has written that universities must "respond to the changing contexts of external society. Much of the history of higher education is written by the confrontations of internal logic versus external pressure."[10] A recent Pew Roundtable report similarly suggests that "no institution will emerge unscathed from its confrontation with an external environment that is substantially altered and in many ways more hostile to colleges and universities. . . . The danger is that colleges and universities have become less relevant to society precisely because they have yet to understand the new demands being placed on them."[11]

Indeed, polling recently undertaken for California higher education in preparation for ballot measures indicates that voters view public universities like they view other public agencies: as a bureaucracy that is wasting a large proportion of their tax dollars. Although once held in special esteem, any immunity that higher education may have enjoyed that protected it from the voter resentment faced by other agencies in the public sector appears to be fading. Correspondingly, a large and increasing segment of voters polled viewed private universities as elitist and out of touch, overpriced, pampered, and irrelevant to the average American.

[9] Former president of the University of California and chairman of the Carnegie Commission on the Future of Higher Education.
[10] Clark Kerr, *Higher Education Cannot Escape History: Issues for the Twenty-first Century* (Albany, N.Y.: State University of New York Press, 1994).
[11] The Pew Higher Education Roundtable, *Policy Perspectives*, April 1994.

At a time when the current president of the United States was a governor chairing its board, the Education Commission of the States reported:

> We sense a growing frustration, even anger, among many of the nation's governors, state legislators, and major corporate leaders that higher education is seemingly disengaged from the battle. Colleges and universities are perceived more often than not as the source of the problem rather than the part of the solution. The issues raised are usually specific: lack of involvement in solutions of the problems of urban schools; failure to lead in the reform of teacher education; skepticism regarding faculty workload and productivity; a lack of commitment to teaching or the escalating and seemingly uncontrollable cost of a college education. But whatever the issue, the overall sense of many outside of colleges and universities is either that dramatic action will be needed to shake higher education from its internal lethargy and focus, or that the system must be bypassed for other institutional forms and alternatives.[12]

Restricted General Revenue

Tax reform has dramatically altered the way the public sector operates, because no longer can anyone predict or project public funding availability with any degree of confidence. Even more essentially, across the country various initiatives, propositions, and referenda have severely limited the amount of revenue that states can raise.

For example, in California,[13] Proposition 13 capped property taxes and transformed support patterns at the city and county levels. Still frustrated with what they saw as gridlock and ineptitude in the management of state finances, voters in California then began to pass a series of initiatives that mandated fixed percentages of state spending for various programs (e.g., earmarking gas taxes for roads, a minimum of 40 percent of the general fund budget for K-12, etc.). Many of the "locked-up" spending guidelines included built-in escalators, which has produced a situation in which the legislature and governor have discretionary control over only 15 percent of the state's budget, and that percentage is decreasing each year. Higher education is in that ever-shrinking discretionary portion, squeezed by its only major competition in that category—corrections. Ironically, in the past half decade our portion of the state budget has

[12] *Higher Education Agenda*, November 1989 (a planning report presented by Education Commission of the States).
[13] Note that throughout this chapter, I will use California as an example because (1) it is the environment in which I operate and, more important, because (2) things that happen in California have a way of spreading to other states.

gone from 13 percent to less than 9 percent, while the portion for prisons has *risen* the same rate, from 4 percent to 8 percent.

In the coming decade, funding for higher education will be under continued pressure. To keep businesses globally competitive, there will be huge pressure against any increases in taxes. Combined with the federal deficit and the growth in entitlements, this means that there is little prospect for an infusion of new public funds such as those that fueled the previous historic changes in higher education. In California, there has been sufficient concern regarding structural restrictions on revenue and expenditures that the political leadership has established a special Constitutional Revision Commission. Charged with examining possible reshaping of the way in which this state raises and spends its money, the commission presents a rare opportunity to address legal impediments to educational support. At the moment, it is very hard to find anyone optimistic about the likely outcome.

With the continued erosion of public investment, the contribution of students and their families to some portion of instructional cost plays a more significant role in higher education's funding equation. The market, in concert with the political process, now shapes pricing and aid policies far more extensively. The tax reform implications for public university's costs and price have led to tense debate around the catch phrase "High Tuition, High Aid." Like many shorthand references, the implications have been severely misleading. The actual question is: Can society afford any longer to subsidize all students regardless of ability to pay, and will increasingly scarce financial aid dollars go to those *qualified* students with greatest need?

Price Versus Access

There are three key ingredients to California's vaunted Master Plan: comprehensive access, for a quality education, at a low cost. With the loss of the state's ability to finance entry at any one of the four educational components (independent colleges, public research, public comprehensive, and community colleges) with dramatic subsidies while maintaining first-rate programs, a key ingredient of the Master Plan has collapsed. This shift must now force a reexamination of how to finance higher education while ensuring access and quality. That general policy review—complete with a reaffirmed commitment to the latter two ingredients—has yet to occur. With many stakeholders, an intensification of media scrutiny, and a fragmentation of political coalitions, a replication of the timely and tight 1959–1960 master planning process is ever less likely.

Like California, many states are running out of the ability and the will to subsidize students who are at the top of the socioeconomic ladder.

The justification for reducing investment in pressing social problems in order to support very wealthy students—of whatever academic skill—is less and less persuasive. An increasing number of national observers argue that the access issue is not one of favoring those who are poor over those who work hard, but rather of selecting those with greatest need from a pool that is *totally qualified*. The issue is not one of price but of *affordability*. Later in this chapter we examine a possible response to this dilemma.

It was Franklin Roosevelt who observed that "the test of our progress . . . is whether we provide enough for those who have too little." As public resources decline, fee and aid policies must be linked to ensure that cost alone does not keep qualified students out of school.

Public–Private Partnerships and Fund-Raising

Once the sole province of private institutions, with some competitive efforts at major land grant research universities, fund-raising is now a critical component in the support of most public institutions. Development can provide a rare source of discretionary funding, and there is for most public universities a growing expectation that some operating budget components will be met through alumni, corporate, and foundation contributions.

So important are these new private partnerships within the California State University that we are now expecting our campuses to raise and earn up to 10 percent of their budgets from external sources (10 years ago this was well under 5 percent across the system, and virtually zero on some campuses), and success at a range of development activities has been formally added as a criterion in the selection and evaluation of our presidents. Although there is nothing unique in this approach, it raises issues of how the fiscal interaction with the state will evolve, how leadership expectations should be adjusted, how management is structured to enhance these new trustee expectations, and how the vital public–private partnerships will affect faculty workload and compensation patterns.

Although fraught with complications, these expanding partnerships hold great promise, not just between public universities and the corporate world (which is a natural link that many campuses have undertaken) but also between public and independent universities. Examples run from sharing the costs of a research facility to collaborative use of technology and joint degree programs. Indeed, cooperative use of resources and collaboration on joint programs should constitute increasingly important considerations alongside more traditional development priorities for all universities in this shrinking resource environment.

A Look at Expenditures

David Reisman has written that higher education becomes more and more omnivorous of resources as it becomes less and less able to elicit community support. Simply stated, high-quality education, particularly in an era of rapidly improving technologies, is expensive and particularly so as it is also more specialized. While internally we can argue that costs are increasing faster than revenue due to tax policies, that quality measures are highly investment sensitive, and that higher education is generally a capital- and labor-intensive enterprise, the public, together with our elected officials, are beginning to demand better explanations of our pricing policies and greater accountability for our outcome and value-added assertions. If the driving principles of cost containment and the investigation of cross-subsidies between levels of instruction are left ultimately to examiners outside the system, less knowledgeable and less sympathetic processes will have a perilous impact on historic academic values.

Influence over Product. The Pew Higher Education Roundtable reports that "parents now ask institutions with growing bluntness, 'what exactly are we paying for?' and they measure the quality of higher education in terms of their children's ability to garner secure, and well-paying jobs."[14] They want to know not only the value added by their investment in education but also worry about a growing gap between the reasons they send personal and tax dollars to an institution and the way in which those funds are actually spent. As they learn about the subsidy patterns for freshman instruction balanced against the teaching assignments for doctoral faculty, their curiosity is intensified. They are not alone in that uncertainty. Legislators across the country are beginning to ask similar questions and express the same concerns.

Perhaps the most intriguing shift occurring in the 1990s is a heightened sense among students, their families, and the general public about what a university education should be. Unlike earlier debates on this topic, the issue now is not only why go to college, but who should decide and who should shape the college experience. A recent poll conducted in California shows that voter priorities for public higher education are not focused solely on academic prestige but rather, are increasingly employment and career oriented in nature. Voters want higher education to train students for jobs and careers, to give young people the opportunity to move up in the world, to provide retraining opportunities for adults seeking new careers, and to improve the economy through a more competitive workforce. Most constituents want socioeconomic mobility and the chance to fulfill the American dream, but they no longer see the

---

[14] Pew, *Policy Perspectives.*

■ 33 ■

accomplishment of that objective tied automatically to the abstract concept of a degree or to a historical interpretation of elite status. Conversations ranging from "school to work" to programs shaped by employers and students (rather than faculty alone) make 1960s discussions of curricular reform look two-dimensional by comparison.

Clark Kerr has issued the most striking and critical prediction regarding the university of the 1990s (in a direct challenge to the more comprehensive institutions): "In general, I believe that the greatest single trend in the reorientation of program efforts within American higher education, as already in Western Europe, will (and should) be toward more emphasis on training polytechnic type skills and toward more polytechnic type applied research and technology transfer. This is where the competitive battles will focus increased attention."[15]

Who Is the Client?   Responding to the changing priorities of our clients (clients identified as the student, the employer, the fiscal patron, and the community at large) will require the earlier mentioned reallocation of resources and redesign of rewards at a delicate "triage" stage. Those watching this pressure from the corporate and political worlds consider us the least willing and the least able to look at such fundamental change. Many consider this ironic—and distressing—since internationally our business leaders are often criticized as conservative and slow moving. Nonetheless, from the American business perspective, the academic world is the least likely to shut something down, turn something off, or ask whether a program could be provided differently. Employers and students expect to be treated as customers and higher education has adjusted slowly to the new customer orientation brought about dramatically by the quality management approaches (such as TQM) employed by so many businesses.

The basic question here may be whether the producers or the consumers should control the nature of the product. In a commercial setting (e.g., automobile manufacturing) the answer would be so clear that the question would be silly. For higher education, where faculty design curricula, set standards, and shape schedules, the issue is far more complex. *What* range of programs, *what* unique facilities, *what* use of space, *what* criteria for evaluation—all very sensitive issues, all subjects of intense debate and scrutiny.

When such analysis is undertaken by various constituents, with fewer dollars to allocate and substantial cynicism about our interest in reform, we are at a severe disadvantage. For example, to demonstrate much greater differentiation of function among the institutions of higher education will require a far more candid and sharper willingness to say

---

[15] Clark Kerr, *Troubled Times for American Higher Education.*

what we do well and what we do not do well, what we should do together, and what we should stop doing. For the polytechnic model to play an appropriate role in society's requirements, senior faculty mentors will have to establish value expectations and professional models that reward and honor the application of knowledge and imaginative classroom techniques for its delivery.

Why have these modifications been so difficult to introduce even though our audiences urge their consideration? The virtually automatic generational cloning of research masters by graduate student apprentices, and the rabid pursuit of research prestige by aspiring liberal arts and comprehensive colleges made it extremely unlikely that our academic governance system opened traditional values to genuine inquiry. Now they must be reconsidered by us, or the current pattern will be altered by others with far less insight and care. We are going to have to learn, as Clark Kerr notes, to "subtract as well as add, to reduce less-useful areas in order to make way for the more useful."[16] More generally, the balance of power between provider and consumer is about to be shaken, and the current national debate over health care may be a startling forerunner of the confrontation awaiting higher education.

2.4   WHAT MUST WE EXAMINE?

> Settlers in the 1870s used to build the schoolhouse before any other public structure; today our states try to fund education with lottos and dog racing. . . . Three of four new jobs will require some postsecondary education (no surprise, considering what secondary education is today), but the skills will not be available. We might find out that dollars depend on learning, on justice, on morals, on character.[17]

Designing strategies for managing change in higher education under even placid circumstances has been compared to herding cats or making a quick U-turn with a supertanker. Without commenting further on those particular metaphors, anyone attempting to guide the movement of a contemporary university will have to examine five major issues:

1. How will we establish a value and reward system consistent with priority goals?

2. What leverage and constraint mechanisms will be required to effect change and improve client orientation in response to consumer and patron expectations?

[16] Ibid.
[17] Gramm, *Gettysburg*.

3. How will price and cost relate to subsidy and access?

4. What should the relationships be between demonstrating public accountability through the reallocation of resources and the measurement of tangible outcomes and the justification for enhanced public and private investment?

5. How will we use technology to improve productivity? Indeed, how will we define productivity in an academic setting?

Value and Reward System

It will be impossible to approach effectively the challenge of overseeing transformation and reassigning resources within the academic community without a serious national discussion of what Ernest Boyer[18] has described as the *prestige ladder*. This is not a new topic, but one on which there is stronger pressure and focus. Creative incentives and sanctions (discussed under "Leverage and Constraint Mechanisms" in Section 2.4) will be required to encourage more than one model of reward for faculty, to legitimize more than one measure of prestige, and to realize feasible alternative paths for graduate student growth.

For many years, national policy leaders have asked institutions to recognize that great teachers are just as important as superb basic researchers. Nonetheless, the concepts of multiple-parallel values and rewards have never taken hold, and as a result—in an era of shifting priorities and limited resources—our public and private patrons, our customers, and our clients are growing restless enough to impose their interpretation of appropriate hierarchy and value upon us. As mentioned above, our leadership strategies will have to include greater respect and reward for those carrying out the highest-priority tasks—defined according to external public interests and requirements, not just internal guild standards and desires.

Leverage and Constraint Mechanisms

No discussion of changes in higher education's operations can be undertaken without a serious consideration of faculty productivity and the strategies available to strengthen vital aspects of the current academic mosaic. Critics charge us with resisting the application of technology, avoiding measures of accountability, and refusing to discuss the concept of tenure itself. Some argue that the very nature of pedagogy resists productivity improvements. This *perceived* automatic opposition to any

[18] Chairman of the Carnegie Foundation, former U.S. Commissioner of Education, and chancellor of the SUNY system.

basic adjustment in the manner in which faculty function threatens to undermine institutional vitality until the educational community effectively counters such skepticism with tangible examples of how we manage change. University executives know that evidence is available, but they are still struggling uphill against the common indictment that if faculty do as they have always done, society will get no more than it has always had. In response, public expectations must be linked more directly to the criteria for institutional prestige, and faculty rewards must be linked more directly to the highest-priority social requirements. Unless courageous leadership from innovative faculty is recognized more creatively and honored publicly, the tendency to protect traditional turf and defend historical processes[19] will be irresistible—and very destructive.

A leading corporate CEO who has engineered massive restructuring at two of America's largest companies recently described to me the leverage and constraint mechanisms (more often described in the business environment as reward and punishment) necessary to bring about change. He said: "I have concluded that there are three and only three things in the end that matter to those key employees upon whom essential change rests: pride, fear, and greed."

Pride in the value of the institution, fear of relocation or dismissal, and greed for greater personal support are not often the stated considerations when presidents and chancellors attempt to bring about change in a classroom, an educational organization, or an independent or public university. But without candid analysis of how we hire and promote employees, pay and protect faculty and staff, and improve or dismantle programs, there is little hope for establishing a healthier relationship between the social priorities (which trigger public investment) and the way in which colleges and universities do business. For academic employees and their supervisors, what we seek are factors shaping individual behavior, influencing choices, and molding decisions—all directed toward facilitating, not obstructing, transformation. Although their exploration has rarely been invited into polite academic discussions, incentives and sanctions are central to managing change most emphatically when money is tight and competition is tough.

Aid and Affordability

After suffering a severe loss in state support, public universities in California have been forced to raise fees and rethink the manner in which students are subsidized. Thus we arrive once again at the important

[19] As one of many examples, to many public policy analysts the notion that student–faculty ratio is a defensible and comprehensible measure of academic quality grows more questionable with each passing day.

question regarding affordability and access to the university. Historically, the increase in access to higher education has profoundly reshaped our society, and indeed, reshaped our institutions. Just as the earlier infusion of federal money greatly exploded entry to college, revenue limitations and shifting political priorities are becoming a major determinant in reducing access. In this setting it has been surprisingly difficult to adjust the nature of the partnership between public and family contributions, or to identify the proportion of the cost of instruction to be accepted by students. Institutions cannot, should not, simply increase the price just to fill ever-larger gaps in public support, but they must reconsider the nature and balance of subsidies—from each external sector, to each economic class and educational level.

Many opinion leaders will argue that the lower the fee, the greater the access. But when general revenue and tax dollars are tight (as is currently the situation in most states), that simply is not true; the lower the fee when general revenue is held constant, the less money the institution takes in. The less money the university has, the fewer faculty it can hire. The fewer faculty hired, the fewer classes available. The fewer classes available, the fewer students that can enroll and the lower the access to higher education.

To address the affordability issue, universities must develop a more thoughtful and analytical basis for setting fees and for gauging the likely level of public investment (as well as what new expectations must be met in return). At the CSU, our board policy calls for students eventually to pay one-third of the cost of instruction (we will take several years to phase-in this level, which is currently at about 20 percent), with the state subsidizing the remaining two-thirds. To ensure that middle- and lower-income students are not cut off from the university, we are putting aside one-third of all new fee revenue to fund additional financial aid, and reshaping our relationships to local high schools. (A broader issue of K-12 reform is addressed elsewhere.) The amount we receive from the state will then determine our enrollment level, and student fees will go to increased aid and ensuring the quality of instruction. At the same time, our supporters continue to argue vehemently for enhanced financial aid from the state, which is absolutely essential to this equation. Although this strategy might not seem dramatic in some parts of the country, these shifts require intense scrutiny of educational cost and subsidy assumptions and therefore will bring fundamental revisions to California's honored Master Plan.

Public Accountability

As Machiavelli wrote: "There is nothing more difficult to take in hand, more perilous to conduct, or more uncertain in its success than to take the lead in the introduction of a new order of things."

2.4 WHAT MUST WE EXAMINE?

A new era is upon us, one of accountability, and greater accountability must be introduced at all levels of higher education. If there ever was an age when the ideal of a group of scholars engaged in essential discovery and passing along that discovery to others was enough to satisfy corporate givers, legislative bodies, alumnae groups, and students, it does not describe the harsher reality of the 1990s. Not only has the general emphasis shifted from basic and applied research to instruction and service, but inquiries from stakeholders and constituencies now center around outcome measures, value-added components, and market applicability. Even for those institutions made famous by their traditional functions (and they are still vital to the future of America), parents, employers, patrons, and politicians are seeking, and usually insisting upon, quantifiable and verifiable indices of performance and success. Concepts historically foreign to universities, such as academic return on investment and comparative strategic advantage, are creeping or leaping into the vocabularies and skills of contemporary college administrators.

For better or worse, our institutions are going to be held to standards comparable to those that corporations apply to their businesses or that governments are beginning to apply to their agencies. We are not immune from the productivity pressures that already exist throughout the world and will have to be more market responsive in our publications and our offerings. More complexity and greater detail will be expected in our cost accounting and pricing decisions. If colleges and universities are to prosper or even survive in this new setting, we should teach patrons and consumers alike how to measure our performance and show them a sophisticated interaction between concepts of accountability and systems for incentive. At multicampus systems, where a growing number of American students are attending school, concepts of decentralization and performance audits will be essential; the same arguments that higher education is making to state agencies will be made by individual campuses to the system administration. In both cases, systems and campuses will seek flexibility in their operations while offering in exchange performance measures and standards of accountability. Once again, our trustees who lived through recent corporate cycles of complex conglomerates and vertical specialization find our problems in this area mystifying.

In laypersons' terms, if resources are invested by stakeholders and constituents based on specific interests, we must demonstrate how our institutions are responding and whether the employees most responsible for those specific successes are rewarded appropriately. With state universities and major national universities that are state funded always competing for limited tax dollars, an increasing number of questions about subsidy are going to be asked. Just as students and their families want to know what value is added, legislators want to know what they are paying for and what return it has for the community. Those universities that fail to adjust to these changing societal needs in a timely and imaginative manner will be in grave trouble in the coming decade.

Use of Technology

The use of technology holds great promise for keeping universities competitive and greatly expanding access. In terms of price and performance, costs are predicted to decrease by double digits each year for the foreseeable future. Therefore, using technology becomes ever more critical for universities that are squeezed by market pressures on student fees and tax policy. Interestingly enough, the accountability concerns expressed earlier tie directly into technology issues as well.

No one can reasonably expect higher education to be exempt from productivity pressure. Technology has been the most significant component of productivity improvement in other industries (e.g., agriculture and manufacturing). The question at hand is the degree to which technology can aid productivity in a service environment such as higher education and the degree to which the information explosion and the access it provides to data will change the very nature of the university. If we need empirical proof of technology's role in our economy, consider the fact that in 1991, U.S. companies for the first time spent more on computing and communications gear—the capital goods of the new era—than on industrial, mining, farm, and construction machines (Exhibit 2–2). By 1992 the gap between the two had exploded and will continue to widen in the years ahead.

What are the implications of the computer and telecommunications revolution for America's colleges? Some campuses are already beginning to provide some of their department's classes to other universities via video and computer. Every issue of the *Chronicle of Higher Education*, and many of the *Wall Street Journal*, describes outreach innovations and instructional experiments that raise profound but inevitable questions about intellectual property rights, faculty workload, library configurations, compensation priorities, and definitions of residency.

Technology will have an equally complex effect upon institutional planning to meet capital requirements. In an environment of extreme resource limitations, the building of new classrooms can become as problematic as the delivery of instruction. Discussions of capital outlay cannot continue at most universities without a concomitant examination of alternative physical configuration. For example, an interesting opportunity has been created near Silicon Valley by the interplay between cutting-edge technology and defense conversion. California State University is taking over 1500 acres of the old Fort Ord Army Base in Monterey and converting it (with substantial assistance from federal defense conversion funds) into

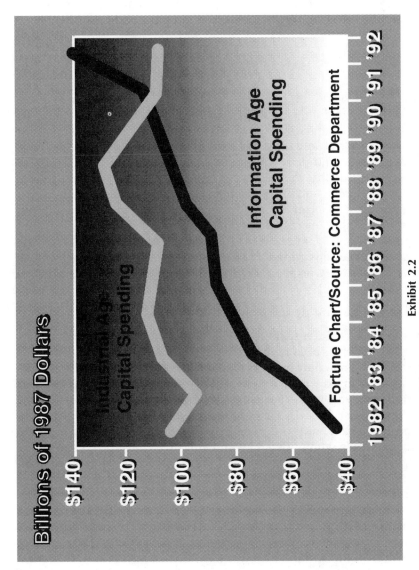

Exhibit 2.2
Rise of the Economy

a new campus. This new facility will be a model of twenty-first-century mechanics, reducing building requirements at the site (by using such things as a robotics-controlled off-site library) while incorporating the technological capacity to reach students across the entire state through a two-way satellite and microwave telecommunications network.

2.5 LEADERSHIP–MANAGEMENT QUESTIONS

To the outside world, in a corporate and political context, higher education has responded quite tentatively to one of its greatest challenges. To our critics, our campuses still look too much the same. Consistent with Governor Kean's observation, we teach many of the same subjects, with the same format and delivery, and hire people the same way. To those who would argue that this very slow moving and stable system protects society from trendy and ill-considered superficial adjustments, the skeptics ask whether we can at least demonstrate a sensible combination of long-term stability and timely transformations. The key question thus becomes how do we preserve our role in society and maintain our essential values while conveying an ability to consider new strategies and to react sharply to new expectations?

Finding and Rewarding the New Executive

Clark Kerr has written that "leadership in the special situations within higher education, is becoming both more important and more difficult."[20] Recruiting and retaining appropriate executive officers and testing different models of management are essential if colleges and universities are to respond creatively to the challenges outlined above.

Unless we acknowledge the requirement to design search processes and professional training programs that bring to our chief executive officer positions people who understand and are comfortable with concepts of public accountability, consumer and client expectations, relationships between pricing and access, and the balance between traditional faculty expectations and contemporary social requirements, we will be unable to keep our academic institutions competitive in this age of triage resource allocation. Trustees tend to prefer leaders with strong management backgrounds; faculty prefer those with scholarly achievements. The only way we will have leaders who are imaginative, courageous, and professionally trained will be to depart from higher education's traditional view of presidential responsibility as "the last bastion of amateur management." Recruitment and assessment committees should acknowledge that sys-

[20] Clark Kerr, *Troubled Times for American Higher Education*.

tematically learning about running a department or a college is a credible and desirable professional objective, that internships with strong presidents can be a marvelous education, that assignments in student and financial affairs—indeed, in corporate or government service—can be as useful as academic affairs training. Career tracks for administration should be driven by design rather than by chance. Otherwise, we doom ourselves to mismatched and ultimately unhappy relationships at too many institutions.

Indeed, one of the reasons why both the corporate and political worlds view college and university management with considerable skepticism is that our institutions tend to undermine those people who set about to learn the major components of university administrative requirements and discuss their leadership ambitions publicly. In a business setting where one deliberately assumes positions in marketing, and then in engineering, or in finance and audit, and then in manufacturing, the issue of leadership development and succession becomes one of extraordinary high priority around the governing board table. At most colleges and universities, a comparable professionalization of academic administration would be frowned upon, many times misunderstood, and far too often criticized as inappropriate to the historical values of university administration. Trustees who simultaneously run their own global conglomerates and serve on academic boards remain baffled by the contrast between these two management worlds.

Kerr refers to the new model of university leader as the "academic statesman." This person works from the same basic goals as an earlier college executive—the proper use of resources, effective policies, consent-driven quality, and reform—but his or her methods of pursuing these goals have changed. The academic statesman is far more out in the open, deals far more with mediation and with political leadership, and indeed, is far more preoccupied with image building and public relations. This new breed of leader is more likely to be in the newspaper and on television than in his or her own office or at the faculty club. They must be capable of marshaling mass support and gaining the public's trust rather than negotiating in private. They must also be found in the middle of messy public debates, balancing social priorities and asserting a strong influence over their institutions. (Although insiders may understand the governance implications, presidents of major universities who tell corporate leaders that they have no real power at their academic institution—that instead, the faculty is powerful—are viewed as either inept or dishonest.)

If we deny the responsibilities of leadership or if we deny the legitimacy of that leadership in the public education arena, we have no reason to believe that others in public and corporate leadership will pay attention to our description of needs and our recommendations for future direction. We cannot have it both ways. The new model of presidential leadership involves people who are willing to take risks, be accountable, sell the university to its many publics, and develop workable leverage and constraint mechanisms to alter the internal structure. They must be willing to ruffle feathers, reconsider the earlier boundaries of academe, and be willing to test the old assumptions with a courageous coherent vision.

Executive Evaluation and Accountability

Looking at one of Cezanne's paintings, a critic once told him, "That doesn't look anything like a sunset." Cezanne reflected on the comment and then replied: "Then you don't see sunsets the way I do." Higher education has to have people at the top who can look at the picture we all know and, like Cezanne, see it differently.

Similarly, governing boards must be willing to look at presidents differently, both when they are selected and as they continue in office. During selection and evaluation, trustees should understand the essential link between how constrained dollars are spent, priorities are established, expectations are understood, and evaluations are undertaken—and in each instance who carries out those assignments. The nuts and bolts of the leverage and constraint mechanism, where relevant and flexible incentives and sanctions determine who we hire, who we promote, how we pay, and in what we invest—all of these administrative tools cry out for imaginative leadership in this Age of Triage.

The need for effective review of university leadership has been a topic of concern for decades, but in this age of multicampus systems and rapidly altered priorities, formal executive assessment serves both professional development and governance review functions. In 1978, Joseph Kauffman wrote: "Our colleges and universities are in desperate need of leadership. Assessment activity must contribute to improve leadership and heightened morale if it is to be worthy of support."[21] In an ideal world, presidential self-assessment might be sufficient, but in the Age of Triage, trustees must review leadership vigorously and publicly—much more creatively and aggressively than they have in the past, and with a greater sense of clarity. The factors that define success must be reconsidered continually—fundamentally for the executive's sake. Recent literature shows remarkable agreement on the key points: There should be objective procedures and criteria; presidents must develop commonly understood policies and priorities with an awareness of new constituencies; they must confirm that internal and external audiences understand the changes occurring within their institutions; they must be at carefully

[21] Joseph F. Kauffman, "Presidential assessment and development," in C. F. Fisher, ed., New Directions for Higher Education: Developing and Evaluating Administrative Leadership, No. 22 (San Francisco: Jossey-Bass, 1978).

considered intervals (in our case, three and six years); and they must translate difficult decisions contemporaneously to professional insiders and lay patrons.

Unmentionables on the Table

Niels Bohr, the influential Nobel Prize–winning physicist, said: "Never make predictions, particularly about the future." Despite that warning, it would be useful to suggest a number of controversial and delicate issues that must be analyzed in the near future if people assuming management positions in our new context are to lead with ultimate success.

Each of these topics deserves a separate chapter of its own, and each is fraught with complication and controversy. Nonetheless, they are lurking below or slightly above the surface of contemporary tensions, and too many academic Titanics will falter on these icebergs if their presence is ignored. As the Pew Higher Education Roundtable sharply notes: "Neither legislative critics nor would-be customers are interested in hearing detailed explanations of why things cost so much, why the processes of research and discovery are so important, or why it is best to do things in the future as they have been done in the past."[22]

1. With all the talk of "virtual universities" and the excitement regarding technology's impact on academic delivery systems and productivity, how will the faculty and administration describe workload and compensation expectations when traditional classroom configurations are competing directly with a variety of public and proprietary inventions to deliver instruction?

2. When many academic institutions—particularly those with faculty members in an organized professional union—consider the traditional value of tenure from both political protection and academic security perspectives, how long will we be able to secure academic freedom without implying comprehensive job security regardless of available resources? Alternatives such as rolling appointments—with or without periodic evaluation—move closer to the bargaining table and the daily life of academic administrators with each passing day. When contracts spell out detailed procedures for laying off tenured faculty at times of economic and/or programmatic distress, it becomes vital to distinguish the traditional tenure protection of academic freedom from the tangible negotiation of employment guarantees.

3. As patrons and clients of higher education inquire pointedly about the nature of their investment and subsidy for academic institu-

---

[22] Pew, *Policy Perspectives*.

tions, and examine more closely whether the returns they are expecting in fact are those of highest priority to the institutions, the traditional balance among instruction, research, and service becomes more tenuous and explosive. As both public dollars and public confidence become more scarce, institutions and their employees jeopardize stable bases of support if they stray too far from the functions most essential to society. Foundation and legislative staffs learn to monitor closely how their dollars are allocated. Roland Schmidt, who chaired the National Science Board and now administers the Mellon Foundation, recently warned: "Trends may signal a shift or a diversification of expectations for the academic enterprise, creating an uncertain system of incentives and rewards for those in the university community."

As stakeholder interests have diversified, the general public and policymakers at the state and federal level are increasingly committed to academic work relevant for job creation and economic competitiveness. It may be time, therefore, for a fundamental reexamination of the relationship between higher education's traditional prestige hierarchy and our constituencies' interest in hiring and rewarding faculty whose interests and expertise are linked more directly to contemporary requirements.

4. A particular dilemma will be faced by those state land grant universities whose extraordinary international research strength has directed public attention more toward their graduate and research training than toward their undergraduate classroom commitment or their relationship to K-12 restructuring. Indeed, Government–University–Industry Research Roundtable leadership indicates that the level of stress and dissatisfaction on our strongest academic research campuses has intensified dramatically even when they have experienced a real growth in financial support. In some states this dilemma has led to serious discussion of the "semiprivatization" of publicly supported graduate research institutions, to balance in a more creative and healthy way basic academic priorities with variable sources of funding. Intrigued by such exploration in Michigan, Virginia, and California, a new national commission of business and university leaders has just been established by the Council for Aid to Education to reexamine the total pattern of funding for higher education.

5. The length of time taken to complete graduate degrees and the time requirements at the baccalaureate level have recently led to a national debate regarding a three-year bachelor of arts degree, as well as cutting back the time for doctoral study. At a time when the dominant student profile is older, of a changing ethnic background and gender, working, and less mobile, the issue may very well be one of greater student control over time to degree, whether or not the consumer takes three or nine years, part-time or full-time, day or night, in the classroom or using technologically based "learning at a distance." The Office of Science and

Engineering Personnel, sponsored by the National Academy of Sciences and the National Academy of Engineering, recently discussed the growing conflict between concern over lengthened time to Ph.D.s and greater interest in broadening graduate curriculum and sharpening instructional skills. The real question in each case is emerging as manifest influence over one's own "time-to-degree destiny."

6. As those interested in national policy confront the diverging goals of stakeholders in the academic system, and colleges face traumatic gyrations in the funding environment, the concepts of "value added" and school-to-work transition increase in importance. The pragmatic, polytechnic attitude toward manufacturing skills, practical training, effect on K-12 education, and general socioeconomic mobility will require meaningfully different definitions and measurements of institutional quality to match scarce dollars with social priorities.

7. Finally, although unheard of in higher education's past, altered consumer demands combined with constrained state and federal budgets may very well lead to the closure of public institutions. Increased attention toward the proprietary sector, as well as technological effect and enhanced market sensitivity, will ultimately force institutions that never contemplated an end to their existence to either adapt their essential core or disappear.

2.6 CONCLUSION: WE ARE STILL A UNIVERSITY

In her keynote address to a National Academy of Science Conference, Mary Good, undersecretary of commerce for technology (and former chair of the National Science Board), argued that "the status quo is not going to be maintained . . . get out there with a vision of the future, not a justification of the past." She called for "some statesmanlike leadership. . . to begin to articulate what the real, appropriate role of the university is in today's society," suggesting to her distinguished audience that "if the service that you provide over time does not satisfy the customer, who is the public, then the customer won't pay."

Despite the dramatic changes that will continue to occur, forcing colleges and universities to reconsider how they do business, much that we have reaped from our institutions will inexorably be maintained, and the traditional missions of discovering, disseminating, and applying knowledge should remain at the heart of our commitments, However, nothing is guaranteed. By choosing courage over convenience and responding creatively to the aspirations of future scholars, learners, and employers, our institutions can prosper while society is served more effectively. In the Age of Triage, conflict is inevitable between competitive instincts to survive and to expand. Those leaders who determine where to find and how to distribute scarce supplies, equipment, and other economic resources must have confidence in higher education's ability to provide and deliver a transformational vision or they will turn to other urgent public priorities.

To ensure their continued health, universities must continue to be forces for improvement in the outside world and significant players in framing a candid debate involving increasingly difficult issues. This task will be impossible unless we simultaneously foster a new generation of leaders who can reposition higher education as a major participant in national policy development with the same degree of confidence that they reposition their universities to meet the pressing needs of students, legislators, and employees. At the very center must always be the faculty. As teachers and as mentors, it rests in their hands to join traditional values with creative new responses and bring forth the twenty-first-century educational institution.

When he was worrying about the dissolution of the British Empire in the postwar era, Winston Churchill said: "The empires of the future are the empires of the mind." If we address explicitly those concerns and expectations lurking treacherously below the social surface, and encourage our faculty and their presidents to speak and work accordingly to their best imaginative spirits, America's universities will be the driving force behind those empires.

Governing and Administering Change

MARILYN McCOY

Northwestern University

3.1 What Kind of Change?

3.2 An American Higher Education System Evolves

3.3 Organizational Models in Higher Education

3.4 Governing Boards
Evolution
Growing Board Influence
Corporate Boards
Higher Education Governing Boards
Composition of Boards
Trustee Roles
Board Effectiveness

3.5 Institutional Leadership
A Delegated Role
Conceptions of College and University Presidencies
Effective Leadership
Theories of Leadership
Transformational Leadership
Creating Readiness
Overcoming Resistance to Change
Articulating a Vision
Generating Commitment
Institutionalizing Implementation

3.6 Maxims of Change

Hard times are producing nothing less than a complete change in the character of our institutions of higher learning. Every aspect of their work is being affected. Their faculty, their students, their organization, their methods, their teaching, and their research are experiencing such alteration that we who knew them in the good old days shall shortly be unable to recognize them. Many of these changes are for the better. Others may wreck the whole system.[1]

3.1 WHAT KIND OF CHANGE?

Today, as in 1933 when Robert Hutchins wrote about higher education in the foregoing quote, hard times have intensified concern about the future mission and operation of our colleges and universities. The litany of financial pressures is well known—the growing costs of the enterprise, tuition charges increasing at rates that significantly exceed inflation, declines in state and federal government support, shifts in charitable giving, slowing rates of investment return, the removal of mandatory retirement in an industry that has granted lifetime tenure to its faculty, and the deteriorating condition of facilities, among others. It is, however, the broader question of trust that is even more compelling—a decline in public confidence in higher education, a sense that higher education has overvalued research at the expense of teaching, visible incidences of research fraud and inappropriate charges, and calls for greater accountability relating to both the efficiency and effectiveness of what institutions do. Chait notes: "Unfavorable attitudes towards higher education are based primarily on questions of purpose rather than questions of efficiency."[2] As Alpert has further noted: "Efficiency is an internal standard, effectiveness an external one."[3]

Kerr attributes the questioning of higher education's traditional governance to increasing litigation, loss of public respect for the conduct of faculties and athletics programs, concern about tuition policy, declining influence of presidents, more fractionalization on campus along ethnic lines, and less consensus about institutional mission.[4] Hansen and Stampen note that "higher education is currently in a transitional period, with a growing emphasis on improving quality after a long period that emphasized equity and access."[5] Anderson and Meyerson also see a

---

[1] Robert Hutchins, 1933, as quoted in Richard E. Anderson, "Does money matter?" *Journal of Higher Education*, Vol. 56, No. 6, 1985, pp. 623–639.

[2] Richard P. Chait, as cited in Anthony W. Morgan, "Resource allocation reforms: zero-base budgeting and marginal utility analysis in higher education," *Proceedings of the Association for the Study of Higher Education Conference*, 1978, p. 32.

[3] Daniel Alpert, "Performance and paralysis," *Journal of Higher Education*, Vol. 56, No. 3, 1985, pp. 241–281.

[4] Clark Kerr, in Richard T. Ingram and Associates, *Governing Independent Colleges and Universities: A Handbook for Trustees, Chief Executives, and Other Campus Leaders* (San Francisco: Jossey-Bass, 1993), p. xvii.

[5] W. Lee Hansen, and Jacob O. Stampen, "The financial squeeze on higher education institutions and students: balancing quality and access in the financing of higher education," *Journal of Education Finance*, Vol. 15, No. 1, 1989, pp. 3–20.

growing focus on productivity and accountability for colleges and universities during the decade of the 1990s.[6]

Throughout all of this, new challenges and opportunities are arising for higher education. The number of high school graduates is projected to grow by 34 percent through 2008, with a growing proportion of minority students among them.[7] Moreover, increasing globalization of all enterprises presents a clear call to higher education to rethink its programs, services, clientele, personnel, and locales. With the availability of highly advanced information technology, there are increasing opportunities to harness technology in the educational and administrative spheres of our institutions. The application of technology to the classroom has been limited to date, but its potential for application raises the specter of significant new competitors entering the higher education market. As noted by Cameron and Ulrich, "without alternative sources of funding it is unlikely that [higher education] institutions will be able to afford the high initial costs [of widespread application of technology]. The competitive advantage is simply being seized by organizations other than colleges and universities."[8]

Changing technological developments, similarly, are important in influencing institutional resource allocation. As Massy,[9] Bowen,[10] McPherson and Winston,[11] and others have noted, higher education, while remaining a labor-intensive industry, is also becoming increasingly capital intensive. However, thus far these changes appear to have added to the cost structure without yielding improvements in productivity. As Bowen notes, "our education may be a constant productivity industry surrounded by others in which productivity is in fact improving."[12]

---

[6] Richard E. Anderson and Joel W. Meyerson, eds., "Financial planning under economic uncertainty," *New Directions for Higher Education*, No. 69, Vol. XVIII, No. 1 (San Francisco: Jossey-Bass, 1990).

[7] Western Interstate Commission for Higher Education, *High School Graduates: Projections by State, 1992–2009* (Boulder, Colo.: joint publication of WICHE, TIAA, and the College Board, 1993).

[8] Kim S. Cameron, and David O. Ulrich, "Transformational leadership in colleges and universities," in John C. Smart, ed., *Higher Education: Handbook of Theory and Research*, Vol. II (New York: Agathon Press, 1986), pp. 1–42.

[9] William F. Massy, "A strategy for productivity improvement in college and university academic departments," paper presented at the Forum for Postsecondary Governance, 1989.

[10] Howard R. Bowen, *The Costs of Higher Education: How Much Do Colleges Spend per Student and How Much Should They Spend?* (San Francisco: Jossey-Bass, 1980).

[11] Michael S. McPherson and Gordon C. Winston, *The Economics of Cost, Price and Quality in U.S. Higher Education*, Williams Project on the Economics of Higher Education, Discussion Paper 13, 1991.

[12] Howard R. Bowen, *The Costs of Higher Education*, p. 196.

Yet, as noted by Zammuto, higher education is more vulnerable to shocks from its environment and less able to take advantage of market opportunities because of a reduction in "slack" associated with recent financial difficulties.[13] El-Khawas indicates that 40 percent of public institutions and 9 percent of private institutions report declines in their annual operating budgets.[14] Another third of these institutions reported only small increments to their budgets. When queried about the cumulative impact of recent financial events, only 29 percent of administrators at public four-year schools and 46 percent of those at private institutions were confident about the financial condition of their campuses.[15]

When higher education's weakened financial condition is viewed together with its inherent structural and cultural attributes, it is apparent that our institutions are not mobilized for change. Shared governance with its attendant consultative style, extensive external requirements and constraints, and the nonhierarchical structure of our institutions all mean that the nature and speed of institutional decision making differs vastly from that prevailing in profit-making entities. Many elements of this profile serve as key strengths of our enterprise. By design, higher education institutions represent the continuity of civilizations and cultures. But when faced with a playing field that potentially includes new competitors in the form of business and other organizations, this traditional style of decision making could represent a dramatic challenge to institutional modes of operation—if not a threat to their ultimate survival.

For most institutions, change occurs through nibbling rather than massive bites.[16] For higher education, the question is whether more familiar patterns of evolution will be sufficient or whether the academy is really confronting a major sea change. This concern has been raised by a wide number of authors, including Cameron and Ulrich,[17] Peterson,[18]

---

[13] Raymond F. Zammuto, "Managing decline in American higher education," in John C. Smart, ed., *Higher Education: Handbook of Theory and Research*, Vol. II (New York: Agathon Press, 1986), pp. 43–84.

[14] Elaine El-Khawas, "Campus trends, 1993," *Higher Education Panel Report*, No. 83, 1993.

[15] Ibid.

[16] Charles E. Lindblom, "The Science of 'Muddling Through,'" *Public Administration Review*, Vol. 19, No. 2, 1959, pp. 79–88.

[17] Kim S. Cameron and David O. Ulrich, "Transformational leadership in colleges and universities."

[18] Marvin W. Peterson, "Contextual planning: preparing for a new postsecondary paradigm," unpublished paper presented at the Annual Conference of the Society for College and University Planning, 1993.

and Simsek and Heydinger.[19] Each of them argues that the changes institutions are confronting are indeed profound, requiring a significant paradigm shift. As characterized by Cameron and Ulrich,

> the fundamental transformation occurring in the broader context in which colleges and universities exist threatens to change the very nature of higher education in America—from particularism to universalism, from monadism to pluralism, from domestic to a global outlook, and from a monopolistic orientation to a competitive one. This fundamental shift in context will have a profound impact on colleges and universities in the future. The basic premise is that a new kind of leadership—transformational leadership—will be required in higher education to adapt to these new conditions. Both the quality of higher education and the survival of the industry in its present form are at stake.[20]

In this chapter we discuss the "leadership" of higher education, concentrating on the governing board, the president, and other chief institutional officers in the context of such evolutionary or revolutionary change.

3.2 AN AMERICAN HIGHER EDUCATION SYSTEM EVOLVES

Higher education in the United States is rooted in very diverse state and regional contexts, influenced by a history of strong public and religious aims. It is reliant on varying sources of funding, and it reflects particular structural and organizational patterns developed to cope with the differing circumstances of each institution. Private institutions were initially financed much like public ones. For example, as noted by Tolbert, "during the colonial period, state governments provided substantial subsidies to private institutions."[21] However, in 1819, their autonomy was clearly established and the states rapidly withdrew their support.[22]

The development of the U.S. system of higher education reflects directly both the federal system of states and the powerful influence of the

---

[19] Hasan Simsek and Richard B. Heydinger, "An analysis of the paradigmatic evolution of U.S. higher education and implications for the year 2000," in John C. Smart, ed., *Higher Education: Handbook of Theory and Research*, Vol. IX (New York: Agathon Press, 1993), pp. 1–49.

[20] Kim S. Cameron and David O. Ulrich, "Transformational leadership in colleges and universities," p. 1.

[21] Pamela S. Tolbert, "Institutional environments and resource dependence: source of administrative structure in institutions of higher education," *Administrative Science Quarterly*, Vol. 30, 1985, pp. 1–13.

[22] Ibid.

missionary movements.[23] These forces led to the creation of a wide range of institutions to address local and religious interests and in so doing created one of the signature characteristics of American higher education: *its diversity*. No other system of higher education embraces such scale and variety. The imperative for each institution was (and still is) to find its own way in the broader context.

Thus from the beginning, institutions benefited from a panoply of potential sponsors and clients as well as purposes to which to commit their energies. This environment created diverse institutional alternatives for students. Since there was not a single model, there were perforce many options. As Rudolph noted, "Americans seem much more desirous that their affairs be managed by themselves than that they should be well-managed."[24] This concern with autonomy and devaluation of managerial efficiency is similarly a key feature of the U.S. system of higher education. Another important characteristic of the academy is its view of college as "an agency of social and economic mobility."[25] Although the specific purposes assigned to higher education shift over time, the casting and recasting of its societal role is significant in affecting the character of institutions and the dynamics they confront.[26]

In marked contrast to the centralized systems of higher education that predominate elsewhere, the American system evolved in very local and specialized ways. Absent reliance on a single governance system and its funding support, institutions in this country had to scramble to survive. And in the process they experimented with novel funding mechanisms (e.g., the support of wealthy individuals), various "business" efforts (e.g., selling electric power, raising silkworms and mulberries), and unusual mechanisms of support by different government entities (e.g., lotteries, granting of lands).[27] In full flower today, there are more than 3000 institutions, with varying degrees of autonomy, a wide web of different governmental and private relationships, focused on very different missions and clienteles, and funded in a rich variety of patterns.

3.3 ORGANIZATIONAL MODELS IN HIGHER EDUCATION

Before the Civil War, most institutions were simply organized, with an average of four administrators: a president, a treasurer, and a part-time

[23] Frederick Rudolph, *The American College and University* (New York: Vintage Books, 1962).

[24] Ibid., p. 35.

[25] Ibid., p. 485.

[26] Clark Kerr, *The Uses of the University* (Cambridge, Mass.: Harvard University Press, 1982); and Marvin W. Peterson, "Contextual planning."

[27] Frederick Rudolph, *The American College and University*.

librarian accounting for three positions.[28] By 1933, this structure had evolved to encompass an average of 33.5 persons.[29] One of the influencing mechanisms was the growth of benefactors in the early twentieth century and the associated requirements of institutional stewardship.[30] But wealthy benefactors represented only one source of funding even then. More recently, the growth of research as a largely federally sponsored enterprise, the assumption of a broad set of roles from health care to technology transfer, and a host of externally imposed regulations have all added to the staffing and organizational complexity of higher education operations.[31]

Clark has characterized universities as "hybrid organizations," given their multiple roles spanning undergraduate, graduate, and professional education, research, and public service.[32] As he notes, "holding these operations together against their strong centrifugal tendencies . . . is an elaborate authority structure, parceled out implicitly and explicitly among multiple stakeholders."[33] McPherson and Winston also note that while most universities are multiproduct, providing many services, "even simpler institutions like community colleges or liberal arts colleges have multiple objectives"[34] and thus they, too, face elements of complexity.

As Birnbaum notes, "governance is not solely an administrative prerogative, but rather a shared responsibility and joint effort that properly involves all important campus constituencies, with particular emphasis given to the participation of the faculty."[35] This point is reinforced by Zemsky, Porter, and Oedel;[36] they describe colleges and universities as inherently decentralized and dominated by horizontal versus vertical relationships. This is so because academic decisions are the domain of the faculty in individual departments and schools. Massy goes further in

[28] Ibid., p. 435.

[29] Ibid.

[30] Ibid., p. 424.

[31] William F. Massy, "Productivity improvement strategies for college and university administration and support services," paper presented at the Forum for College Financing, 1989.

[32] Burton R. Clark, "Higher education American style: a structural model for the world," *Educational Record*, Fall 1990, p. 24.

[33] Ibid., p.25.

[34] Michael S. McPherson and Gordon C. Winston, *The Economics of Cost*, p.3.

[35] Robert Birnbaum, "Responsibility without authority: the impossible job of the college president," in John C. Smart, ed., *Higher Education: Handbook of Theory and Research*, Vol. V (New York: Agathon Press; 1989), pp. 31–56.

[36] Robert Zemsky, Randall Porter, and Laura P. Oedel, "Decentralized planning: to share responsibility," *Educational Record*, Vol. 59, 1978, pp. 229–253.

recognizing that "academic work dictates that many of the tradeoffs between quality and quantity [are] resolved at the level of the individual faculty member."[37] Birnbaum[38] takes it a step further and portrays teaching as a departmental function, research as a faculty and center/institute function, and public service as a shared function among a variety of entities. Zemsky, Porter, and Oedel[39] see the large size and complexity of many universities as incompatible with the development of a consistent set of institutional priorities to guide resource allocation. As a result, institutional preference for market-based and decentralized models is reinforced. However, Perrow,[40] in an opposing viewpoint, argues that universities are far more hierarchical and less collegial than is generally believed.

Among the more salient characteristics distinguishing institutions in the United States is their "control" status as public or independent. Although public and independent institutions operate in a common external environment, they relate to it very differently because of major differences in their internal economies.[41] Fuller notes the greater focus on institutional mission of private institutions,[42] while McPherson and Winston distinguish between the outcomes that public and private institutions achieve.[43] They also note that "quality is a problem in public higher education because student demand matters too little and cost is a problem in private higher education because student demand matters too much." Pfeffer and Salancik see more external constraints on public than on private institutions (as well as on newer and less prestigious institutions of either type).[44] The topic of "control" will be touched upon in both the governing and managerial sections that follow because it is so critical in how these systems function.

[37] William F. Massy, *A New Look at the Academic Department*, published report prepared for the Higher Education Research Program, sponsored by the Pew Charitable Trusts, 1990, p. 21.

[38] Robert Birnbaum, *How Colleges Work: The Cybernetics of Academic Organization and Leadership* (San Francisco: Jossey-Bass, 1988), p. 13.

[39] Robert Zemsky, Randall Porter, and Laura P. Oedel, "Decentralized planning."

[40] Charles Perrow, "Departmental power and perspective in industrial firms," in Mayer N. Zald, ed., *Power in Organizations* (Nashville: Vanderbilt University Press, pp. 59–89.

[41] Katherine H. Hanson, in Richard T. Ingram and Associates, *Governing Independent Colleges and Universities*, p. 38.

[42] Jon W. Fuller, in Richard T. Ingram and Associates, *Governing Independent Colleges and Universities*, p. 23.

[43] Michael S. McPherson and Gordon C. Winston, *The Economics of Cost*, p. 2.

[44] Jeffrey Pfeffer and Gerald R. Salancik, "Organizational decision making as a political process," p. 150.

3.4 GOVERNING BOARDS

Evolution

Until the Civil War, trustees were largely in control of direction setting and decision making at their institutions.[45] From the 1860s until World War I, the number of institutions expanded and the range of their missions diverged, accompanied by the emergence of strong presidents.[46] Kerr then traced the growth of faculty power through the 1960s when state governments began to assert their supervision and control. Kerr sees the current time frame as one in which trustees are again gaining influence.

Growing Board Influence

Kerr is not alone in anticipating a stronger trustee role. Richard Chait joins Kerr in seeing the 1990s as the *decade of trustees,* especially given the turbulence in the external environment for higher education.[47] Similarly, Richard Ingram cites the changing conditions in higher education and notes the value of trustee positions in helping to address the current environment.[48] For example, in an unusual move recently, a group of 36 Goldman-Sachs partners, each of whom serve on one or more college or university boards of trustees, published an open letter in the *AGB Reports* calling for trustees to play a more active role in the restructuring of higher education in the future.[49]

Corporate Boards

The call to action for trustees in higher education mirrors recent patterns of concern about corporate board roles. As part of the restructuring of corporate America, there have been many discussions of needed changes in the role and composition of its boards. A study by Heidrick & Struggles[50] focused on the role and importance of outside directors as well as on improvements to the selection of directors based on their special expertise

[45] Clark Kerr, in Richard T. Ingram and Associates, *Governing Independent Colleges and Universities,* p. xviii.
[46] Ibid.
[47] Richard P. Chait, (1991). "The 1990s: the decade of trustees," in Larry W. Jones and Franz A. Nowotny, eds., *New Directions for Higher Education,* Vol. 70, 1991, pp. 25–32.
[48] Richard T. Ingram, "The end of sanctuary," *AGB Reports,* Vol. 34, No. 3, 1992, pp. 19–23.
[49] Association of Governing Boards. (1992). Higher Education Must Change. *AGB Reports* 34(3): 6–10.
[50] Heidrick & Struggles, Inc., *The Changing Board* (Boston: H & S, 1987).

rather than their general status. Lorsch and MacIver[51] noted an increasing reliance in corporate America on outside directors, a predominant use of CEOs as directors, and a broadening concept of shareholders' interests as well as corporate responsibility. Their study focused on the constraints of directors' powers, notably limited time, limited knowledge and expertise, a lack of consensus on goals, group norms against criticizing the CEO, as well as the strong position of the CEO in the functioning of the board and the selection of directors.

Demb and Neubauer[52] attribute the furor over the relative ineffectiveness of corporate boards to the transitions that are taking place not only in the boardroom but in the wider environment faced by corporations. A January 16, 1994, *New York Times Viewpoint*, "Drawing the Line on Corporate Boards," described results from a Korn–Ferry survey of top executives which showed that 82 percent of them believe that boards will become increasingly critical of management performance. Clearly, each of these commentaries illustrate that as the external environment for profit and not-for-profit organizations becomes more stringent and dynamic, not only is the role of management questioned, but the proper purview and functioning of their boards is under review as well.

That same article went even further, noting that the new challenge may not be sleepy boards but hyperactive ones. While such a cry has not generally been voiced in the private sector of higher education, it is sometimes voiced among members of public institutional boards.

Higher Education Governing Boards

Anticipating many changes and challenges confronting higher education institutions in the foreseeable future, what roles and changes are in store for boards of trustees in fostering constructive change at our institutions? As Kerr has noted, there is no prototypical board in higher education. Governing boards vary in both function and composition, mirroring the diversity of the institutions they represent.

Composition of Boards

The composition of college and university boards has been widely documented. For example, a 1986 profile published by the Association of

[51] Jay W. Lorsch and Elizabeth MacIver, *Pawns or Potentates: The Reality of America's Corporate Boards* (Boston: Harvard Business School Press, 1989)
[52] Ada Demb, and F. Friedrich Neubauer, *The Corporate Board: Confronting Paradoxes* (New York: Oxford University Press, 1992).

Governing Boards[53] noted that boards at private institutions are approximately three times larger than those at public institutions, with the former having, on average, 28 trustees compared to nine trustees in the public sector. This study documented an increasing reliance on business executives as trustees, increasing from 34 percent in 1977 to 41 percent in 1985, with those over age 50 representing two-thirds of trustees. Nearly a third of trustees are alumni of the institutions they serve. The survey highlights that while boards representing multicampuses comprise less than 10 percent of higher education's boards, they govern one-third of all campuses and serve almost exclusively public systems. The survey also showed small gains in the number of women trustees, but not minority members. Trustees in the private sector are largely self-perpetuating boards, while those in the public sector are usually either elected or appointed by the governor or legislature.

Trustee Roles

College and university trustee responsibilities have been widely described in the literature. They can be broadly described as encompassing responsibility for:

- The advancement of the institution

- The protection and enhancement of its assets

- Preservation of institutional integrity

- Fostering effective board/president relations

- Being attentive to the functioning of the board itself

While the foregoing broadly describes trustee responsibilities, it is important to look at the subactivities encompassed within these broad rubrics.

Institutional Advancement. One of the most frequently cited areas of higher education board responsibility is to review periodically the administration's efforts to establish and implement strategies and plans to advance the mission and quality of the institution. It is interesting to note that this is clearly a responsibility for corporate boards as well. Associated with this responsibility are efforts to ensure that the faculty and administration are attentive to the development and sustenance of quality aca-

[53] Association of Governing Boards, *Composition of Governing Boards, 1985* (Washington, D.C.: Association of Governing Boards of Universities and Colleges, 1986).

demic programs that are responsive to changing market needs. The development of a high-quality faculty to carry out these tasks should also be ensured by the board. Another important board advancement task is monitoring the well-being of students, faculty, and staff, assuring the institution's capacity to attract and retain students, faculty, and staff of the highest caliber. In sum, these represent some of the most proactive areas for trustee involvement in looking at how the institution addresses and attempts to influence its role in the external environment. Because board members are drawn externally, they represent a valuable resource to the institution in interpreting and navigating the external environment.

Protection and Enhancement of Assets. The second broad category of board responsibility, protection, and enhancement of assets, is one that is often cited as a primary responsibility for trustees. Particularly in the case of private institutions (and increasingly public as well), maintenance of the real dollar value of institutional endowments and invested funds is considered a key stewardship responsibility of the board. However, it has been recognized increasingly that "assets" should not be confined to financial assets. The quality of faculty, the strength of the institution's student market position, and the condition of its facilities also are key assets for trustee attention.

Other critical responsibilities in this category include trustee involvement in assisting with institutional efforts to cultivate donors, conduct fund-raising campaigns, and obtain contributions from government, corporate, and other sources. They should also assure strong financial management by the administration in meeting current obligations, protecting financial stability over the longer term, and assessing the capacity of operating and capital budgets to support the long- and short-run goals of the institution. Other trustee responsibilities should include reviewing the status and development of the physical assets of the institution, including property use, approval of new construction activity, and the maintenance and renovation of existing facilities.

Finally, a major responsibility of the board is working with the external auditor and the administration to ensure that proper accounting procedures and controls are utilized at the institution. As noted by Johnson, "although the specific responsibilities of audit committees vary, they generally fall within the areas of financial reporting, internal accounting controls, standards of conduct, and financial management."[54] These board committee functions encompass not only the "financial" risks faced by colleges and universities but also their broader "business" risks, such

[54] Sandra Johnson, "The audit committee: a key to financial accountability in nonprofit organizations, (Washington, D.C.: National Center for Nonprofit Boards, 1993), p. 4

as handling of environmental hazards, systems backup and security, and compliance with federal laws.

Preservation of Institutional Integrity. Under the third major category of trustee responsibilities, the preservation of institutional integrity, the board ensures that academic freedom is protected by the institution. In this regard, the board makes sure that the institution remains independent from groups that may try to use the institution for inappropriate political, business, religious, or personal purposes. It also assesses the integrity of the management of institutional programs and assets, including the application of proper fiduciary and conflict-of-interest standards.

Board–President Relations. The selection and, if necessary, the removal of the president are widely recognized trustee responsibilities. The board should also evaluate the president's performance on a regular basis. Finally, and increasingly emphasized in the literature, is the role of trustees to provide input and counsel to the president at their initiative as well as in response to requests by the president. It is in this area that the literature notes a historically greater emphasis on the appointment of the president, and now calls for a parallel degree of trustee involvement in assuring the success of the president, once appointed.

Drawing the line between board and president/administrative areas of responsibility is a sensitive issue and one that has been addressed by higher education researchers. Chait and Taylor[55] repeatedly emphasize the importance of not-for-profit boards focusing primarily on higher policy levels and selectively on executing and monitoring these policies. Cleary[56] also addressed this issue in his survey of board and administrative members of 213 institutions in the Middle Atlantic area. In assessing 16 different decision areas spanning appointments, academic program, budget, admissions, planning, facilities, and selected moral areas, he asked each respondent to categorize the decision areas as either a board or an administrative dimension. His results showed significant areas of agreement, but also enough disagreement on some items to encourage trustees and presidents to examine these matters at length. To avoid potential conflict, trustees and presidents should jointly clarify their respective agendas and areas of purview.

Functioning of the Board. The final major area of trustee responsibility, attention to the functioning of the board, is also receiving increasing

[55] Richard P. Chait, and Barbara E. Taylor, "Charting the territory of nonprofit boards," *Harvard Business Review*, 1989, pp. 44–54.
[56] Robert E. Cleary, "Trustee–president authority relations," in Marvin W. Peterson, ed., *ASHE Reader on Organization and Governance in Higher Education* (Lexington, Mass.: Ginn Press, 1989).

attention in the literature. Especially at private institutions, where the appointment of new members is handled directly by the board, the process of identifying new members is a significant and important responsibility. Once appointed, the board and administration have a shared responsibility to orient new trustees and to foster their effective inclusion on the board. The chair of the board, in particular, should develop future trustee leadership through committee assignments, appointments of committee chairs, and involvement of individual members in the work of the board. Finally, concern with the effective functioning of the board, both in its totality as well as of individual members, is an area receiving greater research attention. Associated with this area are calls for formal reviews of board effectiveness.

Board Effectiveness

Although the literature has strongly emphasized descriptions of board characteristics and discussions of roles, including a wide number of commentaries by knowledgeable parties, there has not been a great deal of analytical work that charts or describes *effective* trusteeship. One notable exception to this is the study done by Chait, Holland, and Taylor[57] representing a significant research-based analysis of boards of trustees in private higher education. Using a sophisticated methodology, the study sought to identify qualities of effective trusteeship. They identified the following six competencies:

1. *Contextual dimension*. The board understands and takes into account the culture and norms of the organization it governs.

2. *Educational dimension*. The board takes the necessary steps to ensure that trustees are well informed about the institution, the professors, and the board's roles, responsibilities, and performance.

3. *Interpersonal dimension*. The board structures the development of trustees as a group, attends to the board's collective welfare, and fosters a sense of cohesiveness.

4. *Analytical dimension*. The board recognizes complexities and subtleties in the issues it faces and draws upon multiple perspectives to dissect complex problems and to synthesize appropriate responses.

[57] Richard P. Chait, Thomas P. Holland, and Barbara E. Taylor, *The Effective Board of Trustees* (New York: MacMillan Publishing Company, 1991).

5. *Political dimension*. The board accepts as one of its primary responsibilities the need to develop and monitor healthy relationships among key constituencies.

6. *Strategic dimension*. The board helps envision and shape institutional direction and helps ensure a strategic approach to the organization's future.

Chait, Holland, and Taylor[58] then dissected and discussed these competencies using specific examples encountered in their campus interviews. In addition, the authors attempted to relate trustee self-evaluation to institutional performance, but could not validate the utility of such self-reviews. The study is one of the most significant in the field for its careful efforts to define and revalidate its findings. In toto, this study defines important roles and cultural dimensions found to be valuable in effective board functioning.

Kerr[59] noted some important differences between public and private college and university boards that define their character. First, he found that private institutional boards are more concerned about the preservation and enhancement of the institution versus the "watchdog" role more typically assumed by public institutional boards. This fundamental difference in orientation is a source of serious dissatisfaction for the leadership of many public institutions. Kerr also found a greater interest in student affairs, educational policy, fund-raising, and investments by private institutional boards. He noted a greater devotion to institutional heritage and that, by the very nature of their independent control, they are less subject to government influence and therefore function in an environment more conducive to decision making. He, nonetheless, feels that volunteer trusteeship is undergoing a stringent test of its viability at the current time, and made four recommendations in this context.[60]

1. The board needs to think and act more strategically.

2. It needs to be better informed.

3. It needs to be a more assertive advocate for the institution.

4. It needs to take a more active and careful interest in assessment of its own activities.

---

[58] Ibid.
[59] Clark Kerr, in Richard T. Ingram and Associates, *Governing Independent Colleges and Universities*.
[60] Ibid., p. xxii.

Ingram,[61] in his introduction, reiterates many of these same points. He cites the need for greater strategic vision, recognition of the importance of restructuring within higher education, involvement in addressing diversity at colleges and universities, acceptance of fund-raising responsibility, greater attention and concern for the position of presidents, and a recommendation of a greater and more proactive role in public policy.

In responding to suggestions that boards of trustees at colleges and universities need to be better informed, Carol Frances and others[62] have developed a compendium of key questions for trustees to assist them in structuring their information needs. Meyerson and Johnson[63] have elaborated on this need, noting that "there are few commonly accepted performance measures set by the market—therefore trustees and executives must rely on self-analysis, noting the satisfaction of key constituents within the institution and the institution's financial stability and public image." The widespread publishing of ratings in the popular press is furthering the interest in quantifiable measures of performance.

In sum, then, current literature on trusteeship appears to be in substantial agreement on the need for a more activist board. This clearly parallels trends in corporate board roles and appears to be reflective of the challenging environments felt in both spheres. In corporate and educational environments, a board can provide a particularly valuable perspective to a college or university through its independence from the institution. Certainly, in comparison to the administration, the board should provide a separate sounding board and source of counsel. Given the clout and expertise often represented on higher education boards, and the diverse environments from which they come, trustees represent a potentially valuable set of connections to the external environment. As institutions attempt to cope with the myriad changes they are facing, and to develop cooperative arrangements and other forms of external strategic alliances, the board, both as a collective and as individual trustees, can be extremely valuable in helping to negotiate and facilitate these venues.

It seems highly likely that higher education will parallel the growing focus in the corporate sector on greater board activism, resulting in a greater involvement in accountability issues. If they were not already engaged in such efforts on their own, college and university boards are being drawn into the accountability mode by federal initiatives setting up

[61] Richard T. Ingram, "The end of sanctuary."
[62] Carol Frances, *Strategic Decision Making: Keep Questions and Indicators for Trustees*, (Washington, DC.: Association of Governing Boards of Universities and Colleges, 1987).
[63] Joel Meyerson and Sandra Johnson, in Richard T. Ingram and Associates, *Governing Independent Colleges and Universities*, p. 81.

state postsecondary review entities (SPREs). As the focus within higher education moves toward greater accountability, it is clear that the board's role in this arena will probably increase and become more clearly defined. Providing a regular set of qualitative and quantitative information to boards so that they can mark the progress of the institution as well as pinpointing areas needing attention is a trend that senior management should anticipate.

Given the perpetual life assumed for most institutions, the board's role in assuring the continued viability of the institution is a critical one. This is particularly true in light of the short terms of office held by many presidents these days, averaging four to seven years. In these situations the board becomes an important point of continuity and guardianship for the institution.

3.5 INSTITUTIONAL LEADERSHIP

A Delegated Role

Although the foregoing discussion has pointed to increasing activism on the part of the governing or coordinating boards of our colleges and universities, it is the president of the institution along with the top administrative team that carries the direct authority and responsibility for institutional leadership. As noted by Fincher, "administrative leadership in American colleges and universities is a direct function of presidential leadership, the personal quality of presidents, and their interpersonal effectiveness with other administrators and leaders within the academic community."[64]

These responsibilities represent a direct delegation of authority from the board or underlying charter of the institution. Birnbaum noted that "there is no standard definition of the presidency, or description of the expectations placed on the performance of its incumbents. Institutional statutes or by-laws commonly identify the president as the chief executive and administrative officer of the board as well as the chief academic officer of the faculty, and delegates to the president, all powers necessary to perform these functions."[65] This latitude in role definition, in combination with the wide variety of institutional types and settings makes it wholly understandable that the conduct of presidencies at institutions would vary widely. Fincher reemphasizes this point, citing Kerr and Gade in their study of the college presidency, in which they refuted "all lingering

[64] Cameron Fincher, "Administrative leadership in higher education," in John C. Smart, ed., *Higher Education: Handbook of Theory and Research*, Vol. III (New York: Agathon Press; 1987), pp. 155–198.
[65] Robert Birnbaum, "Responsibility without authority," p. 33.

notions that college presidencies are unitary positions occupied by universal types of presidents."[66]

Conceptions of College and University Presidencies

According to Birnbaum[67] one simple characterization of the presidential role is to view it as comprised of "internal" and "external" responsibilities. Strategic planning, academic program coordination, and financial management would be among the internal tasks of the presidency, with fund-raising, legislative relations, and alumni interaction among the external responsibilities of the presidency. Quoting from Cohen and March,[68] Birnbaum goes on to offer another view of presidential tasks as having administrative, political, and entrepreneurial components. Birnbaum then notes, however, that presidential activities are, to a great extent, contingent on the characteristics of their institution. In citing Mintzberg,[69] he notes that "the pace, intensity, and comprehensiveness of the presidency are in many ways comparable to those of managers and executives in other settings."[70]

However, he notes that there is a fundamental difference: "On a college campus the exercise of authority and governance is not solely an administrative prerogative, but rather a shared responsibility and joint effort that properly involves all important campus constituencies."[71] The complexity of the role was clearly acknowledged by Cameron and Ulrich in noting: "On the one hand, leaders will require the ability to maintain efficiency, stability and smooth functioning. On the other hand, they will be required to be visionary, discordant, and innovative."[72]

Effective Leadership

Although M.D. Cohen and J.G. March,[73] with their model of colleges and universities as "organized anarchies," were not persuaded by the efficacy

[66] Clark Kerr, and Marian L. Gade, *The Many Lives of Academic Presidents: Time, Place, Character* (Washington, D.C.: Association of Governing Boards of Universities and Colleges, 1986), p. 187.

[67] Robert Birnbaum, *How Colleges Work*, p. 33.

[68] Michael Cohen, and James March, *Leadership and Ambiguity: The American College President* (New York: McGraw-Hill, 1974).

[69] H. Mintzberg, *The Nature of Managerial Work* (New York: Harper and Row, 1973).

[70] Robert Birnbaum, *How Colleges Work*, p. 34.

[71] Ibid., p. 35.

[72] Kim S. Cameron and David O. Ulrich, "Transformational leadership in colleges and universities," p. 11.

[73] Michael D. Cohen and James G. March, *Leadership and Ambiguity: The American College Presidency* (New York: McGraw Hill, 1974).

of leadership, many other observers are more positive about its contribution. In citing research by Cameron and Whettan[74] and Cameron and O'Reilly[75] on college and university effectiveness, Cameron and Ulrich note that this work has "clearly demonstrated the power and importance of top administrative strategy in institutional performance."[76] Fincher[77] cites the work of Benezet, Katz, and Magnusson[78] in concluding that presidents do make a difference in institutional effectiveness. Birnbaum notes that "successful presidents are likely to be realists than idealists. They accept a decentralized structure, conflicting authority systems, and loose coupling as inherent organizational characteristics, and try to work within these constraints."[79] He goes on to note that effective presidents "recognize they can have an impact on the institution if they focus on a small number of limited objectives or programs and devote extraordinary energy to them." Birnbaum further notes that effective presidents "understand the culture of their institution and the symbolic aspects of their positions."

This point is reinforced in studies by Chaffee[80] which suggest that "presidents who focus on resource acquisition strategies alone to resolve financial crises are not as successful as those who also combine them with interpretive strategies that change campus perceptions and attitudes."[81] Birnbaum notes further that presidential effectiveness "is based as much on influence as upon authority, and influence in an academic institution depends on mutual and reciprocal processes of social exchange."[82] Birnbaum goes on to note that "the strategies of unsuccessful presidents are likely to be the reverse images of successful ones. They do not accept the institution's characteristics, but consider them as indications of institutional pathology. They attempt comprehensive rather than incremental

[74] Kim S. Cameron, and David A. Whetten, "Models of the organizational life cycle: applications to higher education," *Review of Higher Education*, Vol. 6, 1983, pp. 269–299.

[75] Kim S. Cameron, and B. O'Reilly, "The problems of higher education in America: another look," working paper (Ann Arbor, Mich.: Center for the Study of Higher Education, University of Michigan, 1985).

[76] Kim S. Cameron and David O. Ulrich, "Transformational leadership in colleges and universities," p. 40.

[77] Cameron Fincher, "Administrative leadership in higher education," p. 183.

[78] Louis T. Benezet, Joseph Katz, and Frances W. Magnusson, *Style and Substance: Leadership in the College Presidency* (Washington, D.C.: American Council on Education, 1981).

[79] Robert Birnbaum, *How Colleges Work*, p. 46.

[80] Ellen E. Chaffee, "Successful strategic management in small private colleges," *Journal of Higher Education*, Vol. 55, No. 2, 1984, pp. 212–241.

[81] As quoted in Robert Birnbaum, *How Colleges Work*, p. 47.

[82] Ibid.

change, violate norms and procedural expectations, try to prevent error by complex management systems, control and filter communication, and emphasize one-way rather than two-way influence."[83]

Theories of Leadership

In his review of the management and higher education literature on leadership, Fincher[84] developed a typology of seven types or broad categories of leadership theories.

1. *Fate-and-destiny theories*. Traditional or conventional notions of human mind, character, and heritage as the source of leadership, with special characteristics that are manifest in early life; leaders are born, and history is biography of great men.

2. *Time-and-place theories*. The emergence of leadership in a time of need; given the opportunities, threats, or risks of occasion, leaders will be found; history is the saga of persons who appeared at the right time, and situational demands usually determine who will lead.

3. *Group-and-organization theories*. Often a matter of size, complexity, and perceived challenges of the group or organization; personal qualities and interpersonal skills are secondary to, if not determined by, group demands and expectations.

4. *System-and-process theories*. Leadership is a minor factor in a context larger than leaders, groups, and organizations; roles, norms, expectations, and values are submerged in the systemic features of an ongoing process.

5. *Selection-and-training theories*. May have begun with Plato's philosopher-kings and statesmen who were carefully groomed and did not ascend to leadership until they were 50; . . . often seen in the assessment of talent and managerial, executive, and administrative development programs.

6. *Here-and-now theories*. Have many vestiges of great-man theories and hero worship; successful or popular leadership is more often depicted than effective leadership, and the power of positive thinking is overestimated.

7. *Interaction-and-effectiveness theories*. Recognize the nonlinear effects of personal characteristics, situational variables, and group

---

[83] Ibid., p. 48.
[84] Cameron Fincher, "Administrative leadership in higher education."

or organizational complexities; the effectiveness of leadership is an outcome of person–situation–group–goal interactions that are often difficult to ferret out.[85]

What is apparent in Fincher's synthesis is that conceptions of leadership have evolved from the heroic individual view to more complex interactions among the characteristics of the individual as well as the internal and external settings in which the individual functions. Kerr and Gade[86] present four models of leadership in colleges and universities: a hierarchial model, a collegial consensus model, a polycentric model, and a limited power (or organized anarchy) model of presidential leadership. These models are fairly similar to those synthesized by Hardy[87] as bureaucratic, rational, political, "garbage can," and collegial. However, such models are, in her opinion, relatively superficial and inadequately represent the unique variables of particular institutions. She concludes that the predominant mode in universities is the bureaucratic model.

The challenge of institutional leadership has been aptly characterized in Cameron and Ulrich.[88] Their prescription emphasizes the simultaneous tasks of administration (i.e., administering existing policies and procedures), management (i.e., managing multiple constituencies both reactively and proactively), and leadership (i.e., creating new visions of the future in a readiness for change). This conception is reinforced by Chaffee,[89] who emphasizes the importance of leadership roles that are attentive to the symbolic and interpretative aspects of leadership as well as expressing concern for efficiency and internal factors. Although Cameron acknowledges the importance of the administrative and managerial functions, he laments the lack of transformational leadership in higher education. Such leadership "is seen to be as much about the management of meaning as it is the management of substance."[90]

---

[85] Ibid., p. 161.

[86] Clark Kerr and Marian L. Gade, The Many Lives of Academic Presidents, as cited in Cameron Fincher, "Administrative leadership in higher education," p. 189.

[87] Cynthia Hardy, "Putting power into university governance," in John C. Smart, ed., *Higher Education: Handbook of Theory and Research*, Vol. VI (New York: Agathon Press, 1990), pp. 393–426.

[88] Kim S. Cameron and David O. Ulrich, "Transformational leadership in colleges and universities," p. 12.

[89] Ellen E. Chaffee, "Successful strategic management."

[90] Kim S. Cameron and David O. Ulrich, "Transformational leadership in colleges and universities," p. 12.

Transformational Leadership

Simsek and Heydinger[91] identify a framework for developing an institutional approach to addressing the rapidly changing environment confronting higher education. The first step they enunciate is one of identifying the larger forces at work, specifying the important and broad changes that are under way. In the second step, they identify five key strategies to build on these emerging characteristics:

1. Focus on the customer;

2. Be specific and demanding about quality;

3. Build from collaboration;

4. Use technology to the fullest;

5. Recognize the inherent power of accountability measures.

In the third step, they encourage the institution to assess which characteristics have the most salience for the emerging paradigms in order to identify the characteristics of the educational system which, if changed, would yield the greatest likelihood of needed institutional redefinition.[92]

Cameron and Ulrich,[93] by contrast, focus on more general components of change. They identify five specific steps to apply to leadership in colleges and universities:

1. Creating readiness;

2. Overcoming resistance;

3. Articulating a vision;

4. Generating commitment;

5. Institutionalizing implementation.

Each of these steps to significant change is described below, together with specific examples and suggestions for operationalizing this process.

---

[91] Hasan Simsek and Richard B. Heydinger, "An analysis of the paradigmatic evolution of U.S. higher education," pp. 40–42.
[92] Ibid., p. 44.
[93] Kim S. Cameron and David O. Ulrich, "Transformational leadership in colleges and universities," p. 13.

Creating Readiness

Cameron and Ulrich[94] encourage the leader to "unfreeze the organization and create enough dissatisfaction with the *status quo* so that individuals are motivated to change." They describe five mechanisms for accomplishing this, including (1) the use of benchmarks or referents to detail the inadequacies of the performance of the organization as a spur to seek improvement, (2) the introduction of new players to the organization to bring fresh ideas and different modes of operation, (3) the use of different imagery to open ways of thinking, (4) the reliance on personnel training and development to teach new approaches, and (5) the identification of external threats to the organization's well-being.

Each of these approaches is frequently employed in higher education. The use of comparative data and rankings have long been used within higher education and have been growing in frequency in recent years with the publication of institutional rankings in *U.S. News & World Report* as well as other generally available industry statistics. The hiring of significant new players at various layers within the institution is likewise a familiar strategy; the hiring of new major administrative officers, including deans, the recruitment of an outside department chair or center director, as well as the hiring of a star faculty member are examples. A third tactic cited by Cameron and Ulrich, the use of new language and imagery, is similarly a very popular strategy. Higher education has gone through a series of buzzwords and methodologies as a spur to action for rethinking old ways of operating. The use of "quality" methodologies, "benchmarking," and "reengineering" are examples of the approaches currently being used with increasing frequency in higher education to induce such change.

Interestingly, for an industry focused on education, reliance on widespread personnel training and human resource development (Cameron's and Ulrich's fourth point) has not been practiced extensively within higher education. Instead, very little energy has been expended on staff development and enhancing skill levels. This is an area where universities in particular can draw on their faculties to upgrade the skills of their staffs. With the TQM movement, there has been a growing emphasis on the value of enhanced training. Also, as higher education has attempted to cope with an increasingly diverse population of students, faculty, and staff, diversity training is gaining some currency within the industry.

The last tactic mentioned by Cameron and Ulrich to create readiness for change, the early identification of external threats is similarly very familiar to higher education. The much discussed introduction of technology into higher education is probably the external threat that is receiving the greatest attention currently. The specter of students telecommuting

---

[94] Ibid., p. 13.

around the globe from their homes rather than residing on college campuses is regularly cited as an important spur to action for higher education.

Overcoming Resistance to Change

Because change disrupts normal levels of performance, communication channels, organizational values, power relationships, and careers, Cameron and Ulrich recognize the likelihood of organizations and individuals resisting change. And as noted earlier, colleges and universities are inherently conservative in their operation. Drawing on work by Tichy,[95] Cameron and Ulrich[96] identify three types of resistance: (1) technical, (2) political, and (3) cultural. Examples of technical resistance they cite are those associated with the sunk cost of current technology, existing organizational structures and reporting relationships, and the absence of technical skills needed for a changing work environment. They note that these are among the most obvious forms of resistance and the easiest to overcome.

Political resistance is described as changes in organizational resources such as "power, money, career opportunities and recognition."[97] Such changes threaten the autonomy and control of participants in the process and on that basis are resisted. Given the strong autonomy of higher education's culture, this is clearly a significant source of resistance.

The third category, cultural resistance, "emerges from the values, norms, biases, and underlying assumptions that develop in organizations."[98] These forms of identification and traditional pride reflect the inherently conservative style of operation within our colleges and universities. Changes in the single-sex identity of particular colleges, in the religious orientation of the institution, or on revising the college's focus on liberal arts in favor of professional fields are examples of changes in higher education that encounter cultural resistance.

Based on their review of the literature, Cameron and Ulrich[99] have identified seven principles for fostering change: (1) encouraging participation and information dissemination, (2) fostering autonomy and discretion, (3) providing hierarchial support, (4) using the support of group influences, (5) building advocates versus opponents, (6) creating interesting and nonthreatening approaches, and (7) demonstrating desirable values.

With higher education's tradition of shared governance, reliance on participation and communication has long been a core strategy. Commit-

[95] Noel M. Tichy, *Managing Strategic Change* (New York: Wiley, 1983).
[96] Kim S. Cameron and David O. Ulrich, "Transformational leadership in colleges and universities."
[97] Ibid., p. 19.
[98] Ibid.
[99] Ibid., pp. 13–23.

tees and task forces, white papers, retreats, and similar mechanisms are commonly used to foster interaction and communication. The second strategy they identify, efforts to foster autonomy and participant discretion, is a widely recognized tactic within higher education and is a variant on the participation principle just articulated. Often, a problem or issue is presented to an individual or group, such as a department, which is then asked to address the issue and identify alternative approaches. The third principle, hierarchical support, recognizes the value of support from those in acknowledged leadership positions as well as from informal opinion leaders in the institution. Presidential statements and position papers signed by influential and well-regarded faculty members are among the strategies used in higher education for generating such support. Getting the leadership of the institution out front is generally viewed as a necessary, although not usually a sufficient, step. These and other strategies, such as those presented below, have been articulated by Cameron and Ulrich as likely to lead to the kinds of transformational change that is required.

Articulating a Vision

Cameron and Ulrich[100] also discuss the importance of articulating a vision. They use the word *vision* to connote a sense of values and meanings more significant than operational goals. Given the social and moral purposes served by our institutions, it is to be expected that transformational leaders must call on fundamental values in seeking to evoke change. Cameron and Ulrich talk about the importance of marrying formal institutional processes such as strategic planning, analysis, and communication with more evocative steps to rally a sense of purpose and commitment.

Generating Commitment

Cameron and Ulrich[101] talk about five different strategies for inducing commitment in the organization: (1) public declarations by leaders in the organization of their commitment and support of the vision, (2) meetings and other mechanisms to encourage participation and involvement, (3) the setting of effective goals (i.e., goals that are specific, set jointly, challenging, and can be measured), (4) efforts to inform key individuals in the organization about the transformation, and (5) the demonstration of simple successes or "quick wins" to build momentum.

There has been a great deal of discussion, particularly in large institutions, about decentralization as an effective management strategy.

---

[100] Ibid., pp. 23–27.
[101] Ibid., pp. 27–30.

Schick, however, notes that "letting managers manage does not necessarily mean that they will."[102] Successful decentralization is heavily dependent on the quality of leadership in the various operating units as well as on the degree to which management is actually participatory. Academic deans and department chairs play key roles in decentralized organizations in higher education. However, Hearn[103] notes that very little of the literature expounds on the role of deans or department chairs. Finding mechanisms for involvement at this level, as well as at the level of individual faculty, is essential to successful change processes in higher education. As the intellectual boundaries across various fields have begun to disappear, an institution's capacity to foster cross-unit collaborative efforts in the face of organizational structures that do not facilitate such interactions has been problematic. Marrying appropriate organizational structures with associated budget inducements is one common mechanism for trying to foster such cross-unit interaction. At the same time, there is a price to be paid to the extent to which these supraorganizations undercut the role and functioning of the base departments.

Institutionalizing Implementation

The final principle articulated by Cameron and Ulrich[104] is a set of steps oriented toward institutionalizing the vision. Their discussion focuses on the human resource systems in operation as well as on the organizational frameworks that need to be managed in order to institutionalize change. In the latter category, they refer to Waterman et al.,[105] who proposed the "seven-S framework" of strategy, structure, systems, style, staff, skills, and shared values that are needed for successful change. There has been significant recognition within higher education about the importance of building appropriate reinforcing incentives into personnel systems. A repeated and justified lament of the faculty in the discussions about teaching versus research is the inadequate recognition given to teaching excellence at research universities in salary and promotion decisions. The need to reinforce desired behavior through the incentive and reward structures at higher education institutions is apparent.

[102] Allen Schick, "Budgeting for results: recent developments in five industrialized countries," *Public Administration Review*, Vol. 50, No. 1, 1990, pp. 26–34.
[103] James C. Hearn, "Strategy and resources: economic issues in strategic planning and management in higher education," in John C. Smart, ed., *Higher Education: Handbook of Theory and Research*, Vol. IV (New York: Agathon Press, 1988), pp. 212–281.
[104] Kim S. Cameron and David O. Ulrich, "Transformational leadership in colleges and universities," pp. 30–33.
[105] R. H. Waterman, T. J. Peters, and J. R. Philips, "Structure is not organization," *Business Horizons*, June, 1980 pp. 50–63.

One of the critical impediments to change is the turnover of leadership at the top of the institution. Frequent leadership turnover works against the establishment of ongoing processes that can be employed effectively and confidently by the institution. Instead, with each new administration, a new set of people and processes are brought to bear and the prior processes in place are upended. When these cycles are repeated, cynicism and skepticism is bred, hampering change.

3.6 MAXIMS OF CHANGE

From the foregoing discussion as well as the observations of the author, the following points are reemphasized as key dimensions for enhancing change in our colleges and universities:

1. *Normalization of change.* Change and experimentation need to become the "norm" within our colleges and universities rather than a necessity during crises. During periods of duress, it is more difficult to build the needed interactive processes so valued by our constituents. Yet higher education's track record in motivating change without a crisis is not impressive. The leadership of the institution needs to develop ongoing systems and processes that focus attention on important agenda priorities and constant improvement as opposed to episodic and short-lived approaches. Program review, quality programs, and ongoing feedback systems are among the approaches that can keep an institution in a "learning" mode. As change is attempted, the use of pilot tests is one key mechanism to explore alternatives and build support. In sum, the process of change needs to be conceived of as one of opportunity rather than constraint.

2. *External focus.* Many of the forces affecting our colleges and universities are external in origin. For this reason it is critical that institutions build functioning linkages to external enterprises as a means of keeping colleges and universities current and in touch. Using board members and visiting committees, tapping consultants, building alliances, and other means of interconnection are all useful strategies to encourage an outward-looking, even global, focus. Similarly, attention to defining our customers and understanding their needs is another important strategy for inducing change. The development of effective, usable information about students, industry, and other current or potential clients of our institutions is a key infrastructure to establish and update on an ongoing basis.

3. *Importance of leadership.* Although this premise has been underscored throughout this chapter, the capacities of those in leadership roles

at varying levels within our colleges and universities are critical to the success of the institution. The willingness to make tough choices, including the capacity to make differential versus across-the-board decisions, is critical. The related capacity to engage the community in these directions is also essential to effective change. Although the caliber of the top-level administration, including deans, is often emphasized, the leadership of departments and centers is of equal concern since so much of the life and timber of our institutions is defined at that level. Proactive processes to recruit and develop top-notch talent should be a central component of each institution's agenda.

4. *Management of the tension between centralization and decentralization.* In large institutions, there is an inherent need to decentralize decision making to the local level. At the same time, with the need to build interactive institutions, it is essential to establish incentives and vehicles that foster cross-unit collaboration and interaction as well as commitment to institutional objectives. Although there are no easy prescriptions, financial incentives and the development of organizational mechanisms for interaction are key. Since the financial and budgeting systems of the institution play a central role in this context, they should be examined for their inherent incentives and disincentives and realigned as appropriate. There is an active debate as to whether movements to "responsibility centered management" overly sacrifices institutional needs and goals for the desirable benefit of fostering local unit initiative and incentives.

5. *Faculty engagement.* Real change in our institutions will not occur without the active leadership of the faculty. As noted previously, the role established by individual faculty defines the nature of programs at our institutions. In general, there have been differences noted between liberal arts faculty and those in professional fields in their closeness to outside forces and therefore in their willingness to recognize and respond to change. Whatever the case, it is clear that mechanisms are needed to ensure that members of the academy have the opportunity to assess the conditions to which they are asked to respond, confronting both the costs and the benefits of alternative courses of action. In this context, the use of task forces and pilot tests are especially valuable, ensuring the involvement of faculty leaders in these efforts.

6. *Role of technology.* It is widely acknowledged in higher education that colleges and universities have not been very aggressive in the application of technology to either academic or administrative processes. Given the rapid expansion of information technology capabilities, a more forceful effort to apply such tools to our enterprise is warranted. However, because of the large up-front costs, the development of cooperative partnerships to spread these costs is now being explored in a number of venues and can be expected to increase.

7. *Importance of management function.* Although colleges and universities have not widely been considered hotbeds of managerial prowess, the capacity to improve the asset (financial, human, facilities, etc.) position of the institution is extremely valuable in creating a base of flexibility useful in undergirding change. To the extent that a positive economic climate can be developed of a sustainable nature, the openness of our campuses to change can be enhanced. Similarly, the development of discretionary funds to encourage pilot programs and experiments is another vehicle to jump-start new approaches. At the same time, there is an inexorable tendency to view such changes as add-ons versus substitutes in the functioning of our institutions. Developing the commitment to discontinue lower-priority endeavors is an important component of managerial discipline. The linkage of academic directions with budget and related resource levers is similarly important.

8. *Focus on implementation.* Developing a sustained effort committed to addressing needed changes is one of the hardest challenges colleges and universities face. Given the shortening tenure of leadership in higher education, it is increasingly difficult to develop the culture of change needed in our institutions. Too often one process is put in place and before effective change can be demonstrated, the will to persist is dissipated given the change in leadership. The building of leaner but more manageable processes is more likely to be productive and with successes in hand such efforts can be expanded upon.

9. *Dynamics of accountability.* As was noted in the discussion on board roles, there is strong and growing pressure to demonstrate the accountability of higher education. There is a shift underway now from one of measuring "process" to one focused on "outcomes." There is a decreasing focus on time in the process and fulfilling "course units" to a concern with demonstrating student learning as an example that is often cited. Similarly, in research, issues of utility and value of published material are being aggressively raised by critics of our system. As a result, the academy needs to take a stronger leadership role in defining the terms by which the enterprise and its components will be judged. As we are now seeing in the health care industry, such shifts can have massive implications for the functioning of an enterprise.

10. *Forging new cooperative endeavors.* As colleges and universities confront the constantly changing environment, it is essential that they begin to rethink the traditional organizational boundaries which have defined our operations. Within the institution, the value of department and other such demarcations are increasingly being upended by the dictates of cross-disciplinary activities, from fields like philosophy where definitions of ethics are being enlivened by professional contexts in busi-

ness, medicine and law as examples, to the sciences which now reach into engineering, management, and health fields, to the social sciences which increasingly depend on the integration across traditional fields such as economics, psychology, and anthropology as well as integrating with law, management, and science.

But even more dramatic are the strategic alliances being developed outside institutions—with business and industry, with other educational and cultural institutions, and with various consortia. The leadership of our colleges and universities needs to be creative and proactive in building programmatic and resource ties to other organizations—to reduce costs, spread risk, and gain access to expertise and markets, among other goals. The development of library consortia, the increasing efforts to promote technology transfer, and cooperative instructional technology development efforts across institutions are examples fitting the above model.

That we will face significant change in the near term is widely acknowledged. The pace of such change and the degree of redefinition that it will entail is not yet certain. Developing a more nimble capacity to address these forces and to turn constraints into opportunities is the task we face collectively and individually in our colleges and universities.

In sum, people are the key to change. They must identify what to change, create new processes, and adapt to them. A critical management challenge then is to prepare those who work at colleges and universities for change. According to a Chinese proverb:

> If you want one year of prosperity, grow grain.
> If you want ten years of prosperity, grow trees.
> If you want one hundred years of prosperity, grow people.[106]

---

[106] James M. Kouzes and Barry Z. Posner, *The Leadership Challenge* (San Francisco: Jossey-Bass, 1990), p. 161.

CHAPTER FOUR

Preparing for Administrative Restructuring: A Strategic Approach

JOHN A. FRY

Coopers & Lybrand L.L.P.

4.1 Introduction
How to Restructure
  Administratively
Categorizing Processes
A Restructuring Approach

**4.2 Establishing Context and
  Developing Guiding
  Principles and Goals**

**4.3 Identifying and Prioritizing
  Meaningful Opportunities for
  Improvement and
  Implementing Quick Wins**
Strategic Questions
Baseline Analysis
Quick Wins
Longer-Term Enhancements
Preparing a Business Case

**4.4 Planning and Introducing the
  Implementation Program**

Project Prioritization,
  Sequencing, and Goals
Process Treatments,
  Methodologies, and
  Work Plans
Training and Technology
  Transfer
Governance, Organization, and
  Staffing
Accountability Measures
Communications Network
Human Resource Redeployment
  and Outplacement
Key Transition Program
  Resources

**4.5 Gaining Agreement on the
  Business Model**

**4.6 What Colleges and Universities
  Have Learned**

4.1 INTRODUCTION

The question facing the majority of boards, presidents, and senior administrators from our nation's colleges and universities is not whether they should begin the process of restructuring their organizations, but *when* and *how*. Competitive pressures for attracting faculty, students, and external financial support as well as price sensitivity, call for greater accountability from public and private agencies alike and a stream of negative publicity are all unlikely to abate, and if anything may continue to grow. An institution that recognizes this and is willing to weather the gales of change caused by restructuring will find itself rewarded by more effective, less costly operations, and perhaps even an enhanced competitive position. Those that hope that the environment will make an exception for them may not survive the storm, and if they do hold on and remain intact will probably emerge weakened competitively.

So if not *whether*, then *when?* This is a decision that will vary from institution to institution. Some will restructure in reaction to a crisis (e.g., a precipitous decline in enrollment or midyear reductions in state aid), others during a leadership transition, and some in response to a mandate from a board or state entity. Exemplary institutions will restructure as a normal course of business, because improvement is part of the institutional history and culture. There is no best response to the "when" question other than to suggest that the timing of a restructuring effort must be thought through carefully, and leadership for the effort must be sustained for a period of years. In essence, *when* is a personal choice, based on the circumstances of the institution.

The focus of this chapter is on the *how*, specifically how to get started, because this has been a befuddling question to many. Like their counterparts in the corporate and governmental sectors, colleges and universities are often susceptible to the latest management fad proffered by the hottest management gurus. However, there are no "silver bullet" solutions when it comes to restructuring: What is needed is a strategic, multidisciplinary and data-based process that focuses on both the revenue and expense sides of the institution, is sensitive to the constituencies that will be affected by the process, and strives to be fair but tough-minded in its execution.

Note that in this chapter we discuss only administrative restructuring, the logic being that the administration must show the faculty that it is willing to "walk the talk" before asking the faculty to subject itself to scrutiny. This may be a faulty premise in some institutions, but in similar cases the administration will be challenged if it suggests changes in academic programs and faculty personnel without having demonstrated goodwill and credibility by first taking a hard look at administrative costs and service levels. Even when the administration has done its fair share or more, there are no guarantees that the faculty will follow suit. Nonetheless, this approach provides a sensible first step in a comprehensive institution-wide restructuring process.

4.1   INTRODUCTION

How to Restructure Administratively

So *how?* The philosophical basis for administrative restructuring can be captured in three simple, interrelated questions that institutions should ask themselves:

1. *Do we have to do this at all?* Does this program or service (herein referred to as a "process") add as much value now as it did when it was conceived, and if not, can it be eliminated without materially affecting the institution's ability to deliver high-quality teaching and research? If yes, eliminate it. If no, seriously consider outsourcing or reengineering.

2. *If we have to do this process, is there an alternative mode of delivery other than self-operation?* Strategic, mission-focused institutions are constantly asking themselves what "businesses" they are in and what core competencies they possess. Everything outside of these categories should be reviewed to determine whether self-operation or contract management is the better choice. If our constituencies need and want this process, can we outsource or privatize it? If yes, then solicit and evaluate bids from qualified providers, and select the one that is most competitive on the decision-making criteria (willingness to invest, cost, quality of service, etc.). If not, for whatever reason (usually, the lack of interest in or availability of a qualified provider, or the institution's own philosophical, political, or practical trepidations), there is one last question to ask, the following one—to which the answer will always be a resounding, yes!

3. *If we have to self-operate this process, can it be reengineered or at least incrementally improved?* There is always room for improvement in an institution's processes, be it incremental or more dramatic. In most higher education management processes, substantial opportunities for improvement are usually possible, in part because no one has ever done a serious examination of process quality, cost, and timeliness, and in part because technology has either not been introduced, or if it has, the utilization of that technology has been suboptimal.

Categorizing Processes

The ability to answer these three questions depends on an institution's willingness to evaluate its processes along a scale of salience, that is, how central these processes are to the mission and competitive advantage of the organization. Based on the work of Ellen Knapp, Coopers & Lybrand's vice chairman for technology, and other collaborators, processes can be categorized in four ways.

1. An *identity* process is what an institution stands for, "who" it is, and how its clients[1] think about it. The college's or university's vision,

[1] Clients are recipients of services, be they faculty, staff, students, or alumni.

mission, values, priorities, and sense of shared culture all relate to these processes. Identity processes are akin to an institution's assets. They provide a distinctive value to it in terms of capability, reputation, and competitive differentiation, and therefore must be maintained consciously. Clearly, an academic institution's identity processes include instruction, the creation of new knowledge, and service to local, state, and national communities. Relative to the three fundamental restructuring questions, identity processes are never eliminated or outsourced, but are candidates for reengineering.

2. A *priority* process is an important element of the college's or university's activities and therefore makes a material difference in how well it is executed. Specific examples include enrollment management, institutional advancement, personnel and career counseling, and grant proposal preparation. Priority processes are never eliminated, almost never outsourced (unless seriously flawed), but often can be reengineered.

3. A *background* process is most of what an institution does administratively, but something in which it does not want to invest a lot of time, attention, or resources. Because they are "background" to everyday work, people in the institution tend to take these processes as givens and not subject them to the same type of scrutiny that an identity process might attract. These processes tend to harbor the most waste and therefore the greatest opportunity for improvement. Examples include procurement/disbursement, facilities work order management, security, and auxiliary services. Background processes are amenable to outsourcing and reengineering, and occasionally even to elimination.

4. A *mandated* process is executed only because the government or other external agent requires the institution to do so. Regulation is the major source of these processes, and the institution's primary goal in this case is to reduce their cost. Post-award management of grants can be considered a mandated process. Mandated processes cannot be eliminated, but they can be reengineered and potentially, outsourced.

A Restructuring Approach

With these underpinnings in place, the following approach to preparing for restructuring the major administrative processes (priority, background, and mandated) of a college or university is recommended. Each of the following steps will be elaborated on in the remainder of the chapter:

1. Establish context and develop guiding principles and goals.

2. Identify and prioritize meaningful opportunities for improvement and implement quick wins.

3. Plan and introduce the implementation program.

4. Gain agreement on the business model.

4.2 ESTABLISHING CONTEXT AND DEVELOPING GUIDING PRINCIPLES AND GOALS

The president who is planning to restructure an institution's administration must first lay out the context for the effort, as well as a series of principles and goals that will guide subsequent decision making. The context for the effort is usually explained in terms of external environmental factors (increased competition for funds, need to free up internally committed resources for reallocation to priority areas in order to maintain or enhance program quality, etc.), internal factors (dissatisfaction with quality and cost of campus services, transition in leadership calls for a fresh look, etc.), or a combination of both. In either case, these factors should be credible, compelling, and if possible, quantitatively supported. The context statement should be hard-hitting without causing panic: It should be a call to action. Finally, the context for the restructuring should be repeated—ad nauseum—and the message should never fundamentally change. Consistency and repetitiveness are key.

Guiding principles help provide the scope and boundaries for the restructuring effort and clearly signal the president's priorities. They should also be hard-hitting and focused on the institution's most critical restructuring opportunities. Above all, they should be action oriented, signaling a clear intent to move forward decisively. Examples of guiding principles might include the following:

- Eliminate "nice to have" but nonessential services.

- Outsource administrative services where higher-quality, more cost-efficient alternatives are available.

- Flatten and simplify the administrative organization by reducing hierarchical structures and broadening spans of control.

- Break down unnecessary organizational barriers by combining similar functions.

- Centralize delivery of "back office" functions where possible, and decentralize services that require intensive customer interaction.

- Maximize the institution's present investment in people and technology through continuous, "just-in-time" training and meaningful employee development programs.

- Clearly delineate the roles, responsibilities, and authority for administrative activity throughout the university, and hold people accountable for their decisions and actions.

- Embrace an organizational culture that emphasizes self-supporting business units that are constantly subject to market competition and have full responsibility, authority, and accountability for winning and retaining a client's (e.g., a department chair's, faculty member's, or student's) business.

- Provide appropriate opportunities for retraining, redeployment, and outplacement for employees who lack the capability or drive to perform at acceptable levels or whose positions become obsolete due to restructuring.

- Establish clear performance standards and provide meaningful incentives for meeting or exceeding them.

Finally, the president must establish, even at a high level, explicit goals that will provide a way to measure the success of the restructuring effort. Goals might deal with service level improvements (responsiveness, timeliness, service quality), revenue enhancement, cost reduction, and client handling. Whenever possible, goals should be quantitative and measurable (e.g., reduce the costs of administering the university by 10 percent over the next three years) and related to the mission of the institution (e.g., freed up resources will be reallocated to the College of Arts and Sciences for investment in learning technologies and associated faculty development). While subsequent analysis of the institution's business opportunities will undoubtedly result in much greater specificity of goals, this initial goal-setting exercise by the president should symbolize the CEO's commitment to monitor progress, measure results, hold people accountable, and reward meritorious performance.

4.3 IDENTIFYING AND PRIORITIZING MEANINGFUL OPPORTUNITIES FOR IMPROVEMENT AND IMPLEMENTING QUICK WINS

The president should charge the senior management team and/or a carefully chosen institutional group of staff and service recipients to undertake a comprehensive but fast-paced "performance assessment" of all major administrative units. The purpose of the performance assessment is to give the institution direction for the restructuring by identifying the most significant and meaningful opportunities for service improvement, revenue enhancement, and cost reduction. By establishing early on the focus of the restructuring effort as well as the potential "return on investment," the institution can move forward with confidence, knowing that the inevitable pain caused by restructuring will be offset generously by substantial results.

As a rule of thumb, a performance assessment should take anywhere from two to six months, depending on the size and complexity of the institution and the scope of the assessment. Beyond six months, there is a risk of "analysis paralysis," not to mention the inevitable strain on the people undertaking the work as well as on those whose units are being scrutinized. Some institutions address the timeliness issue by reviewing parts of the institution in a sequenced program (development first, then finance and administration, followed by student services, etc.), and subsequently moving to implementation on a division-by-division basis. This approach may, however, weaken the restructuring effort; many of the most substantial improvement opportunities lie in eliminating redundant non-value-adding activities that cross divisions, making a horizontal look across divisions the key issue rather than a "vertical" or functional asessment of each division.

The purpose of the performance assessment is to provide a quick evaluation of the operation of key processes (buying goods and services and paying for them) and their associated functional areas (purchasing and accounts payable) using quantitative analyses to identify opportunities for service improvement, revenue enhancement, or cost savings. Once these analyses have been performed, the institution can begin to prioritize its future improvement efforts, and build it a clear restructuring agenda going forward.

Strategic Questions

The specific objective is to answer several strategic questions:

- What do our clients care about most, and what are their most pressing administrative support needs?

- In each process and function, what benefits can the institution expect to reap in terms of cost, service, and quality?

- Where can we realize the greatest return on our investment of time, energy, and dollars in the restructuring effort?

- What should be our priorities for restructuring?

Baseline Analysis

Answers to the first three questions can be derived by applying a proven set of analytical tools to major processes and functions, to create a *baseline* of information. Essentially, there are three components of the baseline analysis, which taken together provide a comprehensive view of the overall administrative effectiveness of the college or university:

- Structural/managerial
- Process
- Technology

Structural/Managerial Analysis. The first component is an analysis of the existing structure and management practices of the institution to understand how well they support its mission and primary activities. Important elements of the structural analysis for each major process and function include:

- Composition and logic of divisional activities
- Distribution of responsibility and authority by management level
- Reporting relationships
- Spans of control
- Staffing patterns
- Committee structure and interface with line structure
- Cross-functional interactions, especially on key issues (student retention, institutional planning and budgeting, etc.)

Key management practices that are examined include:

- Planning and budgeting
- Communication
- Teamwork and coordination
- Delegation of responsibility and authority and degree of employee autonomy
- Human resources management, including employee evaluation, accountability practices, and performance incentives
- Client satisfaction measurement
- Program- and service-level evaluation
- Documentation of key policies and procedures, especially for control and training purposes
- Management and financial controls

Process Analysis. The second component of a comprehensive performance assessment focuses on process, or the end-to-end stream of activities that allow institutions to accomplish their major work. In this chapter we focus on priority, background, and mandated processes. Examples of process tools include:

- *Process flowcharting*: documents the way in which work is actually done by following a transaction step by step through an entire process. Produces a wealth of data on process characteristics, including costs, time, and error rates.

- *Work distribution analysis*: collects comprehensive, institution-wide data from employees regarding how they allocate their time among various administrative processes.

- *Client analysis*: measures current client satisfaction, identifies key areas for improvement, and identifies potential needs going forward.

- *Value-added/non-value-added analysis*: defines each step in the process as either value-added (essential and required by clients) or non-value-added (not required by clients and therefore not valuable, such as rework, redundant data entry, duplicate file keeping, etc.).

- *Cost of quality analysis*: categorizes and quantifies the cost of various types of non-value-added activities, to estimate potential savings created by eliminating non-value-added work.

- *First-run yield analysis*: identifies the number of transactions that do not make it through the process the first time around, due to errors. Evaluates the nature and cause for errors in the process and then identifies methods to eliminate these "root causes."

- *Volume analysis*: evaluates the various types and numbers of transactions that flow through a process and affect employee workload. Helps to determine various types of special handling procedures for transactions, appropriate approval requirements, and reasonability of employee workload.

- *Benchmarking*: compares the performance of one process to that of other institutions, including colleges, universities, and even for-profit organizations.

Technology Analysis. The final component of the performance assessment has to do with technology. Basic elements of the technology analysis include:

- Diagramming the "logical architecture" of existing information technology applications

- Assessing the degree to which the campus is networked and the potential for voice, data, and video networking

- The software applications and hardware currently in use in the computing organization as well as in other departmental offices that support administrative activities

- The quality, accuracy, and availability of applications data and documentation

- Strategy for future enhancements or replacement of existing systems

- Assessment of current skills, services, and employee staffing levels and capabilities in the information technology organization

Quick Wins

Once the assessment is completed and reviewed, two basic determinations must be made, the first being: *What can we do right away, or within a relatively short period of time, to show progress and create momentum for restructuring?* In many performance assessments, opportunities for "quick wins" that provide an immediate return on the institution's investment in the assessment will be identified. Quick wins may include changes in cash management practices that will provide additional short-term resources to the institution; modifications of procurement practices to allow clients greater ease and flexibility in purchasing goods and services; and resolution of long-standing performance problems in a visible administrative unit by reorganizing the department and reassigning or terminating employees. The key is to show results in visible areas of the institution, to underscore the president's commitment to change, and to create momentum for change, or a "get on the bandwagon" mentality, within the organization. Ideally, these quick wins can be announced throughout the performance assessment, rather than waiting for the final work product to be developed. A half-dozen or so quick wins is enough to set the right tone for the restructuring effort.

Longer-Term Enhancements

The second basic determination to be made is: *Over the long run, what administrative areas hold the greatest potential for substantial and visible improvement in service levels, revenue enhancements, and cost-effectiveness?* While quick wins set the symbolic tone for the restructuring, the substance of the assessment lies in identifying the most important priorities for restructuring going forward. If done correctly, the performance assessment will reveal to the institution those administrative processes that hold the greatest potential for improved service, revenue enhancement, and cost-effectiveness. Institutions can usually identify more than enough opportunities for improvement, but may struggle to prioritize them and to marshal the resources necessary to implement the improvement program. The following criteria may provide some guidance for prioritizing the restructuring effort:

1. *Nature of process/centrality of function.* If the process or function in question is a crucial "backbone" factor in the institution's overall improvement program (i.e., human resources, information systems, financial management), it should be a priority. Without it, other improvement processes may falter. For example, the restructuring process at any college or university is dependent on a capable human resources department that can successfully manage difficult employee transition issues, such as retraining, redeployment, and outplacement. Without a first-class human resources function, the institution that undertakes restructuring risks its chances for success. Similarly, the information systems function is crucial to the success of any reengineering effort and therefore must be capably, hopefully creatively, managed.

2. *Degree of risk.* Especially for institutions undertaking restructuring for the first time, the risk of failure must be carefully gauged. It is important that the restructuring program get off to a good start. A carefully sequenced program will include a number of areas that should result in clear wins for the institution, although not without significant effort and investment. Good advice in the initial round of restructuring is to refrain from "priority" processes (e.g., student services), and instead, focus on high-visibility "background" processes (e.g., procurement, gift processing) as well as "mandated" processes (e.g., grants management). Once the institution has substantive restructuring experience under its belt, more mission-central processes or functions can be tackled. Also, beware of areas that for whatever reason are politicized, due either to past history or present difficulties (e.g., labor relations problems). This is not to suggest that the institution ignore risky or politically charged situations, but perhaps it should hold off on these until it has some credibility and experience with restructuring.

3. *Client needs.* Achieving buy-in from faculty, students, and administrators (internal clients) is crucial to the ultimate success of restructuring. If time and time again clients have identified several areas of concern, if not outright dissatisfaction, this should be noted and weighed carefully relative to other areas of potential improvement.

4. *Required investment.* All restructuring initiatives require an investment—at the very least some significant time from internal staff. Some areas require more extraordinary investments, especially if the process has been neglected over time. If the campus community equates restructuring with allocating more resources for administration in return for vague, long-term payoffs, its support may not be forthcoming.

Overall, an institution that is serious about long-term restructuring is well advised to select a careful mix of priorities for action, weighing carefully such factors as dependencies, risk, required investment, and client needs. *Above all, do not take on too much during the first round of restructuring—keep it to two or three substantive initiatives, no more.*

Preparing a Business Case

The last step is to prepare a strong business case for each of the restructuring priorities, both quick wins and longer-term initiatives. The business case is a persuasive, quantitatively based argument that both educates and persuades campus constituencies that the restructuring initiatives were selected for compelling, nonpolitical reasons. (Benchmarking is especially powerful in this regard; it can be used to demonstrate performance gaps and, consequently, the possibilities for improvement.) The business case is a crucial factor in launching a successful restructuring initiative, and the necessary time and effort should be put into its development. Without a strong business case, the institution's leadership may be accused of unfairly targeting a particular department for restructuring.

4.4 PLANNING AND INTRODUCING THE IMPLEMENTATION PROGRAM

Although an institution should immediately launch its strategy for achieving quick wins, it should not be hasty when it comes to planning for the implementation of its long-term restructuring initiatives. These initiatives are likely to be complex and time consuming and therefore require careful planning up front. This is especially the case if the institution intends to drive the restructuring program itself, without relying on external advisors. The elements of a comprehensive restructuring plan include the following.

Project Prioritization, Sequencing, and Goals

Over a three- to five-year period, what are the restructuring projects the institution wants to take on, and how should they be sequenced? As project prioritization and sequencing have already been addressed, we focus only on the issue of establishing goals here. In a *Harvard Business Review* article several years ago, Robert Schaffer and Harvey Thompson argued that most corporate change programs mistake means for ends and become "activity centered" (activities that "sound good, look good, and allow managers to feel good—but in fact contribute little or nothing to bottom-line performance") rather than results driven.[2] This is an especially dangerous trap for higher education and one that it is susceptible to given its emphasis on collegial decision making and inclusiveness and its relative lack of experience with restructuring. Beyond strong, steel-willed leadership, the other key success factor in avoiding the "activity-centered fallacy" is to specify goals and performance parameters that the institution expects to see for each restructuring initiative. Goals should be specific enough so that progress can be measured throughout the implementation cycle and changes made to the program or people involved if progress is not sufficient.

Process Treatments, Methodologies, and Work Plans

It is important to remember that total quality management, activity-based costing, business process reengineering, and outsourcing are not ends in themselves, only means to the greater end of fundamental restructuring of the institution. The effectiveness of total quality management, a method used to achieve continuous, incremental improvements, will be minimal if applied to a process that requires dramatic rethinking and aggressive utilization of technology. Similarly, an exercise to determine the feasibility and desirability of outsourcing a targeted function is fruitless if the market of external providers for that service is immature and therefore questionable in terms of quality. In both of these cases, reengineering is really the more appropriate *process treatment*. But each case may vary: The important point, and first step, *is to match the restructuring initiative with the appropriate process treatment*. Beyond outsourcing, reengineering, or continuous improvement, alternative process treatments may include creating hubs (bringing work to a single point rather than moving it in steps through departments and functions), importing successful processes from other industries [e.g., using automated teller machines (ATMs) to register students], turning an expensive background or mandated process into a product (e.g., providing security services for neighboring institutions in return for a fee), and inventing a new process by "breaking" an existing process and creating a new one.

Once the process treatment has been identified, methodologies and tools must be selected and tailored for the specific projects to be under-

[2] *Harvard Business Review*, January–February 1992, p. 180.

taken. The only caution here is to avoid taking a "corporate" approach untested in the higher education environment and plugging it in without first tailoring and testing it. To achieve its goals, each initiative needs to be managed aggressively. Be sure that a detailed work plan is in place, which delineates work steps, time lines, staffing, critical path linkages, key decision points, expected outcomes, and specific deliverables.

Training and Technology Transfer

Restructuring should not be something that an external party "does" to the institution, but a self-sustaining, internally driven program of change and improvement. To achieve the latter, the institution must, over time, build its own capabilities by investing in training, certification, and perhaps with help from an external partner, *technology transfer*, or the transfer of sound restructuring methodologies and tools from the partner to the institution. A training curriculum with an applied focus should be designed and administered to those who will participate in the restructuring program on a "just-in-time" basis. Critical components of the curriculum include awareness training (i.e., setting the basic rational for each "process treatment" and how it should be applied), facilitator team leader training, team building, and practical application of tools and techniques (benchmarking, activity-based costing, etc.). To ensure rigorous application of restructuring methods, some institutions have established certification programs, which allows them to create a cadre of well-trained people who in turn can serve as technical experts and trainers in other areas of the institution.

Governance, Organization, and Staffing

A governance and organizational structure for restructuring needs to be established to make decisions, communicate results and reinforce the institution's commitment to this effort. Generally, the creation of new organizations and committees to drive restructuring is not necessary. The existing line management structure should be responsible and accountable for putting management reforms in place. However, in cases where the line structure is ineffective or in a state of transition, a coordinating entity may be appropriate. New structures that may be introduced without usurping managerial prerogatives include the following:

1. *Client advisory committee*: a representative group of institutional constituencies (faculty department chairs, resident advisors, business managers from academic units, etc.) who are clients of campus service organizations. The committee's role should be advisory and focus on whether the restructuring initiatives, in both the conceptual and imple-

mentation stages, are going far enough to satisfy the legitimate needs and demands of clients.

2. *Program coordinator*: a relatively senior institutional manager charged with the day-to-day management of the restructuring effort, including structuring projects, recruiting staff for improvement teams, training, monitoring, and evaluating progress, shaping communications, and coordinating all efforts with the appropriate line organizations on campus (human resources, information systems, etc.). This person should have a modest organization and staffing complement lest the institution be accused of building bureaucracy when it is ostensibly trying to tear it down. Leveraging in external resources during the first year or two to get the program started is a feasible strategy as long as the migration path and time line to a self-sustaining capability is clear and reasonable.

3. *Expertise network*: to institutionalize the notion of restructuring, colleges and universities must substantively involve their employees and clients in the effort. The two most critical concerns are expertise and time. The expertise issue can be addressed over a period of approximately two years by training and experience, perhaps supplemented by external support when a particularly nettlesome problem emerges. The commitment of an employee's time to an intensive restructuring project is more problematic, especially if their present assignment includes significant line responsibilities. There is no easy answer here other than to have the president personally request the support of the senior team in allowing personnel from their departments to take a temporary leave to participate on a restructuring team, perhaps in exchange for some budgetary relief that would allow temporary support to be brought in to backfill the donated employee's position. Although difficult, most institutions are able to develop a reasonable approach to staffing teams that allows the initiative to progress without materially impairing the day-to-day work of the institution.

Accountability Measures

Without clear measures for ascertaining progress and ensuring that participants are held accountable for results, the restructuring program risks becoming nothing more than a training and team-building exercise. Each restructuring initiative must begin with a clear set of measurable performance benchmarks (i.e., response time, cost per transaction, error rates, client satisfaction measured quantitatively, etc.) that can be achieved within a reasonable period of time. In reviewing the progress of each initiative, the president and senior management team should focus not on how many people were trained in quality methods or how many improvement teams are in place, but on how close the teams are to achieving the desired performance benchmarks. Although process is important and requires careful management, in the end, results count most: Did the institution achieve its goals in the restructuring initiative?

Communications Network

Without a doubt, the news that a president plans a major restructuring initiative will send tremors, if not convulsions, throughout the institution. As a result, senior management must pay significant attention to the issue of campus communications, not only at the inception of the process but also throughout its duration and after, hopefully to announce positive results. There are three cardinal rules when communicating about restructuring. *First, the restructuring initiative must be related directly to the mission and strategy of the institution*, so it becomes an imperative: We cannot achieve our full potential as an institution unless we carry out this restructuring initiative successfully. *Second, consistent themes and messages must be developed and delivered* by the senior administrative leadership of the institution. Inconsistency is just what detractors want, so agree on a few clear messages and stick with them. *Third, communicate until they can't stand it anymore, then communicate again.* The key is to be ubiquitous with the communications so that no one can claim ignorance of the reasons for restructuring, the approach to doing it, and the progress being made. Another key success factor in communications is to segment constituencies according to the media vehicle (campus newspaper, union newsletter, local radio station, alumni newspaper) to which they are most likely to pay attention, and make sure that the institution's communications on restructuring are being picked up by those media. In other words, don't just use the "house organ" to communicate. This multiple-media strategy, in turn, makes the three cardinal rules (i.e., high-mindedness, consistency, redundancy) even more important to follow.

Human Resource Redeployment and Outplacement

Without a doubt, this is the component of the restructuring program that is most controversial and poses the greatest risk to the institution. (It does not help that human resources management in some institutions is not as professionalized as it is in the corporate sector, although a number of institutions are doing some very progressive things.) The success of an institution's restructuring effort is dependent on a comprehensive employee transition program. Without such an expression of commitment and concern for its employees, the institution leaves itself open to significant internal and external criticism that could derail an otherwise first-rate restructuring program.

The institution should start with a logical series of carefully thought-out commitment statements, for example:

- To the extent possible, downsizing will be accomplished through attrition, early retirement, and other incentives.

- All employees who are affected by restructuring will be given the option of voluntary separation from the university with an appropriate severance package and/or outplacement services, depending on their seniority.

- The institution is committed to finding alternative employment within the university for qualified employees displaced by restructuring, assuming that positions are available and the candidate is qualified.

- Redeployed employees will be given preference for internal positions over other internal and external candidates, all skill sets being equal. This is not tantamount to a right of first refusal.

- Any employee who is unable to be placed within the university in a reasonable period of time will be provided with career counseling and outplacement services and a severance package.

Key Transition Program Resources

Key resources required in a transition program include the following:

1. *Career counseling and outplacement services.* An external firm can be contracted to provide career counseling and outplacement services for all employees who elect to separate from the institution voluntarily or for whom no vacant positions can be found. Services include career counseling, mock interviews, access to job databases, résumé writing, and office support.

2. *Redeployment pool.* Employees who wish to remain with the institution may be placed in a redeployment pool for a fixed period of time. During that time, management will endeavor to find another position within the institution that can reasonably be performed by the employee given their current skill set, perhaps supplemented by targeted retraining. To facilitate this process, the institution should create a fund to share a portion of the employee's first-year salary with the hiring unit during a probationary period.

3. *Severance package.* Employees who voluntarily separate or who are unable to be hired within the redeployment period should be given a severance package based on their seniority.

There are obviously other options for employee transition that an institution can provide (recall rights, etc.). The list above is not intended to be exhaustive. What is important is that an institution begin actively to plan for employee transition well before it is confronted with a recommendation from a reengineering team that 25 percent of a department's work can be eliminated, therefore freeing up a dozen employees, many of whom have long tenures with the institution and have been loyal, hard workers.

4.5 GAINING AGREEMENT ON THE BUSINESS MODEL

Many institutions wrestle with the roles and responsibilities of the central administration vis-à-vis the schools or departments regarding the provision of administrative services. The corporate sector is moving toward smaller "headquarters" operations, either eliminating work or pushing it out into line operations to focus more leadership time on strategy development, external relations, and other enterprise-wide activities. The important point here is that successful corporations have made explicit organizational design decisions that if implemented appropriately will eliminate the expensive and unnecessary duplication that is one of the important cost drivers in any complex organization. They have adopted, in effect, a business model for managing their enterprises.

This same set of issues is germane to educational institutions, particularly those that are contemplating administrative restructuring initiatives. It is difficult to reengineer a process when the essential roles and responsibilities of the process participants are unclear and subject to constant reinterpretation. Therefore, as part of the restructuring process, an institution should attempt to define a business model that clarifies responsibility, authority, and accountability at all levels of the organization, to eliminate redundant effort and non-value-added work. By way of an example, Exhibit 4–1 provides some elements of a financial management business model in a large university.

A long-term question for higher education in defining its business model is the extent to which institutions are willing and able to organize themselves around a core administrative process and move gradually away from a functional, "hands off the client" organization (current functional areas include recruitment, admissions, financial aid, registrar, advising, career counseling, and alumni relations) to a seamless "process" organization (combining the functional areas into one: student services). Given the imperative to contain, if not reduce, costs while becoming more responsive to clients, the idea of organizing along core processes, at least partially, is quite attractive given the resultant decline in supervisory levels, consolidation of fragmented tasks and elimination

Exhibit 4–1
ELEMENTS OF A FINANCIAL MANAGEMENT MODEL FOR A UNIVERSITY

Central University	Responsibility Centers[a]
▪ Establish consistent standards, policies and procedures, controls, and "best practices" (centralized infrastructure to support decentralized management)	▪ Execute transaction within financial management framework established by the university
	▪ Establish tailored office procedures, consistent with overall university framework
▪ Support decentralized, on-line data entry with adequate controls, tracking and quality checks, and provide for centralized processing of financial transactions	▪ Engage in on-line entry, editing, and validation of financial transaction utilizing common system (obviates need for shadow systems)
	▪ Establish a single point for data entry and one-time entry of source data
▪ Support a single integrated database to provide data integrity, to meet the information needs of the entire university, and to allow for effective central monitoring and oversight	▪ Utilize on-line access/inquiry to current and historical financial and operating information supported by user-friendly analytical tools to manipulate and/or consolidate information
▪ Provide technical advice, training, and professional development to responsibility center business managers	▪ Invest in "knowledge workers"
▪ Develop and maintain integrated information systems that link financial data to nonfinancial data	▪ Over time, discontinue investment in redundant systems by utilizing tools that allow users to develop customized reports, "what if's," etc.
▪ Provide responsibility centers with capabilities to interact with systems on a decentralized basis	▪ Utilize university-maintained integrated systems and diagnostic tools to manage business and spot problems and trends as they evolve
▪ Monitor and spot-check fiscal performance of responsibility center	▪ Manage daily activities within context of business plans and established protocols for resource management
▪ Certify/"accredit" responsibility centers based on adherence to standards, policies and procedures, and best practices	
▪ Focus efforts on enhancements to internal systems, processes, and activities to support improved customer service	

Exhibit 4–1 (Continued)

Central University	Responsibility Centers[a]
■ Develop consolidated reports and provide responsibility centers with flexible reporting capabilities	■ Develop flexible reports to meet special needs
■ Greater focus on accountability for upholding standards and achieving plan, and less on operations, data manipulation, etc.	■ Equal focus on accountability—greater emphasis on "doing it right" operationally and meeting established goals
■ Establish framework within which decisions will be made and resolve exceptions	■ Initiate and make decisions

[a] Academic schools or large administrative units, such as physical plant and auxiliary services.

of non-value-added work. While functional organization structures are quite strong in higher education, the need to gain competitive advantage through service improvements and cost effectiveness is driving institutions to experiment with the use of self-managed accountable teams, oriented toward clients as the primary drivers (and measurement sources) of performance.

Another longer-term business model question, and one that cannot be given justice in this single chapter, is the role of outsourcing in helping redefine the role of campus administration. The fundamental question of whether the external market can provide more cost-effective service at the same or a better level of quality is one that not enough institutions have seriously entertained. As external providers move into more and more areas (technology delivery, professional services such as tax and internal audit, specialized areas such as residential management and child care), the options for institutions increase. If one believes in the notion of core competencies, the only things not up for scrutiny relative to outsourcing in a college or university are teaching, research, and service (and even teaching may be subject to change, depending on how far and fast distance learning technology goes). One can envision a university that contracts for its administrative services with a network of business partners whose core competencies are background, mandated, and perhaps even priority processes, thus allowing the institution to focus on its identity processes, free at last from struggling with eight-part purchasing forms.

One last point on outsourcing: Why not treat internal service providers like stand-alone business units, subject to periodic market tests like real businesses, with no guaranteed monopoly on service? This will motivate these units to restructure themselves long before any formal institutional initiative is launched; they will be motivated to do so, lest they lose their client base due to shoddy service or high prices. This "in-sourcing" approach might provide some real incentives to enhance performance, competition and a sense of ownership of the service. Whether the service is managed internally or provided by an external vendor, the institution using this approach should be able to improve its quality, timeliness, and cost, provided that it pays attention to aggressively managing all its service providers.

4.6 WHAT COLLEGES AND UNIVERSITIES HAVE LEARNED

In preparing for restructuring, institutions should keep in mind the following lessons:

- Provide a clear focus, direction, and logical sequencing for the restructuring program.

- Build a data-based, analytical case for change.

- Secure senior management consensus and commitment to change.

- Establish explicit and measurable service improvement and cost-reduction goals and clearly defined terms to guide the process.

- Utilize proven, credible, and broad-based restructuring methodologies (policies, structures, processes, technologies, and people) to realize expected benefits.

- Recognize that cultural and organizational change are integral components of successful restructuring and should therefore be given significant attention.

- Search outside the academy for best practices and innovative approaches to leading and managing complex decentralized organizations.

- Adopt a strong client focus to ensure that internal and external customer needs are driving the initiative and that value is being measured from the client's perspective.

- Communicate clearly, frequently, and vigorously the goals of the program and its results.

- Take into account the likelihood that people may be displaced and develop an employee transition plan to meet their needs.

- Install measurements, measure results, and hold people accountable for results.

Above all, successful administrative restructuring in an academic environment is dependent on knowing where the most significant opportunities are, establishing clear goals and performance measures to monitor progress, having a comprehensive plan for addressing communications and human resources issues, and forging consensus on the most appropriate business model for delivering services. Perhaps most important, a successful restructuring program is attuned to the needs of its clients—whether they be faculty, students, or other administrators—and capable of stretching for the best solutions to address their needs.

Rethinking the Academy's Administrative Structure

JILLINDA J. KIDWELL

Coopers & Lybrand L.L.P.

DAVID J. O'BRIEN

Stanford University School of Medicine

5.1 **The Growth of Administrative Inefficiency**

Understanding Administrative Growth

Departmental Process Navigators and Central Specialists

5.2 **The Business Case for Change**

5.3 **The Reengineered Organization**

The Corporate Experience

The Applicability of Reengineering to Higher Education

The Reengineering Process: An Overview

Evaluating and Fixing Processes

Higher Education's Process Map

5.4 **The Stanford University School of Medicine Experience**

The School's Process Map

Perceptions of the School's Administrative Processes

Implications of Administrative Fragmentation

A New Organizational Construct

5.5 **Conclusions**

5.1 THE GROWTH OF ADMINISTRATIVE INEFFICIENCY

For well over two centuries, including the most recent 40 years of extra-ordinary post–World War II growth, the basic *academic* organizational structure of U.S. higher education has remained essentially unchanged. Academic endeavors continue to function, with notable success, through a loosely coupled system of individual faculty interacting within intellectual disciplines organized into academic programs, divisions, departments, schools, colleges, and universities.

For most of its long history, a recognizable *administrative* support organization for an institution's academic endeavors has been notably absent. In the past 20 years, however, administrative support organizations have emerged as a significant component in most institutions, and administrative operations are an increasingly expensive portion of the institutional budget.

Understanding Administrative Growth

Administrative resources within academia have traditionally been aligned as directly as possible in support of faculty activities. The long-held principles of academic freedom grant each faculty member an enormous degree of latitude over the direction and content of their academic pursuits. Under this guiding principle, as the business of academia has grown, so has the amount of administrative resources allocated and controlled at the faculty level. The need to manage dramatically increasing amounts of programmatically controlled academic resources has produced increasingly large administrative support groups attached to individual faculty and program groups, to divisional and departmental chairs, and to school deans. Similar specialized administrative groups support university offices under the direction of provosts, vice presidents, and presidents. Over time, bureaucratic expansion has resulted in a lack of clarity in the current business model, that is, in the distribution of responsibility, authority, and workload among the university, its schools, and its departments.

Institutions of higher education now conduct their critical and complicated administrative operations through a hierarchical organizational structure that directly parallels, and is appended to, its fundamental, underlying academic structure. Since ultimate institutional accountability is held centrally and most resource and spending authority is delegated locally (to faculty), seemingly reasonable operational control objectives have produced elaborate administrative processes that tend to wind their way up through successive layers of administrative oversight groups until, at a sufficiently high level of the organization, approval is given and the desired action takes place.

Departmental Process Navigators and Central Specialists

Process Navigators. These labyrinthine processes have gradually required a change in academic departmental administrative structures. The faculty secretaries of old have given rise to local administrative assistants, or *process navigators*, on whom the faculty rely to move things through (or around) the administrative system. Process navigators provide to the faculty their only safe, reliable, and responsive access to byzantine university administrative systems. They are administrative generalists who know enough about all the university administrative systems to get the paperwork started and keep it moving. Whether it is a research proposal submission, a travel reimbursement, a simple equipment purchase, or a personnel requisition, the road to administrative approval begins at the door of the process navigator.

If the paperwork is not managed by a process navigator and is left to wend its own way through the university process, the results are disastrous. In the hiring process, for example, the faculty process navigator knows *who* to contact in central employment and *when* to contact them to get the posting date retroactively dated, thereby cutting nearly two weeks off the posting time (or even better, how to waive out of the posting period altogether). The ultimate triumph of a process navigator is to exceed the expectations of the faculty member and develop an expedient work-around process that gets the job done. Process navigators are ferociously loyal to faculty and will go to whatever lengths are necessary to shepherd the paperwork through the system and keep the frustrations and inefficiencies of the system away from their employers. The final outcome of this business model is that process navigators need departmental resources to build "shadow systems," maintain logs, manage databases that track the progress of paperwork, or provide access to up-to-date management information to make the process itself invisible to the faculty member or department chair.

Central Specialists. The road process navigators must travel leads through numerous "central" offices, corresponding to the traditional hierarchy of the academic organization, and across the desks of administrators who specialize in specific administrative areas, such as sponsored projects, travel reimbursement, capital equipment, or personnel. As loyal as the local administrators are to their faculty, *central specialists* are equally loyal and committed to their bosses. Central specialists are defined by their ability to protect the university's administrative/control interests within their particular areas of expertise. Consequently, their paperwork reviews more often than not result in redirection of the paperwork back down the road to unsuspecting faculty and their process navigators for additional information or corrections. For the local process navigator the process proceeds with two steps forward and one step back, until the end of the road is eventually reached. Throughout it all, process navigators have two purposes: to get to the end of the road as quickly as possible and not to burden faculty with their problems in getting there.

In the past several years, attempts have been made to reduce the high costs associated with this business model. Central university administrators have been stymied in their attempts to "fix" their processes because they exert control over—or "own"—a relatively small portion of the administrative activities that comprise the end-to-end process. Typically, only 20 percent of the overall process is under the control of most central university offices. The remaining process activities are controlled by the dean's office staff, academic departmental chairs, or individual faculty members.

5.2 THE BUSINESS CASE FOR CHANGE

Reducing the costs built into its complicated hierarchy is one of the most significant challenges facing U.S. higher education today. The task of rationalizing the costs of administration in light of a dramatically shifting underlying economic picture is daunting. The past years of administrative growth have been fueled, in large part, through a fortuitous combination of factors, including a robust national economy, high interest rates, strong federal investments in cost-reimbursed basic research, and a steadily expanding and cost-reimbursed national health care agenda that has funded growth in medical schools.

However, beginning as early as the mid-1980s, planners in higher education began to raise concerns about the potential dampening of these fundamental growth factors. The preceding decades of growth had produced an even more rapidly expanding community of academics forced to compete ever more aggressively for smaller pieces of the higher education pie. As interest rates began to come down, so did expendable earnings from institutional endowments. Student tolerances for double-digit inflation in tuition and fees have similarly decreased with declining interest rates. The growth in federal support of research has begun to flatten (in constant-dollar spending) and become refocused on direct costs at the expense of institutional overhead cost, a trend that was most recently reflected in the capping of administrative costs recoverable from federally sponsored research. A slower economy has significantly constrained state and local funding available for public higher education. Tax code changes have similarly dampened philanthropic support to private higher education. For institutions involved in health care delivery, the continuing shift from cost-reimbursed to capitated health care systems, both federally funded and private, have eroded a significant source of support to academic programs.

The economic picture for higher education in the 1990s differs in almost every way from that which supported the past decades of programmatic and administrative growth. The administrative organization which emerged from that period was largely unplanned and it remains unchallenged. It is characterized by administrative processes that are so interwoven into the fabric of academic departmental administration as to be nearly inseparable. The new economic realities confronting higher education require a serious rethinking of the way that work is done, the way it is organized, and the systems needed to support the academic enterprise. To develop successfully a new business model appropriate to the economics of the future, this rethinking needs to question the academic departmental base as the underlying condition for the delivery of administrative support services.

5.3   THE REENGINEERED ORGANIZATION

Several years ago, administrators responded to the cost crisis as if it was a temporary problem and financial resources would ultimately return to their previous levels, enabling them to spring forward to even higher levels of administrative support. Their early response to budget imbalances was to implement across-the-board cost-cutting measures or to freeze administrative budgets. Each of these approaches may have balanced the budget temporarily but did little to provide long-term budget relief. These approaches produced unsatisfactory results because administrative work did not go away. Instead, fewer staff remained and were required to do more with reduced resources. Although some forward-thinking institutions implemented innovative strategies in response to the cost crisis, such as total quality management (TQM) initiatives, the results have been incremental. To achieve the systemic changes needed in higher education today requires more dramatic approaches than TQM and other traditional measures.

As evidence mounts that the cost crisis is long term and structural in nature, more and more institutions are seeking ways to initiate radical organizational restructuring. The current administrative hierarchical organization requires more than tinkering around the margins. To accomplish change of the magnitude required in administrative structures today, colleges and universities need to question the underlying assumptions regarding the structure of administrative tasks. The outcome of this questioning should lead to organizational restructuring, management delayering, employee empowerment, and a culture that is less bureaucratic. Those who embark on this road need to be prepared to restructure their business services and administrative operations radically, even to the point of giving up certain responsibilities, taking on new responsibilities, or collaborating in heretofore unheard of ways (e.g., "hub" structures to provide administrative services to a group of three or more departments).

The Corporate Experience

Death of the Corporate Hierarchy.   Many corporations have faced and overcome the challenges currently confronting higher education. An army of writers is declaring the death of corporate bureaucracy. The U.S. corporate structure—defined by complex organizations, hierarchical chains of command, narrowly defined roles and responsibilities, numerous layers of management, and excessive division of labor—is considered a superfluous artifact of a bygone era that is becoming increasingly irrelevant in today's demanding environment. According to reengineering gurus Hammer and Champy:

> Advanced technologies, the disappearance of boundaries between national markets, and the altered expectations of customers who now have more choices than ever before have combined to make the goals, methods, and basic organizing principles of the classical American corporation sadly obsolete. Renewing their competitive capabilities isn't an issue of getting people in these companies to work harder, but of learning to work differently. This means that companies and their employees must unlearn many of the principles and techniques that brought them success for so long.[1]

In his book *The Rebirth of the Corporation*, D. Quinn Mills disdains the traditional hierarchy and considers it a threat to our economic survival. He proclaims:

> The traditional hierarchical structure of our companies is more than just a system that has outlived its usefulness—it is a clear and present danger to the economic welfare of all of us. . . .
> Perhaps in the past companies needed to be organized as if they were old-time military units. People were poorly educated and required precise direction. They were reluctant to work and poorly self-disciplined, so they needed close supervision. Because communications were slow and information difficult to obtain, many people were needed to collect information and prepare reports for top executives. The result was a pyramid of supervisory managers who kept business humming and rewarded themselves with good salaries and high status.[2]

Emergence of a New Way of Work.   Today's corporate reengineers are taking apart current hierarchical business models and are developing in their stead *process-oriented* organization structures. Although some corpora-

---

[1] Michael Hammer and James Champy, *Re-engineering the Corporation: A Manifesto for Business Revolution* (New York: HarperCollins, 1993), p. 11.
[2] D. Quinn Mills, *Rebirth of the Corporation* (New York: Wiley, 1991), pp. 13–14.

tions have reengineered superficially, at other corporations, corporate structures are being turned on their sides and upside down. Customers who were previously viewed as the downstream receivers of the output of the organization are moving upstream to the front end of the process to help define product requirements. Organizational boundaries are blurring and the edges of the corporation are merging with suppliers, becoming boundaryless organizations.

People in these organizations are adopting new ways of work. As they become focused on the needs and desires of their customers and are empowered to design responsive systems, their need for a traditional boss wanes. As the end-to-end process is organized into a single unit, narrow bands of specialization vanish and staff are responsible for the overall performance of the process and the results it delivers to customers. Ultimately, employees are organized as self-managed process teams that no longer rely on the directives of a middle manager to inform their daily, monthly, or annual activities. Concomitant with this change, old functional departments disappear, managers become more like coaches, and the traditional hierarchy begins to flatten. Ultimately, as the people who deliver the process implement a reengineered process and provide service that exceeds expectations, the need for process navigators evaporates. If an institution is committed to organizational change, the cost to deliver service is reduced dramatically.

Gifford and Elizabeth Pinchot explain this new way of work in compelling terms. They believe that bureaucracies are giving way to the rise of an intelligent organization. Employees in these new organizations

> . . . put their heads together to milk opportunities, co-create products and services, find and solve problems. The "get in over their heads" and help each other emerge with stronger skills and a bit more wisdom. Employees run their areas like small businesses, service their internal and external customers with care and work with others across the organization to make sure the whole system is going well. Everyone, not just the people at the top, is exercising his or her intelligence and responsibility at work.[3]

The Applicability of Reengineering to Higher Education

The Pinchots' description of the emerging work system for the corporate sector sounds almost too good to be true. It may seem difficult to achieve in the higher education sector. It is sometimes hard to imagine that staff will be able produce the results promised by reengineering. Higher education's elaborate system of controls, checks, and balances does not lend itself readily to the creation of an empowered workforce. Approvals are

---

[3] Gifford Pinchot and Elizabeth Pinchot, *The End of Bureaucracy and the Rise of the Intelligent Organization* (San Francisco: Berrett-Koehler Publishers, 1993), p. 5.

required because there are no consequences for abuses to the system. Numerous signatures create the illusion of control.

Higher education's reliance on numerous signatures also leads to the creation of tracking systems to monitor the process. Most processes are characterized by a series of handoffs and black holes. Tracking the transaction becomes an activity in its own right. Staff members develop systems so they are able to respond to queries regarding the status of the transaction and assure the caller that their small piece of the activity is done and they have sent the paperwork on its way.

It is resoundingly apparent that *radical*, systemic change is needed in higher education's underlying processes to overcome the built-in inefficiencies of the processes and to achieve the vision described by the Pinchots and other proponents of reengineering. But process change in not enough. The current culture of mistrust and control leads to "checkers" checking "checkers" and to a system that rewards the creation of work-around processes. This culture is a strong impediment to change.

To realize the results of process reengineering, accompanying changes are required in the systems, organization structures, cultures, and values that undergird higher education's current business model. New technology that provides decision-making information to the person closest to the customer is needed. Expert systems that contain simple rules for choosing options can tell faculty and staff immediately what to do rather than taking hours paging through various manuals and policy books or turning to central specialists to find the answer.

Finally, higher education's underlying management values need to change before its workforce has the luxury to operate in the manner described by the Pinchots. Classification systems need to become less restrictive, and people working in self-directed teams need new methods of feedback in their performance evaluations. Abuses require consequences. Exceptional work needs to be rewarded.

The Reengineering Process: An Overview

The new corporate organization is customer driven, results focused, and performance based. Importantly, the new organization will shift its focus from a functional or "vertical" orientation to a process view and will "go horizontal." Processes that have been fragmented across several departments will be restructured into a cohesive whole and will be designed to provide services to end customers in the most cost-effective manner.

This new *process mantra* is the basis of reengineering and has transformed many organizational structures into process-based organizations. Reengineering therefore begins with the identification of an organization's processes. A process is a series of linked activities in which an input is transformed into an output and a tangible product is delivered to an external customer.

But processes are hard to define. Rigorous application of Adam Smith's principles of division of labor has built a hierarchical structure in which excessive departmentalization makes it nearly impossible to identify the end-to-end process. The beginning of the process often has no connection to its end. Because most processes are characterized by hand-offs among numerous departments and obscured by complicated work steps, many organizations spend days simply defining their processes.

Process definition begins with the identification of an organization's outputs and the identification of the external customer to whom those outputs are delivered. In higher education, attaining agreement on the definition of the institution's customer often proves to be an arduous task. For some institutions, even the mention of the word *customer* is distasteful because it connotes a businesslike attitude that many college and university faculty and administrators abhor.

This reluctance to accept the existence of an external customer and the rejection of the idea that an institution produces measurable outputs and products is an obstacle to higher education's reengineering efforts. For example, a reengineering team that fails to define its customers correctly will—by default—fail to define the university's core processes correctly. Reengineering teams that abdicate their responsibility and do not own up to the customer definition task will be hampered in their reengineering efforts. For example, a team that agrees to an amorphous customer definition, such as the state's taxpayers or the general public, will find it difficult to define the product that is delivered to the customer or the process that creates the product. Unless accurate definitions of customers and outputs are achieved, defining processes and creating an institutional process map is nearly impossible.

Despite the difficulties in defining an institution's processes, it *is* an approach that is applicable to colleges and universities and provides interesting results, as described in the example later in this chapter.

Evaluating and Fixing Processes

Once an institution's processes have been defined, they can be evaluated according to their degree of criticality to its mission. A process framework allows an institution to evaluate its processes along a scale of salience, that is: How central are they to the mission and competitive advantage of the institution? The degree of saliency indicates the value an institution's processes deliver. In deciding what to reengineer, an institution can use process saliency to help determine the amount of investment they intend to make in reinventing the process. Investments should be made to improve the institution's most value-creating processes. Investment in other processes should not exceed the value they provide the institution.

Processes can be categorized as core and non-core. Core processes can be further segmented into identity and priority processes. Likewise, non-core processes can be further segmented into background and mandated processes. These are defined as:[4]

1. An *identity* process is what an institution stand for, "who" it is, and how customers think about it. The institution's vision, mission, values, priorities, and sense of shared culture all relate to its identity processes. This category of processes must be consciously maintained as an asset and strategically positioned to avoid becoming a liability.

2. *Priority* processes are important elements of an institution's business and link directly to and support its identity processes. These processes make a material difference in the ability of an institution to achieve a leadership position in its identity processes.

3. *Background* processes are part of what an institution does but do not directly support its identity processes. As such, background processes should not consume undue time, resources, or attention, nor divert critical resources away from the institution's identity and priority processes. Interestingly, background processes tend to harbor the most waste. As such, reengineering efforts are often centered around ways in which to reduce costs for background processes at the lowest investment possible.

4. *Mandated* processes are performed only because the government or other external agencies impose them on an institution. Regulation is the major source of such processes, which rarely adds economic value. Care should be taken to reduce the amount of effort and expense expended on these processes and yet comply adequately with regulation.

Not all processes should be reengineered. As reengineering teams begin the task of evaluating an institution's processes and designing new ones, they should initially ask hard questions designed to identify processes for elimination or outsourcing. Teams should challenge the status quo by asking whether the service needs to be done at all. If not, it should be eliminated. In these times of financial stringency, institutions should cut back (if not cut out) "nice to have" but nonessential services.

If the activity or service is essential but not an identity or priority process, can it be outsourced? This requires looking beyond traditionally outsourced services such as bookstores and dining services and examining whether services such as physical plant, payroll, human resources, audit, computing, security, "back office processing," and a host of other

---

[4] These terms were coined by Ellen M. Knapp of Coopers & Lybrand L.L.P.

activities are suitable candidates for outsourcing. According to a recent *Business Week* article:

> Hundreds of big companies have outsourced noncore operations: Continental Bank Corp. has contracted its legal, audit, cafeteria, and mailroom operations to outside companies. In September, American Airlines Inc. announced it would do the same with customer service jobs at 30 airports. . . . Outsourcing can work wonders for the bottom line: So-called contingent workers get pay comparable to full-time staff's, but without benefits that typically add 40% to labor costs. A contingent workforce, too, is more flexible: When business sags, the temps go first. Blue Cross/Blue Shield of Rhode Island cut its workforce by 40% over five years without laying off a single full timer.[5]

If the essential activity or service cannot or should not be outsourced, how can it be made more cost-effective, customer responsive, and efficient? For example, can redundant administrative work taking place in a multitude of departments be "in-sourced" to a process team to provide end-to-end process service while increasing timeliness and service delivery? Can the process be completely automated using advanced technology? Can the organizational model be restructured by creating a single customer service desk for students that handles registration, housing, service privileges (library card), dining, financial aid, and other essential student services? Is it possible to design a hybrid process in which a central organization sets standards and provides necessary infrastructure, yet which is decentralized to the end user?

There are numerous types of process solutions; one size does not fit all. Each institution will make unique decisions based on its mission, values, and the degree of supporting technology that exists. Importantly, the decision regarding which solutions are needed to fix the process begin by defining the customer and determining how the process creates value for the customer.

Higher Education's Process Map

Before processes can be redesigned, they need to be defined and the degree to which they are interrelated must be understood. One of the key tools of reengineering is the creation of a high-level business process map. According to Hammer and Champy:

> Process maps don't require months of work to construct; several weeks is the norm. But this task does induce headaches, because it requires people to think across the organizational grain. It's not a picture of the organization, which is what people are used to seeing and drawing, but a depiction of the

[5] "Special Report: Rethinking Work," *Business Week*, October 17, 1994, p. 85.

work that is being done. When it's finished, the process map should not surprise anyone. In fact, people may wonder why drawing it took as long as it did, since the finished map will be so easy to understand, even obvious. "Of course," people should say, "that's just a model of what we do around here."[6]

To create the map, it is necessary to identify the outputs created by the institution's core processes and define the customers to whom these outputs are delivered. The map, by definition, does not show departments, but rather, shows how work is done in the organization. Because processes have been obscured by organizational structures, employees often have a difficult time creating the first process map. The first step is to ignore department, college, or divisional reporting relationships and think about the processes that define the organization.

Most colleges and universities are able to distill their identity and priority processes into five to ten core processes. The way in which an institution implements each of these processes helps establish its reputation in the academic community. These core identity and priority processes are listed in Exhibit 5–1. Their distinct relationships to each other are expressed in a high-level process map in Exhibit 5–2 and described in the next paragraph.

Although the reputation of an institution is based on a number of factors, its implementation of its core processes contribute directly to and affect its reputation. How does this happen? One of higher education's core processes is its ability to create and sustain a dynamic and compelling intellectual community. The establishment of that community—accomplished by its strategic planning and budget setting process—is one of the primary assets that enable an institution to attract and retain faculty. Subsequently, these faculty members generate knowledge through research, educate students, and provide community service. Their teaching, research, and service activities produce distinct and measurable products (outputs) to the institution's customers, including the business community that employs its students, federal agencies that fund its research, patients that receive medical care, and community members that receive direct service, to name a few. Finally, customer satisfaction levels, changing customer needs, and the emergence of new customers inform its strategic planning process.

Each of the processes on the high-level process map in Exhibit 5–2 explode to create detailed maps of the corresponding subprocesses (Exhibit 5–3). These detailed subprocess maps can be blown up even further to identify the tasks required by each person in each department to complete the process.

[6] Hammer and Champy, *Re-engineering the Corporation*, p. 121.

Exhibit 5–1
ACTIVITY DICTIONARY: HIGHER EDUCATION'S FIVE IDENTITY PROCESSES

Conduct strategic planning and allocate resources to create, sustain, and revise the institutional intellectual community/environment.

Assess environment. Environmental scanning to determine future academic and research needs. Communicating with external customers. Identify opportunities and threats.

Set academic vision and priorities. Based on the environmental scan and a review of the institution's strengths and weaknesses, develop a vision for the future and identify priorities.

Establish/revise academic structure. Implement change to the academic structure of the institution, add/eliminate programs, schools, etc.

Formulate budgeting strategy and monitor results. Create strategic and operational plans departmentally, schoolwide, and campus-wide. Assess projections versus actual activities, prepare management reports, evaluate performance.

Output: The output of these sets of planning and budgeting activities is the creation of an intellectual community by which an institution attracts and retains its faculty.

Manage faculty resources.

Recruit faculty and retain faculty.

Implement promotion and tenure process.

Generate new knowledge.

Through the *conduct of research*, faculty generate new knowledge. See Exhibit 5–3 for a list of the subprocesses that comprise this core process.

Educate students.

Provide services to local, state, and national communities.

Exhibit 5-2

HIGHER EDUCATION'S PROCESS MAP

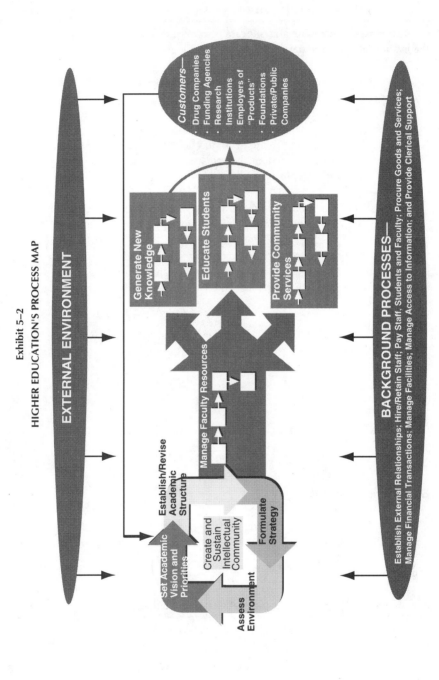

Exhibit 5–3

SUBPROCESS MAP: GENERATE NEW KNOWLEDGE THROUGH RESEARCH

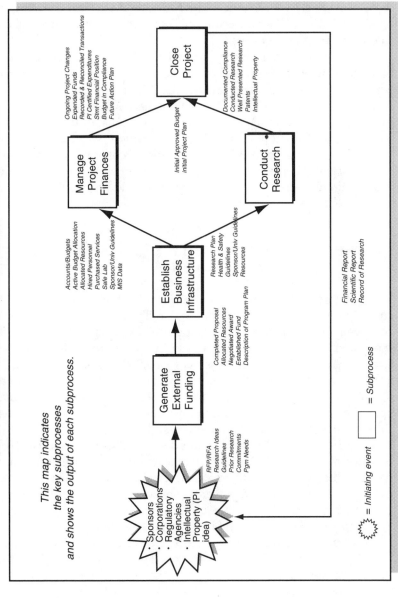

This map indicates the key subprocesses and shows the output of each subprocess.

The high-level process map provides a framework in which to discuss transforming higher education because it shows how processes link to and support the institution. Importantly, the map depicts the way in which work is done. By reengineering processes and reorganizing around the way in which work is done, higher education can create new organizational structures that ignore traditional hierarchical boundaries and follow the horizontal nature of work.

This process philosophy formed the basis for discussion of the Stanford University School of Medicine study. The Stanford University School of Medicine situation provides a microcosm of what is happening in higher education today. The school has experienced phenomenal growth but is in the midst of a significant cost crisis. In 1994 a representative group of the school's staff began to explore ways to deal with its budget crisis. The group evaluated traditional cost-saving strategies and rejected them. Their research led them to conclude that radical restructuring of administrative support was the only valid response to the budget problem.

5.4 THE STANFORD UNIVERSITY SCHOOL OF MEDICINE EXPERIENCE

In 1961–1962 the Stanford University School of Medicine reported a total consolidated budget of just under $7.1 million. At that time, the school consisted of 118 faculty members supported by 72 administrative staff. Of these staff, nearly 80 percent were faculty and departmental secretaries. Consequently, in 1961–1962, less than $500,000 was budgeted for administrative staff throughout the school. This amounted to less than 6 percent of the school's total spending and just 4 percent of all departmental spending. The entire central administration of the school consisted of three administrative deans and seven support staff.

By 1991–1992, although Stanford's School of Medicine faculty size had increased by nearly 400 percent over its 1961–1962 size, to 571 faculty, its consolidated budget had grown to a total of $231.2 million (a constant-dollar increase of over 600 percent). This expanded enterprise was supported with a 1000 percent increase in administrative staff, now totaling 835 people in 76 different job types, and a 1700 percent (constant dollar) increase in total administrative costs. Secretaries (although budgeted within five different job grades) comprised just 20 percent of the administrative workforce. The predominate departmental job groups are now administrative assistants, office assistants, and accountants. Administrative costs now consume nearly 15 percent of all school spending and over 25 percent of departmental spending. The rise in faculty process navigators has produced a constant-dollar increase of over 300 percent in departmental administrative costs per faculty member.

Despite a conventionally organized, well-developed, well-funded, and well-staffed administration supported with all the latest advances in automated administrative systems, in 1990, a series of procedural and accounting problems came to light at Stanford University which called into question the integrity of the cost-accounting da:a supporting the university's sponsored research indirect cost rate. As a result, the federal government unexpectedly and retroactively reduced the university's effective indirect cost rate by over 30 percent, which at the Stanford School of Medicine, resulted in an immediate and sustained loss of some $12 million in budgeted unrestricted annual income. This represented a loss of nearly 20 percent of the support behind the school's general funds.

Although it had recently undertaken a downsizing effort in response to more subtle changes in its financial forecasts, the school's administration responded to the lost indirect cost recoveries with an immediate 5 percent reduction in central administrative staff, followed shortly thereafter by an across-the-board 7 percent reduction in general funds allocations to academic departments, a one-time salary freeze, reductions in planned faculty billet increases, and an additional 6 percent reduction in central administrative units. Combined with other adjustments in the school's financial plans and reserves management practices, by 1993 these actions left the school with a continuing base budget shortfall of about $2 million.

At the request of the school's dean, a group of departmental and central administrators convened to study the school's administrative costs and to advise the dean on options for reducing costs further to achieve a balanced budget. In addition to continuing to pursue conventional downsizing approaches and exploring opportunities for reducing costs through TQM-type approaches, this study included an assessment of the applicability of business process reengineering (BPR) approaches to administrative restructuring at the School of Medicine. The results of the study have proven to be invaluable in helping the school's academic and administrative leaders to better understand the limitations of continuing with their prevailing model and to identify the risks and opportunities of pursuing a new and different approach.

The School's Process Map

The hierarchy of activities and taxonomy of administrative processes presented earlier provided a unifying framework for studying the School of Medicine's administrative costs and structure. Stanford's study began with the development of a process map of the School of Medicine's activities. Traditional administrative inventories usually ask the question,

"What do we do?" and tend to produce effort measures within the existing organizational chart. A high-level process-based view of the school was produced by repeatedly asking the question, "To what end do we do what we do?" and yielded a unique view of the critical outputs of the school. The school's data indicated that between 525 and 590 full time equivalents (FTEs) of staff effort was expended in administrative tasks. These FTEs cost the school between $30 million and $35 million. Despite the relative importance of the priority processes to the success of the school's academic mission, nearly three-fourths of the FTEs and two-thirds of the staff costs were attributable to the administration of background processes. In Exhibit 5–4 these processes are depicted on a process map to indicate how each process links to and supports other processes and to show the output to the school's customers. It also shows the costs (in millions of dollars) of the school's administrative activities.

Perceptions of the School's Administrative Processes

Focus groups representing the recipients (customers) of the school's administrative efforts indicated a high degree of customer dissatisfaction with the performance of nearly all of the school's administrative processes. The faculty's confidence in the administration's value, ability, and willingness to get things done decreased in direct correlation to the distance at which the process activity took place from their own offices. From the faculty's perspective, the most valuable participant in the process was their local administrator. The only way to get anything done was to rely on their local administrator—the process navigator—as a go-between, bridging the gulf between their academic program needs and an unfathomable and unresponsive administrative bureaucracy.

Local administrators clearly viewed faculty as their customers and expressed their frustrations with this go-between role and the extraordinary effort expended in meeting the demands of faculty. Faculty and their local administrators expressed a distrust of the motives and abilities of central medical school administration and suggested that if they could simply be left to do their jobs, things would run just fine. Local administrators evidenced a particular pride in the private shadow systems they developed to support their work in ways in which the official university systems could not. They frequently measured their successes by their heroic abilities at shortcutting the university's processes, often through their knowledge of key persons at critical steps in the process. "Process busting" was a skill valued by faculty and an activity from which local administrators derived professional pride.

Focus groups representing the providers of central medical school administrative services generally saw the university or external agencies

Exhibit 5–4
STANFORD UNIVERSITY, SCHOOL OF MEDICINE:
HIGH-LEVEL PROCESS MAP

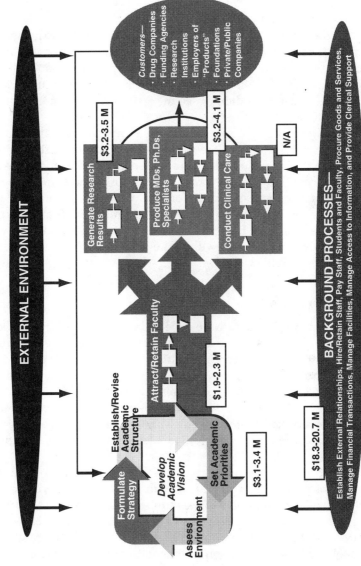

as their customers. They expressed great frustration with the attitudes and capabilities of the faculty and their local administrators. They felt that if the faculty and staff would just learn the university's policies and procedures, the jobs in the medical school's central offices would be made much easier. While these central administrators acknowledged their effect on the pace of administration and the frustrations expressed by the local staff as a result of their prolonged reviews and frequent returns of work, they consistently rated the quality of their work as "high." This is an understandable difference in perception from the faculty view since central administrators did not see the faculty and local administrators as their customers.

In all the focus groups, individuals expressed a clear understanding of their specific jobs. They knew in infinite detail their particular pieces of processes that usually began and ended elsewhere in the institution. They did not, however, express a sense of ownership of the overall conduct of any process. From a process view, the School of Medicine's administration consisted of a vast array of individuals all working very hard at their assigned tasks, with little or no understanding or ownership of their contributory role within the larger processes that define the success of the school.

Implications of Administrative Fragmentation

Detailed staff effort data were collected and analyzed by the School of Medicine reengineering team. They helped express the administrative effort and costs of the school in light of the processes involved. Reinforcing the findings of the focus groups, the data gathered indicated a great deal of process fragmentation within the School of Medicine. Within an organizational unit (i.e., a division or a department) numerous individual staff members were involved in the various phases of the processes. Also, staff from across all levels of the organization indicated participation in the process.

Not surprising, then, were the data indicating a similarly high degree of position fragmentation with the school's processes. Position fragmentation is a measure of the number of people required to yield a full FTE of administrative effort within a process area. The lower the ratio, the better. Exhibit 5–5 shows a sample process fragmentation table. At the School of Medicine, position fragmentation ratios ranged from a low of 1.75 (recruiting M.D. and Ph.D. students) to a high of 10.37 (research project closeout). Across all processes the school averaged a fragmentation ratio of 1.57. Within its priority processes, however, the ratios were 2.66 (educating students), 3.42 (establishing vision and recruiting and retaining faculty), and 3.81 (generating research results).

Exhibit 5–5
SAMPLE PROCESS FRAGMENTATION TABLE

Process	Individuals[a] (1)	FTE[b] (2)	Fragmentation Ratio[c] (3)	Average Percent[d] (4)
Recruit/retain faculty[e]	94	19.2	4.9	20
Generate external funds[e]	89	17.1	5.2	19
Establish infrastructure[e]	24	3.4	7.1	14
Manage project finances[e]	102	25.5	4.0	25
Close project finances[f]	31	3.0	10.4	10
Hire/retain postdoctoral candidates[e]	43	11.6	3.7	26
Hire/retain staff[f]	74	19.5	3.8	25
Procure goods[f]	291	41.0	7.1	14
Manage facilities[f]	155	23.0	6.8	15
Manage access to information[f]	79	37.6	2.1	48

[a] Number of staff who indicated that they participated in the process.
[b] Converts the number of staff in the process to an FTE based on the percent of time spent on the process.
[c] Fragmentation ratio calculated by dividing column 1 by column 2. Indicates the degree to which the process is fragmented; that is, the process does not require or is not structured such that a person spends most of his or her time on the process. The higher the ratio, the more fragmented the process.
[d] Average percent is calculated by dividing column 2 by column 1. Indicates the average percentage of time a person spends on the process.
[e] Priority process.
[f] Background process.

These ratios were a concern for two significant reasons. First, they indicate that even within the priority areas so critical to the success of the school, the average administrator was only spending one-fourth to one-third of his or her time "doing" the priority process. The rest of their time was spent in largely administrative tasks outside a particular priority process area.

The second reason for concern was the implication of the ratios on the potential for successful sustained downsizing efforts. Traditional downsizing efforts were not possible because across-the-board cost cuts do not eliminate administrative work. Similarly, reducing administrative costs by implementing incremental process improvement (TQM) did not offer the prospect of sustained cost savings. Although minor process change can improve performance, it is impossible to translate those efficiency improvements into reduced staff costs. This is because radical improvement in work flows in at least three or four processes is required to achieve significant staff reductions. The school's data showed that efforts to achieve cost savings from incremental process improvement in a highly fragmented work environment is hindered by the fact that these improvements usually affect only a portion of a person's job.

It became increasingly apparent that without dramatic changes in work flow *and* organization, the school would not be able to achieve the level of savings it so sorely needed. The fragmentation data indicated that without larger-scale organizational changes, neither traditional downsizing nor TQM techniques appeared to offer real opportunities for the School of Medicine to achieve and sustain its administrative cost saving.

A New Organizational Construct

Faced with low customer satisfaction, high costs, and high fragmentation data, the School of Medicine explored the implications of business process reengineering on its staffing, costs, and organization. It was fortuitous that Stanford University was already engaged in several campuswide process reengineering initiatives: the process by which staff and faculty "buy/pay" for goods and services and the methods by which proposals for research funding are generated and submitted. Each of the university reengineering teams had produced a conceptual model identifying a radical new process by which to procure and pay for goods and to develop and submit research proposals. Using the university's conceptual redesigns, the school began an exercise designed to identify the ways in which these new campuswide processes could enable it to restructure its administration. Concurrent with receipt of the university's redesigned processes, a front-end financial software package would become available which would allow the school to change significantly the way in which departments manage financial transactions. The financial management system would eliminate the need for shadow systems and time-consuming reconciliation processes. Subsequently, it would enable departments to eliminate positions that exist solely to maintain the shadow systems.

The result of the school's effort to model the effect of the proposed Stanford University redesigns on the school's organization resulted in the conceptualization of an administrative organizational model that would:

1. Uncouple the administrative organization from the academic organization.

2. Organize administrative units around priority processes focused on the support of individual faculty.

3. Organize administrative units around background processes focused on maintaining reliable and responsive institutional sys-

tems that deliver minimally invasive services and support to the priority processes.

4. Staff administrative units with fewer people more focused on a specific process area and operating with much greater authority to support the desired products and outputs.

At the heart of this model is the creation of several process teams to support the school's identity processes. For example, the school envisions a team of talented staff who would act as research process managers (RPMs) and support the end-to-end pre- and post-award process. These process managers would have delegated signature authority and be empowered to bust away bureaucracy, although they would report to a process owner, the associate dean for research, and would be accountable to their customer (the faculty) for getting proposals out in a timely manner and for providing support to principal investigators (PIs) in the management of their research funds. Technology would be a key enabler for the process. In addition to providing templates for proposals, new software solutions would help process managers oversee the day-to-day financial operations of the project. Research process managers would not have academic departmental reporting relationships. They may serve faculty from a number of departments. Decoupling research administration support from the narrow boundaries of the academic department would enable the school to reduce the number of staff members participating in the process by 50 percent. The school envisions involving other process managers in the student recruitment and retention process as well as in the faculty recruitment and retention process.

The high-level conceptual design of the new organization is presented in Exhibit 5–6. The success of the School of Medicine's model depends on Stanford University's continuing campuswide reengineering efforts. The maintenance of large numbers of staff to participate in "broken" university background processes is an expense that the school can no longer afford. The new high-level buy/pay process intends to deliver a process so simple and straightforward that every member of the Stanford community will become "a shopper" and will be able to procure most goods without the help of process navigators or procurement specialists.

The efforts of the school's team to untangle administrative costs from its academic departments provide lessons for other institutions contemplating reengineering. To date most reengineering efforts stop at the door of a school or academic department; little work has been undertaken to realize the results promised by reengineering. The school's hard look at the structure and organization of the administrative tasks within an academic department indicates that substantial change is possible. In general, radical change is possible in higher education if institutions are

Exhibit 5–6

STANFORD UNIVERSITY, SCHOOL OF MEDICINE:
PROPOSED ADMINISTRATIVE ORGANIZATION CHART

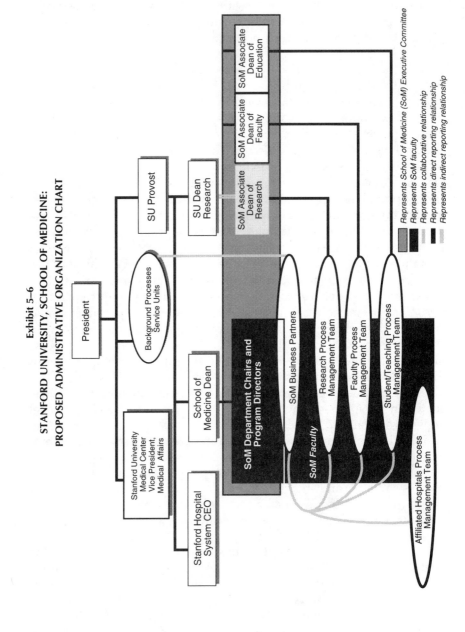

Represents School of Medicine (SoM) Executive Committee
Represents SoM faculty
Represents collaborative relationship
Represents direct reporting relationship
Represents indirect reporting relationship

President

SU Provost

SU Dean Research

Stanford University Medical Center Vice President, Medical Affairs

School of Medicine Dean

Stanford Hospital System CEO

Background Processes Service Units

SoM Associate Dean of Research

SoM Associate Dean of Faculty

SoM Associate Dean of Education

SoM Department Chairs and Program Directors

SoM Business Partners

Research Process Management Team

Faculty Process Management Team

Student/Teaching Process Management Team

SoM Faculty

Affiliated Hospitals Process Management Team

bold in their approach to redesign and do not set limits or boundaries on the process.

5.5 CONCLUSIONS

Is it actually possible for higher education to achieve the results promised by reengineering? Does corporate restructuring have any relevance for academia? Is a radically different organization model possible?

The answers to these questions are: Yes. Yes. And, yes. Radical change is possible. This transformation will not be an easy task, nor will it happen overnight. In fact, the road to a transformed institution can be treacherous. It requires both stamina and a dedication to goals that may at times seem impossible to attain in higher education. The road to transformation begins by requiring that college and university administrators establish a healthy skepticism regarding the status quo and be ready to let go of traditional approaches. An essential ingredient for success will be the desire, inclination, and ability of people from disparate functions across the institution to work together cohesively to develop a new business model.

Therein is the most difficult challenge. *Designing* the new model is easy. *Achieving consensus* around a new business model, however, is fraught with difficulty. Most colleges and universities are characterized by a highly decentralized, boundary-sensitive environment in which responsibility centers usually focus on maximizing their own benefits rather than taking a "What's best for the institution view?" In most institutions, there is an apparent lack of a "tiebreaking" structure to make tough decisions. Unlike the corporate sector, in which top-down decisions to change are made more readily, higher education's current business model does not provide an efficient decision-making mechanism for change.

However, restructuring will cause an institution's leadership to wrestle with important issues regarding the role and responsibilities of its campus-wide, university-provided functions, school-based central administrative functions, and departmentally-based administrative functions. In short, by reengineering, an institution's leadership will be answering the fundamental underlying question: What is the most appropriate business model for a complex, decentralized organization?

The answer will ultimately be one of organizational design: To what extent is the institution willing to "go horizontal," moving from a functionally oriented organization (vertical) to a "process" organization? How much will employees be empowered to operate in teams and make decisions about their processes without going through the organizational hierarchy? These can be difficult questions. Failure to address them consciously throughout the organizational change process may thwart the success of any attempt to change. However, confronting these questions directly and aggressively can enable an institution to reengineer itself successfully, saving substantial costs and positioning itself strategically for the future.

PART THREE

Funding the Enterprise

Chapter Six
Revenue Opportunities for the Public Institution

Chapter Seven
Strategies for Optimizing Revenues in the Tuition-
Dependent Institution

Revenue Opportunities for the Public Institution

WELDON E. IHRIG

**Vice Chancellor for Finance and Administration
Oregon State System of Higher Education**

JAMES F. SULLIVAN

**Vice Chancellor of Administration (Retired)
University of California, Riverside**

6.1 Introduction
6.2 Historical Context
6.3 Current Situation
6.4 Seeking Revenue Opportunities
6.5 New Revenue Opportunities
  Information
  Teaching
  Alumni
  Campus Population
  Land and Facilities
6.6 Expanding Current Revenue Sources
6.7 Conclusions

6.1 INTRODUCTION

Although there are more independent than public colleges and universities in the United States, far more students, in fact over 80 percent of those enrolled, attend public institutions. Enrollment on just the 100 largest public university campuses exceeds that of all independent colleges and universities taken together.[1]

---

[1] *Digest of Higher Education Statistics*, 1993 National Center for Education Statistics, Washington, DC. Calculated from table 211.

Public colleges and universities serve a much more diverse population, in terms of minority students, age of students, and full-time/part-time students, than do their independent counterparts. For example, part-time enrollment more than doubled at public institutions between 1970 and 1991, compared to a 65 percent increase at independent institutions.[2]

Although serving a larger, more diverse population requires more resources, public higher education's share of state budgets has fallen in recent years. As a result, some public institutions are becoming more resourceful and entrepreneurial. They are looking at their human, technological, and plant assets in new ways, seeking to generate new revenue opportunities by using these assets more creatively. In this chapter we explore new revenue opportunities, focusing on public colleges and universities.

6.2 HISTORICAL CONTEXT

The only constant for higher education is change, and change at an ever-increasing rate, as reflected by public higher education's declining share of traditional state and local revenue sources. The 1980s were a period of increasing costs for public institutions and of attempts to increase state support and tuition to cover the increasing costs. State support did not increase, however. In fact, the decline in state support represented the single largest financial constraint on public colleges and universities. In 1985–1986, public institutions received 48.8 percent of their revenues from state and local governments[3]; by 1991–1992, that share of revenues dropped to 41.9 percent.[4] The decline in state and local government support is likely to continue as pressures expand on available government resources to address other societal needs. Another factor is the reluctance of taxpayers to increase taxation in support of public needs.

As the 1990s arrived, the reality was that state and local support for public higher education continued to decrease while costs continued to increase, resulting in a greater shift of the funding burden to students. These events occurred at a time when increasing numbers of students and their families were unable to pay higher tuition prices. Between 1985–1986

---

[2] *Digest of Higher Education Statistics*, 1993, National Center for Education Statistics, Washington, DC. Calculated from table 174.

[3] "Public support of private colleges," *Change*, Vol. 20, No. 2, March–April 1988, Chart 1, p. 38.

[4] "Revenues and expenditures of colleges and universities, 1991–92," *The Chronicle of Higher Education Almanac*, September 1, 1994, p. 37.

and 1991–1992, student tuition and fees grew from 14.5 percent to 17.1 percent of overall revenues for public institutions. Tuition as a share of median family income increased from 3.8 percent in 1980 to 5.0 percent in 1990, primarily because tuition at public institutions increased 141 percent during the decade of the 1980s while inflation increased 64 percent.[5] The tuition increases of the 1980s were driven, in part, by general increases in college and university costs. But cost shifting from state and local government to students greatly exacerbated the situation. Then and now the middle class feels hard-pressed to find ways to adjust to the rate of tuition increases facing them. As a result, the tendency is to attribute the cause of tuition increases to out-of-control spending on the part of the public colleges and universities.

Support from private gifts has increased from 3.2 percent to 4.0 percent of total public institution revenues, while sales and services revenues have risen from 20 percent to 23.3 percent. Although some might conclude that direct sales and services are replacing some of the traditional revenue sources, these revenues must be applied to fund the services provided. They do not support the costs of instruction.

The decline in state and local government support, the inability of tuition increases to replace this decline, and the modest changes in other traditional income sources are likely to continue indefinitely. These circumstances suggest strongly the need for public higher education to place increasing emphasis on seeking and expanding new revenue sources. The leaders of public higher education are being challenged to alter their focus, to seek new and expanded revenue opportunities that can contribute to funding their primary mission, instruction.

6.3 CURRENT SITUATION

As the pressures increase on state and local governments to address greater demands for expanded social services, including primary and secondary education and crime prevention, higher education continues to find itself receiving a lower share of state and local support each year. There are few, if any, indications that the trend will change in the foreseeable future. The result will be an even greater shift in the share of the cost to the often underfinanced private person who wants high-quality education, but at a low price.

As the dual trends affecting tuition and government support continue and are, perhaps, made worse, expenditure pressures on public higher education continue to mount. Retaining faculty means providing

---

[5] Ernest R. House, "Policy and productivity in higher education," *Research News and Comment*, June–July 1994, p. 29.

competitive salaries and leading-edge equipment, including modern computers connected to worldwide information networks. At the same time, institutions must address accumulated deferred maintenance problems and modernize campus infrastructures to accommodate future technological changes in the classroom, office, and research laboratory.

Replacing more state and local government funding with higher tuition increases will continue to be difficult to sell to legislators and the public they represent. However, students who believe that the education they receive is worth the increased costs of tuition will pay more for access, especially to high-quality education. On the other hand, the position of students with lower family incomes continues to worsen; as tuition rises, the availability of student financial aid from both the federal and state governments is not likely to keep pace.

Such trends increase the pressure on public institutions to rely less on state and local government resources. Even government leaders are encouraging public colleges and universities to self-generate a higher proportion of institutional revenues. Some states provide flexibility, urging campuses to operate in a more entrepreneurial manner by reducing state requirements and delegating greater authority to public institutions.

However, government leaders who encourage public colleges and universities to enhance their nontraditional revenue sources must be willing to provide positive incentives to encourage new ideas. An obvious disincentive for future creative revenue enhancements exists whenever a legislature or governor reduces the amount of state support by an amount equal to new institutional revenues generated from other sources. Therefore, it is important that state and local governments encourage revenue enhancement strategies by making it clear to institutions that any new revenues generated can be applied to meeting unfunded needs or lowering future tuition increases. Government must also recognize that certain revenue enhancement activities require startup costs for which campuses will need to divert budgeted funds to act as seed monies.

To the extent that the increased revenue comes from students, in the form of special fees, for example, they may become more sophisticated consumers and insist upon higher-quality services for their fees. This could force faculty and staff to become more directly involved in the institution's financial situation since the link between the quality of the instruction and services provided and the revenues generated will be clearer. In this new environment, faculty and staff may also see the value of providing greater support to those areas with high revenue-generating potential.

Given reductions in governmental resources and strained tuition levels, many efforts have gone into reducing the costs of instruction, support services, and administration. Institutions will need to continue to reduce costs, find new ways to teach, and reduce their overhead expenses. However, such actions will not by themselves counteract the declines in state and local support or the pressures to hold down the rates of increases on tuition. Therefore, colleges and universities need to focus on the dual strategies of *reducing* expenditures as well as *diversifying* and increasing their revenue sources. Planning for the twenty-first century requires public colleges and universities to seek new revenue opportunities and expand existing revenues as a critical component of developing strategies for success.

6.4 SEEKING REVENUE OPPORTUNITIES

There is some resistance to finding new revenue sources. Some people believe doing so relieves government from its historical responsibility to fund public higher education. Other people are concerned that new income-generating activities may be out of character for colleges and universities, making them too much a part of the world of commerce. Some suggest that public institutions may be ill-advised to pursue profits in activities that could be provided by private enterprise (see Chapter 16 for a discussion of the tax implications of this topic).

These criticisms have some merit and must be kept in mind when considering what new revenue source to pursue. However, the expansion of revenues remains an appropriate recourse because the revenue shortfall of colleges and universities will not disappear easily or quickly. Further, in this era of change, all appropriate revenue sources have not yet been found. Finally, colleges and universities must be able to plan their future, to the extent possible, in a rational manner and not continue to be the victims of financial problems unrelated to their own operations.

This viewpoint appears to be gaining acceptance in higher education. *The Chronicle of Higher Education* reported in July 1994 that 50 percent of all colleges and universities, including 49 percent of public institutions, have expanded revenue-generating academic programs and that 48 percent of all colleges and universities "plan[ned] academic programs with business."

Whose responsibility is it to look for new revenue sources? Few campuses have thought about this subject systematically. In the past, finding new income streams or expanding existing ones has generally occurred on an ad hoc basis. But for this function to be given the time and resources necessary to produce the results needed, it must be assigned to the appropriate levels of the administration.

Senior administrators each have a stake in taking responsibility for finding new income streams. They are also well prepared to fill major roles in this new endeavor, for they possess a breadth of knowledge of the campus, its operations, and resources. They also should have both the imagination to see opportunities where others do not and the patience to approach the task in an orderly fashion. Presidents must add revenue enhancement to their leadership as a primary focus. Adding this responsibility to an already overcommitted position is necessary for several reasons. First, it is vital to the future financial success of the campus. Second, the president is the primary person to convince constituencies on-campus and off-campus of the appropriateness of these new activities. Third, the president has a unique view of the entire campus and its constituencies. Finally, the president is the best person to orchestrate a combined effort by all campus senior administrators.

The other major administrator to play a role in generating new revenue is the chief business and financial officer. This person should become knowledgeable about what other campuses are doing, or thinking of doing. The task is not to find unique revenue sources, just sources new to one's campus. Approach this task as a research project. Do a library search. Read the appropriate publications, such as *The Chronicle of Higher Education*, for the past few years. Perhaps hire a clipping service. Read the publications of appropriate professional associations, such as the *Business Officer* of the National Association of College and University Business Officers (NACUBO). Seek information from the professional associations and attend a few carefully selected seminars and annual meetings. Research what other nonprofit entities outside higher education are doing. Consider hiring a consultant who specializes in this area. Because of the researchlike nature of this work, an institution might consider hiring or giving release time to a faculty member, one with the ability and interest to do the job properly. In this way, it is possible to become knowledgeable about what is going on and what others are thinking regarding new revenue sources for colleges and universities.

Some colleges and universities have created a separate legal corporation for the purpose of raising money for the campus. These separate legal entities can run businesses, sell products, create contractual obligations, and embrace other activities that public institutions may not wish to do for political or public relations reasons and/or which may create legal problems for the campus. A separate corporation generally has fewer administrative regulations (i.e., a less bureaucratized approval process, a more flexible personnel process, etc.) than public colleges and universities. This separate legal entity can be a valuable tool for implementing new revenue opportunities.

Another initial step in looking for new or expanded income streams involves borrowing some strategic planning techniques. What does a campus have that is valuable to the world, that is unique, or at least in short supply? Does it have faculty with unusual expertise? Is the campus located on valuable land? Do the alumni have special characteristics? Think about potentially valuable campus assets. What can be done with each of these assets that is appropriate, legitimate, tasteful, and would raise significant revenue for the campus?

6.5   NEW REVENUE OPPORTUNITIES

In the remainder of this chapter we suggest possible new income sources. Whether they should be implemented depends on the characteristics, needs, and values of individual campuses.

Information

One valuable resource of colleges and universities is information. Higher education institutions store information, primarily in their libraries; disseminate information, primarily through teaching; and create information, primarily through research. Information is a valuable commodity in society. It is a vital element of decision making in business, the health and medical fields, and government. People use it for personal decisions about job opportunities, vacation planning, leisure-time activities, and so on. Colleges and universities hold more information, create more of it, and have a more sophisticated dissemination process for it than any other organization in society. This cornucopia of information should be carefully reviewed to determine how it can help expand the revenue sources available to colleges and universities.

One aspect of information that is receiving considerable attention today is intellectual property. Intellectual property—research results, computer programs, and so on—is generally created by full-time employees on campus time using campus equipment. In the past, because of a firm belief in free access to knowledge and because public funds support the creation of this knowledge, campuses have been very reluctant to charge for its use. When others took this information and made a profit from it, it was of little concern to higher education. But given the fiscal future of higher education, campuses should consider whether their legitimate ownership of this valuable commodity gives them the right to share in the income generated with this newly created knowledge.

Financial arrangements for the sharing of intellectual property can take many forms. Licensing, where anyone using the intellectual property signs an agreement with the institution covering the use of the information and stipulating what payments will be made to the institution, is one example. Another example involves giving the institution or its foundation partial ownership, or stock, in a company in return for the company's use of the university's intellectual property. For example, Rutgers University has an ownership stake in four companies that were started with information gained by its research.

Approximately 100 colleges and universities have offices responsible for patent processing, negotiating license agreements with private companies, and working with people who want to commercialize campus research results. These offices also advise faculty about the patent potential of their research and encourage them to share their research results with the patent office. These patent/technology transfer offices have been successful. American colleges and universities received four times as many patents in 1992 as in 1980. Income from licensing such campus-generated knowledge is also growing, particularly among the leading research universities. In 1992–1993, the most successful 100 of these institutions received over $172 million just from licensing their inventions. For example, Columbia University received over $14 million and Michigan State University received over $13 million.

In some cases there has been so much use of campus-generated intellectual property that research parks have been developed on or near universities. Campuses receive not only income from the intellectual property used by the companies in the research park, but also research grants and contracts to support their efforts to create new information so valuable to these companies. Occasionally, the companies are so appreciative of how the university has assisted them that they provide it with gifts for non-research-related programs.

If a campus does not have a strong research component, it normally has faculty, and sometimes staff, who keep track of basic research done at other institutions. They often understand, before others do, the implications of this basic research. These faculty and staff can provide a valuable bridge between those who generate new knowledge and those who would find it valuable. This ability could translate into a campus service that gathers and reports research data, and perhaps interprets it for regional businesses or other groups. Another possibility is to teach regional businesses and governmental units how to use new information (e.g., how to handle the toxic wastes they generate).

Teaching

The basic mission of colleges and universities is teaching. Institutions generally have the most knowledgeable faculty, the best equipment, and the most extensive educational facilities in their area. Instead of limiting themselves to students who choose to matriculate to the campus, institutions could use their already organized educational operation to meet the needs of external constituencies. More and more private companies are realizing that their staffs must possess the latest knowledge in a field. The half-life of knowledge is decreasing, causing corporate know-how to become obsolete quickly. In some cases businesses are expanding and want a steady supply of employees trained to move into newly created positions. Campuses should be able to meet some of these needs by contracting to teach corporate employees. Many campuses, the University of California–Irvine, for example, provide such a service to companies in their area.

It is generally agreed that the United States has the best system of higher education in the world. Many companies and governmental agencies from other countries would like their employees to be trained in specific subjects in U.S. colleges and universities. Given the declining value of the dollar, more people from other nations than ever before can afford to come to the United States for education. Some campuses already contract with foreign companies to train their employees in such subjects as agriculture, banking, and transportation. For example, the Davis campus of the University of California had a long-term contract with the Kingdom of Saudi Arabia to teach Saudi bank executives about agriculture and agricultural economics. Federal assistance to underwrite such programs is sometimes available. For example, certain federal agencies might want to underwrite economic training for citizens of Eastern European countries. A campus's high-quality academic departments could be used to train foreigners; if the campus also has or can create a living environment that would be attractive to people from other cultures, it may have all the ingredients it needs to create such a training program.

Some campuses have been successful in winning domestic government training or retraining contracts. These contracts cover different population groups—from early childhood education through worker retraining to courses for senior citizens. Continuing part-time education for working adults is also an expanding opportunity. Many adults seek an educational background to enhance their eligibility for promotion, to strike out in new career directions, or to get the basic higher education they bypassed after high school. Some professionals are required by state law to take courses periodically to maintain their proficiency. Colleges and universities are the best institutions in society to provide these people with the continuing education they seek.

Another educational opportunity for colleges and universities is the Elderhostel program. Elderhostel provides inexpensive, short-term academic programs for older adults hosted by educational institutions around the world. This new income stream is being tapped by more and more campuses throughout the United States, for example, Johns Hopkins University, the University of Alaska, and the Yavapai Community College in Prescott, Arizona, among others.

Some campuses have unique specialties or locations that create unusual opportunities for nontraditional course offerings. For example, a campus may have a department of enology (wine-making) or be located adjacent to a national park with special geographic features or an historical site. Such campuses can provide specialized short-term, nondegree courses; institutions should not overlook these kinds of opportunities, not only because of their financial benefits but also because of the interests of the public in learning what a campus is uniquely able to provide.

Alumni

Colleges and universities also should not overlook their alumni. A special relationship exists between alumni and the higher education institutions they attended. For years, this relationship was tapped primarily by alumni fund drives, reunions, attendance at major campus sporting events, and occasionally, assistance in recruiting students or placing students upon graduation. More recently, the relationship between alumni and institutions has broadened. Campuses are providing continuing education for their graduates; and increasing numbers of alumni are interested in continuing their learning experience. Additionally, some alumni look to their alma mater for certain professional services and for housing after retirement. Campuses are beginning to respond to these interests.

Alumni continuing education is taking two major forms. The first is establishing an alumni college and inviting alumni, for a fee, to take short courses geared to their interests, generally when the college is not in normal academic session. Dartmouth College is one of a sizable number of institutions that operates an alumni college. The second format is campus-sponsored tours to interesting educational locations using faculty experts as guides. The University of Colorado, Boulder, has such a program. Both types of alumni continuing education not only provide income to the campus, but also renew ties between alumni and the campus.

Some campuses are offering alumni certain professional services. These include professional midcareer placement services, home mortgage service, personal insurance policies, and credit cards. For example, alumni associations at Duke University, the University of Notre Dame, and the University of Arizona refer alumni who are job hunting to a private firm with which the association has a contract. Credit cards received through alumni association affiliation, called affinity credit cards, are available to graduates of a number of institutions, including Georgetown University, the University of South Carolina, and Northwestern University.

Alumni usually have pleasant memories and good friends from their student days. Such factors may cause them to think of their alma mater when it comes to retirement housing. Some alumni have moved several times during their careers and no longer have a place that seems like home. In contemplating where they might retire, their former college campus could have a great deal to offer compared with other potential retirement locations.

Living on or near the campus allows alumni to participate in college life again by attending sporting events, plays, concerts, and so on. They can use the library and perhaps enroll in classes. They might even find a role to play in helping current students. If the campus has a medical school, they would be close to high-quality medical care. In addition to these advantages, they might also be able to convince some of their fellow alumni friends to retire to their alma mater. This has a great deal of appeal to some alumni.

A campus can anticipate this interest and create a high-quality housing development for alumni on or near the campus. In creating such a development, the campus should take retired alumni interests into account, creating special ties to the campus for people living in retirement housing (e.g., special block seating at sporting events).

The potential financial payoff to the campus in alumni housing is considerable. First, there is the income from the housing development itself. In planning the development, consider ground lease of campus land, selling lots subdivided on campus-owned land, turnkey construction with the campus selling the homes or condominiums, and campus-owned homes or condominiums leased to alumni. Second, there is greater potential for annual gifts from these alumni, particularly when they become interested in particular campus programs (e.g., support of a concert series, scholarships for students in a specific major, funds for a research project, support for a student activity with which the alumnus is associated). They might help in job placement of students or, if the alumnus is truly an expert, give a lecture in a campus course. The largest fiscal windfall might be estate gifts from the alumni who have been reintegrated into the campus. A number of colleges and universities currently have active alumni housing developments, including the University of Virginia, Oberlin College, and Iowa State University.

Campus Population

Colleges and universities have a relatively large population in a concentrated area. Campuses usually have thousands of students, staff, and faculty who come to the campus each day, constituting a major customer base. In addition, many campus activities attract visitors—sporting events, conferences, alumni activities, and so on. All of these people require services while they are on campus. A campus may generate enough overnight visitors to support a small hotel on campus. For example, Johns Hopkins University turned four old townhouses on campus into a hotel for their continuing education clientele. If land is in tight supply, perhaps there is space in campus buildings to lease to private firms to provide commercial services. Banks are usually eager to locate automatic teller machines on campus. Fast-food franchises generally look forward to leasing space on campus. The possibilities are as broad as are the interests of the campus population—a greeting card store, beauty parlor, dry cleaner, or a pharmacy are just a few examples of what might be offered to campus visitors.

Land and Facilities

Colleges and universities own considerable land and facilities. Undeveloped campus land can be translated into income. The regional shopping center at Stanford University is a good example. But many campuses do not have enough land for their present activities. Even if no land is vacant, there is the question of whether it is being properly utilized. Are there new, better uses of existing space that could create new revenue sources? Older campuses, in particular, may have a major facility (e.g., a sports stadium) which, because of growth in the adjacent community and/or highway realignments, sits on land with great commercial potential. If any part of a campus contains land that could be used to generate a significant income stream, management might consider carefully how it could be made available for that purpose. Most campuses have a "sacred cow" or two. But with thorough analysis, unique solutions to roadblocks, and inspired selling of a good idea, sometimes the impossible happens, especially in changing times.

Increasingly, campuses are buying or accepting gifts of land and/or buildings, primarily for their commercial potential. South West Texas State University purchased a 90-acre resort, which includes an amusement park. Drexel University purchased a building in Philadelphia for $7 million that it plans to lease out as a long-term investment. Whitman College in Washington owns 15,000 acres of farmland, most of it received as gifts, which the college farms. Harvard University owns two office buildings outside Washington, D.C., which it presently leases to the Navy Department for $20.5 million per year.

Earlier in this chapter, the point was made that because of their knowledge-generating capabilities, colleges and universities may foster the development of research parks, sometimes on university land. Campuses also have created business incubator facilities in buildings they own. For a share in the ownership of a new business, the campus will provide an individual or small group which has a potentially workable business idea with space, services, and occasionally capital to get the business started. Rensselaer Polytechnic Institute in Troy, New York has been a pioneer in this type of development.

Occasionally, a campus will have a facility on campus that is underutilized for part of the week or for the entire year. For example, a campus parking lot may see little use on weekends and could be rented to a commercial establishment that needs extra parking then. Or athletic facilities may be underutilized in the summer and can be leased to local government or to a private sports club for that period. The best approach is to look first for underused facilities on campus and, if some are found, seek a market for them. (Exhibit 6–1 summarizes new revenue opportunities.)

6.6 EXPANDING CURRENT REVENUE SOURCES

All campuses have revenue-generating operations. In seeking new monies, it is very useful to review existing campus services to see if they can be expanded. For example, many campuses allow their typing pool to do private work for students, staff, and faculty, particularly for academically oriented typing. If the campus has its own travel agency, it might be used by students, staff, and faculty for personal travel arrangements. If a campus does not have a travel agency, it should consider creating one. Not only can a travel agency charge the usual commission for selling travel tickets, but an institution can be more certain their employees traveling on campus business are using the least expensive

Exhibit 6–1
NEW REVENUE OPPORTUNITIES

- Selling information
  - —Intellectual property
  - —Research parks
  - —Interpreting data for regional businesses
- Teaching
  - —Corporate training programs, domestic or foreign
  - —Continuing part-time education for working adults
  - —Elderhostel programs
- Using alumni resources
  - —Alumni continuing education
  - —Professional services for alumni
  - —Retirement housing
- Providing services to employees, students, and visitors
  - —Hotels
  - —Leasing space to private businesses
- Using campus land and facilities
  - —Utilizing existing land to its fullest income potential
  - —Buying or accepting gifts of land with income potential
  - —Business incubators

airline fare, modest hotel rates, and the cheapest auto rental rates. The agency could also be responsible for negotiating discount contracts with hotels, airlines, and auto rental firms. One variation of an on-site campus travel agency is to contract with an existing off-site travel agency to handle all campus business. Not only does this contract income represent a new revenue source for the campus, but if the travel agency does its job properly, the total cost of campus travel (which is often substantial) will decrease.

Some colleges and universities have a campus shuttle bus service. This auxiliary service might be expanded to run off campus, carrying students, staff, and faculty throughout the community. The city of Davis, California paid the campus bus service to serve the city, making it available to the citizens of the entire community. The payoff to the campus was not only additional revenue but also less traffic congestion and fewer parking spaces needed on campus.

A number of campuses have signed contracts with private companies, giving them special privileges for a fee. Examples include making only one cola drink available for sale on campus, or advertising messages on the scoreboard at intercollegiate athletic contests. In 1994, the 14-campus system of Pennsylvania State University negotiated a 10-year contract with Pepsi giving the soft-drink maker exclusive rights to sell beverages on the campuses. The new revenue to the system will be at least $7.5 million plus a percentage of the income from the drinks sold.

Another business possibility for a campus is the generation of electricity that is sold to the local utility as a credit against the campus utility bill. Several campuses, such as SUNY–Stonybrook, have built profitable cogeneration facilities. Generally, the analysis of the construction of such a plant shows that it will pay for itself in several years and make a profit thereafter. On the basis of such analyses, some public institutions have received state capital outlay funds to construct a campus cogeneration plant.

Another way to add to the profits from existing campus auxiliary enterprises is to adopt customer service techniques used in private business. For example, to make it easier for faculty, staff, and students to shop at the campus bookstore, an institution could create a program to let them order items for their personal use through their desktop computer. A campus might start a delivery service, sending the item ordered to the person's campus address. Similar customer service innovations might be used by the campus travel agency, printing plant, or typing pool.

Another tool of private business being adopted by campuses is the debit card system. It works much as a credit card. Students, to whom the cards are issued, must first deposit money into their debit card account. Then they use the card, up to the deposited amount, to purchase food, books, and other items from campus auxiliary enterprises. New income is generated for the campus through interest earned on the unused money in the student's debit account. Also, the cards encourage students to spend more money in campus enterprises because they are so convenient to use. Among the campuses using a debit card for students are Clemson University, Vanderbilt University, and the University of Miami. Florida State University uses this system with an additional feature; it is tied in with a national telephone system. In addition to its other uses, students can charge long-distance telephone calls with the card. Florida State University received about $200,000 in 1993 from this arrangement with the telephone company.

Credit cards present another opportunity to utilize the revenue power of not only the campus population but also alumni. Institutions, working with a bank or other financial institution, can create a vanity credit card for use by alumni and students. The campus generates income by receiving a percentage of the expenditures charged against the card as well as the initiation fee for receiving the card. Using the charge card as the card of preference for student transactions, either as a charge or debit card, can also save an institution the cost of operating an internal debit card for students while generating new unrestricted institutional revenues.

Some campuses have expanded the net revenue from auxiliary services by privatizing them, that is, leasing their operation to a private company. Leasing the campus bookstore to a company specializing in bookstore management may provide additional income to the campus. The same may be true of campus food services operated under contract by private companies. Privatizing other operations on campus, such as utility plant operations or campus grounds operations, may save money in utility or operating costs, at least in the short run, but are not designed to increase the flow of money to the campus.

One revenue source that is being used by large universities but also may have some potential for smaller ones is licensing companies to use college trademarks on products such as T-shirts, mugs, and stationery. The Collegiate Licensing Company of Atlanta estimated that in 1992–1993, licensing royalties of $55 to $65 million were paid for goods bearing college and university insignias. To assist community colleges in California to tap into this income stream, the Community College League of California is working with private concerns to attempt to license use of the trademarks for all community colleges in the state. Elsewhere in the United States, smaller colleges might use existing consortia of campuses, or create new ones, to market their trademarks or other products.

A unique income possibility being offered by an educational exchange company in Chicago is the bartering of goods between educational institutions and private companies. The company signs up educational and business organizations as members of the program and facilitates their trading. For example, college tuition credits can be traded for goods and services from companies in the system. In 1993, two colleges, the College of Du Page and Carl Sandberg College, had joined the program.

Yet another innovative income stream, which underscores the importance of being selective in choosing which innovations to adopt, was reported by Consummes River College, a community college in Sacramento, California. Consummes River College rented to vendors advertising space on the walls and stalls of six campus rest rooms for $6000 per year.

Cash management is another traditional campus operation which, if handled expertly, can provide additional funds for the campus. Components of such a program include monitoring checking account balances to keep them as low as possible; negotiating, as a large, preferred bank customer, higher interest rates on money in campus bank accounts; getting checks from each campus department deposited in a timely manner; initiating procedures to ensure that accounts receivable balances are kept at a minimum; and making payments no earlier than conventional business practices require.

Yet another means for colleges and universities to expand current conventional revenue-generating operations is to encourage faculty to focus on research eligible for state matching funds. Economic development is vital to each state, especially development in areas crucial to emerging local technologies, for this assures high-quality jobs for the future. Increasingly, states are utilizing their economic development resources on an incentive basis by matching university research dollars from nonstate sources that support economic development. Such matching funds provide seed monies for faculty to develop even more research ideas and encourage increased sponsored research projects from private businesses interested in tapping into the state matching monies.

A similar advantage to the campus is achieved if state or campus money is pledged to match private gifts received by the college or university. When used to match gifts to the endowment fund, this method helps create a stable funding source for the future. The institution's source of funds to pledge for matching endowment gifts could be other gift receipts, the use of which was undesignated by the donor. (See Exhibit 6–2 for a summary of ideas for expanding current revenue sources.)

6.7 CONCLUSIONS

A new and increasingly vital component to strategic planning and decision making for public higher education is the development of new revenue sources. While public higher education has traditionally used auxiliary operations and, more recently, has emphasized fund-raising,

6.7 CONCLUSIONS

Exhibit 6–2
EXPANDING CURRENT REVENUE SOURCES

- Travel agencies
- Campus community bus service
- Private contracts granting special privileges for a fee
- Generation of electricity
- Adoption of customer service techniques
- Debit card system
- Vanity cards
- Privatizing certain auxiliary services
- Licensing of college trademarks on products
- Bartering of goods between institutions and private companies
- Cash management
- State matching funds for economic development
- Gift funds to match other gift funds

increasingly, the need is to create new revenue opportunities to support the primary mission of instruction. As state and local governments face ever-greater demands from taxpayers while those taxpayers demonstrate increasing reluctance to pay for the public services they demand, one result has been public tuition rate increases that far exceed the rate of inflation. As a result, greater pressure by students, parents, and legislators has slowed down the rates of tuition increase.

Therefore, public higher education is being challenged to define new revenue opportunities that will enhance the funding available to support instruction and related educational services. As strategies are developed to address the ever-changing educational needs of students, public higher education leadership needs to begin to plan for revenue enhancement. As the traditional revenue sources are stressed, senior management needs to think outside the usual parameters and begin to treat revenue opportunities as a major item for executive strategic planning.

The future of public higher education will require that as state and local governments decrease support for higher education, they will have to increase institutional flexibility to encourage the senior administration and faculty to consider new revenue opportunities. Those public higher education institutions that exhibit the creativity and willingness to explore new revenue opportunities will be successful in the twenty-first century.

CHAPTER SEVEN

Strategies for Optimizing Revenues in the Tuition-Dependent Institution

NORMAN R. SMITH

Wagner College

7.1 Introduction

7.2 Fund-Raising Almost Never Offsets Enrollment Revenue

7.3 There Is No Alternative to Net Enrollment Income

7.4 The Secret Lies in Controlling Discounts

7.5 Optimizing Net Enrollment Revenue

7.6 The Only Solution Is Recruiting Paying Customers

7.7 Can Enough Paying Customers Be Recruited?

7.8 Retaining Students Gains In Important

7.9 Can Everyone Aspire to Optimize Revenues?

7.1 INTRODUCTION

Of the approximately 3500 colleges and universities in the United States, over half are private colleges with enrollments under 3600 students. As anyone associated with most of these institutions knows firsthand, the past decade has not been kind to them. Operating costs have sky-rocketed, often beyond the control of even the most cost-conscious managers. Health insurance premiums, obligations to retirees, and campus operations and maintenance, including utilities, are among the hard-to-control expenses that have led reluctant college leaders to increase their primary source of revenue, tuition rates, to levels forcing most college-bound families to conclude that private higher education is beyond their economic reach unless heavily subsidized by financial aid.

Unfortunately for private colleges, financial aid opportunities for college-bound students have been drying up during this period. At the federal level, nonresearch aid to higher education, as measured in constant 1993 dollars, went down 13 percent between 1980 and 1993 (American Council on Education). Many state appropriations have been even more draconian. Since the beginning of the 1990s, New York's appropriations to private colleges and universities dropped 68 percent while the public university system experienced a 30 percent increase.

Elsewhere, the statistics are just as ominous. According to the National Association of Independent Colleges and Universities, federal and state appropriations, based on constant dollars, dropped about 24 percent during the 1980s, one of the primary reasons why private colleges and universities were forced to raise tuition 45 percent on average during this period. Tuition increases, however, were significantly diluted by increases in "college-funded" student financial aid of over 90 percent.

Financial aid increases during the past decade have largely fallen on the shoulders of the private colleges and universities themselves. College-funded grant aid jumped from $397 million in the early 1970s to over $3 billion by the late 1980s, a 666 percent increase. Adjusted for inflation the increase is still a whopping 140 percent.[1]

All this adds up to a set of forces that are individually and collectively bringing private higher education to its fiscal knees. The 1990s show little hope for improvement. If anything, these forces will continue to intensify, victimizing especially the smaller, heavily tuition-dependent private colleges that comprise the majority of private colleges in the United States. The survivors will be those institutions that manage to sustain their revenue streams. It seems clear that the alternative, cost cutting, will not make up for a significant decrease in revenue at most private colleges.

Of the over 14 million college students in the United States,[2] less than one-fourth of them attend approximately 2000 private colleges and universities[3] that comprise over half of the 3600 higher education institutions.[4] With so many private institutions for such a small proportion of the college-bound population, it is a "buyer's market" for students.

When colleges cut costs, they inevitably cut services and standards that the private college consumer will probably find at other colleges. Like it or not, the private college student cohort is increasingly an upper-middle-income (or higher) group that is attracted to perceptions of

[1] National Association of Independent Colleges and Universities,
[2] From a table in *The Chronicle of Higher Education* (February 23, 1994 issue, p. A31) Washington, DC.
[3] From an article in *The Chronicle of Higher Education* (April 6, 1994 issue, p. A17).
[4] From a conversation with the Carnegie Foundation for the Advancement of Teaching in Princeton, New Jersey on 12/6/94.

quality. Those private colleges that successfully convey images of quality, real or perceived or both, will be most attractive to this discriminating consumer. To that end, cost cutting that visibly affects the perceived quality of the college could impair enrollment revenues at amounts greater than the expenses saved.

The cost of running a private college is expensive and is not going to get significantly cheaper. Colleges that try to reduce their costs by cutting faculty and lowering tuition may find themselves increasingly perceived by college-bound students as lacking the quality and substance they seek in a good private college. (Bennington College in Vermont is among a number of institutions that have pursued this strategy.)

The perception of quality can also be impaired by strategies for generating alternative revenues that alter the character of the institution. For instance, many private colleges have contracted with European and Asian recruiters to enroll large numbers of international students as an alternative to the traditional-age college students they are losing. Although cultural diversity is greatly enhanced by international students and can greatly add to the appeal of a campus culture, there is a limit to the relative proportion of international students to American students that can be accommodated by institutions and be accepted by many traditional college students. The University of Bridgeport was a pioneer in heavy enrollments of international students and in the process may have lost their traditional U.S. undergraduate student population. Bridgeport's enrollment declines during the 1980s were so dramatic that their financial problems ultimately overwhelmed them.

The 20 percent of college students attracted to private residential colleges are most attracted, in my view, to college settings where the student population is most like them. Along with such factors as the condition of the campus facilities and residence halls, the atmosphere created by the students currently enrolled plays a key role in college choice. Thus even a heavy emphasis on adult and part-time programs can deter those potential full-time residential students who are seeking a traditional private college.

The survivors among the large number of private colleges and universities vying for only 20 percent of the college population will be those that successfully present themselves as offering the most for a comparable price. Therefore, the best tactic to remain competitive is to design a strategy aimed at optimizing revenues that in turn permit incurring costs necessary to deliver high quality. Although many academicians may shudder at the prospect of private colleges considering themselves "products" in the "marketplace," that is exactly the way in which they are being evaluated by college-bound students and their families.

When small to midsize private colleges seek to optimize their revenues, there is really only one place to look that will make a meaningful difference to the bottom line: *enrollment revenue*. The exception may be the several dozen colleges with major endowments of $100 million or more. These privileged institutions, including Swarthmore, Wellesley, and Amherst, have the enviable "challenge" of optimizing their revenues by retaining the best portfolio investor. For the 90 percent of small private colleges without significant endowments, there really *isn't* a revenue-optimizing alternative to the tuition, fees, room and board, and auxiliary income generated from the students enrolled.

However, in today's investment market, even a $100 million endowment will probably generate not much more than $5 million, for operating purposes, if the college's investment policy is prudent and includes preservation of the value of the principal. Thus a $100 million endowment would keep all but the smallest colleges over 75 percent tuition dependent. That is a lot better than an unendowed college's virtual tuition dependence, but it does not create freedom from enrollment revenue dependence.

Only 250 or so colleges and universities in America have built endowments exceeding $50 million, and only 150 of those have more than $100 million. Thus over 90 percent of all colleges and universities in the United States have endowments too small to have a meaningful impact.

Yet even the significant impact of a large endowment does not eliminate tuition dependence. Harvard's massive $5.8 billion endowment earned about $400 million in 1993. If every penny of endowment income had been applied to operating costs (which rarely occurs in the interest, instead, of corpus preservation), less than one-third of Harvard's $1.2 billion annual budget would have been underwritten, leaving even ultra-endowed Harvard tuition dependent.

"Tuition-dependent" colleges are often over 90 percent reliant on enrollment-generated revenues. This fact has many college presidents and boards of trustees placing a priority on the search for alternative sources of income in order to be less dependent for so much operating revenue from a single source. Although understandable and justifiable, nonenrollment revenue will never significantly alter the proportions of revenue at most colleges and universities. And too much effort spent pursuing alternative sources of revenue can take an institution's eye off its lifeline—enrollment.

A commonplace pursuit of alternative revenues is fund-raising. However, obtaining the multimillion-dollar gifts that can truly replace enrollment revenue is about as improbable as winning the lottery. Yet every time someone like Walter Annenberg or Henry Rowan gives $100 million or so to a school, thousands of college presidents and development officers receive newspaper clippings from trustees asking why their institution can't "pull off" a similar coup. Such a challenge inevitably launches an exhaustive review of the 100 or 200 richest men and women in the world capable of such a gift—and, usually, the discovery that none of them graduated from your college.

Heed this. In the past 30 years, only 36 donations to colleges and universities have exceeded $35 million. Of the 36 gifts, only four have gone to moderately-sized institutions—Spelman, Pomona, Regent, and Asbury Theological. Any college hoping to be the fifth such recipient confronts very long odds.

7.2   FUND-RAISING ALMOST NEVER OFFSETS ENROLLMENT REVENUE

Although fund-raising will rarely save a tuition-dependent college with an enrollment revenue problem, the effort is worthy and can provide important revenues to any college. Fund-raising should, however, be put in its proper context: as an embellishment to an overall revenue generation plan.

What *can* be expected from fund-raising? A tuition-dependent college is doing well, it seems to me, if 10 percent of its net revenue comes from fund-raising. In fact, a college might be quite relieved if 5 percent of the total operating expenses are annually underwritten by unrestricted or comparable giving. Note the emphasis on *net* revenue. Too many fund-raising efforts cost up to half or even more of the monies raised. Some gifts even add costs to the institution. How many colleges have accepted expensive equipment as a gift without realizing that the equipment costs $25,000 a year to operate and maintain? Funding to support those operating costs rarely accompanies the gift.

When setting fund-raising goals, be realistic and be patient. Generally, annual giving builds slowly. If 10 percent of your alumni give annual gifts averaging $50, there is little you can hope to do to double this level in one year, even though the average should be much better. Broad-based giving evolves slowly. Therefore, do not build quantum fund-raising leaps into the operating budget.

Also, any giving goal that is not a modest increment above existing trends probably has to be based on a realization that most of your giving comes from a few of your donors. Thus for every million dollars' worth of annual giving, you had better, in most cases, have some donors of $100,000 or more upon whom you can rely. Ambitious giving goals, with few exceptions, are not possible without donor sources among trustees and successful alumni.

Trustees often divert presidents and development officers away from trustee giving, proposing instead that foundations and corporations be tapped for major gifts. However, only a few dozen foundations in the entire United States give grants exceeding $100,000 to colleges, and most such gifts are not for operating purposes. Also realize that the development offices of all 3500 American colleges and universities are approaching these very few major foundations. Most, needless to say, are turned away.

Corporations tend to spread their giving thinly among as many worthy institutions as possible. More often than not, corporate support is directed to easing social problems "in the news." Because of this, their giving to higher education is usually confined to colleges where employees are recruited, colleges in the communities surrounding their corporate centers, and through matching gifts from employees who give to their alma mater.

Unfortunately, to most corporate givers private higher education is perceived as being in fine shape. As a result, corporate giving priorities have gravitated away from private colleges and toward public universities because corporations presume pressing urban and social problems are better addressed at state universities. This trend is revealed in that corporate giving to private colleges has shrunk from 67 percent in 1975–1976 to only 47 percent of total giving to higher education in 1990–1991. According to the Council for Advancement and Support of Education, over half of corporate giving to higher education now goes to the public universities.

In most cases, corporate and foundation giving is destined to be modest, and although worth pursuing (cost effectively), the revenues generated will not offset effective enrollment revenue management. Therefore, any college without major donors on their board of trustees, and without a tradition of building close relationships among their most successful and prosperous alumni, had better plan to spend decades methodically building donor cohorts before they hope to see the kind of giving revenues that build sizable endowments or generate annual gifts that have a meaningful impact on annual operating budgets.

7.3 THERE IS NO ALTERNATIVE TO NET ENROLLMENT INCOME

Having considered the prospect of optimizing revenue through fundraising, let's return to reality. Too many small private colleges are not properly monitoring the aorta of their lifeline—namely, full-time enrollment—to assure that enrollment revenues are indeed being optimized. That is, colleges usually measure the effectiveness of their admissions recruiting program in terms of applications received and students subsequently enrolled. Gross versus net income has yet to become a common measurement comparison in admissions and enrollment planning.

Whenever a president or admissions dean tells me that their fall enrollment is up 10 percent, my first question is: Gross or net? Rarely do I hear an acknowledgment of this important distinction. Some have considered the distinction irrelevant.

Gross versus net is an essential consideration for any tuition-dependent college aspiring to optimize revenue. *Gross* is bodies. *Net* is *tuition-equivalent* bodies. College-funded financial aid is the difference between the two.

For tuition-dependent institutions, college-funded grant aid is a misnomer implying that a *fund* exists somewhere in the college's coffers from which dollars can be drawn as an alternative to cash from student tuition payments. Only the heavily endowed colleges have investment income to fund their scholarship awards. Everyone else is discounting and, in doing so, is forgoing tuition income they probably need.

College accounting obscures this fact. On the revenue side of a college's financial statements is an income line that logs 100 percent of tuition as if every college actually collected full tuition from every student and offered no college-funded grants. College-funded grants are then posted as an expense. This works for accounting purposes but misleads many college managers and trustees into thinking that they are making more than they are and can thereby control expenses more than they can.

For example, a college could boast an increase in enrollment from 1000 to 1100 students, appearing to increase operating revenues by 10 percent. At first glance, the books reinforce the perception. On the revenue side, the 100 new students at, say $10,000 tuition, is posted as $1 million in additional revenues, leaving some to assume that $1 million was actually collected.

Then, somewhere on the expense side of the ledger is what can sometimes be as much as 40 percent or more of that tuition revenue which is "expensed" as college-funded grants. If it is 40 percent, that expense represents $400,000 of the $1 million posted as revenue that never existed. Instead, that $400,000 is a discount that resulted in the college actually realizing only $600,000 in new tuition revenues. The $1 million on the books was gross. The net was $600,000. The nonexistent $400,000 probably should never have been counted in any way. This example demonstrates the essential relevance of gross versus net (Exhibit 7–1).

A 10 percent increase in students that would generate additional gross revenue could be totally offset by increases in college-funded aid. In such cases, more students can actually result in less net revenue. Since more students usually create the added expense of more faculty and staff, a poorly conceived enrollment growth strategy can have many adverse effects that can include less revenue and higher expenses. To that end, what appears to be a successful admissions recruiting effort, when measured by traditional head-count methods, could have disastrous revenue outcomes.

Exhibit 7-1
KEEP YOUR EYE ON THE BOTTOM LINE

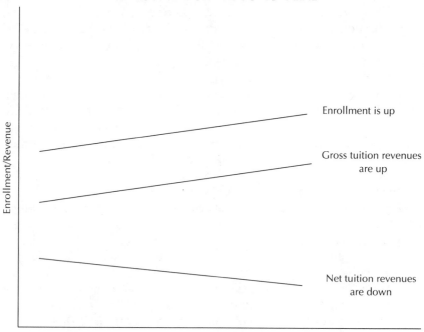

Private businesses face the same principles, but their financial re-ports more clearly post actual cash revenues received. A department store, for example, would not post the recommended retail price of every product sold as cash received. That is, a shirt originally priced at $25 that is sold at a half-price sale would be posted as $12.50 revenue realized. If retailers followed the college finance model, however, they would post the shirt as having realized $25 on the revenue side with a $12.50 discount on the expense side of the ledger. Needless to say, retailers don't do this, because it misrepresents their actual revenue realizations. Perhaps colleges would be better served with a similar model.

7.4 THE SECRET LIES IN CONTROLLING DISCOUNTS

However, the problem of revenue optimization does not stop with chang-ing a fundamental accounting principal. The most difficult aspect of discounting experienced by both retailers and colleges is minimizing discounts and thereby maximizing net revenues.

Some retailers, including Macy's, have nearly gone bankrupt (instead, Macy's is merging) trying to increase sales through heavy discounting. Consumers got smart quickly and waited for sales before purchasing most of their sought-after products. In a short time, Macy's greatly increased their gross sales while actually losing ground in net revenues.

The fundamentals of this strategy illustrate basic principles of Marketing Management 101. If you sell 100 items for a dollar each, you make $100. If you discount by 10 percent, you make $90. If you decide you want to increase sales by improving the discount, be careful to watch your net revenue instead of your gross. A 20 percent increase in sales could be construed as increasing sales volume to 120 items. However, a 30 percent discount implemented to effect that increase will result in a net income of $84, $6 *less* than selling 100 items at a 10 percent discount.

Such fundamental strategic planning for optimizing revenue has yet to be implemented routinely into many admissions recruiting programs. In fact, many admissions offices presume no responsibility whatsoever for the revenue equivalent of their recruitment efforts: "That's the responsibility of the financial aid office and the billing office." Everyone's pointing the finger and no one really knows what has happened until it is too late to control or prevent.

There once may have been a time when admissions offices could divorce themselves from revenue considerations. Even at private colleges, federal and state grant programs overseen by the financial aid office weighed heavily in net revenue outcomes.

As already documented, private college tuitions increased dramatically during the 1980s at a time when federal and state financial aid sources, particularly grant aid, went in the opposite direction. In the past decade, essentially all of the tuition increases effected by private colleges and universities have been absorbed by either the paying student or the college itself in the form of more grant aid because the federal and state contributions have at best remained the same. Today, even the most needy students cannot rely on government financial aid for more than 40 to 50 percent, at best, of the total bill—unfortunately, usually much less. Most colleges cannot ante up the other 50 percent and stay afloat, although too many lack admissions recruiting policies that prevent such a potential outcome.

To make matters worse, college-funded grant aid has been a relatively freewheeling operation at most colleges that have found it virtually impossible to set budget limits on the amount of discounting authorized. Too many colleges are still trying to manage their enrollment on a "need-blind" basis, a noble goal but a financially unfeasible one at a time when federal and state financial aid programs have been cut to the point where tuition-dependent colleges can't hope to make up the difference. At best, financial aid offices are given guidelines in the form of maximum grant limits, but these limits often exceed 50 percent of tuition in high-need circumstances.

7.5 OPTIMIZING NET ENROLLMENT REVENUE

Presuming the sobering realities of net versus gross are cemented in your consciousness, how do you go about implementing admissions and enrollment policies that optimize net enrollment revenues? (See Exhibit 7–2.) To begin with, you must determine how much net revenue you absolutely need from enrollment. As a rule of thumb, it seems to me that a tuition-dependent college cannot afford to discount more than a third of its gross tuition revenues, probably less.

Staying with the 1000-student, $10,000-annual-tuition model utilized earlier in this chapter, college-funded grant expense should not exceed $3 million of the $10 million being posted as gross tuition revenues. Needless to say, a rule of thumb depends on many factors that make each institution distinctive in its limits. Colleges in rural settings have lower operating costs that permit them to realize less net revenue. Colleges with above-average tuition rates can also afford higher discounts. However, any college discounting above 30 percent is probably getting too close to its respective red line unless it is among the heavily endowed or has unusually low operating costs.

Colleges above 40 percent are close to "selling the product" for less than it must be costing them to "make the product." In such cases, the college has either an annual operating deficit or is not incurring the necessary educational expenditures to give students the quality of education that will keep them enrolled through graduation. Therefore, simply

Exhibit 7–2
OPTIMIZING NET REVENUE

- Keep discounting under 30 percent, preferably 25 percent.
- Focus on full-time traditional undergraduates.
- Maintain the standards and stature sought by students who can pay a substantial portion of their tuition.
- Increase the proportion of merit discounts.
- Link discounts to the admissions process rather than to financial aid applications.
- Focus yield strategies on a middle-of-the-bell-curve applicant and admissions pool.
- Hold admissions accountable for net tuition-equivalent head count, not gross head count.
- Market the institution to already enrolled students to retain them.

stated, keep your discounting below 25 percent and you are probably optimizing revenues.

Easier said than done. But like it or not, tuition-dependent private colleges face the unenviable reality that they have to successfully recruit students who can pay most of their total annual tuition. Emphasis on enrolling paying customers is a very unpopular and politically incorrect notion among academics. That any private college should restrict admission to academically promising students because of its financial limitations is a spark that can ignite faculty censures of administrations daring to propose such socially unconscionable policies. However, paychecks and other expenses can only be paid with real money collected from students who pay tuition.

7.6   THE ONLY SOLUTION IS RECRUITING PAYING CUSTOMERS

Unless state and federal government sources of financial aid improve, tuition-dependent colleges are left with no choice but to build enrollments among students who can pay a substantial portion of tuition. Colleges enrolling too many high-need students will be forced to offer them more discounts than they can afford to expense.

One could argue that overenrolling high-need students is not just a disservice to the fiscal health of tuition-dependent institutions but also a disservice to the students themselves. Many ambitious students will stretch themselves beyond their financial limits in order to enroll at the private college of their choice. These economic ceilings are hit long before the end of a four-year college career. As tuition and other college costs continue to spiral upward each year, high-need students require more financial aid and call upon the college to increase grant aid when the college is already offering more than it can afford.

Some colleges worry, however, that without students of high need, they will be without *any* students. To that end, tuition-dependent colleges are between the proverbial "rock and a hard place." Colleges overly dependent on students unable to pay private college tuition will be forced to discount beyond their means. Eventually, lack of necessary revenues will impair institutional quality in ways that deter students of higher academic quality and financial means.

Tuition-dependent colleges can no longer afford to be idealistic without a strategy to assure adequate revenues in order to operate with high standards of academic excellence. Running a good college costs money that tuition-dependent colleges realize only if they are enrolling enough paying customers to underwrite such standards.

How, then, does a college redirect its enrollment management effort to optimize revenues? First and foremost, the admissions recruiting plan must target applicant markets populated by college-bound students capable of paying tuition. Next, the grant-aid or discounting decisions have to be more closely linked to the admissions recruiting strategy of enrolling paying customers. Sadly, need-blind enrollment management strategies are just no longer possible for most private colleges and universities; to survive, the philosophy must be abandoned.

Many institutions have found that yield is increasingly the most critical factor in the admissions recruiting process. "Inquiries" are the easiest statistic to increase and are often cited by pressured admissions offices as an indicator of progress. Application rates can also be built to levels that appear more impressive than they really are by soliciting applicants who are actually not likely to enroll but seek fall-back institutions.

Nowadays, college-bound students often apply to as many as five or six institutions. Some schools have been startled to discover that most of the applicants they admitted had little intention of choosing them from among the half-dozen or so institutions to which they admitted. Colleges with an overflow of such "phantom" applicants can find themselves with an enrollment that is not even close to what their bountiful application or admissions pool implied.

At many of these colleges, the discounting effort (still called "college-funded grants" in most cases) is overseen mainly by the financial aid office. Whereas financial aid is often part of the admissions organizational structure, decisions about aid levels are often based solely on need. This can often direct the lion's share of discounts toward the most needy students, who may not be the strongest academically and can also be among the least likely to be able to afford their share of four years of tuition.

Like it or not, more colleges must realistically assess the prospects of an applicant's wherewithal to pay tuition for the full four years of a typical college undergraduate career. Think of the admissions pool of incoming students as a bell curve for a moment. At one end of the bell curve are the extremely high-need students, who are probably receiving the largest portion of the college's discounts. At the other end of the bell curve are the top academic students, who may be receiving presidential scholarship types of awards, designed to yield a cohort of academically gifted applicants.

These two extremes of the bell curve will probably comprise no more than 40 to 50 percent of the average total admissions pool. However, because students at both extremes have received grant offers, the ends of the curve can be seen to generate the highest yield. The high-need students have been lured because of need-based discounts. The academically high-achieving students are drawn as a result of their presidential scholarships.

The middle of the bell curve comprises an admissions group usually not needy enough to receive need-based discounts and not academically distinguished enough to be granted academic scholarships. On the other hand, the middle of the bell curve comprises a solid applicant cohort. Yet this largest portion of the bell curve, often more than half of all admissions, is populated by students who have been offered the fewest financial incentives to choose a given institution over the five or six others being considered.

In the process of studying its yield outcomes, one college found a 40 percent yield of students admitted on each extreme of the bell curve but only a 10 percent yield in the middle (Exhibit 7–3). Upon redistributing student tuition discounts in order that the middle of the bell curve received more grants, the yield of admitted students dropped less than 10 percent on the need side and remained the same on the academic side. The middle of the curve, however, jumped 25 percent. What happened? The average student of average income level suddenly had a financial incentive to favor one institution over others.

Offering a discount to students of lesser need at the expense of students with greater financial need may not conform to the social ideals

Exhibit 7-3
YIELD OF ADMITTED STUDENTS

The largest cohort of admits: Not needy enough for aid based on FAFS and not distinguished enough for presidential-type scholarships; thus, the yield of admitted students is 10%

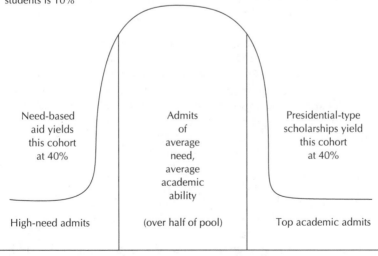

| Need-based aid yields this cohort at 40% | Admits of average need, average academic ability | Presidential-type scholarships yield this cohort at 40% |
| High-need admits | (over half of pool) | Top academic admits |

Redirecting aid to middle of bell-curve yields higher rate in the most populous cohort; the result is more admits than are available at the tails of the curve of many academicians, but it may be a key to optimizing revenue or even financial survival. Think of it this way. If successful at keeping discounts below 30 percent, a 1000-student population could be construed as a cohort of 700 paying students and 300 "free rides." The free rides are being underwritten by the paying customers, not by the college and its faculty.

Obviously, students with the greatest incentive to remain at a college are those receiving close to full grant-aid scholarships. Alternatively, students who pay tuition are in the best position to transfer to other colleges. The more "paying customers" who leave, the fewer dollars are available to underwrite the nonpaying students. Thus discounts more widely spread throughout the student cohort provide every student with a "piece of the pie" and a stronger incentive to enroll and remain throughout a four-year college career.

7.7 CAN ENOUGH PAYING CUSTOMERS BE RECRUITED?

Many private colleges and universities rightfully fear that refocusing their admissions recruiting efforts on paying customers of relatively high academic quality may result in declining enrollments. Are there enough such students for the large number of private colleges and universities in the United States? The good news is that the demographics of high school enrollments is slowly trending upward after over a decade of decline. However, there may never again be enough students to accommodate the existing capacity in private colleges, partly because much of the demographic growth is among students who probably cannot afford private college tuition.

Colleges perceived to be among the best are continuing to experience increases in their application rates while they are also usually among the most expensive. "I'm willing to pay more because I feel I might get a better job if I go to one of the more prestigious schools" is an increasingly common feeling among those students able to consider the cost and debt of a private college education. Recently, the Associated Press reported that over half of 13- to 15-year-olds believed that "the higher the tuition costs of a college, the better the quality of education a student will receive."

Any private college able to sucessfully position itself among those institutions regarded as the highest-quality institutions is in a better position to survive. Part of being perceived as a good institution is to enroll good-quality students.

Unless public policy changes and the outlook on accessibility to private higher education improves, tuition-dependent colleges have no choice but to focus their attention on recruiting and enrolling students who can afford to pay a significant portion of their tuition. Institutions that for ideological reasons resist accepting this reality are "jumping off a bridge to prove the law of gravity."

7.8   RETAINING STUDENTS GAINS IN IMPORTANCE.

Colleges spend enormous resources recruiting students. They have no choice in today's highly competitive market. When staff, advertising, and publication costs are totaled, it is not unusual for a college to spend thousands of dollars per successfully recruited student. On the other hand, many colleges spend little "re-recruiting" students. By *re-recruiting*, I refer to what most colleges define as *retention*. However, retention is more often seen as a student affairs or academic advisement function headed by an administrator quite different from the people working the admissions operation. In fact, most retention officers do not think of themselves as having marketing responsibilities.

A successfully enrolled full-time freshman is, for all intents and purposes, an $80,000 sale (presuming $20,000 annual revenue from tuition, room, board, fees, books, and incidentals sold at the college). However, every freshman who transfers out at the end of the first year constitutes a $60,000 refund. Lose 20 freshman and you have lost over $1 million.

Many colleges do little to re-market the college to already enrolled students and their parents. Should a college send a new version of the admissions viewbook to parents of upper-class students? A new catalog? A new video? It may sound costly, but in a business where a 40 percent yield among new applicants is considered high, successfully re-recruiting the upperclass students could constitute a yield that is well over double the new student rate.

Do not assume that all enrolled students are relatively firm in their conviction to remain at the college. Saving 20 or more students every year will more than pay for itself in refunds that never become necessary. Since two-thirds or more of most private college enrollments are upper-class students, and since most of them are relatively committed to the institution (or they wouldn't have enrolled), an admissions-recruiting program aimed at keeping students is clearly more cost-effective than the extremely expensive effort of locating new students to replace transfers that might have been prevented.

7.9   CAN EVERYONE ASPIRE TO OPTIMIZE REVENUES?

For too many years now, prognosticators have been predicting the demise of private higher education in the United States, only to be shown that most colleges are still living, albeit perhaps ailing. That the world has not come to an end for more private colleges has the more hopeful among us wanting to believe that such a day of reckoning is greatly exaggerated by those who remain steadfast in their ominous predictions.

However, the changes in the higher education financial landscape over the past decade have not improved for private colleges; they have worsened in a big way. They continue to "add straws to an already overburdened camel's back" that eventually has to break.

The fact is that, economically, college-bound families are being forced to select lower-cost public education, even if it is overcrowded. Government policy is unlikely to change its practice of favoring public education over private education. Thus private colleges are left with no choice but to enroll paying customers, realizing that there may not be enough paying customers out there to fill the capacity.

Increasing numbers of private colleges are "steering themselves into the rocks" attempting to shore up their enrollment declines by admitting students who are oversubsidized by college-funded discounts. Private colleges simply can no longer afford to enroll students who cannot afford to pay. Yet some colleges are not facing this unpopular reality. One of the first institutional victims of this practice that has come to media attention is Upsala College in New Jersey, which for several years has been enrolling a disproportionate number of academically marginal students with high economic need.

Upsala apparently had hoped to sustain itself on the federal and state grants available to these students, realizing that little would come from their personal resources. At first, newspapers including *The New York Times* heralded the impressive enrollment growth at Upsala and characterized the phenomenon as a turnaround for the college. Within a year Upsala's method of increasing enrollment proved to be its downfall. More students may have been recruited, but less revenue was emanating from them.

No one, including the media, seems to have asked about *net* enrollment. Upsala was not collecting enough revenue to pay the bills. At the end of the 1993–1994 academic year, Upsala ran out of money and credit lines while having a burdensome unpaid debt, all of this forcing the Middle States Commission on Higher Education to remove accreditation.

Needless to say, more students are not always better. For tuition-dependent colleges such as Upsala, more students are good only if they are paying customers. This may sound like a crude and philistine consideration, but the alternative is financial demise.

Throughout the 1990s, there will be more Upsala College tragedies as small tuition-dependent colleges discover the hard way that they cannot generate enough revenue when they seek to enroll students who cannot afford private college tuition without more financial aid than state and federal government sources provide them.

Who will survive? (see Exhibit 7–4.) The private tuition-dependent colleges that stay intact will be those that have competed successfully for an enrollment populated primarily by college students in the economic position to finance most of their tuition and fees. Private colleges are alone and the prospects are dim for a public policy change that gives low- and middle-income students the aid necessary for them to choose a private college.

Private colleges can learn some important lessons from the retail consuming environment in the United States. Just like the 80 percent of today's college student cohort who attend low-cost public universities, the majority of Americans shop at Sears, Penney's, and Wal-Mart. More Americans own a Sears credit card than that of any other department store.

However, a notable representation of the American public want more than Sears and are willing to pay for the higher quality they perceive is available from Saks Fifth Avenue, Nordstrom's, Lord & Taylor, Bloomingdale's, and other upscale retailers, not to mention boutique chains from Tiffany and Cartier to Louis Vuitton, Fendi, and Georgio Armani. Like private colleges, there are many more upscale retailers serving a proportionately smaller total of the consuming public and, by and large, they are prospering, even in times of economic downturn.

Although most academicians are understandably repelled by the notion of comparing their colleges to Neiman-Marcus (and, needless to say, there are myriad differences between consumer retailing and higher education), there are nonetheless some intriguing similarities. Like the success stories in upscale retailing, the survivors in private higher education, will be those who are seen as providing high quality, justifying the cost.

Private colleges that try to recruit the 80 percent of college students drawn to public universities will probably collapse (and some already have) the way Macy's failed to increase their sales by trying to compete for Sears and Wal-Mart customers. Their nonstop sales sold merchandise but at a price too low to generate profits. Private colleges that offer too much

Exhibit 7–4
WHO WILL SURVIVE?

- Colleges perceived to be of high quality and worth the price to those who can afford it
- Merged institutions that can cut operating costs while maintaining standards
- Heavily endowed institutions
- Colleges that focus on recruiting and enrolling students who pay most of the tuition being charged

aid to students while wanting private tuition to be competitive with public university costs are destined to generate less revenue than is needed to operate at a standard of quality expected of a private college.

If government does change its priorities, it will only be after witnessing a significant deterioration in the private college landscape. If and when that happens, it will be too late for many smaller colleges that are already stretching the limits of their resources. Most sobering is the fact that these victims will not come back to life.

The only hope for many private colleges is a rather dramatic and unlikely change in the public's perception of private higher education:

1. If foundations and corporations recognized the importance of the private higher education community and its vulnerability, they might become more interested in offering academically promising but financial needy students the opportunity to choose a private institution, where, in most cases, their prospects for graduating improve. Also, the long run might be better served if "fire prevention" replaced "firefighting." If private higher education is ignored by donors and is thereby forced to lower standards, America may lose one of the dimishing number of assets it still has that remains world class in quality.

2. State governments need to recognize that private higher education may be cost-effective to taxpayers. In New York State, for example, existing capacity in private colleges has been disregarded by public policy planners, who instead build new $500 million public university campuses while declaring that there are no revenues available to sustain grant programs for needy students preferring private colleges. Much less than the annual interest revenue from one $500 million building program would enable thousands of students to take advantage of existing private college capacity.

Someone has to pay for the operating costs of private higher education. For now, the money has to come from students and their families. To that end, the private colleges that survive and prosper will be those finding a way to enroll students who are attracted to the merits of private colleges and are willing and able to pay tuition.

Some private colleges near other educational institutions may be able to merge. These mergers will result in cost benefits similar to the motivations that have so many major corporate entities in a flurry of marriages (i.e., mergers) in response to the economic climate of the 1990s. For example, Macy's and Federated Stores recently merged to bring down their operating costs in order to compete more successfully against giant discount retailers such as Wal-Mart. Anchor and Dime Savings Banks also merged to form the largest thrift outside California. Their motivation was consolidation of operations that, among other "benefits," reduced operating costs by over 500 jobs while enhancing revenue streams.

The Wal-Marts of retailing are doing to traditional department stores what public policy is doing to private colleges. They are selling what the consuming public considers to be the same product for less. Until considerations such as overcrowding in public universities deters college-bound students and has them returning to less-crowded private colleges, the only hope for survival is to be among the private colleges perceived by a relatively limited number of college-bound students as worth the price.

Those private colleges unable to establish the cache of quality worthy of the higher cost will not succeed in generating the revenues necessary to survive intact. In today's economic times, cheaper is winning—at least for now. However, there will always be those who want quality and are willing and able to pay for it. Surviving private colleges have to understand the market and make the necessary investments to attract it.

Unless federal and state governments give students the ability to select the college of their choice, there is no panacea for private colleges except to be among those perceived as the best. Any college unable to aspire to that challenge will eventually cease to exist.

Managing Institutional Capital

Chapter Eight
Endowment Management in a Global Economy

Chapter Nine
Managing Debt in Changing Financial Markets

Chapter Ten
Developing, Not Controlling, Human Resources

Chapter Eleven
Facilities Management: Preserving the Past,
Building the Future

Chapter Twelve
Organizational and Technological Strategies for Higher
Education in the Information Age

Endowment Management in a Global Economy[1]

WILLIAM F. MASSY

Stanford Institute for Higher Education Research

8.1 Introduction

8.2 Historical Perspective

8.3 Current Situation and Practical Guidance

Spending and Accumulation Policies

8.4 Capital Structure Strategy

8.5 Uses of Endowment

8.6 Modern Investment Theory

Mean–Variance Principle

Capital Asset Pricing Model

Arbitrage Pricing Theory

Tactical Asset Allocation Models

8.7 Investment Policies

8.8 The Future

8.9 Conclusions

8.1 INTRODUCTION

Those institutions that do not have endowments covet them; those that do, seek to sustain and expand them to enhance institutional flexibility. As college and university resources become more constrained, endowments are increasingly under the spotlight. The critical underlying issue is that as the financial markets change—becoming increasingly complex, global, and volatile—institutions must balance appropriate levels of risk with appropriate levels of endowment return.

In many ways, endowment management is a constant. The issue has always been risk versus return. Prudent and sound investing has

[1] This chapter is based on *Endowment: Perspectives, Policies, and Management* by William F. Massy, published by the Association of Governing Boards of Universities and Colleges in 1990. However, Dr. Massy has updated the information from his 1990 book for this chapter.

historically been the objective of endowment management, and it remains so today. What has changed, and continues to change, is the external environment. Not only are investment markets subject to continuous and unpredictable change, it is unlikely that substantial new money will be added to most endowments. The days of rich entrepreneurs funding (and naming) a university and endowing it heavily are long gone. Although wealthy individuals continue to give generously to endowments, the phenomenal past gifts of such legendaries as Matthew Vassar, Leland Stanford, Ezra Cornell, Johns Hopkins, and John D. Rockefeller are few and far between. As a result, institutional endowments must be carefully nurtured, grown by the addition of new but smaller gifts and by thoughtful investing and management to protect the long-term purchasing power of the endowment.

Endowments are a vital ingredient of institutional flexibility and a substantial asset at many institutions. According to the 1993 National Association of College and University Business Officers (NACUBO) annual endowment study, over 150 institutions have endowments over $100 million; over 240 have endowments over $50 million. The largest, Harvard, has an endowment approaching $6 billion. Endowment levels of $100 million and above enable an institution to contribute perhaps 5 to 10 percent of its overall revenues from its endowment income. Such dollars directly reduce institutional reliance on tuition, in particular. In effect, endowment dollars enable an institution to leverage tuition revenue and buffer it from an uncertain external environment.

When thinking about endowment management, consider what has happened with campus facilities. Facilities are an equally (if not more) substantial institutional asset. However, over the last several decades, institutions have systematically diverted funds from their facilities to other areas of institutional need, allowing deferred maintenance to accumulate and risking the value of their facility assets. The challenge for institutions will be to not allow a similar calamity to befall the endowment asset. Maintaining endowment purchasing power to benefit today's students as well as tomorrow's is key.

8.2 HISTORICAL PERSPECTIVE

The concept of endowment arose in the Middle Ages. Wealthy patrons donated land to religious groups that would use the rental income from the land to support their religious endeavors. In the early years of American higher education, land was a major part of the endowment, although financial investments were also an important component of the mix.

Endowments in the United States were managed according to English trust law, under which institutions could invest only in certain prescribed securities. In the 1830 case *Harvard College* v. *Amory*, however, the notion of the "prudent man rule" was established, giving institutions choices about their investments as long as they invested as a prudent person would.

In the early twentieth century, most endowment funds were still invested in relatively safe bonds and mortgages. After World War II, endowment fund managers began to diversify their portfolios, and by the late 1960s, stocks became a key component. Stocks became a more common investment vehicle following the recommendations of the Ford Foundation in 1969; the Ford Foundation report concluded that most institutions were investing too conservatively. The Uniform Management of Institutional Funds Act was introduced soon thereafter in 1972, and subsequently passed in many states.[2] This act helped to open up other, somewhat riskier investment opportunities. Today, the management of endowment funds has evolved still further and become increasingly complex as managers weigh a myriad of investment decisions as well as discussions about spending alternatives and capital accumulation.

8.3 CURRENT SITUATION AND PRACTICAL GUIDANCE

Endowment funds[3] provide an invaluable contribution to an institution's financial health and flexibility. Ranging in amounts from several thousand to several billion dollars, they subsidize an institution's operating budget, particularly when funds can be used to support *nonincremental* (i.e., existing) activities rather than *incremental*, add-on activities. Non-incremental endowment gifts allow general funds to be allocated or used to mitigate tuition increases. If, on the other hand, donors give endowment funds with so many restrictions that institutions are hampered by them, it is far better to negotiate with the donor for more flexibility or to reject an endowment gift outright.

---

[2] The Uniform Management of Institutional Funds Act provided that (1) endowment funds can be pooled for investment purposes, (2) the prudent man standard applies to the portfolio as a whole instead of to individual components, (3) it is possible to spend capital appreciation on the endowment, and (4) investment management decisions can be delegated.

[3] There are three types of endowment funds. The principal of *true endowments* cannot be spent. *Quasi-endowments* are funds set aside by the institution's governing board to function as endowment funds, although the board may chose to lift the restriction at any time. The principal of *term endowments* may be spent when a given period of time has passed or certain donor-imposed stipulations have been met.

Endowments also grant an institution some freedom from political and economic forces. Endowment gifts represent one of the few institutional revenue sources that can be used to support academic freedom. Large endowments reduce an institution's reliance on government support and on future donor gifts, thus reducing government and donor influence over its activities. Institutions that do not have endowments must often base their decisions on economics rather than academics. Institutions with endowments can weigh academic priorities more strongly.

Third, endowment funds improve the balance sheet, strengthening the asset side of the balance sheet and making it more attractive to creditors. Managing the balance sheet means accumulating equity capital by making periodic transfers from the current operating budget to the capital budget and maintaining a capital structure that is attractive to creditors. In this way, debt financing can be obtained when needed. The long-term assets/liabilities ratio, which is increased by a healthy endowment, indicates a balance sheet's strength.

In summary, endowments are critical to an institution's financial health and flexibility, granting more flexibility to institutions with larger endowments and less flexibility to institutions with smaller endowments. Despite the importance of endowment, relatively few institutions have truly sizable endowments. Exhibit 8–1 summarizes information about the 20 U.S. institutions with the largest endowments.

Spending and Accumulation Policies

Deciding how much to spend and how much to save is the most important endowment management decision. Ideally, institutions should maintain the purchasing power of their endowment funds over time. If endowment funds are pooled for investment purposes, each pool's share value should be matched to a broadly based cost-rise average. For example, sufficient reinvestment of endowment fund earnings must be made so that the cost of supporting an endowed professor's salary with endowment income can be fully supported today as well as in 10 or 20 years.

Another consideration in deciding how much to save is *intergenerational equity*. Future students and faculty should enjoy the same benefits as present ones. But if too much is spent today, the future purchasing power of the endowment will be reduced. In addition to reinvesting current earnings, adding gifts raised in a capital campaign to an endowment is a feasible way to save for the future.

Within these constraints, how much of its endowment earnings should an institution spend? The spending rate that allows an institution to maintain equal growth rates of income and expense, in other words, *the*

Exhibit 8–1
SUMMARY OF ENDOWMENTS FOR THE TOP 20 INSTITUTIONS

Institution	Market Value at End of Fiscal 1993 (thousands)	Endowment per Full-time-enrolled Student
Harvard University	$5,778,257	$321,389
University of Texas System	$4,007,472	$10,820
Princeton University	$3,286,327	$508,012
Yale University	$3,219,400	$298,535
Stanford University	$2,853,366	$219,456
The Texas A&M University System and Foundations	$1,848,525	$30,162
Columbia University	$1,846,600	$113,039
University of California-Berkeley	$1,834,955	$11,405
Emory University	$1,763,518	$194,520
Massachusetts Institute of Technology	$1,752,943	$183,324
Washington University	$1,687,413	$176,674
Northwestern University	$1,308,363	$87,580
Rice University	$1,302,576	$317,779
University of Chicago	$1,224,036	$118,025
Cornell University	$1,214,600	$64,717
University of Pennsylvania	$1,095,796	$56,267
University of Notre Dame	$828,554	$83,981
Vanderbilt University	$800,632	$86,284
University of Michigan	$797,149	$17,449
Dartmouth College	$743,670	$138,486

Source: 1993 NACUBO Endowment Study, prepared by Cambridge Associates and published in 1994.

equilibrium spending rate, is optimal. If an institution uses the total return concept[4] the equilibrium spending rate is as follows:

equilibrium spending rate = real total return − real cost rise

An institution does not need to find the equilibrium spending rate by trial and error. When an institution is in long-run financial equilibrium, the growth rates of its sources and uses of funds are equal. Real total return is determined by the portfolio investment mix. Inflation is a given. Real cost rise is a function of many variables, leaving the equilibrium

[4] Under the total return concept, endowment income includes dividends, interest, and appreciation made on investments, usually on a pooled basis.

Exhibit 8–2
USING GROWTH RATES TO SET THE EQUILIBRIUM SPENDING RATE

Sources of Funds		Uses of Funds	
Inflation	3.5%	Inflation	3.5%
Real total return[a]	5.5%	Real cost rise[b]	1.5%
		Equilibrium spending rate	4.0%
Total sources	9.0%	Total uses	9.0%

[a] Real total return includes dividends, interest, and appreciation on investments made on a pooled basis.

[b] Real cost rise is the increase in the cost of a certain activity or group of activities after inflation.

spending rate as the unknown element for which to solve. Exhibit 8–2 shows how the equilibrium spending rate was derived for one institution, assuming an inflation rate of 3.5 percent.

A comprehensive policy for accumulating endowment funds and spending endowment income consists of four components:

1. *Base an endowment spending policy on total return, not yield.*[5] Using a total return policy provides less budget volatility for an institution, opens up investment opportunities, and is more in keeping with the philosophy of maintaining long-term financial equilibrium than is a spending policy based a yield that can fluctuate widely. To use the total return concept, it is best to make investments on a pooled basis. The pooled shares are marked to market periodically, and additions to the endowment and withdrawals from it are made by buying and selling shares. Total return and the spending rate are quoted on a per-share basis.

2. *Support the operating budget with a relatively level share of endowment income.* If reinvestments in the endowment from earnings and the addition of new funds are adequate, the share of the institutional operating budget supported by endowment income should be relatively level over time. This is the ideal for which to strive.

The endowment support ratio[6] is a good way to monitor how much of an institutional budget is supported by the endowment. For example, given a $100 million endowment, a 5 percent spending rate, and a $500 million budget, 1 percent of the institutional budget is supported by the endowment (using the formula in footnote 6). Increasing the spending rate to, for example, 10 percent, increases this ratio to 2 percent. On the

[5] Yield is dividends and interest; it excludes realized and unrealized capital gains.
[6] The endowment support ratio = [spending rate × endowment ($)] divided by budget ($).

other hand, spending more means that less is available for reinvestment. If the endowment is not increased through gifts or reinvestment, it will grow at a smaller rate, making it difficult to maintain the endowment support ratio at a constant level.

Adding gifts raised through a capital campaign eases the burden on the endowment support ratio. For example, take a spending rate of 5 percent, a $500 million budget, and an endowment that has grown to $150 million through a highly successful capital campaign. Instead of the 1 percent contribution of the endowment to the institutional budget, the endowment support ratio now approaches a 1.5 percent contribution.

If an institution is in financial difficulty, however, it may have little choice but to increase the immediate endowment support ratio at the expense of future endowment purchasing power. If approved (and an institution should consider this strategy carefully because it is difficult to reverse a decline in the endowment support ratio), the institution can set the spending rate above its equilibrium level and divert gifts (that ideally, would be added to the endowment) to support current operations—or else take funds from quasi-endowment. Funding a deficit from quasi-endowment is the most common cause of sharp declines in future endowment support ratios.

Since there is never enough endowment to support every worthy institutional program, focusing on maintaining the endowment support ratio at a relatively constant level is the minimum for which to strive; increasing it by increasing the size of the endowment is optimal. However, these goals depend very much on institutional circumstances. In any case, the board should set targets for the endowment support ratio. The worst-case scenario would be that the endowment support ratio would change by default.

3. *Maintain the purchasing power of each existing endowment fund.* If an institution can successfully maintain the purchasing power of its individual funds, it will be easier to maintain the endowment support ratio.

4. *Apply a smoothing rule to mitigate the effects of short-term market volatility on spending from endowment.* Investment returns can vary dramatically from year to year. Even if the total return concept is used, a smoothing rule mitigates these variations and allows the spending rule to deviate from the equilibrium rate in a controlled fashion.

To put in perspective our discussion of endowment thus far, it is useful to examine some institutional data about the size of institutional endowments, spending rates, and nominal returns. According to a sample of institutions that participated in the annual NACUBO endowment study, endowment assets totaled $82.2 billion at fiscal 1993 year end. Average endowment spending rates ranged from 4 to 5.2 percent, depending on the size of the endowment. (In general, those with smaller endowments tended to have slightly higher spending rates.) As would be expected, the larger the endowment, the higher the nominal return on it in most cases. Exhibit 8–3 shows the average endowment size, spending rates, and nominal returns of the institutions in the 1993 annual NACUBO endowment study.

8.4 CAPITAL STRUCTURE STRATEGY

Capital structure relates to the size and form of an institution's assets and liabilities. As a key component of capital structure, decisions about how much endowment to accumulate and how much to spend affect an institution's capital structure directly and substantially.

When optimizing the use of assets, a key decision is how much to invest in endowment and how much to invest in physical plant. It makes little sense to invest only in endowment when campus facilities are deteriorating beyond repair or when equipment is obsolete. However, the decision to invest in endowment or plant is a subjective one; each option has significant advantages and disadvantages. In brief, building new facilities or updating old ones can increase operating costs as well as produce benefits for the institution (i.e., high-quality facilities attract students and faculty). If the facilities are for auxiliary purposes, they can increase operating income. Endowment investments are more liquid and hence reversible; plant assets are not liquid and hence are not reversible.

One consideration is what happens to the endowment support ratio under various scenarios. Institutions may want to ask: Are facility needs

Exhibit 8–3
AVERAGE ENDOWMENT SIZE, SPENDING RATES, AND ONE-YEAR NORMAL RETURNS

Endowment Size	Endowment Assets	Endowment Spending Rates, Fiscal 1993	Investment Pool Nominal Returns, Fiscal 1993
$25 million and under	$1.4 billion	5.2%	12.0%
Over $25 million to $100 million	$9.9 billion	4.3%	12.8%
Over $100 million to $400 million	$23.3 billion	4.4%	14.6%
Over $400 million	$47.5 billion	4.0%	14.5%

Source: 1993 NACUBO Endowment Study, prepared by Cambridge Associates and published in 1994.

at the margin more or less important than improving the endowment support ratio? The less healthy an institution's endowment, the greater the need to add to it. Conversely, if an institution's endowment is healthy and its plant is deteriorating, it makes sense to make plant a higher funding priority.

In recent years, colleges and universities have significantly increased the amount of debt on their balance sheets. The advantage of debt is that it permits an institution to build now and pay later, allowing it to leverage its available assets. The two kinds of borrowing can be summarized as follows:

1. Borrowing for projects, such as dormitories, that will generate enough incremental income to pay for debt service.

2. Borrowing for projects, such as libraries and general-purpose academic buildings, that do not add to an institution's revenue stream. In this case, debt service is a drain on institutional operating funds.

An institution's ability to borrow depends on the market's assessment of its financial health. Healthier institutions will pay less for debt than those judged to be less healthy. An institution's credit rating can be improved, and its borrowing costs lowered, if it uses its endowment as collateral. Even without collateralization, endowment makes a very real difference to rating agencies; they view it as added flexibility, just as institutions do. Debt capacity is thus another reason for an institution to maintain or increase its endowment and to maintain or increase its endowment support ratio.

8.5 USES OF ENDOWMENT

After an institution sets an endowment spending policy, the most important question becomes how best to spend endowment income. Consider the two kinds of spending: (1) endowment income that is *restricted* for such uses as faculty chairs, student financial aid, buying library books and equipment, and general support of donor-designated programs, and (2) endowment income that is *unrestricted*. Although the value of restricted endowment income cannot be denied, unrestricted endowment income provides the most operating budget relief.

Increasingly, institutional growth today must come from substitution instead of from adding new programs. Endowment can figure prominently in the necessary budget allocations. Seeking endowed chairs for faculty who are already employed is a kind of "reallocation in advance." We mentioned earlier the concept of nonincremental (i.e., an existing activity) versus incremental (i.e., an add-on activity). Encouraging donors to endow nonincremental faculty chairs instead of adding a new faculty position is a good way to increase growth by substitution and allocate resources accordingly.

Endowment for student aid can be nonincremental as well. Institutional policy can be to use restricted aid moneys first, then current gifts, and finally, fill the remaining needs with available general funds. In the case of library acquisitions and equipment, the amounts are apt to be quite small, and stressing reallocation might not be as beneficial as it is in other areas.

Spending from endowment, whether it is restricted or not, should be included in an institution's integrated operating budget. The operating budget is an important tool for decision making, control, and resource allocation. Including all endowment spending in the operating budget provides an institution with an overview of how its resources are used. Such budgeting is aided by a good information system that tracks (1) how much is in each endowment fund and how it is invested, (2) the amount appropriated for spending from each endowment fund, and (3) the appropriations into expenditure control accounts that show the amount of spending budgeted for the year and the amount actually spent in the current month and in the year to date.

The information system should also be able to answer "what if" questions. For example: What if general funds budgets must be cut by x percent? Ideally, the endowment fund accounts should be tagged with information about restrictions and who has the authority to deploy income within these restrictions. This kind of information is invaluable during downsizing, the situation many institutions find themselves confronting today. Such information permits a dean or department chair to consider deploying existing resources in new ways that are still consistent with the donor's wishes.

Restricted endowment income defrays the direct costs (i.e., such items as salary and benefits for an endowed faculty chair) of the activity supported. But what about the indirect costs (i.e., such items as a secretary's salary, a portion of central administration costs, and a portion of facility costs) associated with the restricted activity? When it is not specifically precluded by the donor, a good case can be made for using restricted endowment income to support the indirect as well as the direct costs of a restricted activity.

Investing endowment monies can also be used to promote social goals. The role of U.S. corporations in South Africa and apartheid gave rise to the idea of investment responsibility. On the one hand, trustees' responsibility is still to seek maximum investment return consistent with risk. However, various constituencies also think that a goal of investing should be to solve social problems. Some institutions have incorporated into their policies statements about responsible investing. For example, an institution's policy could be that when a corporation's policies or practices cause social injury (the term *social injury* should be defined), this factor should be weighed thoughtfully when deciding whether or not to invest in a particular company. Similarly, stocks in some companies that are already in the institution's portfolio may need to be divested if an institution is to maintain the objective of investing responsibly.

8.6 MODERN INVESTMENT THEORY

As mentioned earlier, the prudent man rule was first applied in *Harvard College* v. *Amory* in 1830; it gave institutions more discretion in their investing than had been allowed previously. The court held in this case that "[a]ll that can be required of a trustee to invest is that he shall conduct himself faithfully and exercise a sound discretion. He is to observe how men of prudence, discretion, and intelligence manage their own affairs, not in regard to speculation but in regard to the permanent disposition of their funds, considering the probable income, as well as the probable safety of the capital invested."[7] The prudent man standard was followed (mainly in Massachusetts) until the 1940s.

The competing doctrine called for investments to be perfectly safe, largely ruling out stocks. However, recognition that bonds were not safe either was brought home when a wave of bond defaults occurred in the 1930s. After that, the prudent man rule was once again in vogue, and institutional portfolios reflected investments in stock, bonds, and real estate.

The changing doctrines are indicated by Harvard's and Princeton's asset allocations from 1830 to 1989, as shown Exhibit 8–4. The two institutions started out with very different investment mixes; Harvard held mostly real estate while Princeton focused on stocks. By 1884, Harvard held mostly bonds with a sizable number of stocks; Princeton held primarily bonds. By 1940 when the prudent man rule was more widely accepted, the two portfolios were quite similar; each was almost half invested in stocks. Stocks as a percentage of the portfolios increased thereafter. By 1989, approximately 59 percent of Harvard's portfolio consisted of stocks compared to about 68 percent for Princeton.

Modern investment theory has raised new questions about the prudent man rule. The work of Benjamin Graham and David Dodd, among others, in the 1930s indicated that the prudent man rule did not

[7] William F. Massy, *Endowment: Perspectives, Policies and Management* (Washington, D.C.: Association of Governing Boards of Universities and Colleges, 1990), p. 90.

Exhibit 8–4
ASSET ALLOCATIONS FOR HARVARD AND PRINCETON (1830–1989)

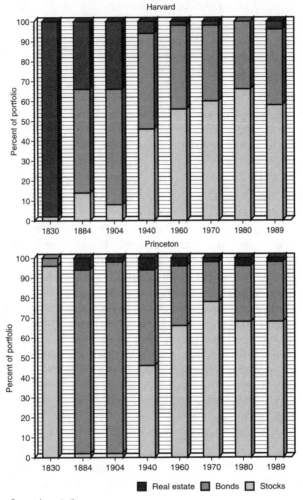

Source: Longstreth,
1986, Tables 2.2 and 2.3, updated to 1989

Source: William F. Massey, *Endowment: Perspectives, Policies, and Management* (Washington, D.C.: Association of Governing Boards of Universities and Colleges, 1990), p. 91.

fully consider such principles as: diversification pays, [expe]cted reward depends on risk, and investors should focus on total [retur]n, not just income. Also, new investment opportunities introduced [in th]e last two decades, such as international stocks and bonds, ventur[e cap]ital, and leveraged buyouts, do not always fit neatly into the cat[egorie]s envisioned by the prudent man rule. Although "prudent men" inv[est in] these newer investment vehicles today, such investments do not [meet] the historical standard. When the prudent man rule was first p[assed], trustees made all investment decisions. Now investment manage[ment is] delegated, although trustees still oversee it. This change also w[as not] envisioned by the prudent man rule.

In summary, the following generalizations can be made about m[od]ern investment principles following development of the prudent man ru[le] and theories raised since then:

1. *Diversification is important*; it reduces risk relative to expected returns. Diversification is achieved by adding different investment vehicles to a portfolio (i.e., stocks, bonds, etc.) and by ensuring that the investments within each category differ sufficiently (i.e., a portfolio consisting of two automobile manufacturers' stocks is less diversified than one that includes an automobile manufacturer's stock and a high-technology stock).

2. *The investor's portfolio should reflect the investor's tolerance for risk and the size of the portfolio.* The two are very closely related; the degree of risk tolerance for an institution depends, at least in part, on the size of its portfolio.

3. *An asset's riskiness can best be judged in the context of the overall portfolio.*

4. *If risk is increased in a portfolio, expected return will also improve.*

5. *Investment performance should be judged over a period of a year or more—not in the short term.*

6. *If used prudently, short selling, borrowing, leverage, and derivatives such as options and futures can be useful in a portfolio.*

7. *It is extremely difficult to time market cycles.*

Given these broad principles, certain theories have developed, including the mean–variance principle, the capital asset pricing model, arbitrage pricing theory, and tactical asset allocation models. We now explore each of these.

Mean–Variance Principle

Investing is inherently risky. According to the mean–variance principle, investment decisions should be made based on the expected value, or *mean* of total return, as well as on a measure of risk, the *variance* of possible returns. Neither the mean nor the variance can be known precisely, but long-term estimates are available. For this reason, investors should also keep in mind two basic principles: (1) the greater the risk, the greater the expected return, and (2) diversification reduces risk.

Capital Asset Pricing Model

One approach to asset allocation is the capital asset pricing model (CAPM). Among other assumptions, this model assumes that investors make decisions based on expected total return and risk (i.e., the mean–variance principle). Under this model, investors are compensated for tying up their money in investments and for taking on risk. The "best" investment is the *market portfolio*, which is roughly equivalent to an all-encompassing index fund. At the core of CAPM is the efficient market hypothesis. An efficient market is one in which security prices reflect publicly available information so quickly that it is difficult for people to "beat the market." The CAPM has several limitations, one of which is that the definition of what constitutes "the market" is incomplete. Another is that the market is not always efficient.

Arbitrage Pricing Theory

Under the arbitrage pricing theory (APM), investors do not necessarily make investment decisions based on the mean–variance principle. Instead, investors "arbitrage" away differences in the expected return of assets they believe have roughly equivalent risks. This means that the market portfolio is not necessarily the best investment for all investors. APM frees modern investment principles from the market portfolio, recognizing that index funds are not always, in theory or practice, the best investment vehicle.

Tactical Asset Allocation Models

Until recently it was assumed that efforts to time market swings did not pay off. The judgment-based procedures used to make timing decisions did not offset the increased risk of trying to time market swings. However, computer modeling involving large-scale data screening and extensive mathematical procedures for allocating the mix of stocks, bonds, and cash are potentially valuable. For example, computer modeling protected some portfolios during the October 1987 market crash.

8.7   INVESTMENT POLICIES

Most institutions delegate the management of their endowment portfolio to an investment manager. The board's investment committee usually has overall responsibility for the institution's investments. This committee should address two basic questions: (1) how to delegate endowment management, and (2) how to oversee the process. The board should consider establishing adequate procedures for determining how to delegate; selecting the right delegates considering such factors as style, philosophy, and track record; subsequently monitoring their performance against predetermined criteria, often on a quarterly basis; and finally, making changes as necessary.

To facilitate this process, the board should set percentage targets for each kind of investment vehicle (i.e., stocks, bonds, real estate, etc.) Setting asset-allocation targets involves considering the institution's tolerance for risk (the most important decision point), how the institution views each of its asset classes (i.e., is the purpose to act as a hedge against inflation or deflation, for example, or more simply, to diversify), and finally, how much competence the institution has to invest in a certain asset class. A small institution with a small endowment may not be able to afford a top-notch advisor for more arcane investment vehicles, for example, although it may be able to invest with others in limited partnerships. Developing a carefully reasoned strategy provides insurance for an institution during times of crisis and it also allows for more thoughtful discussions about the institution's investment decisions.

8.8   THE FUTURE

Managing endowments for the future has two critical components. The first relates to changes in how investments decisions are made internally within an institution, and the second relates to changes in the financial markets themselves. Internally, the future lies in the further integration of decisions regarding endowment and plant with decisions about operations. Traditionally, capital and operational decision making was kept separate. One result of not looking at the combined financial picture was that institutions allowed deferred maintenance to accumulate; another was that institutions tended not to invest adequately in equipment.

Integrating decision making about endowment, plant, and operations makes the questions about how much endowment to spend and how much to save even more critical. Institutions will have to craft policies about endowment spending and saving. They should thoughtfully and strategically protect the value of their endowment while addressing facility and operational needs.

Externally, it is clear that the financial markets are changing rapidly, are increasingly volatile, and are more complex. Within this environment, the overriding investment trend is toward greater globalization. This trend recognizes that our society is increasingly a global one, and international economic/market forces significantly influence our economy/market as well as create more opportunities abroad. Previously, "hot" investments were found in such countries as Japan and Western Europe. Now, Indonesia, China, Malaysia, South America, and Mexico are playing a stronger role. These countries have less efficient markets, and as a result, there are more opportunities to "exploit" the market.

A secondary trend in the financial markets is the proliferation of investment vehicles. Index funds are not as widely touted as they were previously; institutions have more faith in the ability of investment managers to pick winners. Hedge funds have been very active in the last few years, and global investment vehicles involving derivatives have been popular. As the number of investment vehicles increases and as investing becomes increasingly global, diversification as the all-important underlying principle is gaining force.

The future of investment allocation decisions will not be computer driven. Rather, information technology will be used as a screening tool, producing readily accessible data on a host of investment vehicles. Investment decisions will subsequently be made using a blend of judgment and computer-generated data. Successful investment managers will be those people who rely on both judgment and analytical tools.

8.9 CONCLUSIONS

Endowment funds contribute significantly to an institution's financial health and flexibility. Endowment funds also present challenges to institutions, particularly in today's complex and rapidly changing financial markets. Not only must difficult investment decisions be made among a vast array of investment vehicles, institutions must also focus on how much of the resulting endowment income should be spent today and how much should be saved for future generations. Questions also arise about discretionary funds: How much should be set aside as endowment, and how much should be invested in plant and equipment? Managing endowment funds is today, and has always been, a continual balancing act, and setting guidelines and policies about how best to balance risk versus return and spending today versus saving for the future is critical. Although the investment markets have changed substantially, the underlying concept of endowment management has not: Invest prudently and thoughtfully, and spend similarly.

Managing Debt in Changing Financial Markets

PATRICK J. HENNIGAN

Morgan Stanley Group, Inc.

9.1 Introduction

9.2 Historical Context

The Trend Is Toward Stronger Legal Provisions

9.3 Current Situation

Credit Quality of Higher Education Institutions Remains Strong

Institutions Are Assessing Debt Capacity

Comparative Ratios Provide Useful Benchmarks

Higher Education Default Rates on Bond Issues Are Low

Institutions Are Taking Advantage of the Yield Curve

9.4 The Future

Current Demographic Trends Will Affect Debt Issuance

Changing Financial Markets

9.5 Institutions to Examine Broader Range of Risks

9.6 Conclusions: Opportunities and Challenges in Changing Financial Markets

9.1 INTRODUCTION

Global restructuring. Emerging Markets. Twenty-four hour trading. Arbitrage between markets. Information superhighway. Derivative products. Volatility. Hedging. These are a few of the ideas and concepts that define our rapidly "changing financial markets" as we approach the twenty-first century. Within this evolving financial environment, how will the objectives and processes for successful debt management be different from the ways institutions of higher education managed debt in the 1980s?

Three themes appear to be emerging. First, the management of debt will gain a greater role in university-wide strategic planning. No longer will debt management be an isolated function. Rather, it will encompass a broad range of institutional activities, including endowment management and facilities planning. As a result, debt management will become an integral part of the overall institutional strategic planning process.

The second theme focuses on the application of financial products, including those involving debt, to a wider range of risks challenging many colleges and universities. These risks are associated not only with changes in interest rates, but also with changes in foreign currencies and energy prices. Institutions can use such instruments as interest rate swaps, interest rate caps, energy swaps, and currency options to manage risk under different scenarios.

Third, the management of assets and liabilities will become a more integrated function, especially in relation to facilities planning and to the process of assessing debt capacity. Prior to the 1980s, the construction of facilities was financed by cash reserves, gifts, and, in modest amounts, by tax-exempt debt. Public universities typically received sufficient state appropriations for new buildings. As a result, their debt burden was very low.

In the 1980s, however, the capital needs of universities were exacerbated by the demand for state-of-the-art facilities in science and technology and by the need to reduce deferred maintenance. Independent institutions had difficulty raising gifts for plant improvements. Public universities were receiving less in state appropriations for capital needs. As a result, significant amounts of capital were raised through the issuance of debt by both public and independent universities. At the same time, colleges and universities were examining their debt capacity and the relation of debt to endowment and other available monies. The end result was that university finance officers focused more attention on leveraging the institution's available assets and integrating debt and asset management.

These three trends will continue to receive high-level attention at colleges and universities as higher education enters the twenty-first century, especially in relation to the confluence of a greater array of financing techniques available to each institution and diminished sources of traditional external funding. Institutions will be confronted by an increasingly global financial market, creating new opportunities and new challenges. Institutions are also likely to rely more heavily on debt as an essential part of their overall financing structure, raising debt management to a higher priority than ever before. Within this framework, we examine the implications for managing debt strategically.

9.2 HISTORICAL CONTEXT

During the 1980s, colleges and universities sold approximately $41 billion in tax-exempt notes and bonds; 35 percent of the proceeds was used for refundings. Annual volume during that decade increased dramatically, from less than $1 billion in 1980 and 1981 to a high of $11 billion in 1985 prior to passage of the 1986 Tax Reform Act. This act set a $150 million cap on the amount of tax-exempt debt outstanding for private colleges and universities. Following the enactment of the cap, higher education's annual debt volume declined for several years, although the proportion of annual issuance by public universities increased steadily (Exhibits 9–1 and 9–2).

By the end of the 1980s, although the overall volume of debt had increased, only 12 percent of the 3300 institutions of higher education in the nation had entered the tax-exempt market. The most active issuers were the large well-endowed independent research institutions and large public university systems.

Following the imposition of the $150 million volume cap for private institutions in 1986, the higher education sector in the municipal market consisted of three groups of institutions: private universities over the $150 million cap, private universities under the cap, and public universities that were not subject to the cap. Debt management is dramatically different for each of these three subgroups.

The Trend Is Toward Stronger Legal Provisions

As more colleges and universities raised capital in the public markets, they utilized a wider variety of debt instruments and secured them with broader pledges of available revenues. In the 1970s and early 1980s, bonds were issued by universities primarily for revenue-producing enterprises such as dormitories, student centers, and parking systems. These bonds were secured by the specific revenues of each auxiliary enterprise system, and the university set rates sufficient at least to cover debt service. The legal provisions of the bonds had all the standard covenants for rate setting, additional bonds, flow of funds, and debt service reserve requirements. Investors typically assessed the credit risk of the auxiliary enterprises rather than focusing on the overall creditworthiness of the institution or system of campuses because the revenue pledge was narrowly defined as a specific auxiliary enterprise revenue stream.

During the 1980s, higher education issuers were increasingly pledging their "full faith and credit," usually defined as a pledge of all available unrestricted revenues. These revenues include tuition and fees, unrestricted investment income, indirect cost recovery, net revenues of auxiliary enterprises, and other unrestricted monies. Moving from specific revenue pledges to a broader general credit pledge allowed universities to sell lease-rental bonds and bonds for other projects that were not revenue generating, such as academic buildings and research facilities, which were cross-subsidized by other revenue sources. Financing academic

Exhibit 9–1
EDUCATION VOLUME IN THE MUNICIPAL MARKET

Historic Market Share

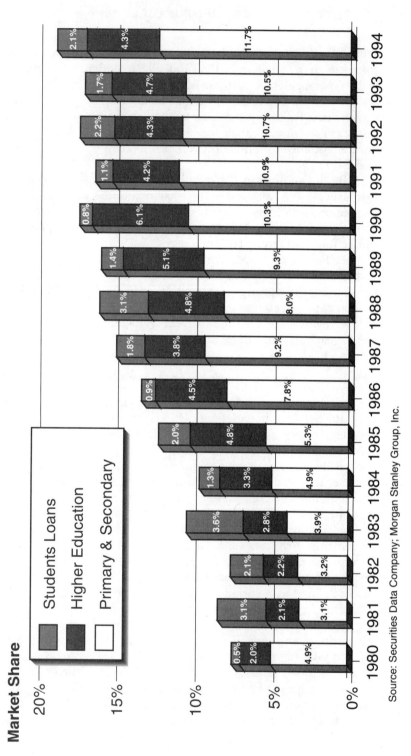

Market Share

Legend:
- Students Loans
- Higher Education
- Primary & Secondary

Year	Students Loans	Higher Education	Primary & Secondary
1980	0.5%	2.0%	4.9%
1981	3.1%	2.1%	3.1%
1982	2.1%	2.2%	3.2%
1983	3.6%	2.8%	3.9%
1984	1.3%	3.3%	4.9%
1985	2.0%	4.8%	5.3%
1986	0.9%	4.5%	7.8%
1987	1.8%	3.8%	9.2%
1988	3.1%	4.8%	8.0%
1989	1.4%	5.1%	9.3%
1990	0.8%	6.1%	10.3%
1991	1.1%	4.2%	10.9%
1992	2.2%	4.3%	10.7%
1993	1.7%	4.7%	10.5%
1994	2.1%	4.3%	11.7%

Source: Securities Data Company; Morgan Stanley Group, Inc.

Exhibit 9–2

TAX-EXEMPT HIGHER EDUCATION BOND VOLUME

New Money vs. Refundings

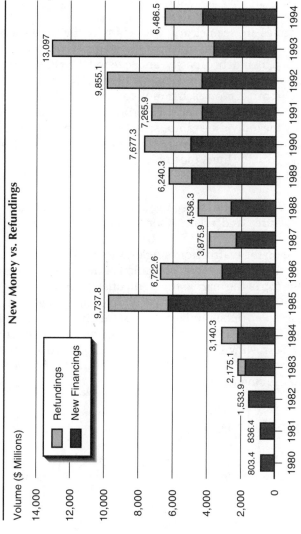

Source: Securities Data Company; Morgan Stanley Group, Inc.

facilities is a relatively recent activity for many public university systems that previously were limited to external financing only for revenue-producing facilities. As a result of the trend toward a broader general obligation pledge, the financial operations of a proposed project must be analyzed within the context of the creditworthiness of the university itself and its capacity to bear additional debt in the future.

Stronger security structures encompassing broader pledges of unrestricted revenues are seen clearly with many of the larger public university systems. Many public university systems have consolidated their debt, increased their debt capacity, and lowered their cost of borrowing by restructuring their security provisions. Previously, each bond issue was sold for specific projects on each campus and secured by a narrow revenue pledge. Those issues were rated based on the specific revenue stream generated by the individual campus. By consolidating the separate issues into a system-wide credit, with a general revenue pledge as strong as state statutes allowed at the time, the university system was able to increase the ratings on the weaker bond issues and obtain an overall lower cost of borrowing.

Exhibit 9–3 identifies seven general types of public higher education security structures and relates them to the rating and cost of capital implications.

Moving up the matrix from single-campus, single-auxiliary revenue project financing to the general obligation of the state or of the university system at the top of the matrix, the credit quality improves and the cost of borrowing decreases while enabling a wider range of debt-financed projects. For example, public university systems in such states as Illinois, Texas, and Missouri attained higher ratings on their debt and reduced their cost of borrowing by restructuring their legal provisions to a higher level on the matrix. In other states, public university systems utilize a variety of these financing structures.

9.3 CURRENT SITUATION

In the mid-1990s, each of the three groups of institutions in higher education are examining different strategies for assessing their capital needs.

1. *Independent institutions near and over the $150 million cap* are reassessing their capital needs and their debt capacity in relation to taxable financing alternatives. The costs of internal borrowing also are being compared to external taxable financings. The total volume of taxable securities issued to date is small in comparison with the tax-exempt market and is concentrated in taxable commercial paper (Exhibit 9–4). A

Exhibit 9–3

PUBLIC HIGHER EDUCATION SECURITY MATRIX

Public Higher Education Debt Financing Methods	Rating	Examples	Cost of Capital
General obligation of the state	Same as state general obligation	WA, FL, MA, OR, WI, VA	Same as state
General obligation of the university	Same as state general obligation to half step below	MN, PA, NJ	5–10 basis points higher than state general obligation
Higher education purpose state appropriation revenue bonds	One step below state general obligation	NY, CA	10–20 basis points higher than state general obligation
Multicampus, multiproject system revenue bonds	One step below state general obligation	MI, MD, TX, MO	15–20 basis points higher than state general obligation
Combined fee system revenue bonds	Half to full step below state general obligation	IL, IN, AL, NY, NV	15–20 basis points higher than state general obligation
System revenue bonds	Half to one and a half steps below state general obligation	CA	20–30 basis points higher than state general obligation
Auxiliary revenue bonds (housing, dining facilities, etc.)	Half to one and a half steps below state general obligation	CO, WA, FL, NC	20–30 basis points higher than state general obligation

Source: This matrix was prepared by the author for the *NACUBO Guide to Issuing and Managing Debt,* National Association of College and University Business Officers, Washington DC, 1994.

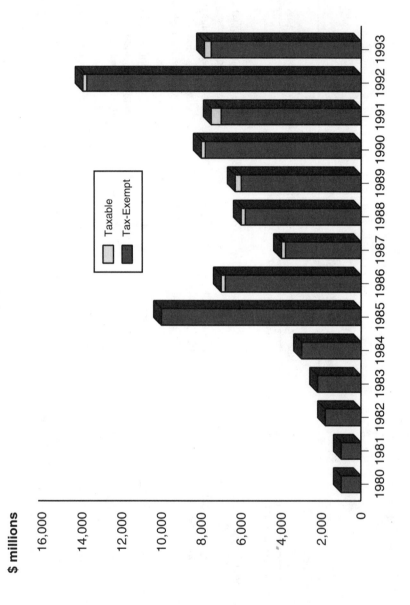

Exhibit 9–4

TAX-EXEMPT AND TAXABLE BONDS ISSUED BY UNIVERSITIES

Source: Securities Data Corporation; Morgan Stanley Group, Inc.

few universities have issued medium-term notes and long-term taxable bonds. Investors have been receptive to the large, well-known research institutions that have made initial forays into the corporate institutional taxable markets. However, investors often have had difficulty understanding the financial statements of universities, especially when applying corporate standards to university financial performance. In addition, the size of university taxable issues is small compared to the size of corporate issues. Also, universities are not in the market as often as corporations. Thus, with less volume and fewer issues trading regularly, university taxable issues are considered less liquid than corporate issues and may not always trade at the same level as corporate bonds rated similarly.

The additional cost of taxable borrowing and the substantial amount of capital needs are the two critical factors that have raised the process of managing debt to a more strategic level in the university decision-making process among independent institutions near and over the $150 million cap. If the cap remains in effect, universities will be seeking more innovative ways to reduce the costs of borrowing and will be assessing their debt capacity more regularly in the future. Finance officers increasingly will be viewing debt as a management tool rather than as a way to finance specific projects.

2. *Independent institutions under the $150 million cap* retain access to the tax-exempt market. As they examine the alternatives available to finance capital projects, many are viewing the tax-exempt market as the most cost-effective source of capital rather than expending plant reserves, quasi-endowment, or gift monies. The key issue for these institutions is their financial strength and related debt capacity. There is a broad range of institutions under the cap. A few have substantial endowments, but the majority are modestly endowed and are more tuition dependent than the larger institutions over the cap. These institutions may benefit by taking advantage of various credit enhancement products, such as bond issuance, letters of credit, or standby bond purchase agreements. Depending on the institution's underlying credit strength, credit enhancement products may lower the institution's overall borrowing costs over the long term.

3. *Public institutions are not subject to the volume cap.* Public university systems increasingly have been accessing the market to raise capital because state legislatures have fewer resources available to appropriate for deferred maintenance and for new facility construction. According to the Center for Higher Education at Illinois State University, average two-year increases in state appropriations to public institutions have slowed to rates of 3 percent or less over the 1991–1994 period compared with

double-digit rates in the mid-1980s. Public institutions are likely to rely more heavily on debt financing in the future, especially in states where the number of college-age students is projected to increase dramatically over the next 15 years.

Credit Quality of Higher Education Institutions Remains Strong

For all three groups of institutions, the general credit quality remains strong, based on the criterion of ratings assigned to outstanding college and university bonds. Over two-thirds of the issues are rated A, AA, or AAA. The remaining one third includes issues rated BBB or lower. Exhibit 9–5 indicates the distribution of ratings for independent colleges and universities bond issues as assigned by the Standard & Poor's Corporation. These ratings represent an assessment of the ability of each university to make debt service payments in a timely fashion over a period. Credit factors in this assessment include financial performance, student demand, selectivity and matriculation ratios, debt burden and capacity, and effectiveness of management.

As Exhibit 9–5 indicates, between 1988 and 1993 there was some weakening in credit quality for independent institutions in the lower A and BBB rating categories. Since 1990, S&P has reported that 19 ratings were downgraded while only 10 ratings were raised. These actions were taken on only 18 percent of the 158 unenhanced long-term ratings maintained by S&P on private colleges and universities. Thus, according to S&P: "Most institutions, however, have not experienced rating changes— a fact that demonstrates the maintenance of credit quality through this difficult period."[1]

Institutions Are Assessing Debt Capacity

Many institutions are examining the strategic questions: How much debt should we incur? How much of the operating budget should be servicing debt? The assessment of debt capacity involves several sets of parameters determined by the university governing board, credit rating agencies, investors, credit enhancers, and governmental oversight authorities. This assessment should also be related to the long-term positioning of the institution. How will the institution's financial ratios change over the next five to ten years in relation to peer institutions as debt is increased?

The framework suggested here is applicable to assessing debt capacity for public and independent institutions. The first step consists of identifying existing parameters:

---

[1] Standard & Poor's, "Credit trends in higher education," *Creditweek Municipal, Special Edition,* (July 1994) p. 19.

Exhibit 9-5

RATING DISTRIBUTION FOR INDEPENDENT COLLEGES AND UNIVERSITIES*

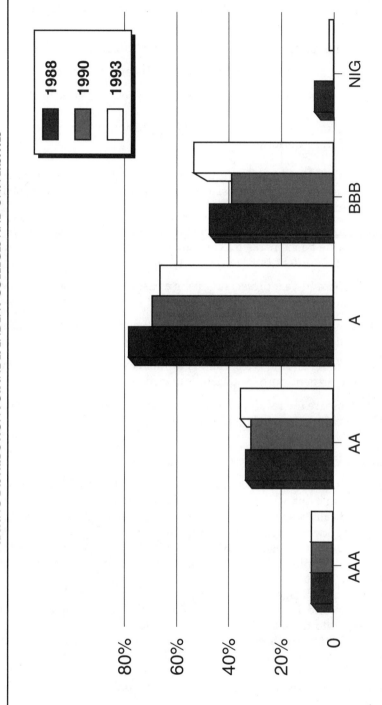

Source: Standard & Poor's, *Creditweek Municipal*, October 25, 1993
*Unenhanced ratings

- Debt limitations established by the institution's governing board

- Covenants in existing legal documents and agreements

- Internal strategic planning assumptions relating to facilities needs

The second step consists of analyzing historical performance and projecting future performance:

- Analyze historical revenue, expenditure, and balance sheet information to identify annual growth rates and trends for the past five years.

- Determine a peer group of institutions based on credit ratings to provide benchmarks for comparative ratio analysis. Develop ratios related to debt burden, liquidity, and operating performance.

- Prepare 10-year projections using a base case of reasonable growth assumptions for major revenues and expenditure categories.

- Identify whether projects will be self-supporting by generating sufficient revenue to cover additional debt service costs.

- Examine alternative scenarios to this base case by varying revenue, expenditure, and debt issuance assumptions.

- Compare the results of various scenarios with peer group median ratios to assess relative positioning.

Comparative Ratios Provide Useful Benchmarks

One integral part of the assessment of debt capacity is the comparison of an institution's financial ratios to outside benchmarks. The rating agencies periodically have published mean and median ratios for various rating categories ranging from the highest rating of Aaa to the lowest investment grade category of Baa (Moody's) and BBB (S&P). Four of the core financial ratios used in debt capacity assessments are listed and defined in Exhibit 9-6. These ratios measure liquidity, leverage, debt burden and coverage. Moody's Investors Service, Standard & Poor's Corporation and Fitch Investors Service have defined other important ratios useful to the assessment of debt capacity.

In addition to these ratios, the concept of *net fixed revenue* may provide additional useful data. In his work on endowment management, William Massy has suggested a single policy parameter that integrates assets and liability management.[2] As more public and independent

[2] William F. Massy, *Endowment: Perspectives, Policies, and Management* (Washington, D.C.: Association of Governing Boards of Universities and Colleges, 1990).

Exhibit 9–6
SELECTED FINANCIAL RATIOS

Ratio	Definition
Liquidity: *Available monies/debt outstanding*	Measures the relationship between available unrestricted monies and debt outstanding; unrestricted monies include fund balances in the current fund, quasi-endowment, and plant funds
Leverage: *Debt/ endowment*	Measures debt outstanding as a percentage of endowment
Debt burden: *Debt service/operating expenses*	Measures the proportion of debt service to the unrestricted current fund expenditures and mandatory transfers
Coverage: *Unrestricted net revenues before mandatory transfers/ debt service*	Measures the coverage of debt service by unrestricted net revenues

institutions examine questions of internal versus external borrowing and the allocation of capital between endowment and facilities, we need to develop measures and benchmarks for monitoring these decisions. Massy defines the concept of net fixed revenue as "appropriated spending from endowment minus debt service." He then relates the measure to the operating budget. The higher the percentage, the greater the net subsidy from the endowment; the lower the percentage, the greater the net leverage. As yet, however, sample medians are not available.

Higher Education Default Rates on Bond Issues Are Low

Despite fiscal strains, institutions of higher education have recorded historically low rates of default on public bond issues. The smaller, less endowed institutions have shown increased vulnerability to declining enrollments and reduced revenue growth during the past three years, although many of these smaller institutions and their larger counterparts have internally consolidated or downsized to reduce their expenditure base while increasing financial aid packages to remain competitive.

The dollar volume of monetary defaults from 1980 through 1994 is low for colleges and universities compared with other major sectors in the municipal market. Anecdotal information indicates there have been a few additional cases where small colleges defaulted to a financing authority and not to the bondholder. In these instances, the authority had the reserves and legal provisions to make timely payments and assist the institution in working out a remedy.

From 1980 to 1994, there were only five institutions in monetary default, totaling $5.2 million. Education issuers currently in default total $2 million, representing only 0.04 percent of the total amount in monetary default, as indicated in Exhibit 9-7.

Institutions Are Taking Advantage of the Yield Curve

The spread between short- and long-term rates and the spread between the tax-exempt and taxable markets are illustrated in Exhibit 9-8. During most of the period from 1982 to the present, the yield curve has been positively sloped. Significant financial innovations in the late 1980s and in the 1990s have allowed colleges and universities to take advantage of this upward-sloping yield curve. Variable-rate demand bonds or floaters were structured to allow the interest rate to be reset daily, weekly, monthly, quarterly, or annually to capture the greater efficiency of the short end of the curve, thereby reducing the costs of long-term borrowing. Exhibit 9-9 illustrates the use of variable rate debt by universities compared with its use by other issuers. These structures also incorporated a "put" feature, which allowed investors to put the securities back to the issuer or the designated remarketing agent on a periodic basis. Both the issuer and the investor enjoyed the increased flexibility and liquidity provided by these innovative structures.

In the 1990s, structured coupon bonds, also known as derivatives, became the latest product of creative financial engineering. In February 1994, the *Bond Buyer* reported that $9.46 billion of municipal derivatives

Exhibit 9–7
OUTSTANDING MUNICIPAL ISSUES CURRENTLY IN MONETARY DEFAULT

Type of Issue	Outstanding Defaulted Amount	Percent of Total	Number of Issues
Housing	$1,487,595,000	29.62	68
Industrial and commercial development	964,395,000	19.20	142
Utilities	913,850,000	18.20	17
Special distributions and others	826,538,000	16.46	41
Health care	774,727,000	15.43	121
COPs/leases	52,855,000	1.05	11
Education	**2,030,000**	**0.04**	**1**
General obligation	0.00	0.00	0
Total	$5,021,990,000	100.00	401

Source: Prepared by Kenny S&P Information Services and Kenny S&P Evaluation Services. Data as of 3/31/94. Published in *The Blue List Extra*, New York, April 1994.

Exhibit 9–8
TAX-EXEMPT AND TAXABLE INTEREST RATES

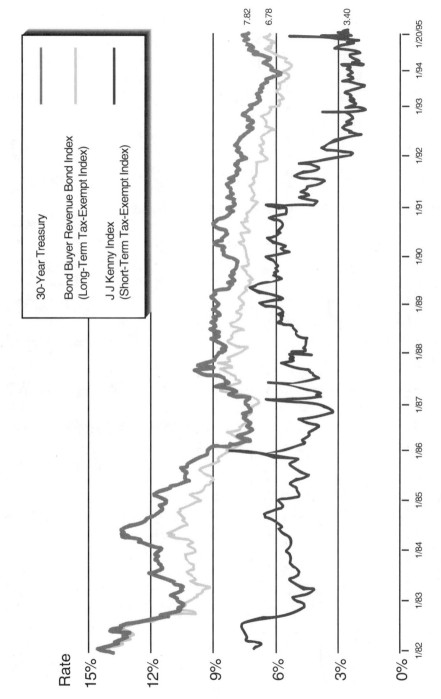

Source: Securities Data Company; *The Bond Buyer*

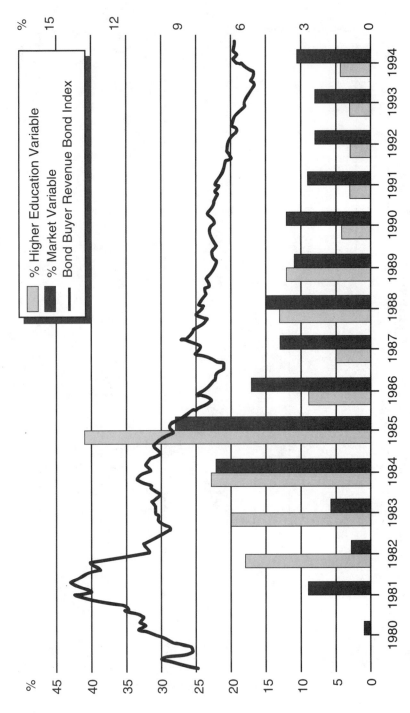

Exhibit 9-9

HISTORICAL TAX-EXEMPT HIGHER EDUCATION BOND ISSUANCE

Variable Rate Debt as % of Market

Source: Securities Data Company; *The Bond Buyer*

■ 200 ■

were sold on 328 issues during 1993, up 39 percent from $6.80 billion sold on 110 issues in 1992. These data do not include interest rate swaps and other derivatives used solely to hedge issuer's own assets and liabilities. Derivatives are tailored to investors' interests and are designed to reduce the cost of borrowing over the long term by taking advantage of unique opportunities in the market, including spread differentials between the taxable and tax-exempt markets.

9.4 THE FUTURE

Current Demographic Trends Will Affect Debt Issuance

The Western Interstate Commission for Higher Education recently has projected that the number of high school graduates is expected to increase by 31 percent between 1994 and 2009, from 2.5 million graduates to approximately 3.3 million. If public colleges and universities continue to enroll over 75 percent of all college students, public university systems in high-growth states will be placing a higher priority on assessing debt capacity and on managing debt over the next 15 years to meet increasing student demand in the face of declining growth in state appropriations for capital projects (Exhibit 9-10).

Solutions will include increasing enrollments at existing campuses, adding new campuses or expanding community college systems. An increase in direct state capital outlays for new buildings seems unlikely considering competing pressures for allocating funds to other vital services, such as health care, prisons, and social services. Thus public university systems will increasingly be forced to rely on proceeds from the sale of either state general obligation bonds, state appropriation bonds, or university revenue bonds to fund an estimated one-third increase in student demand over the next 15 years between 1994 and 2009.

Exhibit 9–11 indicates projected demographic trends by region. The western states and the south-central states are expected to experience the strongest enrollment pressures between 1994 and 2009. As a result, public institutions in these states are likely to need more external financing for new construction than are public institutions in other regions of the country.

Changing Financial Markets

Global restructuring accompanied by technological innovations in telecommunications and computers will have profound effects on financial markets in the twenty-first century. The restructuring of emerging economies in Southeast Asia, Latin American, and Eastern Europe will result

Exhibit 9–10
STATES WITH THE HIGHEST PROJECTED INCREASES
IN HIGH SCHOOL GRADUATES: 1994–2009

State	Percent Increase
Nevada	155
California	76
Florida	71
Maryland	62
Arizona	59
Washington	53
Delaware	49
Georgia	44
Virginia	37
Oregon	36
New Hampshire	36
Texas	35
North Carolina	34
Colorado	30

Source: Data was compiled from High School Graduates: Projections by State, 1992–2009 (Boulder, CO: Western Interstate Commission for Higher Education, 1993).

in their greater integration into the Western economic system. According to David Roche, formerly a strategist at Morgan Stanley, "the immensity of global restructuring cannot be exaggerated. Global restructuring vastly increases the potential world supply of natural resources, agricultural products, and above all, skilled labor. Handled right, this should boost global growth and lower inflation."[3] The demand for global resources will increase dramatically from these major restructuring economies and foreign direct investment will become a key factor in funding global growth.

Barton Biggs of Morgan Stanley believes that over the next 15 years, China, India, Brazil, and Indonesia will become major players in the world's stock markets. During this period, technological advances will facilitate global restructuring and will provide the means to develop innovative financial products to match buyers and sellers from around the world who want to participate in those markets.[4]

[3] These and other factors are analyzed by David C. Roche in Global Strategy and Economics, 2001: An Investment Odyssey (Morgan Stanley International Investment Research, February 1994) p. 11.
[4] Barton M. Biggs, "The myth of the coming capital shortage," U.S. Investment Perspectives, September 21, 1994, Morgan Stanley & Co. Inc.

Exhibit 9-11

High School Graduates by Region

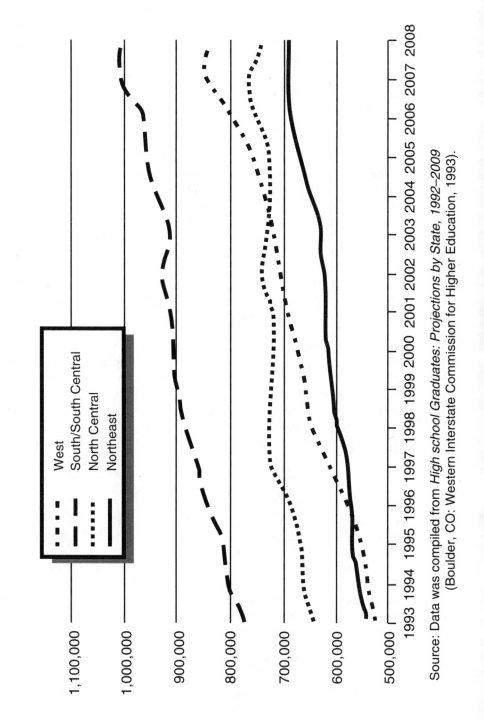

Source: Data was compiled from *High school Graduates: Projections by State, 1992–2009* (Boulder, CO: Western Interstate Commission for Higher Education, 1993).

MANAGING DEBT IN CHANGING FINANCIAL MARKETS

How will changing financial markets affect the management of debt by universities? The implications of these factors appear more obvious for asset managers in universities than for debt managers. University endowment and pension fund managers will have increasing opportunities to invest directly in restructuring economies through direct stock purchase, joint ventures, and limited partnerships or invest indirectly through mutual funds. However, the changing financial markets also raise issues for debt managers at colleges and universities.

As mentioned earlier, the higher education sector in the municipal market is divided into three parts: independent universities over the $150 million cap, independent colleges and universities under the cap, and public colleges and universities not subject to the cap. The management of debt in changing financial markets will be somewhat different for each of these subgroups as long as the cap remains in place.

Institutions over the cap have either entered the taxable market or have been borrowing internally for capital projects. As the near-term probability of lifting the cap diminishes, these institutions will be examining various domestic and international taxable financing opportunities to identify the least costly alternative which also preserves flexibility to refinance in the tax-exempt market. Cap-constrained institutions would benefit most from an enhanced understanding of global markets and by looking for opportunities between markets to structure transactions that capture lower costs of financing. As they compete with corporations and sovereign governments for capital, they will become more knowledgeable about new financial products that are applicable to their borrowing strategy.

For independent institutions below the cap, the use of their limited capacity for tax-exempt debt will become a strategic decision within the overall array of choices related to the use of capital. The focus will be on which projects should be funded with tax-exempt bonds, plant reserves, or gift monies. These institutions will be affected most generally by macro changes in the financial markets as they influence inflation, interest rates, and economic growth. At a more micro level, these institutions will be affected by the rapid development of innovative financial products which they can use to reduce borrowing costs.

For public university systems, the tax-exempt market will remain the most attractive alternative. These institutions also will be able to reduce borrowing costs by becoming familiar with new financial products and their associated benefits and risks. Given the demographic trends described above, it is likely that more public universities will be issuing debt over the next ten years and in larger amounts than during the past ten years. In addition to increasing enrollments, public universities will be facing renewal and replacement of many facilities that were built in the 1950s and 1960s. These institutions will be focusing far more attention on assessing their debt capacity than they have in the past.

9.5   INSTITUTIONS TO EXAMINE BROADER RANGE OF RISKS

Integration of the asset and liability sides of the balance sheet will continue to evolve as institutions of higher education examine their risk management strategies. Here the focus is to identify categories of market risks faced by institutions and to determine which financial products reduce the risk. Over the next decade, the experience of many colleges and universities in utilizing interest rate swaps and structured bond products to lower their cost of borrowing in 1993 and 1994 will lead to the application of similar financial products to other areas of market risk. Below are suggestions for managing risk:

1. *Asset and liability mismatch.* Colleges and universities often employ conservative financing approaches in which long-term fixed-rate debt is issued to finance facilities. Equally conservative on the asset side, cash is often invested in shorter-term floating-rate securities. This result is a balance sheet mismatch in which net income is sensitive to changes in interest rates. By using interest rate swaps, the assets and liabilities can be brought into closer balance with little incremental risk.

2. *Interest rate volatility.* Institutions with variable-rate debt outstanding may be concerned about rising interest rates and want to reduce this risk. They could enter into a floating-to-fixed swap that would set the interest rate for a specified period of time. Also, they might consider an interest rate cap, an agreement by which the cap seller, in return for a payment from the cap buyer, agrees to make payments equal to the amount that a floating-rate index exceeds a predetermined strike rate. This would establish a ceiling on the institution's floating-rate debt service costs. Another alternative would combine the purchase of a cap with the sale of a floor. With this strategy, the university has created an interest rate collar. This is a band within which the university's debt service will range. By giving up some of the gain below the floor, the university reduces the cost of the overall protection with a collar that would be less costly than a cap.

3. *Energy price fluctuations.* Many colleges and universities have substantial expenditures for energy products such as fuel oil. To make these costs more predictable, they might consider using a hedging strategy whereby a college or university contracts for heating oil at a fixed price over the spot price. Through an energy swap, the college exchanges a fixed price for a spot price on a specified volume of oil. The result of the swap is that the college has a net fixed fuel cost over a specified period.

4. *Foreign currency exposure.* Colleges and universities with substantial exposure to foreign currencies might consider currency options to hedge their risk. The university would pay a premium to a bank or dealer

that sells the option. In return, the university may exercise the right to exchange a set amount of a foreign currency for dollars at a predetermined exchange rate on a given day in the future. On that future date, if the university can exchange currencies in the conventional market for a better rate, it can let the option expire.

Following the identification of categories of risk and appropriate management strategies, it is important to quantify clearly the benefits and incremental risks of each strategy. The risks to universities can be classified into four types: market, credit, operational and legal.[5] The market risk of derivatives is based upon their price behavior as markets change. Large users of derivatives should frequently mark their positions to market to accurately assess the valuation. Credit risk involves the loss incurred if a counterparty defaults on a contract. Universities can reduce counterparty credit risk by using credit enhancement approaches such as collateralization triggered by a deadline in credit quality. The measurement of current and potential credit exposure for each transaction is an important component in managing the credit risk. The third risk type is operational risk which involves losses resulting from inadequate systems and poor controls. Legal risk is the fourth type which occurs when a contract cannot be enforced. Unenforceability results from the counterparty being legally incapable of entering into the contract. This was the issue in the case of Hammersmith and Fulham in the United Kingdom which brought the concept of legal authorization into the spotlight in 1991.

9.6 CONCLUSIONS: OPPORTUNITIES AND CHALLENGES IN CHANGING FINANCIAL MARKETS

From a relatively insignificant position in the municipal market prior to the mid-1980s, the higher education sector has increased dramatically in volume over the past 15 years. In addition, many institutions have utilized more sophisticated financial products developed initially in the corporate taxable market and recently transferred to the tax-exempt market. As debt service has become a larger proportion of the operating budget, the management of debt has surfaced as a higher priority. Lessons learned in applying complex financial products to debt management are being applied to other areas of market risk faced by colleges and universities.

For most university debt managers, the implications of these technological changes and global restructurings will consist of (1) greater

---

[5] These categories were defined by the Global Derivatives Study Group in their publication, *Derivatives: Practices and Principals* published by the Group of Thirty, Washington, D.C., July 1993.

9.6 CONCLUSIONS

integration of debt management with asset management to leverage institutional assets more fully and to view an institution's financial condition as a unified whole, one side of the balance sheet influencing and integrated with the other, and (2) the utilization of a broader range of innovative financial products to reduce borrowing costs and to protect the institution from adverse movements in currency rates, commodity prices, and interest rates. These two major trends are consistent with the third theme described early in this chapter, the transition of debt management from the atomized project level to a key component of an institution's long-term strategic planning. Strategic planning is increasingly important to colleges and universities in a changing financial market. Given the many demands on institutional resources and diminished sources of revenue, debt management should be a key component of an institution's strategic plan.

Developing, Not Controlling, Human Resources

JANET FUERSICH

Coopers & Lybrand L.L.P.

RICHARD NORMAN

Rutgers University

10.1 Introduction

10.2 Benefits of Human Resource Planning

10.3 Model for Human Resource Planning

10.4 Compensation and Benefits

10.5 Internal Job Relationships: Job Evaluation

    Job Evaluation Techniques

10.6 External Job Relationships: Labor Market Studies

10.7 Salary Surveys

10.8 Salary Structures

    Salary Ranges

    Constructing a Salary Structure

10.9 Theoretical Versus Practical Considerations

    Pros and Cons

    Salary Structure Design

10.10 Internal and Individual Pay Equity

10.11 Performance Appraisals and Merit Pay

10.12 Tax-Sheltered Annuities: Internal Revenue Code Section 403(b)

10.13 Section 457: Eligible 457 Plans

10.14 Section 457: Ineligible 457 Plans

10.15 Equity and Employment

10.16 Conclusions

10.1   INTRODUCTION

Higher education is very labor intensive; about two-thirds of a college or university budget is related to employee costs. Although human resources has always been an important area in higher education for this reason, it is taking on an increasingly important focus today as colleges and universities adjust to new employee demographics, changes in mission and philosophy, and economic pressures.

In past years, the human resource department was primarily a maintenance function, often decentralized and controlled by individual units and departments within the university. To contribute effectively to the objectives and mission of the institution today, the human resource function must stop being a "controller" and become a "consultant." The function of the human resource department in progressive institutions will be proactive, offering options and alternatives to maximize the effective use of human resources rather than controlling directives on procedures and budgets. Becoming an integral part of the institution and functioning proactively requires a heightened awareness of the strategic mission of the institution and an understanding and commitment to strategic human resource planning.

The functions of the human resource department, depicted in Exhibit 10–1, should reflect the culture of the university or college and provide for the "seamless" delivery of services that support the mission of the institution. In addition, there is an ever-increasing need for the delivery of services to recognize the characteristics of the higher education employee needed to meet the demands of our rapidly changing enterprise. The higher education employee: (1) easily accomodates change; (2) is multi-talented; (3) is able to maintain a university-wide perspective; (4) has the ability to work within a team; (5) is never satisfied with the status quo—always seeking improvement; and (6) has the ability to appreciate and work within state and federal mandates.

10.2   BENEFITS OF HUMAN RESOURCE PLANNING

Significant benefits accrue to institutions that establish formal human resource planning processes. The first benefit from human resource planning is assurance that a sufficient number of qualified personnel will be available to meet future organizational needs. A number of forces, two of which are detailed below, are making planning increasingly necessary to achieve this end.

1. *Technical obsolescence*. Professional knowledge can become outdated very quickly. Institutions of higher education that require the development of new or expanded technology will be required to constantly

Exhibit 10-1
FUNCTIONS OF HUMAN RESOURCES DEPARTMENT

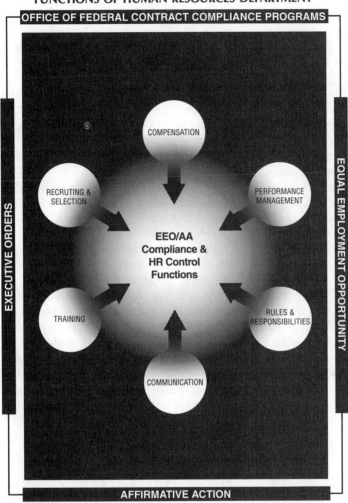

retrain and reeducate portions of their workforce. Even though university systems and technology often lag behind, the most recent developments, the competition of the marketplace will require a continual commitment to keep abreast of an ever-improving technological environment with a concomitant allocation of adequate resources to maintain an ever-improving service level.

2. *Transferability of skills.* As organizations downsize or "rightsize," employees are required to assume multiple responsibilities and learn new skills to transfer "through" organizations rather than "up" organizations.

As colleges and universities continue to adjust their structure and direction and react to fiscal constraints, organizational roles and new or changed job tasks must be planned. Employees within heretofore isolated areas such as student services or financial operations must be prepared to move within the organization to areas of expanded need rather than trying to outlive their usefulness in an area of decreasing need.

The second major benefit of human resource planning is that it identifies problems that hinder the effective use of human resources. To meet changing needs, higher education should analyze the effectiveness of its workforce. The planning process provides an opportunity to identify shortages of skills, over- or understaffing, and other human resource constraints.

Third, human resource planning can establish integrated goals and directions for the activities of traditionally separate human resource functions. This ensures that the institution will be able to allocate the appropriate human resources to departments and units. Too often, the activities of separate human resource functions (i.e., compensation, benefits, and training) are narrowly based, ignoring the longer-term objectives of the institution as well as the effect that the actions of each human resource function has on the other. For example, human resource staff may be recruiting applicants for advanced technology jobs without knowing what training could be done in-house to provide skills to current employees. Or benefits personnel may be developing a flexible benefits program when there is a greater need to increase direct compensation to more competitive levels. Planning can help make the "strategic approach" to human resources more than a philosophy.

The most compelling reason for human resource planning in higher education today is to be able to respond quickly to organizational changes or new directions. Institutions of higher learning are undergoing significant changes. For example, in response to fiscal constraints, they are looking for new revenue opportunities, many of which may require employees with different skills. Only an integrated strategic approach to human resources can provide the needed flexibility for the changing dynamics in higher education.

10.3 MODEL FOR HUMAN RESOURCE PLANNING

Human resource strategic planning is not simply an overview of one year's budgets or activities. Human resource planning is the process by which an organization anticipates future human resource requirements and develops and implements policies and programs to fulfill those requirements. This emphasizes the integration of human resource plans with the development of the human resource programs necessary to achieve those plans. This approach is illustrated in the model of the planning process shown in Exhibit 10–2.

The major components of this model include:

- Developing future human resource needs

- Establishing human resource policies and programs to achieve those plans

- Managing and implementing the programs

- Evaluating the success of the programs

Human resource projections begin with the development of the institution's strategic plan, continue with the identification of skills and jobs necessary to promote the strategic initiatives, and conclude with an assessment of current employee resources in relation to these future needs. In the present changing environment in higher education, institutions cannot be certain that their existing workforce will satisfy their future requirements. They need to consider the projected availability of employees with the necessary skills in the external labor market and to evaluate their internal recruiting, training, and compensation and benefits programs to be sure they will help attract and retain the most qualified employees.

The successful higher education institution will have human resource programs that reflect its current objectives. The institution should be in a proactive, not reactive mode of operation in integrating all of its human resource functions. The relationship between human resource planning and the various functional human resource areas needs constant evaluation.

A critical component of the human resource planning/evaluation process must be a thorough and objective assessment of current staff. Opportunities must be provided for current employees to utilize skills which may in fact be latent but valuable nonetheless. While skills may need to be obtained in the external market, the institution is best served when costs of staff turnover can be avoided whenever possible.

10.4   COMPENSATION AND BENEFITS

Human resource planning can be most visible in the compensation and benefits area. Until very recently, adequate thought has not been given to the importance of compensation and benefits planning. However, there is a great deal to gain by engaging in strategic planning and integration in these two areas as institutions of higher education react to the changing

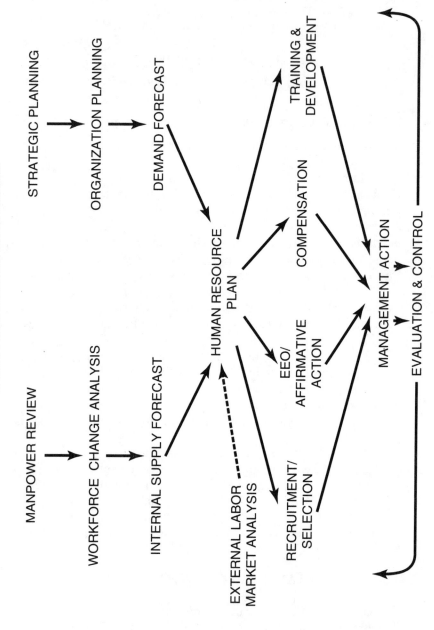

Exhibit 10–2
HUMAN RESOURCE PLANNING PROCESS

STRATEGIC PLANNING

ORGANIZATION PLANNING

DEMAND FORECAST

MANPOWER REVIEW

WORKFORCE CHANGE ANALYSIS

INTERNAL SUPPLY FORECAST

EXTERNAL LABOR MARKET ANALYSIS

HUMAN RESOURCE PLAN

RECRUITMENT/ SELECTION

EEO/ AFFIRMATIVE ACTION

COMPENSATION

TRAINING & DEVELOPMENT

MANAGEMENT ACTION

EVALUATION & CONTROL

education and economic environment. The major benefits of strategic compensation and benefits planning in higher education include providing more relevance in the following areas:

- Program development

- Program costing

- Job analysis and classification

- Program management

With respect to compensation, the relationship between an institution and its employees is reciprocal. Institutions expect a level of commitment from their employees and a "fair day's work for a fair day's pay." Employees expect job security, internal and external equity, and opportunities to grow and develop in the work relationship. Many considerations influence an institution's compensation structure, including the total level of compensation costs, the culture and pay philosophy of the institution, and governmental and statutory regulations. Although this is a complex endeavor, there are two main activities. The task of setting and maintaining salary levels involves (1) considering internal job relationships, generally developed through job evaluation techniques, and (2) the pricing or external market strategy of the institution.

10.5 INTERNAL JOB RELATIONSHIPS: JOB EVALUATION

Job evaluation is an extremely common practice in private industry as well as in higher education. It stems from the idea that job levels and wages should be based on criteria of job worth. These criteria are often expressed as descriptions of skill, effort, responsibility, and working conditions (i.e., the universal job factors). In fact, the many factors used in different job evaluation plans are subsets of these universal factors. For example, education and experience are variants of skill, while budget and financial parameters are variants of responsibility.

Most job evaluation plans create an organizational hierarchy without consideration of external market salary rates and involve the rating and/or ranking of jobs relative to the chosen criteria or job evaluation factors. Job evaluation programs provide information about jobs and job requirements as distinct from the performance and behavior of the employees who hold them. Individual performance and other individual characteristics, such as experience, are relevant in the establishment of equitable pay levels, but they should not influence judgments concerning the jobs themselves. In practice, job evaluations should be based on job analysis and written job descriptions.

Job Evaluation Techniques

There are numerous job evaluation techniques currently in use:

1. *Ranking*. Ranking, the simplest form of job evaluation, involves the ranking of jobs according to their overall value or worth to the institution. Jobs are viewed in their totality rather than by specific job content criteria, hence the name *whole job ranking*. Ranking is the quickest type of job evaluation system to implement, but is useful primarily in institutions with few jobs since it is a one-by-one job ranking process.

2. *Point factor*. Point-factor job evaluation is one of the most widely used evaluation plans in higher education. It is a quantitative method, using weighted numerical points, to assign values to different job dimensions, such as confidentially, or contact with students. The rating is generally done by committee, and the use of many levels allows for fairly fine differentiations among jobs. The committee approach, as well as the multiple factors and levels in this type of plan, are suited to the consensus approach favored in higher education.

3. *Factor comparison*. Factor-comparison job evaluation measures not only examine internal institutional characteristics, but use market rates for the key jobs as a component of the job evaluation process. In effect, it is a double-ranking technique: benchmark jobs being ranked according to content criteria, with continuous iterations for each compensable factor. Next, the market rate is apportioned according to these factors and all evaluations are reranked by the market rate to develop a job comparison scale, which is then used for all nonbenchmark jobs. Factor comparison is one of the most complex techniques and is not commonly used because of the difficulties involved in communication and implementation.

4. *Classification*. The U.S. government uses the classification approach to job evaluation to slot federal jobs. The classification approach is similar to the ranking method in that jobs are considered in their totality in assigning them to predetermined classes. As with ranking, the lack of specificity of criteria in determining differences between jobs presents problems in employee communication and acceptance.

5. *Market guidelines*. Like factor comparison, the guideline method of job evaluation, is a market-pricing approach in that internal evaluations are based directly on current market rates. In the guideline approach, a range of salary rates is determined on the basis of the range of market wages of the jobs that are being evaluated. Jobs that cannot be matched with jobs in the labor market are then placed in ranges based on a slotting technique.

6. *Statistical job evaluation.* Statistical job evaluation is a fairly new technique that utilizes detailed questionnaires concerning job-content dimensions that are filled out by job incumbents. The results of these questionnaires are analyzed statistically to determine numerical scores. Although using this job evaluation technique is quite time consuming and costly, potential bias involved in ranking, rating, and classifying jobs is limited, as the incumbent questionnaire provides more definitive data.

An important issue for any institution is the number of job evaluation programs that should be used. Traditionally, separate job evaluation programs have been designed for groups of employees with different external labor markets: executives and management employees versus administration and production employees. Recently, however, single job evaluation has been espoused as a way to ensure internal equity among all employees through one evaluation instrument that defines criteria applicable to all jobs.

10.6 EXTERNAL JOB RELATIONSHIPS: LABOR MARKET STUDIES

To attract and retain qualified employees, wage structures that are competitive with the external labor market must be established. Organizations, including educational institutions, should establish a compensation and staffing strategy that considers the labor market wage levels with the organization's financial situation. Organizations with a pure internal labor market staffing strategy set competitive compensation rates primarily for entry-level positions. Most higher-level positions are then filled by internal applicants; this practice is quite prevalent in most educational institutions. Organizations that have an external labor market staffing strategy attempt to maintain competitive compensation levels for all positions.

No organization uses a pure internal labor market staffing strategy or a pure external labor market model. Although organizations may promote and fill jobs from within, compensation levels are still market sensitive to ensure the retention and motivation of all employees. The link to the marketplace in either strategy generally consists of identified "benchmark" or key positions that are essential to the staffing requirements of the organization *and* are identifiable in the external labor market. These benchmark jobs are used to monitor the market and are used to determine the compensation posture of the organization. Compensation posture, determined generally by senior administration and the human resources department, considers whether the organization's compensation line leads the market, matches the market, or lags behind the market.

In some organizations, depending on the availability of qualified employees, different compensation postures may be utilized.

10.7 SALARY SURVEYS

Wage and salary surveys are necessary to determine the competitive compensation market for the positioning of an institution's compensation line. There are numerous issues to consider in estimating labor market compensation levels. Compensation surveys should be viewed as planning tools that enable the institution to determine what other organizations pay their employees in general and the level of pay for specific benchmark jobs. Although the pay for an individual job is in many ways an internal matter relating to individual requirements and qualifications, the going or market rate for a job influences to some extent the pay structure of an institution.

Institutions may choose to develop their own salary survey, participate in surveys conducted by others, or purchase salary surveys from consulting, governmental, or industry groups. In all cases there are crucial decision factors to consider in using survey data correctly. Job matching, the matching of the institution's benchmark jobs with jobs in the survey source, is essential to ensure that correct salary levels are obtained. Jobs should never be matched by title, but rather, by functional job duties or responsibilities. Of crucial importance in using survey data are the relevant comparisons, by geographic location, type of institution, and so on. This is particularly crucial in determining the appropriate compensation posture for selected groups of positions. For example, higher education's top administration positions, as well as selected specialty positions, often have national and sometimes international labor markets, while positions in residence life and student service may be regional or local in scope. Such differences may require a different compensation posture for the different positions within the institution.

In reviewing or analyzing survey data, care must also be given to determine that the sample is consistent and representative for the particular institution. The use of multiple survey sources will provide a background to ensure that any individual survey data are reliable and representative. Therefore, attempts should be made to obtain as much survey data on organizational jobs as possible to provide as many data points as possible for development of the institutional salary structure.

10.8 SALARY STRUCTURES

The administration of compensation programs involves the management of salaries for employees within an institution. Accordingly, the compensation program must be designed so that the designated compensation posture and desired internal distributions of salaries are equitable. Salary structures, based on market studies, are control mechanisms that define the parameters of the monetary compensation program in the institution. The techniques used to develop salary structures depend to some extent on the job evaluation technique that is used. With ranking and classification systems, salary structures are normally developed through comparison with the market salary analysis of the benchmark jobs used in the rankings or classifications. Integration of the internal ratings and external market rates, which may be very different from each other, can require some additional fine-tuning. If adjustments are necessary, the internal equity (job evaluation) can be modified in accordance with the external rate, or the external rate may need be ignored. The choice between changing job evaluation results and paying more or less than the market rate to resolve discrepancies is extremely difficult. However, generally, internal equity takes precedence over external equity in the development of salary structures.

Developing a salary structure is not a major consideration if either the factor-comparison or guideline approach is used. In both cases the compensation structure is determined by considering market studies in the job evaluation process itself, and there is less chance of inconsistency between the external market and the internal evaluation. A salary structure can be designed by statistical methods if a point-factor or quantitative job evaluation technique is employed by the use of regression analysis to produce a salary line.

Salary Ranges

In most cases, after completing the job evaluation process, the institution statistically develops a comparison of internal values to external labor market salary levels. A salary structure consists of a logical series of salary ranges, and each salary range usually has the following elements:

- *Minimum.* The minimum of the range represents the lowest salary in the range and may be used as the hiring salary for employees without prior experience.

- *Midpoint.* The midpoint of the range approximates the competitive labor market salaries for jobs included in the salary grade and is an appropriate salary level for fully qualified and experienced employees who have been performing satisfactorily for some time in their position.

- *Maximum.* The maximum of the range represents the highest salary in the range and is usually reserved for those employees who have consistently exceeded their job requirements for a substantial period of time.

Constructing a Salary Structure

There are two basic design issues in constructing a salary structure:

- *Midpoint difference.* How far apart should the midpoint of one grade be to the midpoint of the grade preceding it?

- *Range spreads.* How wide should the range be? (How far apart should the maximum of a salary range be from the minimum?)

The selection of midpoint differences and range spreads can result in a *box structure*, where midpoint differences and range spreads are equal, or a *fan structure*, where midpoint differences and range spreads increase as one moves up through the structure.

10.9 THEORETICAL VERSUS PRACTICAL CONSIDERATIONS

From a theoretical standpoint, jobs at the lower end of the salary structure are more easily mastered than are jobs at the upper end of the structure. Therefore, salary ranges for the lower grades should be narrower to reflect the shorter amount of time required to reach fully satisfactory performance. Salary ranges in the upper grades should be wider to reflect the greater complexity and longer learning periods required in higher-graded jobs.

Similarly, promotional opportunities occur more frequently in lower grades and become scarce in higher grades. Thus, in theory, midpoint differences should be smaller in the lower part of the salary structure and larger in the upper part of the salary structure.

The theoretical arguments above point to a fan structure, with its increasing rate of midpoint difference and increasing range spread. However, fan structures are difficult to administer, maintain, and communicate to managers and employees. In addition, in higher education institutions where promotional opportunities may be limited and longer tenure in one position is the norm, a box structure may be more appropriate.

Where job grades have constant midpoint differences and constant range spreads, as in a box structure, administration, maintenance, and communication are much simpler. Employees can understand that there is a 10 percent salary difference between grades and 50 percent spreads between minimums and maximums. If they get promoted, they know that their future salary opportunity is 10 percent more than it used to be (assuming a one-grade promotion). Compensation analysts maintaining the salary structure can easily update the structure from year to year based on labor market salary movements, economic conditions, and other factors. Salary movement through the range can be managed through simple and direct merit increase grids that relate movement to position in the salary range and performance.

It is important to note that the number of grades in a structure depends on the midpoint difference. A lower midpoint difference (e.g., 8 percent) creates more grades and is usually associated with a narrower range spread (e.g., 40 percent). A higher midpoint difference (e.g., 15 percent) creates fewer grades and is usually associated with wider range spreads (e.g., 60 percent).

Pros and Cons

The primary arguments for a greater number of salary grades (and narrower ranges) are as follows:

- More salary grades create more opportunities to assign any one job into a salary grade containing a group of jobs with similar duties and responsibilities, skill and knowledge requirements, and market rates of pay.

- More grades create more opportunities for employees to be promoted; these opportunities enhance employee motivation and morale. With a shortage of entry-level workers, promotions help attract and retain employees.

Arguments for fewer (and wider) salary grades include the following:

- Greater difference between salary ranges make it easier for employees to perceive differences in job worth (and consequently, there are apt to be fewer requests for reevaluation of jobs).

- Fewer salary grades emphasize pay increases within the salary range based on performance (horizontal salary movement rather than vertical salary movement achieved through promotions). With a large number of employees competing for fewer promotional opportunities, wider salary ranges can continue to reward and motivate plateaued employees.

- Fewer salary grades are easier to maintain, administer, and communicate.

A salary structure with fewer grades and wider range spreads can accommodate increased experience levels among employees through the development of "bands" within each grade that will equate to seniority, experience, and so on. For example, an applications programmer job family can all be included in one salary grade and positioned in an entry, intermediate, and senior band based on experience and qualifications. This approach is especially relevant for positions such as accountants, research support specialists, and so on, where the job function is similar but the topics are progressively more specialized or complicated.

Salary Structure Design

As is the case with job evaluation programs, decisions must also be made about the number of different salary structures used by the institution. Regardless of the number of salary structures, the absolute number of different grades or job classes, with corresponding midpoint or control points for each range of jobs, as well as minimum and maximum levels of pay, must be determined. Traditionally, salary structures have contained many grades or job classes, reflecting the traditional hierarchical structure. The new initiatives in job structuring, including team contributions and skill-based competencies, as well as the flattening of the organizational structure, have created more flexible salary structures. Banding, combining traditional pay grades with skill/job ladders, offers a more flexible alternative to traditional salary structures. Banding is designed to simplify pay administration and to offer realistic opportunities for career and compensation growth.

A banding structure contains several wide bands based on competencies allowing employees to progress to higher levels within each band when they demonstrate certain skills or contribute to institutional goals or strategies. The wider banding structure is very appropriate for higher education, where promotional opportunities are limited, job tenure is generally longer, and incumbents often progress laterally within different divisions or units. Banding can also be an attractive option for educational institutions that wish to decentralize and delegate pay administration to organizational units. Banding versus traditional salary structures can provide significant advantages; however, they must be accompanied by employee training and development initiatives as well as defined performance management programs.

Whatever design is selected, it should be tested against the current employee salary database to determine how the proposed salary structure will affect employees and how much it will cost the institution to implement the structure (such as adjusting salaries for employees who fall below the new range minimums). If the effect is too detrimental to employee motivation and morale and/or too expensive, a different approach should be considered.

10.10   INTERNAL AND INDIVIDUAL PAY EQUITY

Although institutions use different salary structures to provide equity with the external market, no salary structure will ensure internal equity without monitoring and control. Salary distributions or differences within the institution are as important to employees as external equity. These equity differences involve internal equity, equitable wage differences between jobs at different levels in the institution, and individual equity (i.e., equitable difference in wages between employees performing the same job). Wage distributions greatly influence employees' concept of fairness and equity. To deal with equity, institutions administer pay levels between jobs through the job evaluation process, the relationship of pay levels in the salary structure, and performance appraisal. If pay distinctions between jobs are perceived as fair and equitable by employees, internal equity will be achieved.

The compensation function needs to use planning in developing salary programs, determining merit increases, and reviewing the competitiveness of compensation in the external market. However, most of this activity tends to be short term and in reaction to immediate problems or requests from new areas. Compensation planning must consider new forms of pay structures, such as "broadbanding," and new delivery methods, such as incentive compensation and true merit programs. Similar to government organizations, colleges and universities have long provided general across-the-board increases. New initiatives in job structuring, such as the establishment of work teams and skills training for several jobs, require more flexible structures, such as wide compensation bands. This is also an attractive option for institutions that wish to decentralize and delegate compensation decisions to organizational units within the institution.

10.11   PERFORMANCE APPRAISALS AND MERIT PAY

Planning for jobs and the structure of jobs must include evaluations of employee performance. Performance appraisals are conducted for developmental as well as audit and control reasons. Promotion or job change decisions are made on current performance appraisals and assumptions about future performance. More important, at least to employees, performance appraisals provide the basis for compensation decisions. Performance evaluation programs that are consistent, stringent, and relate to job functions and standards are more difficult to implement in collegial environments such as higher education. In addition, limited budgets in higher education have hampered the development of a motivating merit system. The distribution of salaries within jobs must also be monitored

■   223   ■

and controlled through performance appraisal, which provides increases consistent with performance, qualifications, and experience. Individual equity is dependent on relevant performance appraisal systems and trust between supervisors and employees that appraisals are performed objectively and honestly.

Performance management allows institutions to formalize individual competencies and make them part of the institutional reward structure. However, when compensation increases are based on performance, standards of performance must be developed and specific levels of performance must be tied to specific reward levels. Although most higher education institutions provide some form of merit increase, limited budgets have, to a certain extent, hampered the development of a motivating merit system. In addition, "tough" decisions on performance, with limited financial resources, are more difficult within the egalitarian culture of higher education.

All human resource programs must be embedded in the culture of the institution and reflect the reciprocal relationship between the institution and the employees. Buy-in, commitment, and communication are essential or even the best designed programs will fail. This is true not only of employee-sensitive programs such as compensation, employee relations, and diversity, but also of benefits, retirement programs, and health care programs.

Health care cost increases have caused many employers to reduce and/or cap benefits. Although there has been significant debate about universal health care, the benefits and final programs will not become available in the near future. Accordingly, higher education institutions must cope with increased costs for health care, including postretirement medical benefits. Cost sharing with employees for health care costs is an inevitable alternative, even in higher education.

10.12 TAX-SHELTERED ANNUITIES: INTERNAL REVENUE CODE SECTION 403(b)

A tax-sheltered annuity (TSA) is a form of retirement program available to employees of tax-exempt charitable, educational, or religious organizations and to employees of public schools or state or local educational institutions. TSAs include annuity contracts, custodial accounts, or retirement income contracts. Prior to the Tax Reform Act of 1986, employees of tax-exempt entities, including colleges and universities, could elect to defer 25 percent of their compensation, up to a maximum of $30,000. In addition, the employer could contribute to employees' TSA accounts on a selective basis. Since 1986, however, the maximum elective deferral amount has been limited to $9500, and various nondiscrimination rules apply which preclude selective employer contributions. The result of these changes is that the value of a TSA program to most executives has been greatly diminished.

10.13   SECTION 457: ELIGIBLE 457 PLANS

Internal Revenue Code (IRC) Section 457 ("Deferred Compensation Plans of State and Local Governments and Tax-Exempt Organizations") deals with the issue of the timing of payment of taxable income. It addresses the question of when deferred compensation is to be included in the employee's income. The question seems simple enough, but the answer—as is often the case in tax law—is, "it depends." Specifically, it depends on whether the compensation was deferred under an eligible or an ineligible deferred compensation plan.

An eligible 457 plan is an unfunded, nonqualified deferred compensation plan for employees of a state or political subdivision, and independent agency of a state or political subdivision, or any other organization, including a college or university, exempt from tax under Code Section 501. An eligible 457 plan offers employees the opportunity for pretax deferral of compensation up to a maximum of $7500. The sponsoring institution can make matching contribution on an optional and selective basis. Distributions from the plan may not be made to participants or beneficiaries earlier the time of separation from service or when the employee reaches age $70\frac{1}{2}$, with a limited exception for hardship withdrawals.

Compensation deferred under an eligible plan is included in taxable income when paid or made available to the employee. In this regard, the taxation of compensation deferred under an eligible 457 plan is similar to that of a deferred compensation plan of a for-profit company.

The problem with an eligible 457 plan is the limitation on the amount of deferral. First, the $7500 annual maximum is probably less than the amount that most executives would like to save. Second, amounts deferred under a tax-sheltered annuity (which generally has a limit of $9500) offset the $7500 maximum under the eligible 457 plan. Thus an eligible 457 plan is generally of value only for employees who do not participate in a TSA. If both a TSA and an eligible 457 plan are available, most employees would choose to participate in the TSA because the TSA has a higher deferral limit ($9500 for the TSA versus $7500 for the eligible 457 plan) and because the TSA offers more benefit security. The TSA is a qualified plan and is funded with assets in a trust controlled by an independent trustee. The eligible 457 plan is a nonqualified plan and may or may not be funded. If unfunded, the participant's benefits are supported only by the employer's unsecured promise to pay. If the employer has segregated assets to fund the plan, those assets are subject to the claims of creditors in the event of bankruptcy.

10.14   SECTION 457: INELIGIBLE 457 PLANS

An ineligible 457 plan is any deferred compensation plan that does not qualify as an eligible 457 plan. An ineligible 457 plan can be designed to offer benefits similar to those offered by the nonqualified, deferred compensation plans sponsored by many for-profit entities, and under such plans, executives can defer as much compensation as they choose.

To avoid current taxation to the participant, deferrals under an ineligible 457 plan must be subject to a *risk of forfeiture*. This means that an employee's rights to the deferred compensation are contingent upon meeting a predetermined condition in the future, such as the continuation of employment until retirement or for a specified term of years. If, for example, an employee defers $10,000 for a term of five years but terminates employment prior to the end of that five-year period, the deferral will be forfeited. Thus, while an ineligible 457 plan conceptually offers the opportunity for pretax deferral, few are interested in subjecting deferred compensation they have already earned to a risk of forfeiture.

In summary, neither an eligible or ineligible Section 457 plan offers higher education executives a practical or effective savings vehicle.

10.15   EQUITY AND EMPLOYMENT

As human resource managers cope with limited promotional opportunities and the need for multiskilled employees, they must also monitor information on jobs that are becoming of increasing or decreasing importance in the institution because of changes in higher education. New configurations of jobs and functions also require considerations of diversity, training, and management development.

Federal, state, and local regulations enforce equity and nondiscriminatory practices in all human resource programs. Employees are considerably more proactive today, and federal antidiscrimination requirements require more than consent. Active recruiting of minorities and women and comprehensive affirmative action programs will provide opportunities for employees and enhance the delivery of services to an increasingly diversified population.

In addition, statutory regulations require that institutions refrain from any employment practice that adversely affects any member of a protected group unless the employer can show evidence that the practice is necessary to business operations. The protected classes include race, religion, gender, age, and national origin.

In addition to avoiding discriminatory practices, institutions are required to take positive steps to find and hire qualified employees from protected groups and to establish training programs to qualified members of these groups for further promotional opportunities within the organization. Higher education has been very proactive in promoting pay equity and monitoring and analyzing their pay structures to ensure that all employees are treated fairly, especially members of protected classes.

10.16   CONCLUSIONS

Diverse and complicated issues are involved in structuring a strategic human resource program. Human resource management in all organizations, but especially in higher education, is not a simple recordkeeping task anymore. The human investment is often the largest single expenditure as well as the most important asset for any college or university. Strategic planning processes must be established and implemented to ensure the continued success of the institution.

CHAPTER ELEVEN

Facilities Management: Preserving the Past, Building the Future

HARVEY H. KAISER

Syracuse University

11.1 **Introduction**

11.2 **Historical Context**

The Role of Facilities

Legacy of the Past

11.3 **Current Situation**

Critical Issues

Preserving Campus Facilities of the Past

Renewing Facilities for Present and Future Generations of Students

Improving the Productivity of Capital Assets

Building New Facilities for the Future

11.4 **Prospectus of Future Facilities Projects**

Programmatic Improvements

Capital Asset Management

11.5 **Managing for the Future**

11.1 INTRODUCTION

Reinventing the university implies changes in the traditional mission of higher education: teaching, research, and public service. Societal needs, public interest influenced by government intervention, fiscal constraints, demographics, and technology are already changing how institutions provide services and fulfill their missions. The changing environment for higher education will affect campus facilities dramatically.

Higher education's facilities—buildings, fixed equipment, and infrastructure serving over 14 million students—will undergo a continuum of change in teaching methods, transmission of information, and the ways in which students matriculate. Preserving facilities of the past and building for the future are major components of reinventing the university.

Many trends in some stage of introduction or implementation that are currently affecting facilities include:

- Deferral or cancellation of new construction

- Repairs and renovations stepped up to improve facility productivity and the appearance of an institution's capital assets

- Distance learning that reduces campus residential requirements and creates vacant space

Beyond the predictable changes in higher education that affect facilities are more speculative changes. Signals of change now in the air provide hints about the future of higher education facilities, when the shape of the campus as we now know it will be substantially altered.

Discussed elsewhere in this book are the current and evolving trends now under way, altering in predictable ways the core purposes of the creation and dissemination of knowledge. In this chapter we discuss the evolutionary changes in higher education and the possibly revolutionary changes from a facilities perspective. The discussion is introduced by setting a historical context for facilities. Then a discussion of the current situation of higher education facilities is presented. Following is a prospectus of facilities projects based on predictable changes resulting from current observable trends. The chapter concludes with suggestions about managing facilities in the future and contending with the unknown.

11.2 HISTORICAL CONTEXT

American higher education enters the twenty-first century with an admirable accomplishment: contributing to a vast change in the American society. The availability of a college education following World War II was a special hallmark of our nation. The growth of higher education occurred throughout a spectrum of institutions. In the past four decades, construction of new and expansion of existing campuses created academic communities in farmlands and urban centers. The underlying vision was access to an education that would provide credentials for entering the job market, contributing to society, and enhancing personal self-growth.

The Role of Facilities

During American higher education's first three centuries, the role played by facilities in supporting core missions saw relatively little change. The single building founded historically for educating future ministers and housing the entire institution slowly grew into a cluster of buildings differentiated by function. Rural settings inspired horizontal expansion as roles changed from the religious to the secular in the nineteenth century. The oldest campuses in such areas as Cambridge, New Haven, Princeton, and Mr. Jefferson's "Academic Village" were slowly joined by others; by the mid-nineteenth century, there were institutions across the country.

The newer institutions aspired to emulate campuses founded in the seventeenth and eighteenth centuries with clusters of facilities and open space. Buildings for specialized purposes emerged to fulfill the evolving missions of teaching, research, and public service. The heritage of the past began to evolve in the form of stately, solidly constructed buildings.

Two great waves of expansion—the first in the last third of the nineteenth century, and the second after World War II—strongly influenced the current context of higher education. The first began with the passage of the Morrill Act in 1862. This act fostered the concept of campuses of vast acreage to support educational facilities for the agricultural and mechanical arts. This was followed by an era that combined civic pride (many cities and towns wanted a local college or university) and enlightened benevolence (wealthy persons gave generously to found institutions), resulting in the creation of many colleges and universities which today forms the core of America's unparalleled system of higher education. First formed were university-size complexes to support research, the housing of students, and support facilities deemed necessary for the conduct of activities. Added later were facilities for the recreation and entertainment of the student body and alumni in stadiums, fieldhouses, and arenas.

Legacy of the Past

Today's buildings, grounds, infrastructure, and equipment—amassed to house and support academic programs—are the legacy of the dramatic growth of new and existing campuses. More than half of the current campus physical plant was developed after World War II. Enrollment grew 400 percent, from 2.7 million in the 1950s to over 14 million by the mid-1990s. During the same period, the total number of institutions grew from 1800 to 3600. New institutions, primarily publicly supported two-year colleges, opened at a rate of one every two weeks from 1955 to 1974.

The growth in facilities was dramatic. Of the current estimated total of over 3 billion gross square feet of space, 2.5 million was built between 1950 and 1990. Buildings were opened annually, sometimes several in the same year, and construction cranes on the skyline and mud-covered walkways were common campus experiences. Driven by financing demands for capital construction and tight delivery schedules, many of the new facilities were not built with durability and adaptability in mind.

The major share of construction was for new facilities, with little reinvestment allocated for existing facilities. The glamor of planning new facilities and the excitement of ribbon cuttings overshadowed the obsolescence and decay of earlier campus buildings. Old Main was slowly fraying at the edges, while newer facilities began their own cycle of deterioration. Today, many institutions are not only facing the challenge of an increasing debt burden due to an aging physical plant but are also planning to replace or renew their facilities using debt.

11.3 CURRENT SITUATION

Critical Issues

Acknowledgment that higher education is in the midst of what may be its most dramatic period of change is a recurring theme—some call it a crisis. The confluence of fiscal, social, demographic, and technological factors is forcing a fundamental reexamination of higher education's role, mission, and management practices. Effects of enrollment increases or shortfalls, and reduction of government support and research funding, complicate the selection of appropriate solutions. The examination by society of the role, efficiency, and effectiveness of the more than 3000 higher education campuses in America is affecting the future of many institutions. As higher education is changing, so too must its physical plant.

One of the key issues faced by colleges and universities is ongoing budgetary pressures. Escalating operating costs, dwindling revenues, and increased institutional expenditures for financial aid are leading to ever-tighter budgets and reduced operations and maintenance funding. Questioning the price value of a higher education degree has become a strong influence on internal and external reviews of the quality of undergraduate teaching and the research enterprise. Strategic planning is refocusing college and university missions. At risk are the buildings of the past and plans for future facilities.

Higher education must simultaneously face limiting new construction while funding reinvestment in aging facilities. The role of facilities management is to participate in developing and implementing strategic plans preserving existing plant, where feasible, and to plan for future changes in the fabric of an institution. Higher education's overall challenges set the facilities agenda for the next century: building new facilities for the future, preserving the facilities that add character to the campus and are of historical significance, renewing facilities that need to be upgraded to be useful to the present and future generation of students, and improving the productivity of capital assets.

11.3 CURRENT SITUATION

Critical issues related to higher education facilities are summarized as:

- Adjusting to constraints on new construction required for enrollment growth on some campuses, and replacing obsolete facilities

- Adapting facilities to technological changes

- Renovating facilities for program changes and improved space utilization

- Renewing older facilities and reducing deferred maintenance

- Providing effective and efficient maintenance

- Increasing the productivity of capital assets

- Complying with environmental and regulatory requirements

Preserving Campus Facilities of the Past

The "past" for higher education begins the day a facility is put into service. Assuming that facilities are appropriately designed to meet current functions and are well constructed with durable materials, adequate maintenance programs can extend their life to compensate for wear and tear, weather exposure, and the life cycles of facility systems and components. The underfunding of maintenance, or its improper performance, begins the cycle of deterioration and the deferral of work that converts physical assets into liabilities.

The disappointing performance of post–World War II buildings and infrastructure compared to that of earlier campus facilities affects a substantial amount of the physical plant. Sometimes built hastily and with unproven materials and building systems, a large inventory of facilities requires extensive repairs and renovations. A shorter life expectancy for post-1950s buildings is compounded by the fact that most of the campus utilities network was built in the 1920s and now requires renewal or replacement. The expense of updating older buildings to meet current and future needs and the extensive backlog of deferred maintenance for newer facilities adds to the challenge of funding facilities improvements.

Historic Preservation. A motivating force for many capital projects is preserving the past and eliminating obsolescence and deterioration. Historic preservation is achieving a prominent position in our society, inspiring a renaissance of restoration on college and university campuses. The preservation of older buildings, frequently vital to the historic continuity of an institution, is producing notable results in adaption while preserving original character. These structures are often pointed to with greater pride than any of the post–World War II buildings. Their irreplaceable features create emotional ties to a campus. As a result, historical buildings can stimulate appeals for preservation assistance. Many are worthy of National Register of Historic Places status and occasionally receive that distinction.

Despite a revered place on a campus, some historic facilities face a difficult future because of the extraordinary costs for restoring them or converting them to other uses. Restoration and/or replacement of antiquated—and sometimes unsafe—mechanical and electrical systems, decorative exterior trim, and elaborate interior finishes are expensive, labor-intensive projects. The allocation of resources for this type of work requires careful deliberation about the importance of a building to the campus community, especially in an era of restructuring.

A building may have historic significance, or its location may place it in a prominent position in the campus fabric, serving as a campus land-mark and part of its image. However, age should not be the only consid-eration for renewing, replacing, or removing older facilities. A building that obstructs a comprehensive facilities plan for campus development has few redeeming esthetic features or has little functional use is a candi-date for relocation or removal. Investing in restoration should provide a usable facility, with operating and maintenance costs comparable to those of other campus facilities.

Among many noteworthy and successful examples of historic pres-ervation are recent restorations of the Barnard Observatory at the Univer-sity of Mississippi to serve as the Center for Southern Culture, and the Nott Memorial Church at Union College. Another creative example is Syracuse University's relocation of its National Register Holden Observa-tory to provide a building site for expansion of the Maxwell School of Citizenship and Public Affairs.

Deciding to Renew, Replace, or Demolish.   There are some valuable rules of thumb guiding the decision for renewal, replacement, or demolition. Typically, the condition of building components can be evaluated for the extent of renewal necessary to restore a facility to its current or proposed use. A building's foundations, structure, and exterior walls are approx-imately one-third of its value and with reasonable maintenance have a life of 75 to 100 years. The remainder of the building's value requires renova-tion, renewal, or replacement over its life, either because of use changes or because these elements have deteriorated or must be renewed. Two complete renewals of a building are usually required over a 100-year period.

The cost of all the renewal work to bring a building back to its original condition, with all exterior and interior finishes as well as upgrades to meet new technologies, will often exceed the cost of replacing the building. It is at this point that the institution must decide if demolition of the building will be disruptive to the campus fabric. Several strategies are necessary for deciding whether to renew, replace, or demolish facilities. Singly, or in combination, the following strategies will enable colleges and universities to preserve the past and provide facilities that support the academic enterprise.

1. *Assessing renewal, replacement, or demolition as a component of capital planning and budgeting.* A building in the "right" place and with important ties to the historic traditions of the campus should be considered for restoration. In this context, the guidelines of the Secretary of the Interior's Standards for the Treatment of Historic Properties should be kept in mind: "Restoration is defined as the act or process of accurately depicting the form, features, and character of a particular period of time by means of the removal of features from other periods in its history and reconstruction of missing features from the restoration period." Adaption is the reconfiguration of an older building for new purposes.

2. *Reducing the capital burden of deferred maintenance to manageable levels with one-time supplements to the operating budget from reserves or other funding sources.* Repairs and renovations funding in the operating budget should also be increased to prevent future accumulations of unmanageable deferred maintenance. Facility renewal requires an annual reinvestment in building and infrastructure systems and components. A rule of thumb for the annual reinvestment rate is 1.5 to 3 percent of current replacement value. This figure is separate from funding necessary for elimination of deferred maintenance. In other words, a facility's renewal plan must include funding for both one-time deferred maintenance backlog reduction as well as for ongoing adequate funding from the operating budget for repairs and renovations. This concept, often overlooked or misunderstood, is essential to facilities renewal planning.

3. *Assuring that a facilities management program is in place that prevents restored facilities from once again shifting from assets to liabilities.* The program should be based on a strategic facilities management plan, consistent with the overall institutional strategic plan. Adequate organizational structure and resources should be in place; staff should be accountable for doing technically sound and timely work, effectively and efficiently, on all campus facilities. The stewardship role of the governing board and senior administrators requires continuous monitoring of expenditures and of the effectiveness of maintenance management. A maintenance management audit, either self-performed or performed by external reviewers, in five-year cycles is a useful tool.

Renewing Facilities for Present and Future Generations of Students

Renewing facilities is a never-ending task, beginning with routine maintenance and eventually replacing worn-out building elements. Buildings don't disintegrate all at once, unlike the one-hoss shay "that was built in such a logical way it ran a hundred years to a day." They fail by individual components and systems. Failing to provide adequate routine maintenance and repairs as well as renovations to components and systems leads to a backlog of deferred maintenance. As the extent and cost of correcting the deferral of maintenance increase, so do the financial burdens of remedial actions. This has soared into tens and even hundreds of millions of dollars at some institutions.

Deferred Maintenance.   Higher education associations first drew attention to the problem of deferred maintenance in the late 1970s. Physical plants had become a liability in many cases, sometimes consciously as institutions concentrated financial resources on faculty and staff salaries rather than physical plant or were oblivious to the encroaching problems. Maintaining the campus—fixing the leaking roofs and broken pipes—was given a lower priority in the overall institutional strategy.

In 1973, a comprehensive survey of higher education was published by the National Center for Educational Statistics. It came as a shocking revelation that campuses ignoring facility renewal could expect approximately 20 percent of their physical plant replacement value to be in unsatisfactory condition. Sadly, many institutions continue to ignore the realities of stewardship, conducting business affairs as though facilities are an entitlement and not a financial asset.

The call to action for facility renewal has energized many campuses, and deliberate processes have been introduced to cope with deferred maintenance in a systematic manner. Appeals to some state legislatures have begun a flow of much needed funds for tackling deferred maintenance at public institutions through repairs and renovations programs. Independent institutions have tapped reserves, borrowed through bonds, and reallocated operating budgets to fund reduction of deferred maintenance. However, the problem remains substantial and it affects the ability of institutions to meet their missions.

A systematic approach to the continuous renewing of facilities includes the following:

1. *Recognizing that adequately funded and maintained facilities require an integrated program of capital improvements, repairs and renovations, and reduction of deferred maintenance to manageable levels.* The program is a key part of a strategic facilities management plan.

2. *Analyzing the rates of deterioration of building and infrastructure systems and components to determine appropriate annual operating budget requirements for repairs and renovations.* The life cycle of each component (foundations, exterior walls, roofs, interior finishes, etc.) or major building system (mechanical, electrical, plumbing, etc.) is determined and the projected cost of replacement at the time required is calculated. The total of each year's component and system replacement costs results in an annual allowance. Institutional studies indicate that between 1.5 and 3 percent of total current plant replacement value for annual repairs and renovations is necessary to prevent accumulating deferred maintenance.

3. *Conducting regular facilities audits to assess conditions, identify deficiencies, and estimate the costs of remedial work.* An audit is a key element in an inventory of facilities. The inventory also should include drawings, maintenance records, and past repairs and renovation work.

4. *Selecting priorities that assess risks against need, and give life safety and regulatory requirements the highest priority.* A second level of priorities incorporates work that if not corrected immediately will lead to further damage and make a facility unfit for its intended use. Finally, a careful balance is necessary in selecting projects that meet institutional mission requirements, are cost effective, or improve the campus environment.

5. *Developing a funding strategy for short- and long-term needs and identifying funding sources.* Auxiliary enterprises with reserves or opportunities to adjust user costs can be considered as potentially funded. The rest of the work will be for education and general (e & g) facilities. A resource allocation model for e & g facilities is necessary with two alternative scenarios: (a) a target year for eliminating deferred maintenance by an average annual rate of expenditures, and (b) a projected average annual rate of expenditures to eliminate deferred maintenance eventually.

Many campuses and systems of higher education are faced with renewing their facilities with limited resources. Difficult choices must be made. At the same time that restructuring to balance budgets is pervasive throughout the academic enterprise, substantial investments are necessary to compensate for past oversights of deferring maintenance. Buildings constructed before the halcyon days of growth have deteriorated to a sad state and are becoming candidates for replacement. Some are considered central to the image of a campus, part of its history, and complete rebuilding is the only option. Thus, while attempting to reinvent the university and implement visions of the future, higher education also must communicate the need for renewing its existing physical plant.

A useful tool for communicating the facilities renewal program is educating campus constituencies about the relationship between the cost of correcting facilities deficiencies and the current plant replacement value. The facility condition index (FCI), a method of comparing facilities conditions, is based on a ratio of facilities deficiencies to current replacement value (CRV).

$$\text{facility condition index} = \frac{\text{deficiencies}}{\text{current replacement value}}$$

The FCI uses empirical data to measure conditions:

$$\text{FCI} < 5\% \ (0.05) = \text{good condition}$$

$$\text{FCI } 5\text{--}10\% \ (0.05\text{--}0.10) = \text{fair condition}$$

$$\text{FCI} > 10\% \ (0.10) = \text{poor condition}$$

The lower the FCI value, the better the facilities conditions. For example, an institution with $25 million in deficiencies and a current replacement value of $350 million has an FCI value of 0.071, a rating suggesting relatively "good" conditions. The FCI is useful for comparing facilities within institutions or benchmarking conditions with other institutions. Determining costs for correcting deficiencies by conducting a facilities audit and prioritizing projects allows modeling of the variables for annual and total funding needs and the rate of backlog reduction. Calculated annually, the FCI also measures progress toward established goals for a building or an entire campus.

Improving the Productivity of Capital Assets

The capital assets of an institution consist of its buildings, land, infrastructure, and fixed equipment. With an estimated replacement value of well over $300 billion, higher education's plant investment is the single largest asset on its balance sheet. The value of a campus's assets is impaired by deteriorated conditions or low utilization, which changes facilities assets into liabilities. Funding depreciation is one way to increase funds available to finance the restoration or replacement of existing facilities.

Underutilizing capital assets represents one kind of plant liability, because operating budgets are still required for maintenance, energy, security, and other services. Nonessential assets retained in the facilities inventory represent another kind of liability. Improving the productivity of facility assets requires the same astuteness that is applied to the management of an institution's financial assets.

Governing board members, discontent with unstable fiscal conditions, and perennial requests for new construction are challenging administrators with questions based on utilization: Are all facilities at full utilization? What is being done to improve utilization? Can we convert any facilities to other uses for improved utilization? Another set of questions is raised about the retention of capital assets: Does the asset continue to meet its original purpose? Can an alternative assignment of a function to other facilities meet the same purpose? Can we cut operating budget costs by disposing of an asset? Is there a market for the asset that can provide income for other campus purposes? Answers to these questions—disposing of certain plant assets, converting some to other uses, and improving the utilization of others—are integral to the strategic management of facilities.

Disposal. Those assets that no longer serve a useful purpose, or do not have a conceivable future use, should be evaluated for disposal, including demolition. In the interim, facilities deemed nonessential should be allocated minimal resources. Selective allocation of plant resources is based on whether a facility is essential to the mission of the institution or is expendable.

Demolition is a cost-avoidance measure; the space that needs to be heated, cooled, staffed, or maintained is eliminated. A building may be on a site better suited for other uses, or the building may be obsolete and expensive to renovate. When considering demolition, however, costs for complying with regulatory requirements, including removal of asbestos, lead-based paints, toxic substances, or underground tanks, should be part of the analysis. In addition, site preparation for other uses should be added to demolition costs if they are not part of a new project's development budget.

Conversion of a plant liability to a productive asset can be achieved by sale, sale–leaseback, sale–ground lease, or long-term lease. Guiding these decisions are the location of the facility and its relationship to the central activities of the institution. Properties remote from a campus or on the periphery are prime candidates for sale or lease. Leasing offers the potential for eventually recovering land and possibly improving it through a well-structured agreement with the lessee.

Conversion. Another alternative for improving the productivity of capital assets is conversion to other uses. Conversion can require capital expenditures. However, a need can often be met at a lower cost than new construction by creatively using an older facility, leading to opportunities for reducing operating costs and lowering energy cost. The test of converting a facility to a new use is the cost-effectiveness of the project.

Care should be taken in considering conversions with the concept of "what a building wants to be." The rule of thumb is not to renovate a building to a higher level of technical sophistication than the original. A "dry" building should not be converted to a "wet" one, for example.

Another example is modifying an old science building for new laboratory space. This kind of upgrade requires newer mechanical, electrical, plumbing, and safety systems. The original energy and safety requirements for the facility were much less stringent.

Consolidating programs currently held at several buildings into one underutilized building creates the opportunity to terminate some structures. When downsizing occurs, the total amount of campus space can be reduced. Remaining programs consolidated into vacated space can release space for other uses or can be declared as surplus space.

Another possibility for consolidation is terminating the use of "temporary" facilities. Many institutions acquired adjacent property, including wood-frame residential structures during periods of expansion. These buildings provided readily available and, apparently, inexpensive space for small academic units, research programs, and support services. Individuals' preference for a noninstitutional environment and independence from the scrutiny of central administration make the termination of these buildings a difficult task. However, hidden major maintenance and operating costs mask their expensive nature. Consolidating activities performed at temporary facilities into other campus space improves utilization and can free "temporary" space for sale, or demolition if the land is to be retained.

Improved Utilization. Space utilization is the frequency with which a space is occupied and the percentage of capacity in use. The utilization of all campus space is often overlooked because of traditional higher education scheduling practices. Typically, only a small portion of campus space—classrooms, class laboratories, and lecture spaces—is centrally scheduled. Specialized space, including research areas, offices, and departmentally controlled space, is "turf" outside central scheduling.

Opportunities for improving space productivity can be created by reexamining scheduling practices and controlling space assignments. A reasonable request by governing board members and legislators, and one more frequently heard by colleges and universities, is proof that capital requests are not duplicating existing space. Analyses of current utilization levels are demanded as evidence that new facilities are absolutely necessary. The traditional scheduling of blocks of time during certain parts of the day and days of the week at the preference of faculty is a sore spot, especially when governing board members hear complaints of lack of space and they can observe "empty classrooms and laboratories all over the place."

Creating a database on space and its utilization enables analyses of utilization and makes improvements in space productivity possible. Included in such a database should be a complete and comprehensive inventory of existing space as well as evaluations of the functional appropriateness of space for a designated activity. Criteria for space planning and management are also necessary. For example, current planning criteria for the design and utilization of facilities may be outdated because they are based on outmoded space requirements that do not apply to new activities and equipment. A pressing need throughout higher education is for contemporary space standards for planning future facilities requirements, measuring utilization, and planning practices for improved space productivity.

Building New Facilities for the Future

In an era when higher education is considered in a crisis, how can building new facilities be discussed seriously? Answers are evident in the very nature of colleges and universities. The increase in enrollment at certain institutions means that new facilities are needed to accommodate the growth. However, enrollment varies widely across the country, with some institutions experiencing declines and others continuing to add new students. Other justifications for new construction are illustrated by the following examples.

Replacements. Replacement of obsolete facilities, consolidation of programs, or deterioration beyond reclamation can demand new space. There is a legitimate need to build facilities for programs that are ill-housed or remotely located from a campus. As many campuses evolved, programs and support activities were located in temporary facilities or in facilities readily available by acquisition and conversion to interim uses, or else space was leased at a distance from a main campus. Not well suited to their purpose and considered only short term, facilities kept in use only because replacement funds are unavailable should be placed on priority lists for replacement.

The divergence between space standards used for planning growth in the 1950s and current perceived space needs present a concern for campus administrators. Many activities are now considered inadequately housed based on older space planning standards. Improved space utilization is hampered by a lack of contemporary standards for space planning and management. For example, classrooms designed traditionally for an instructor using a blackboard and visual aids and students taking lecture notes are not well suited for today's students who use computer notebooks and require network connections. Similarly, offices at a standard 120 square feet cannot accommodate personal computers and printers. The "information revolution" is causing a drastic review of all campus space standards and planning practices.

New Programs and Technologies. The dynamic nature of the academic enterprise is a unique characteristic of American higher education. The quest for knowledge and service to society, underlying recurrent themes of the academy, is continually leading to innovative areas of research. Eventually, these evolve into new fields of study and disciplines, and space requirements emerge that may not be suited to existing quarters. For example, the concept of "incubator" space to facilitate the transfer of technology from the laboratory to commercial applications did not exist 20 years ago, nor did the new emphasis in nursing on lifelong wellness. Each has created needs for different types of space and accessibility for external campus populations.

Until very recently, methods of teaching and research saw few changes. The widespread use of personal computers and electronic information networks changes higher education significantly. Learning in locations remote from the traditional campus is rapidly expanding. The effect of this innovation can drastically alter the campus and modify space requirements beyond current understandings.

Student Recruitment. A new face is being put on campuses through new facilities and major renovations, creating a more "customer-friendly" environment. The importance of the attractiveness of the campus for student recruitment has placed the admissions officer, frequently now titled the chief officer for enrollment management, in an influential role to spur physical plant improvements. Motivations to increase student retention and improve the academic environment have also induced new construction and renovation projects.

Many existing student life facilities, including housing, dining, student centers, recreation, and assembly spaces, are in need of updating. Changes in these facilities are becoming requisites to attract today's students. Residence halls planned on the model of two students per room, grouped toilets, and modest spaces for lounges and recreation are unappealing to today's students. Creating a more personalized living model is resulting in major renovations to residence halls often designed in the 1950s. Densities are being reduced, spaces converted to smaller group arrangements, and amenities added. Renovating dining centers to replace a cafeteria with eating areas resembling shopping mall food courts is an emerging trend to create more appeal and prevent loss of student meal plan revenues.

11.4 PROSPECTUS OF FUTURE FACILITIES PROJECTS

A prospectus for future college and university facilities projects centers on programmatic improvements and the management of capital assets.

11.4 PROSPECTUS OF FUTURE FACILITIES PROJECTS

Programmatic Improvements

Program Innovations and Enhancements. The dynamic nature of higher education is continually producing new methods of teaching, new areas of intellectual inquiry, and new ways to apply knowledge. New activities create the need for new facilities, adaption of older facilities to new uses, and adequate support facilities and infrastructure. For example, the conversion of traditional models for teaching and inquiry to methods involving electronic technologies is dramatically revising space needs. The rapid growth of some academic departments, institutes, and research programs using new technologies but housed in interim locations will require facilities in more permanent, central locations.

The trend toward combining several disciplines to produce new academic and research programs is driven by the nature of academic inquiry and the overlapping of specialties. Traditional academic departments will be replaced with new configurations requiring major renovations to existing departmental space or new facilities. Adding electronic communications and costly research equipment increases the price tag of these changes for institutions, as do dwindling government, corporate, and foundation funding sources.

Quality of Campus Life. Undergraduate and graduate students, faculty, and staff will demand facilities that meet contemporary standards of space, ambience, and comfort. Inviting the external community to the campus to participate in campus programs will also require space, equipment, and other features that might previously have been considered luxuries in higher education. For example, air conditioning, elevators, and "social" spaces have not traditionally been included in higher education buildings. Adding these features will lower ratios of net to gross space, modifying space design standards, and increasing building and operating costs. Although added capital expenses, these amenities are necessary to generate new revenues.

Motives might include improving the attractiveness of buildings and grounds to enhance enrollment management efforts. As tuition and other costs rise, shabby physical plants and inadequate services will become pivotal issues in student recruitment and faculty and staff morale. Creating a more diverse student body will demand new services along with specialized spaces for learning, housing, and recreation, requiring modifications to existing or new facilities.

Projects that provide a balance between attractive and adequate space for teaching, study, and student life include:

- Modernizing residence halls to lower density, providing more private accommodations, air conditioning, and increased social space

- Building recreation facilities to meet society's emphasis on fitness

- Building or renovating student activity centers combining food service, meeting, and recreational space

- Creating day-care centers to meet the changing student body and workforce

Economic and Social Development. An emerging theme is higher education's role in the economic and social development of communities, regions, and the nation. To improve public perception of the value of higher education and its contributions to society (and to possibly create new revenue sources), public and independent institutions are changing the public service component of college and university missions. Other motivating factors are changing public expectations for higher education to be more responsive to economic and social goals.

Government agendas for economic development will include seeking a return on investment in higher education through programs and facilities that assist in creating job opportunities, retraining displaced workers, and improving skills required for global competition. Government efforts to gain access to campus research capabilities to improve technology transfer from campus laboratories to industry are examples of this trend. The proliferation of university-related research parks is also an outgrowth. Joint efforts by government and institutions to attract industry to a region are another example. The cooperation by state government and the University of Alabama at Tuscaloosa to attract a new North American Mercedes-Benz plant to the region illustrates the potential for successful ventures.

As higher education accepts external funds for joint ventures with government, modifications will be required in campus access and building design to satisfy changing patterns of enrollment. Improvements will be necessary to comply with the Americans with Disabilities Act. Providing overnight accommodations that differ from traditional semester-long housing contracts; offering safe, secure, and convenient parking; and operating academic support and auxiliary services at extended hours for administrative, academic, and auxiliary services will also become increasingly important.

Science and Technology. The White House Science Council Panel on the Health of U.S. Colleges and Universities stated: "The strength of the nation, in trade defense, and health has been directly related to past investments in science and technology." A central theme of the panel was increased support for science teaching and research and the critically important relationships among universities, government, and industry.

11.4 PROSPECTUS OF FUTURE FACILITIES PROJECTS

Science and technology teaching and research facilities, tolerated as marginal or obsolete and reaching the end of their useful life, require replacement on many college and university campuses. The National Science Foundation (NSF) has drawn attention to the critical state of teaching and research laboratories and equipment as well as to the long-term deleterious effects on the nation's economy and international position in technological developments. A 1988 NSF survey of scientific and research facilities estimated expenditures for new construction each year from 1986 to 1989: The projected annual amount was $1.6 billion a year. The same survey reported on the amounts of deferred renewal/replacement and planned spending: for every dollar spent, $3.60 was deferred.

Major laboratory upgrades and expansion to meet space and equipment requirements can be expected, in part as a lever for economic development. Technological advances will create new demands for expensive buildings, equipment, and campus infrastructure systems.

Telecommunications. The reorganization of voice communications into a competitive environment has moved campuses into an era of self-owned telecommunications systems. More and more campuses are becoming private telephone companies and are requiring major capital costs for switches and wiring. Simultaneously, the dramatic evolution of computing technology has placed terminals and workstations in administrative offices, classrooms, and student residence halls. As a result, it will be necessary to combine voice and data with integrated switches (computers) for transmission over comprehensive wiring systems for internal and external connections.

Computer Networks and Reconfiguration of Space. The increased power of personal computers and competitive market pricing has fostered campus-wide computing for faculty, students, and staff. Decreased dependency on mainframes and networks connecting workstations, offices, classrooms, and student housing requires "wiring the campus" for network connectivity. Infrastructure not already in place will be necessary for tying together local area networks, computer terminal clusters, and individual workstations.

Faculty and student access to computing requires changes in space standards and reconfiguration of office space and classrooms as well as the creation of public-access clusters in academic buildings and residence halls. Faculty office space standards will have to be increased to provide room for computers and printers. The conversion of classrooms for computing equipment access at each student station requires redesign of existing space; it also requires support personnel for developing teaching materials and monies for equipment maintenance. As a result, increased operating costs can be expected as well as needs to improve building security and employ more technologically sophisticated facilities management staff.

Distance Learning. The transition from traditional semester-long enrollments and campus residency requirements began to change when institutions aggressively pursued new revenue sources. Students who could come to campus for a short period and continue their programs with prepared study materials and through correspondence were an untapped market. "Weekend colleges" became common throughout the country, illustrated by the numbers of Masters of Business Administration programs requiring only four weeks of campus residency during a two-year stint. These minimal residence requirement programs have only marginal effects on facilities.

The more futuristic concept of students taking degree programs through television and by computer connections without ever setting foot on campus has a far greater potential effect on the need for campus facilities. Rapid expansion of the "information highway" is bringing the future closer to the present. For example, at Edison State Teachers College in Trenton, New Jersey, students are completing degree requirements by home computers connected by E-mail and screen-to-screen communication with faculty. A program announced in 1994 will enable students to earn an academic degree entirely via television. The "Ready to Earn" program developed by the Public Broadcasting Service will enable students to earn an associate of arts degree at any of 60 community colleges. The results are likely to be increasing demands for on-campus equipment and support facilities, and decreasing on-campus space requirements for matriculating students.

Capital Asset Management

Facility Renewal. Facility renewal offsets deterioration and extends the life of facilities. Components of facility renewal are routine maintenance; repairs and renovations of building and infrastructure components on a life-cycle basis; replacement of obsolete facilities and systems, including compliance with regulatory requirements; and (if present) deferred maintenance.

The most thorough approach for determining facility renewal requirements is a facilities audit of existing conditions of buildings, grounds, utilities, and equipment. An alternative method is to use life-cycle analysis in lieu of surveys of actual backlogs of deferred maintenance. By factoring the age and replacement costs of building components, a building renewal allowance can be budgeted to offset facility aging each year. As discussed earlier, empirical studies have produced renewal allowance ranges of 1.5 to 3 percent of plant replacement value to supplement the annual operating budget for operations and maintenance.

At an inflation rate of 3 percent, an annual commitment of between $4 and $5 billion is required nationally to eliminate deferred maintenance during the next decade. In addition, a minimum of 1.5 to 3 percent of the total replacement value of buildings and equipment requires almost $3 billion in annual funding for plant renewal. For a campus with a current replacement value for buildings and equipment of $300 million, this translates into a minimum of $4.5 million a year for capital renewal. Omitted are projections for eliminating deferred maintenance and for program improvements.

A one-time elimination of deferred maintenance priorities does not satisfy long-term facility renewal funding requirements. As campus facilities continue to deteriorate and become obsolete, an annual allocation for renewal is necessary to prevent further accumulation of deferred maintenance. Establishing an appropriate annual level of facilities renewal funding in the beginning of a facilities renewal program may have to include catch-up costs.

Regulatory Standards. The broad mandate of federal and state governments for environment and safety requirements will have a significant effect on facilities funding requirements. Environmental health and safety needs include compliance for asbestos removal, underground storage tanks, and elimination of sources of polychlorinated biphenyls (PCBs). Hazardous wastes and toxic materials also impose new standards for storage and removal. Requirements for accessibility for the disabled created by the Americans with Disabilities Act of 1992 will necessitate additional features in older buildings and in new designs. Life safety improvements include adequate fire protection, exits, and the elimination of unsafe conditions to comply with building codes and other regulatory standards.

Sick buildings affect the quality of working environments and require revisions in air-handling systems in buildings with low-volume air changes. As new environmental hazards are discovered and regulations developed, facilities managers will need to understand them so that they can plan and implement corrective programs.

The increase of regulatory standards by the federal and many state governments has added to the capital burdens of higher education. Although recognized as important initiatives, these capital requirements shift resources from reinvestment in existing facilities and affect the availability of funds for facility renewal, replacement of obsolete facilities, and renovations for changing program requirements.

Historic Preservation. Decisions to renew or replace older facilities will be influenced by increasing concern for the historic aspects of some structures and will affect plans for major maintenance and facilities renewal. Campuses that saw dramatic growth in the 1950s and 1960s will face alumni advocates who want to preserve the campus as they knew it. They will resist alterations and additions drastically affecting older facilities. Despite administrative preferences based on cost/benefit analysis, external constituencies can force restoration or adaptive reuse and compromises in campus planning by insisting on the restoration or adaptive reuse of certain structures.

Restructuring. Because of fiscal conditions, many colleges and universities have instituted varying degrees of restructuring, ranging from selective one-time budget cuts and across the board reductions to complete overhauls of administrative, academic, and auxiliary programs and services. Downsizing is a pervasive theme in higher education. Campus employment has been lowered, programs eliminated or consolidated, and services reduced.

The effects of restructuring on facilities include:

- Undertaking new construction at the lowest possible cost or postponing projects indefinitely

- Reducing budgets for routine and preventive maintenance

- Underfunding of repairs and renovations and an increase in deferred maintenance

- Eliminating facilities to reduce operating costs

11.5 MANAGING FOR THE FUTURE

Evolutionary changes in higher education and their effect on facilities for the next 10 to 15 years are somewhat predictable. The complete diffusion of new technologies and innovations in learning and research will take at least that long to be evident throughout most U.S. colleges and universities. Predicting the trends and innovations that will revolutionize obtaining a liberal arts or professional education is inherently speculative. Although the crystal ball is cloudy, it still hints of the future.

A number of factors are already forcing review of how the learning process and research is conducted. For example, traditional classroom and laboratory relationships are changing as teaching and research shifts from classroom and personal interactions to electronic access to information and experimentation. What was done by a teacher using chalk and blackboard, videos, overhead slides, and print material can now be performed at the pace of the individual learner using a computer. Researchers now share a vast array of information databases through electronic networks, replacing repetitive testing of ideas by rapid computer simulation.

If colleges and universities are to prepare themselves for the coming changes, they should begin planning now. The following is a plan of action to address future critical facilities issues:

- Strategic facilities planning

    —Evaluate institutional master plans to address changing enrollments, program changes, and realistic funding capabilities.

    —Integrate strategic financial and human resources planning with facilities planning.

    —Develop a strategic facilities plan with flexibility for future innovations in learning and research processes.

- Future space requirements

    —Determine which facilities are most critical to support institutional mission.

    —Consider reducing project scope or postponing projects.

    —Dispose of nonessential capital assets.

- Capital funding requirements

    —Establish criteria for prioritizing projects.

    —Prioritize all prospective capital projects, including new construction, additions, major renovations, and facility renewal.

    —Determine potential funding sources.

- Facility renewal

    —Create a database of facilities information.

    —Compile a summary of existing conditions through a facilities audit.

    —Determine an annual renewal allowance for major repairs and renovations.

    —Plan a deferred maintenance backlog reduction program.

- Technological changes

    —Determine the necessary requirements for campus infrastructure to support information networks.

    —Set standards for communications connections.

- Regulatory standards

  —Prepare a summary of all applicable federal, state, and local regulatory requirements.

  —Establish priorities.

  —Select the most cost-effective methods to achieve compliance.

  —Determine funding sources.

- Space utilization

  —Develop space standards and guidelines for space allocation.

- Productivity of capital assets

  —Evaluate facilities for their importance to the institutional mission.

Managing and financing facilities in the future will present a challenge for facilities management. Concerned and informed leadership is necessary to meet changing institutional roles and missions in support of the academic enterprise. The uncertainty of the effects of new technologies and the advent of massive changes introduced by distance learning are indicators of the unpredictable nature of the future. A solution for coping with the unpredictable is a strategic planning process designed with flexibility. Strategic planning is the first step in reinventing the university from a facilities perspective.

C H A P T E R   T W E L V E

Organizational and Technological Strategies for Higher Education in the Information Age

DAVID J. ERNST

Coopers & Lybrand L.L.P.

RICHARD N. KATZ

University of California

JOHN R. SACK

Stanford University

12.1 **Introduction**

12.2 **Trends and Their Implications**

Trend 1: Traditional Funding Sources Are Flat or Decreasing

Trend 2: Public Expectations and State Mandates Are Calling for More Reporting Requirements and Accountability

Trend 3: Consumer Expectations Demand More Sophisticated Services Requiring Greater Access to Data

Trend 4: Evolving Organization Structures Will Significantly Change Traditional Hierarchies

Trend 5: Sophisticated Knowledge Workers Require Expanded Technical and Consulting Support

12.3 **Building Tomorrow's Institution**

ORGANIZATIONAL AND TECHNOLOGICAL STRATEGIES

12.1 INTRODUCTION*

Three forces of change—organizational, technological, and economic—are under way and gaining momentum in higher education today. Each is prompting discussion, study, frustration, and, in some cases, fear. Taken together, these change forces will alter the nature of higher education. They have brought us face to face with hard choices about how to harness and direct these alterations without becoming their victims.

A set of *organizational forces* has moved colleges and universities along a path of greater decentralization, enabling departmental and personal empowerment. *Technological forces* have pushed institutions toward distributed, client/server, and cooperative processing environments. *Economic forces* are affecting both organizations and technology and are challenging the very existence of some institutions.

Campus executives—and information technology (IT) professionals especially—are beginning to comprehend the magnitude of institutional and environmental change in the information age. In many higher education publications and gatherings, the operative words are *transformation, restructuring, reengineering, rethinking,* and *innovation*.

We live and work within a context of accelerating change and a season of choices—there are right paths and wrong paths, critical directions need to be chosen, and time is of the essence. The momentum of change is sufficiently great that it is not enough simply to make wise choices; if we do not also make those choices quickly, we risk being overrun by change rather than being its agents, enablers, or facilitators. This brings to mind Lee Iacocca's admonition to "lead, follow, or get out of the way," and is particularly sobering to those acculturated to the dictates, norms, and values of higher education's unique shared governance model, who rightly and necessarily operate in a time-consuming environment of discussion, intellectualization, consultation, and consensus building.

In this chapter we examine five key trends affecting higher education administration. Each trend is introduced with a question or issue that might be facing a campus chief executive, followed by an assessment of organizational and technological implications, with economic implications discussed where appropriate. In particular, we seek to demonstrate that rather than being part of the problem, information technology is part of the solution. New strategies are proposed to deal with change, using information technology tools to meet the challenges of administering higher education in the information age.

---

*This chapter is adapted from a professional paper published by CAUSE, the association for managing and using information resources in higher education.

12.2 TRENDS AND THEIR IMPLICATIONS

Trend 1: Traditional Funding Sources Are Flat or Decreasing

Whether institutions are public or private, large or small, available funding is falling far behind the requirements. Some institutions are responding by focusing more on information technology (IT) while others are questioning its effectiveness. Can information technology help with this challenge?

Organizational Implications. We live and work today in what some de-scribe as an "era of events." While the historical ideal of the academy as an ivory tower continues to influence our vision of colleges and universities, our institutions have become inextricably linked with the communities we serve. If the global village metaphor is an appropriate one, we may assume that events occurring across the globe can and will affect the behaviors, values, decisions, and priorities of the academy. While a global context may be the proper one for twenty-first century higher education decision making, it is a relatively new planning context for most of us. Few of us have anticipated the organizational and technical requirements and capabilities that will be expected of colleges and universities in a global and event-driven context.

Failing to identify such requirements or to develop these capabilities, there is a risk that college and university leaders will tend to respond to events rather than to plan for them. The failure to institutionalize strategic planning as an element of "normal operations"[1] and other factors have led us to become adhocracies, that is, reactive institutions that grope from event to event, inventing homemade solutions to immediate pressures or opportunities. The immediacy of our problems predisposes us to embrace quick and easy solutions—like across-the-board cuts—in lieu of developing an understanding of the trade-offs between complex priorities set in the context of strategic objectives. Who among us, for example, can articulate our institution's vision and strategy of administration?

As events overtake us, we are discovering the limits of adhocracy as a planning and decision-making paradigm. Some have begun to view our institutions' administration in the context of our academic plans (Exhibit 12–1). It is for this reason that we are now hearing with increasing frequency about emerging productivity enhancement strategies such as infrastructure investment, total quality management (TQM), business process reengineering (BPR), research incubators, outsourcing,

---

[1] Samuel Kirkpatrick, "Strategic planning as normal operations: a revolutionary idea," keynote address to the 1992 meeting of the Society of College and University Planners (SCUP).

Exhibit 12–1
IMPERATIVE: INCREASE ADMINISTRATIVE PRODUCTIVITY

Old Strategies: Adhocratic	New Strategies: Centric Planning
Cut expenses across the board	■ Develop a vision
	■ Identity academic priorities
	■ Rethink mission/markets
	■ Nurture internal growth sectors
Cut administration deeper	■ Redefine administration
	■ Eliminate unnecessary work
	■ Dismantle unproductive policies
	■ Reengineer processes
	■ Leverage the IT infrastructure
	■ Attack paperwork
Tighten procedures and seek scale through centralization	■ Empower employees
	■ Leverage the private market
	■ Embed procedural controls in IT infrastructure

distance education, and other strategic management initiatives and methodologies.

Technological Implications. To sustain the quality of our academic institutions, we must begin to shift the focus of the information technology function away from optimizing machine efficiency and toward enhancing human productivity and effectiveness. Technology investments that help produce more and fancier reports must yield to investments in those technologies that enable faster transactions and better decisions.

In the 1970s and early 1980s, every new thing institutions took on seemed to come with new money. Everything was additive. In the 1990s it is clear that we need to rethink the way we accomplish our work—as Michael Hammer suggests, don't automate it, obliterate it[2]—to free up time and money for new and important goals. We are now leaving behind the mindset that said that the long-term services we have provided must be the most important ones, so when cutting budgets, let's start by cutting the new initiatives. We now know that some of the newest things we are doing have the potential for the greatest payback to our institutions. Budget cutting, at many institutions, has progressed from "last in, first out" to "least valuable in, first out."

[2] Michael Hammer. "Reengineering work: don't automate, obliterate," *Harvard Business Review*, July–August 1990, p. 104.

12.2 TRENDS AND THEIR IMPLICATIONS

In the past two decades much of our effort went into building new computer applications, as we were completing the suite of applications that brought automation to nearly all campus business processes. Now the focus is on leveraging such investments by distributing access to these legacy systems around the campus. The focus is no longer on capturing and storing information as it has been for our transaction systems. We now recognize that information gains value as it moves around the institution and is used by many people in many contexts. The exchange of information between a supplier and a consumer is facilitated by new networking technologies. Leveraging the *installed base* of data and systems provides new value without building entirely new systems.

In the 1970s and early 1980s, new technologies were the most expensive and risky technologies. So to save time and money, institutions avoided trying anything that departed dramatically from their installed base. In recent years, new technologies are often less expensive than the technologies they replace. In some cases new technology—if it isn't "bleeding edge"—can be less risky than what it replaces; that difference is often reflected in the maintenance prices that vendors charge for old hardware versus newer hardware.

When the concept of outsourcing emerged as a business strategy, it was viewed as an all-or-nothing proposition in which information systems functions were potentially provided by an external company under contract. But in the last few years, as in-house information technology (IT) organizations have perforce become more creative in providing improved service at reduced cost, we have recognized that (1) functions can be selectively outsourced, and (2) *sourcing* is a continuum, from *insourcing* through partnering to *outsourcing*. Selectively, one might choose to outsource functions such as printing, or even just those functions that affect printing; many shops have outsourced microfiche printing for years, without even calling it "outsourcing." Similarly, one might elect to use a third party to provide assistance in an architectural transition, having it take over legacy systems maintenance, for example. On a sliding scale from "insourcing" to "outsourcing," an institution can elect to partner with a vendor to develop a system to its specifications, and then the vendor turns the system over to the institution for maintenance, or, in a different outsourcing option, the institution treats the system as a purchased package and pays the vendor for maintenance.

In the 1970s and 1980s we would "harden" our manual business processes into systems that would "automate" the manual function. We made the business more efficient. But in the 1990s—now that most of our manual processes have been automated—the message is that we can save the institution the most money by rethinking, or reengineering, the business process into an effective one before turning it into an efficient process in software.

An institution's first reaction when budgets are reduced is to look for services to cut, or to reduce the number of locations at which it provides service, or the hours during which a service window or phone is open. No doubt these approaches save money. Yet we may be able to use our systems in ways that appear to our customers to be service enhancements, *and* actually save money with the new service. In the banking business, the automated teller machine was an example of this kind of approach. Especially when we are dealing with the most peripatetic of our customers—faculty and students, who are engaged in producing and consuming the very information we manage—they may feel better served by us if we trade off some of our paper-based and expensive processes for electronic ones that are available around and beyond the campus, and also around the clock.

A major reason many campuses are pursuing client/server technologies so vigorously is the scalability of the desktop environment. Why is this important? Because the information economy requires so much more access by so many more people, it is important to bring desktop equipment into the picture. Since the number of users is growing so rapidly, it is that portion of the technical environment that must scale in easy and affordable increments.

In the last decade, many institutions got caught up in rhetoric and too readily believed that by coming up with a utopian vision, they had done the hard work. The sweeping visions of the 1980s don't fit the times now; the visions are not wrong so much as they exceed an institution's real ability to plan, fund, implement, and deliver. The radical visions required revolution, and we can see how slowly that comes to the faculty and other key constituencies. The best approach now should be to look at what successes we have had, and to try to package them, to leverage them, to get our best real products in the hands of more people in our institutions.

Trend 2: Public Expectations and State Mandates Are Calling for More Reporting Requirements and Accountability

Every time an institution turns around it seems there is a new investigation or state or federal audit going on. The need for increased accountability raises fundamental questions about the nature of institutional priorities and about how performance is monitored and communicated to the constituents institutions serve.

Organizational Implications. For the post–World War II period, American colleges and universities operated in a positive growth environment stimulated by (1) the GI Bill, (2) the baby boom, (3) the dramatic increases in federal and private sponsorship of university research, (4) growth in student financial aid, and (5) the growth in many states' tax bases. These demographic trends, plus public policies toward and investments in higher education, made U.S. postsecondary education the envy of the world. In many ways these policies and investments served to create a seller's market for postsecondary instruction and sponsored research. Beginning in the late 1980s, and for the foreseeable future, structural changes to the U.S. economy—changes shaped by burgeoning government deficits, the baby bust, and the emergence of an information economy—threaten to alter, at best, and possibly erode this legacy of investment and support.

The effects of these more recent trends are exacerbated by a perceived inability of colleges and universities to manage their resources responsibly, to control their costs, to balance research priorities with teaching, and to meet the educational needs of young people joining the workplace in the twenty-first century. The ultimate effect of the concurrent rise in tuition and decrease in the availability of college-eligible students will be an increase in public scrutiny of colleges and universities. In what some characterize as an emerging buyer's market for higher education, parents, students, donors, research sponsors, and legislators will demand increasing institutional accountability for the quality of all aspects of campus activity.

Such pressures demand a corresponding rethinking of institutional operations. Just as the event-driven and interdependent nature of campus life suggests the limitations of adhocracy and incrementalism as higher education's prevailing planning and resource management strategies, so does the increased need for public accountability trumpet the limitations of bureaucracy, as higher education's prevailing internal control strategy. In effect, the prevailing business strategy to date has focused on preventing transaction errors to shape and define administrative structures and systems. In creating a never-ending cycle of audits, proceduralization, forms generation, signature authorizations, and centralization of decision making, institutions have lost sight of their constituents and created administration for its own sake and a culture averse to risk taking.

Notwithstanding the very real pressures for transactional accuracy and operational openness, institutions must seek to rethink their operations from a viewpoint of desired outcomes. Such outcomes must be informed by the needs of those served. Institutions must develop the ability to understand, make explicit, communicate, and negotiate the inherent trade-offs between overhead-laden operations that are allegedly "risk free" and streamlined operations that depend increasingly on employee judgment through deeper delegations of authority (Exhibit 12–2).

Reliance on human judgment, rather than procedure, is inherently risky. Some organizational consultants have characterized bureaucracies as "organizations of mistrust." In essence, IT administrators must help

Exhibit 12–2
IMPERATIVE: ENHANCE CONTROLS AND REPORTING

Old Strategies	Emergent Strategies
Introduce new rules	Specify desired outcomes
Introduce new forms	Negotiate acceptable risk
Acquire additional signatures	Embed controls in IT
Centralize approval authority	Measure and evaluate continually

institutional leaders determine how much trust they are willing to invest in their administrative staff, or, conversely, how much they are willing to spend in procedural control to replace that missing trust. Finally, institutions must take advantage of the emerging information technology environment to reduce the risks of error, to eliminate redundant work, and to provide timely and meaningful information to assess their success in achieving the outcomes sought.

Technological Implications. Information technologies and architectures designed for bureaucratic control differ substantially from those designed for employee empowerment. Symbolically, the signature as the embodiment of managerial control and oversight assumes the existence of paper and encumbered former systems with the need for paper-based input documents and outputs. Information technology that is designed to empower people focuses on access to information and on optimizing the flow of processes. The ultimate process optimization is full electronic commerce that is unencumbered by the need for paper-based checks and controls.

In the stovepipe "islands of automation" built in the 1970s and 1980s, the quickest way to determine if two systems contained the same information was to write a report to run against one system and compare it to a report run against the second system. Of course, the comparison was done manually. Many of the reports developed over the past two decades were not for management information, but to balance one automated system against another automated system, or to serve as input into another computer system.

Now, using the techniques of electronic data interchange (EDI), institutions can move transaction information from one system to another without tightly coupling or integrating the two systems. While EDI is most often used to move information between two companies, there is no reason that the same "store and forward" messaging techniques cannot be applied within an institution.

An article on information politics in the *Sloan Management Review* describes five stages of information politics, two of which seem most relevant to universities: feudalism and federalism.[3] The five stages are technocratic utopianism, anarchy, feudalism, monarchy, and federalism. Information sharing and reporting is not a politically neutral activity and is different in each of these. We need to be aware of which phase we are in before we try to "improve" reporting.

In information feudalism, information is managed disjointedly by powerful lords and barons—we know them as deans and vice presidents, perhaps—in individual units. These people define their own information needs and report limited information to the overall commonwealth. Note that the stronger the feudal lords, the weaker the monarch. Many of us see examples of this as we move around our campuses trying to see which fiefdom has dammed the information flow upstream.

Now in information federalism, negotiation and consensus are used to bring parties together; important information is put in easy-to-access data warehouses and there are common expectations for reporting information. Note that this is beyond the monarchy stage, in which, according to Davenport, Eccles, and Prusak, a strong central authority attempts to eliminate politics.

Back in the days when most reporting was from one internal organization to another, and when the reporting requirements were relatively stable, institutions structured transaction applications and data to produce a set of reports regularly and efficiently. Each application had its own reporting mechanism, which understood the typical uses of data in the application.

But now, as reporting requirements mushroom because of external demands and because institutions are using their systems for problem solving and decision support as well as control, it is important to separate reporting mechanisms and data from the transaction mechanisms. This is not only a matter of efficiency and performance; it is also a way of separating things that are very dynamic—like reporting requirements— from things that are relatively more stable—like the transaction processes, controls, and data themselves. In something like a client–server sense, reporting becomes more flexible and scalable when it is separated from the stable base of operational systems and data. And, in the new client–server technologies, the tools for reporting seem to be more mature that those for large-scale transaction processing.

Since Macintosh created the desktop publishing marketplace, institutions have been able to create tons of paper documents very efficiently. And having all these pretty paper documents, distribution publishers had a lot of pride in seeing that everyone had a copy. Our campuses are awash in newsletters and flyers, reporting whatever people have a need

[3] Thomas H. Davenport, Robert G. Eccles, and Laurence Prusak, "Information politics," *Sloan Management Review*, Fall 1992, p. 53.

to tell to anyone who has an interdepartmental mailbox. Publishing more reports in this manner rarely results in people being better informed.

There is now more than enough information to go around. Several campuses are working on a concept called *document repositories*, which store textual information until someone asks for it, and then effectively delivers it to the person who needs to know about it, when he or she needs it. This electronic retrieval and distribution controlled by the end user is a type of *just-in-time* delivery on demand. But the publishing process itself is still just-in-time from the publisher's point of view, and the technology of the document repository allows the same kind of time shifting between a document's author and its readers that we are familiar with the VCR providing between a broadcaster and the viewer.

Trend 3: Consumer Expectations Demand More Sophisticated Services Requiring Greater Access to Data

Faculty and staff in schools and departments continually complain about the non-responsiveness of central offices, especially in information systems.

Organizational Implications. In responding to the pressure for greater information access, institutions need to adopt a greater *consumer* or *customer* orientation. Not surprisingly, the bureaucratic control model and incrementalist problem-solving model foster organizational cultures characterized by guardianship, gatekeeping, controlling, and regulating. These cultures are reinforced by their reward systems, which often favor administrators who have "done nothing wrong." In their most virulent manifestations, institutions are at risk of creating administrative cultures of control that strive to protect it from students and faculty. Compare, if you will, our business partners' talk about "delighting the customer" with some of our talk about "herding cats."

Of the 70 institutions identified by Clark Kerr, president emeritus of the University of California, as having been in continuous existence since the Reformation, 66 are colleges and universities.[4] This record of endurance and stability cannot be ascribed to a unique and enduring bureaucratic control model and administrative service culture. The point here is that there exist uniquely creative and durable elements of campus life and that the mission of campus administration must become, in part, a mission of discovery. In the past 30 years college and university administrators have imported the best and worst of private-sector organizational and decision-making models—such as the specialization of labor and

---

[4] From remarks prepared for a symposium at UCLA by Richard C. Atkinson, University of California, San Diego, June 22–23, 1994, entitled *Reinventing the Research University.*

12.2 TRENDS AND THEIR IMPLICATIONS

Exhibit 12–3
IMPERATIVE: ADOPT A CONSUMER ORIENTATION

Old Strategies	Emergent Strategies
Do things right	Do the right things right
Assure compliance	Become a problem solver
Foster specialization	Empower generalists
Manage by exception	Create centers of competency
Safeguard institutional data	Promote access to information

management by exception. They must now rediscover and codify successful processes and models intrinsic to the academy and blend with them the best of emergent consumer-oriented models, such as TQM and business process reengineering from the private sector (Exhibit 12–3).

A strategy of discovery suggests that institutions seek out those opinion leaders and even renegades on their campuses who succeed outside the formal systems of control and organization and uncover, replicate, and illuminate the competencies they have devised. The challenge is to move our organizations from ones that "just say no" to those that try to say "yes."

Technological Implications. The traditional model of information systems development assumed that the customer of IT design efforts was the functional organization that specified these systems' requirements. The trend of viewing an organizations' work through the lens of horizontal processes rather than through vertical functions places the focus of system development and support on the end-to-end users of these systems: students, faculty, employees, and vendors. The implications of such a changed assumption about the nature of the customer and levels of expected service will affect every choice facing IT organizations.

The message here is: Institutions need to focus on the customer, and his or her needs, rather than on products and their features. In the previous decade, the best institutions produced very well-supported products; now they need to have very well-supported customers.

As institutions are asked to provide more and more sophisticated services, they have to view those services from the perspective of the real consumer. In the 1980s systems were built to automate the operations of back-office users. Now those systems are moving into the hands of people whose jobs are quite different but who need occasional access to the data in these systems. How many systems, for example, would an administrator in the chemistry department have to use to perform the basic departmental task of "hiring a student"? Surely the payroll system and the personnel system, but also the financial aid system and the student records system? And perhaps one or two departmental systems? Perhaps others? If we're going to provide sophisticated services, the services need to be centered on the tasks of the users of those services, such as hiring, rather than the systems function, such as payroll, personnel, and student aid.

In the early 1980s institutions didn't yet have automated systems collecting data on all the university's business processes. On the academic side, they didn't have ready network access to the data delivery systems of scores of other institutions. Now institutions have both of these. The information drought—in which people spent their time trying to find any data at all—has become a data deluge—in which people spend much of their time sifting the data for something of value. Studies have shown that 80 percent of an analyst's time is spent gathering the "right" data, not actual productive time in analyzing the data. The analyst is working the "needle in the haystack" problem and the "wheat from the chaff" problem rather than actually doing analysis. Solutions in the 1990s have to help people select, filter, navigate, and integrate data, not just capture it.

In the 1980s institutions held training classes and wrote large user manuals for "all things to all people" systems. In the 1990s they should design and target subsets—or increments—of system function to users whose needs and abilities match the function and interface of the subset (Exhibit 12–4). Users can thus control when they are ready to take on more and more advanced subsets of system function and complexity. The better the match, the less the training burden; in many cases the system itself can deliver whatever training is needed. For example, only fields relevant to the user's task should appear on a screen. Different fields are needed in a personnel system to hire someone than to terminate someone, yet the same paper forms and online screens may be used to do both, confusing the user who is focused on a particular task.

In the 1980s, we took people out of their offices and brought them to computer classrooms to sit through training lectures; later we introduced our great innovation, hands-on training. There are many more users now, and they are using many more systems per person. They cannot afford to leave their offices for a day each time they need to learn another new

Exhibit 12–4
IMPERATIVE: FACILITATE ORGANIZATIONAL CHANGE

Old Strategies	Emergent Strategies
Add vertical layers	Create a network of networks
Enhance vertical communications	Reduce information float
Create functional "stovepipes"	Promote cross-functional integration
Use the chain of command	Use the network

system component. So training in this decade should be more modular and self-directed; and it should be available at the time and place of need, in the workplace, not the computer classroom.

In the 1980s a "separate but equal" philosophy separating academic computing facilities from administrative facilities persisted in computing long after it was outlawed in our society generally. Supposedly, between academic and administrative computing, the hardware was different, the software was different, and the users' needs and skills were different; in the early 1980s this was true to a large extent. But all these differentiators have moved together as the marketplace eliminated differences without a distinctive value in the market. There are fewer and fewer campuses with separate academic and administrative TCP/IP networks, for example. At the same time colleges and universities have begun to adopt a corporate technology strategy of linking suppliers and customers directly to systems. In higher education, these suppliers and customers are students and faculty to a very great extent, since they produce and consume much of the information in our systems.

Trend 4: Evolving Organization Structures Will Significantly Change Traditional Hierarchies

Presidents are beginning to wonder what all those people are doing who reside organizationally between them and the schools and departments. The only people who wonder about this even more are those in the schools and departments.

Organizational Implications.   Organization charts are useful guides, but they are becoming more and more outmoded. Institutions and firms do not manage through structures anymore; they manage through processes. While this concept might gain easy acceptance in the loosely coupled world of the faculty, it is perhaps antithetical and threatening to many associated with campus administration. If you ask all of the experts in TQM or business process reengineering to describe the typical implications of the new methodologies for organizational structure, in nearly all cases, the answer is, "There are none." The emergent organizational paradigms succeed by empowering people and horizontal processes in ways that are supplemental to—or independent of—the "formal" vertical organization.

By way of analogy, we should consider how faculty might answer these questions: How much of your teaching and research quality can you ascribe to your formal organization, that is, the academic senate? The department? The college?

To enable the organizational transformations we anticipate, institutions need to shift their attention away from the organization chart and toward the creation of an information-rich infrastructure. If institutions can (1) eliminate the technical, cultural, hierarchical, and procedural boundaries that divide or isolate intelligent and motivated people; (2) create a policy environment that stimulates and rewards collaboration; (3) promote easy access to the kind of information people need to make sound decisions; and (4) specify, measure, and reward the achievement of defined and customer-centric objectives, they will go far in implementing many of the emergent organizational capabilities anticipated for the twenty-first century. In this process we may, or may not, have touched the formal organizational chart.

Technological Implications. Note that organizations evolve not just because they change, but because we change our point of view in how we look at the work of an organization.

In the future, work will be directed mainly by cross-functional and self-governing teams. The effectiveness of such teams, in managerial terms, will depend on their members' access to one another, to cross-functional information, and occasionally, to elements of the campus leadership. Such work practices will demand enhanced integration of data across functional systems, robust networking, and technical interfaces that lower the cultural barriers between diverse work cultures.

Remember how you felt when you first went through arena-style registration at college? You went to one window and picked up a form or got one stamped, and then you went to another window down the line and turned in the form you had just picked up and maybe got another one, which you then took to another window, and so on. This is how departmental workflows integrate across central systems: by departmental "hod carrying" as the departments move information from one institution-level system to another. Exhibit 12–5 shows how a departmental business process—such as financial planning—may require a user in an academic department to use four or five institutional systems, sometimes entering duplicate data.

In the 1980s institutions looked for packages that provided a complete set of technical functionality. Packages had to have their own data entry and validation screens, data dictionaries, a built-in database and retrieval language, and a report generating system. These were called *vertically integrated* packages. Now we see what kinds of costs such packages have; they hold the data they contain—which are usually structured for internal processing efficiency and integrity—captive to the manipulation routines that the package vendor has thought to provide. So when the institution that selected the package to suit its needs has changed and finds its needs have changed, the package no longer fits as well as it once did. But the data are locked up in a black box and can only be moved in and out through relatively manual processes. Now we are all looking for packages that at least give us the flexibility of gaining access to the data

Exhibit 12–5

INSTITUTIONAL SYSTEMS AND DEPARTMENTAL PROCESSES

School and Department Processes	Human Resources	Controller's Office	Sponsored Research	Facilities	Health and Safety	Student Resources	Development
Research administration	X	X	X	X	X	X	
Faculty recruitment	X	X	X	X		X	X
Financial planning	X	X	X	X	X	X	X
Space planning	X	X	X	X	X	X	X
Curriculum support	X			X	X	X	
Faculty support	X	X	X	X	X	X	X
Student support	X	X	X	X	X	X	X

Note: Across the top are typical systems provided by the institution's central administrative offices; along the side are typical departmental processes. Note how poorly matched they are to each other.

store through standard database management system query tools and other tools that are part of a more open environment, that is, "liberated" from a type of vendor "lock in."

Twenty years after the concept of separating data from applications was accepted, institutions still build most of their systems so that the database and the application are tightly integrated. This approach to software construction has made it infeasible for a department with a unique need for processing information stored in central databases to be able to use that central data without first (in the best cases!) duplicating it in a departmental database, where it should be maintained, but rarely is. Such data systems are sometimes called *shadow systems*.

The fact that departments—and even individual faculty—are going to have local and unique needs not met by "corporate" information systems isn't going to change. Simply put, individual faculty, departments, and central administration run somewhat different business processes, and one group's process isn't just a subset of another, or a different view of the same data.

So shadow systems are in the nature of a higher education institution. If that is so, then rather than eliminating them, the goals should be to make them less necessary (by making central information more accessible), less labor intensive, and less fragile. How? One way is by constructing "data warehouses" of the central information needed, and making data in these warehouses accessible to systems and programs written by departments and individuals. By making the information available in a standard way—for example, through a structured query language (SQL) database—and in a standard, stable form, central organizations provide a common *data well* that many can draw from, rather than individually customized *point solutions* for each system that needs the data.

In the 1980s, the big word—even before everything was relational— was *integrated*. Every needed business function was tied together by a single vendor into a single package, usually around an "integrated" database. This phenomenon was as true of microcomputer software as of mainframe computer software; every vendor was trying to one-up the integrated Lotus 1-2-3 with more functionality integrated into a single shell. Most of these products failed in the marketplace because they compromised the ability of each of us to assemble our own suite of products from among those we considered "best of breed" for each of the functions we valued. By trying to be jacks of all trades, these products were masters of none. The newer vendors of large-scale business packages seem to realize that their old "protectionism" approach which locked the client into their product suite was in reality a barrier to trade and thus a barrier to the overall expansion of the market. An enlarged market, like a rising tide, raises all boats and provides new opportunity for all vendors, especially the most aggressively "open" and "interoperable" among them.

Ideally, different vendors' modules would "hand off" data as they move from one business process function to another in completing a multifunction task (like, for example, hiring a student). Simply having all the packages using an SQL-compliant database management system won't accomplish this.

The past strategy of buying from established vendors meant that one of the first things institutions would evaluate about a vendor for a major application package was the size of its installed base. A large installed base indicated that a vendor had been in business for a while and had successfully convinced others to buy.

Yet the most successful vendors of the 1980s now recognize that an installed base is a two-edged sword: it provides the cash flow, market visibility, and referenceable accounts an organization needs to fuel growth, but the installed base is a type of ballast that ties a vendor into a cycle of enhancing—rather than replacing—its legacy products. The installed base prefers a steady stream of minor upgrades in the current architecture to a cataclysmic product replacement with a new architecture.

For this reason, the vendors whose application packages are leading the market in open, client/server products are newer companies that could start from scratch in developing a new product to meet today's needs. They were not encumbered by an installed base expecting compatibility and an extended migration period. These small companies move quickly, and thus they represent both higher risk and higher reward than an established, "old architecture" firm.

IT organizations in colleges and universities have for the most part had an architecture specified for years. In most cases, these specifications were about tying modules of an application together and about tying the application into the operating environment. All of these specifications were adequate as long as nearly all the applications ran on the same computer and were developed by the same organization. But these assumptions rarely hold now (if they ever did). Thus, as the organizations that supply and consume information evolve, so must the concept of architecture evolve beyond "coding standards."

The modern notion of architecture recognizes that organizational evolution is something that happens continuously, and the systems that support the changing businesses of changing organizations must be flexible and responsive. The concept of architecture is less like planning to build a home than it is like planning the services and utilities that will support the scale, scope, and fluidity of the activities in a city. Today's architecture is about organizing and connecting components of a system—and the systems themselves—together. Architecture has implications for (1) the way applications, data, tools, and equipment work with each other; (2) the skills needed by technical and office staff; and (3) how systems are developed. It is responsive to business opportunities, needs, and strategy, as well as the marketplace of business and technology suppliers and partners. Its business goal is an institutional framework for planning and linking disparate systems and data, to gain flexibility and responsiveness. Its technical goals are productivity enhancement for users and system developers, and a definition of risks, allowing actions to limit risk.

Many of us have worked wonders building two or three bridges and gateways from one software to two or three others. We have also driven ourselves nearly crazy because a different homebrew gateway is needed between any two packages. If the phone system worked like this, we'd need a different wire to connect our phone to every other telephone we'd like to reach. Our systems are starting to look like rats' nests—or a neophyte networker's wiring closet.

Vendors have this problem, too. One example is the difficulty an E-mail vendor might have in trying to connect a mail system based on a local area network (LAN) to other electronic mail systems on a campus; each additional different system increases the problem geometrically.

Similarly, vendors of database management systems, in trying to prove their "openness," had to build gateways to every other system in the market, so they "architected" their way out by forming the SQL Access Group, which goes well beyond standardizing on an SQL dialect. These new forms of links are not point-to-point links; they are the result of vendors agreeing on a common interchange approach and format. We call this "virtual integration" because, while it seems as if you have an integrated system, you have some of the flexibility that "interchangeable parts" brought to the early automotive industry.

In the 1980s, we thought we could connect anything to anything as long as both ends spoke SQL—interoperability Nirvana. Then we got serious and realized the SQL alone was not flexible enough, nor specific enough, to link our business systems—not just their databases—to each other. So EDI is now the new frontier—essentially a form of machine-to-machine electronic mail in which the message is structured by rules agreed to by each system in the interchange and registered in a standards library.

Trend 5: Sophisticated Knowledge Workers Require Expanded Technical and Consulting Support

If the administrative workforce of tomorrow is to be empowered to make decisions without layers of rules or managers, institutions will need to invest in helping members of this workforce realize their full potential through new tools and capabilities and ongoing training, consulting, and technical support.

Organizational Implications.   To create a sophisticated and continually improving workforce, institutions need to create and nurture learning organizations (Exhibit 12–6). How institutions of higher education engage their workforces in learning activities is one of our sadder ironies. Colleges and universities are, of course, learning organizations by definition. While faculty spend considerable time and effort in discovering how students learn, how much time do administrators spend in the process of discovering how staff learn? Here we are using the term learning in the broadest sense, that is, in the sense of how do employees assimilate the values, norms, and the job skills they need to become the problem solvers we expect them to become?

Institutions make several essential mistakes. First, they equate all learning with either formal teaching or formal training. Second, they focus most of their managerial attention and investments on training. Third, at the first sign of hard times, they cut the training. The point here is that organizational learning takes place right under our noses every working hour of every workday. Most institutions choose, as a matter of convenience, to focus only on formal training, as one component of organizational learning.

If institutions are to develop sophisticated problem solvers, they will need to increase their commitments to the formal training agenda and, once again, discover, uncover, empower, and replicate that complex information system of successful mentorships, peer networks, informal collaborations, and grapevines that exist already in the organization. We have perhaps all heard the apocryphal story, ascribed often to Xerox Corporation, of the efficiency zealot who restricted repair technicians' time at the water cooler only to discover later that repair times went up! The point of this parable, of course, is that learning occurs in a variety of unusual and little-understood ways in organizations. Again, technologists must explore new ways to promote organizational learning and to lever some of the unmanaged learning channels and mechanisms that operate already outside the formal systems of training and teaching.

For some institutions, it will be tempting to interpret this message of discovery as a call for inaction. One might legitimately ask: If this learning

Exhibit 12–6
IMPERATIVE: CREATE "LEARNING" ORGANIZATIONS

Old Strategies	Emergent Strategies
Train your top professionals	Provide training for all
Base pay on job duties	Recognize job skills
Recruit for employees	Engage in open succession planning
Train for job skills	Train for problem solving
Put success behind you	Reward and communicate success stories

is going on without any intervention, then why tamper with success? Our answer to this is that left unmanaged these forms of organizational learning are just that, "unmanaged." As such, these learning processes are at risk of being informed by myth and superstition and of being motivated by power and/or fear.

Technological Implications. Empowerment, with accountability, depends in part on a knowledgeable workforce. The information technology environment of the future should be designed to reduce, wherever possible, the need for unnecessary employee training and should enable, wherever necessary, employee learning. Computer or network instructions and interfaces must be intuitive to their users and access to supplemental expertise must be simple, ubiquitous, and available around the clock. IT organizations should strive to develop applications with sufficiently compatible "look and feel" to foster employee learning and mobility across campus processes and jobs.

This distinction is well articulated by Shoshana Zuboff in her book *In the Age of the Smart Machine: The Future of Work and Power*.[5] Her basic point is that our computer systems not only take over the work of the blue-collar worker when they automate some factory or clerical process, but in doing that, they also collect information about the work itself. This information is grist for the knowledge worker's mill, as he or she takes on the task of trying to improve the basic processes. Zuboff calls this an "informating" process and notes that it changes the jobs of the workers who actually do it. Our task is to ensure that our systems can deliver this kind of basic process information to knowledge workers rather than hiding such information from them.

As IT administrators have been asked to shift their focus from the back-office worker to the knowledge generators and consumers of their institutions, they are now focusing on a different community. Nicholas Negroponte mentioned this in his keynote address at the 1992 CAUSE Annual Conference: a college or university's knowledge workers are peripatetic. But not only do they move around a lot physically, they move around a lot intellectually—jumping from discipline to discipline—and they are usually more "loyal" to their specialty than to their department or institution. In addition, they are not concentrated in one place like the heads-down data entry clerks used to be, but they are scattered in ones and twos throughout our organizations. Think of the senior business managers in each of your large departments as an example.

If IT administrators are going to focus on the needs of these new clients, they will see that these people need a different type of technical assistance structure and content from those they have been aid-

---

[5] Shoshara Zuboff, *In the Age of the Smart Machine* (New York: Basic Books, 1988).

ing through the help desk for so many years. Ultimately, they will have to make independence easier than dependence, fostering the self-sufficiency and enterprise of this type of knowledge worker.

In the 1980s, very generalized tools and solutions were provided to the masses, often encumbering tools with "featuritis" or providing lowest common denominator tools that met no one's needs in particular. Markets of the 1990s appear to be much more specialized and focused than those of the 1980s. Today we hear about vertical-market products that are customized to a specific market and that dominate the market.

What is the equivalent of this in higher education? We can reasonably talk about market segmentation among the different types of knowledge workers in our institutions, based on what they do, what tasks they focus on, who they work for, and what tools and data they use in accomplishing all of this. Some specific technologies that the marketplace wants to provide to us are appropriate only for one or two segments of the higher education knowledge worker "market." If IT administrators have the challenge from their institution to provide better support for knowledge workers, they need to first figure out who the knowledge worker is and then decide whether the best solution for the knowledge worker is, for example, videoconferencing, electronic forms, electronic mail, or collaboration tools.

Exhibit 12–7 is an attempt to segment the higher education market and suggest which tools might be of high value to which segments. For example, if we need to improve the productivity of accounting clerks, we should probably consider EDI and reengineering strategies rather than teaching them how to surf the Internet with a network navigator, or providing them with automated-teller-style interfaces.

Throughout these discussions, we have been comparing an old and a new way of thinking and managing. While it is becoming clear that the "old" way is something we cannot do anymore, unfortunately the "new" way is not entirely feasible yet. As technologists we are, to paraphrase Matthew Arnold, wandering between two technology and business paradigms, one dying, the other waiting to be born. As general managers, however, we are not paid to be standing by; it is part of our jobs to husband, or midwife, or usher, if you will, the best new ways of thinking and working into the standard practice of our institutions, and among our colleagues and staff.

12.3 BUILDING TOMORROW'S INSTITUTION

To be positioned well for the demands of the twenty-first century, institutions should explore a number of strategies and approaches, including the following.

Exhibit 12-7

SUPPORT FOR KNOWLEDGE WORKERS: MATCHING TOOLS TO TASKS

Category	Focus	Orientation	Who?	Tools	Supported by:
Back office	Internal questions	Batch processes	Accounting clerks	Mainframes; process-oriented data	■ Internal and external EDI ■ Process reengineering ■ Distributed electronic forms ■ Scalable servers ■ Interoperable servers and databases ■ Legacy system encapsulation ■ Outsourcing
Front office	Customers and suppliers	Batch processes	Departmental administrators	Client/server systems; cross-functional data	■ Internal and external EDI ■ Windowing, multisystem views ■ Data warehousing ■ Common user interface ■ Graphical user interface (GUI) integration, screen scraping ■ Fax machines, e-mail ■ Integrated data/image ■ Distributed electronic forms ■ Scalable clients ■ Searchable document repositories ■ Open, client/server systems

Knowledge development	Business solutions	Projects		
		Managers, professionals, faculty, students	Desktop tools; external data; enterprise data	■ Decision support system ■ Multimedia e-mail ■ Bulletin boards and electronic conferences ■ Collaborative tools ■ Computer-assisted meetings ■ Videoconferencing ■ Data analysis tools ■ Mobile computing ■ Scalable clients ■ Training-free ATM-like interfaces ■ Network navigators ■ Current-awareness agents ■ Open client tools

Source: Some of the above data has been drawn from Gartner Group material. Used with permission.

1. Open an Import–Export Idea Bank

College and university faculty pride themselves on their critical reasoning abilities. Some administrators, unlike faculty, tend to view critical reasoning as antithetical to, or in conflict with, the rapid incorporation of new ideas into campus business practices. Popular productivity-enhancement strategies or programs such as TQM and BPR have merit. Such strategies should be subjected to an open and critical assessment. New ideas from industry should neither be rejected categorically as "irrelevant to our unique mission and special conditions," nor uncritically embraced as "magic bullets." The most important themes emerging from private industry absolutely deserve a central place in higher education's administrative agenda. These themes admonish us to (1) manage our responsibilities in a disciplined and informed fashion (management by fact); (2) focus our priorities on improving the quality of service to our primary customers; and (3) recognize that stovepiped organizations impede cross-functional and institution-wide breakthroughs. Establishing the culture and infrastructure of an import/export idea bank also suggests a new partnership between the academic and administrative spheres of campus activity. In particular, administrators need not only take better advantage of their faculty's expertise but also need to uncover elements of the faculty learning process itself. That is, we need to emulate in our administrative activities the faculty's ability to identify, assess, diffuse, and assimilate information and knowledge in an era when information is in a condition of oversupply.

2. Remove Obstacles and Build Bridges

Many in central campus administration appear to others to be the operators of feudal baronies which have been optimized for protection against attacks by marauding chancellors, deans, students, faculty, and each other. Instead of walls, moats, and drawbridges, central administrators have constructed policies, procedures, delegations, and information systems to institutionalize (read depersonalize) our intent to say "no." To meet the challenges of the next century, we must begin to interrogate these obstacles honestly and critically and, where appropriate, to dismantle them. Here, information technology professionals must play a leadership role. Together we must design our campuses' technology architecture to optimize for openness and ease of use, and develop a network infrastructure that promotes access. Boundarylessness—across technology applications, organizations, functions, and institutions—should become the central driver of our information technology plans and programs.

3. Reward Behaviors That Promote Innovation and Teamwork

If institutional policies, procedures, forms, delegations, and systems have produced the foundation and bricks for our administrative walls, our personnel policies and programs have provided the mortar and reinforcing bars. These policies and programs have institutionalized our tendencies toward administrative specialization through complex and constraining job classification systems and schemes. Such specialization has fostered a "not in my job description" administrative culture that is antithetical to innovation and which is dehumanizing, ultimately, to administrative personnel at colleges and universities. Institutions have also configured incentives to motivate individual performance and to reward expertise. Such incentives, absent clearly defined goals and objectives, reinforce pressures for specialization of work and workers, put employees in competition with one another, and diminish their capacity to deliver service or to leverage the benefits of new management approaches.

The Trend Toward Greater Accountability

Chapter Thirteen
Transformation of Education in the United Kingdom

Chapter Fourteen
Assessing Outcomes: The SPRE Initiative

Chapter Fifteen
Greater Accountability in Financial Reporting

Chapter Sixteen
The Question of Tax Exemption

Transformation of Education in the United Kingdom

QUENTIN THOMPSON
JULIA TYLER
PETER HOWLETT

Coopers & Lybrand, U.K.

13.1 **Introduction**

13.2 **The U.K. System and Its Funding**
Historical Context
Publicly Funded and National System
University Degrees
Public Funding Streams

13.3 **Income Sources**
Public Funding of Research
Allocation of Public Funds for Teaching
Private Income

13.4 **Management Changes**
Levers for Change

Financial Management
Increasing Individuals' Responsibilities
More Professional Administration

13.5 **Teaching Quality and Standards**
External Examiner System
Funding Council Approach to Quality Assessment
Higher Education Quality Council: Quality Audit
Standards and Specifications

13.6 **Conclusions**

13.1 INTRODUCTION

Universities in the United Kingdom and the United States share certain characteristics. Both face increasing public and government scrutiny, and with it a concomitant loss of autonomy. Their funding from all sources, particularly government, is constrained, forcing them to rely increasingly on private funding. Some universities are more successful at obtaining funding than others, and as a result, a class system is emerging between the haves and the have-nots.

The efforts of universities in both countries to reduce costs may be affecting educational quality in some cases. Planning, monitoring, and controlling spending are becoming more critical, as are thoughtful and well-informed management practices. Both systems of higher education are adopting management techniques that have worked in private industry.

Although universities in the United States and the United Kingdom share challenges, in the United Kingdom the government plays a much more important role. It acts as the primary funding body, sets educational policy, and ensures there are mechanisms to oversee the quality of higher education. Recent examples of the government's policy interventions include its encouragement of performance-related pay and the abolishment of tenure for all new academics. The government also provides incentives for universities to be responsive to the needs of industry and commerce.

Underlying the U.K. system is the belief that higher education should be accessible to all those qualified to attend. (A similar concept applies in the United States but is increasingly not borne out in practice.) To make higher education in the United Kingdom accessible, the tuition of European Union (EU) first-degree students (i.e., undergraduates) is paid for by the government. The government also awards grants for students' living expenses. (However, loans were recently introduced and may eventually be extended to tuition costs in the United Kingdom—loans instead of grants are already prevalent in the United States—as the number of students attending universities increases and government funding becomes more constrained.)

Universities in the United Kingdom form a "quasi-market" system. Block grants are provided to each university, favoring those with lower costs and making the government the major purchaser of teaching. This is key: The government controls expenditure to a great extent in the United Kingdom through its funding system. The government also pays tuition fees to institutions based on enrollment. In this way, it rewards the institutions that attract the most students.

Research is also important to U.K. universities, and again most funding is provided by the government. In another governmental move to impose greater accountability and reward quality, the level of research funding a university receives in its block grant for research is based on the quality of its research as measured by a national assessment.

What lessons can U.S. institutions learn from the United Kingdom? The British system of higher education is not readily transferrable to the United States. It is engrained in the British culture; the American system of higher learning reflects our unique, more free-market culture. However, the increasingly important role of the government in the United

Kingdom in setting educational policy, controlling tuition prices, and demanding greater accountability may spread to the United States. Some trends, particularly accountability, are already well under way here. Others, the ability to control price in particular, are certainly possible, but not yet on the horizon. Nor is the abolition of tenure. However, what has transpired in the United Kingdom bears watching. More government involvement is already occurring in the United States. The feasibility of tenure has been discussed, however cautiously. The growing concern of the American public and its leaders about high tuition costs may lead to serious consideration of price controls in the not-too-distant future.

So, what can we learn from the United Kingdom? Although the differences are substantial, similarities abound. As the economy becomes increasingly global and more volatile and governments feel the pinch of lower tax dollars, there is less discretionary money for social causes such as higher education. Few governments in the world today have sufficient resources to fund all deserving causes. When resources are constrained, governments become increasingly concerned about how their funds are used. Intervention, accountability, and selective funding all become more likely. This may be the key lesson for U.S. institutions: The challenges they face are not unique and neither will be the solutions to them. The United States no longer stands alone but rather, is part of the global village.

13.2   THE U.K. SYSTEM AND ITS FUNDING

In the United Kingdom the term *higher education* refers to those parts of the education system that provide first-degree and/or postgraduate education for students aged 18 and over. The sector consists largely, but not exclusively, of universities. It also includes colleges of higher education undertaking degree-level work, although these often cover relatively specialized fields such as the training of schoolteachers, art and design, or music. This chapter focuses on the issues facing the universities in the United Kingdom, although many of them also apply to the colleges.

Historical Context

For nearly 30 years the United Kingdom had two parallel systems of higher education: universities and polytechnics. For most of this time, the polytechnics were funded by a tier of local government. They were originally set up with a more local and vocational focus than universities. Over the years, this so-called "binary line" became less easy to detect. Eventually, the polytechnics were redesignated as universities after legislation was passed in 1992. The main relevant features of the legislation were:

- Polytechnics and colleges of higher education, formerly under local government control and funded in part through local taxation, were initially incorporated as freestanding institutions with their funding transferred to them by central government.

- Subsequently, the distinction between universities and polytechnics was abolished. Polytechnics and colleges of higher education could apply for university status, and all polytechnics have now been granted such status. As a result, the number of higher education institutions that are classified as universities has increased from 48 in March 1992 to 86 by March 1994.

- For new staff at any of the universities, academic tenure—by which university academic staff were appointed for life, could not be removed from their posts, and could only be replaced if they resigned voluntarily—has been abolished, facilitating a more flexible basis for deploying teaching resources.

- Three separate National Funding Councils (one each for England, Scotland, and Wales) were established to channel public funds to the universities, to act as agents in the implementation of government education policy and to maintain oversight of quality in the higher education sector through regular quality assessments of teaching and of research.

In parallel with these reforms, the government set a long-term target of substantially increasing the proportion of the age cohort attending higher education. This was so successful that a temporary halt was called to contain the dramatic increase in government appropriations to higher education. At the same time, the government also encouraged greater rigor in the ways in which public funds were distributed and used. It sought to raise the status of vocational courses to that of the academic courses, and emphasized that higher education institutions should be more responsive to national economic requirements and to the needs of industry and commerce. Finally, the government promoted the importance of quality both in teaching and in research and decided that quality is not a matter that can be left entirely in the hands of institutions.

The implications of these changes for the management of universities have been substantial. They have heralded new national funding methodologies, which in turn have stimulated moves toward more entrepreneurial, market-oriented management cultures in universities and at the same time have required greater accountability for the use of public funds. This has presented a significant challenge to the U.K. university culture.

13.2   THE U.K. SYSTEM AND ITS FUNDING

Publicly Funded and National System

There is only one privately funded independent university in the United Kingdom, the University of Buckingham. The remainder, a total of 85, receive the bulk of their funding, both for teaching and for research, from public funds. They are regulated by acts of Parliament and (for the older universities) royal charters. Thus U.K. universities, to a greater or lesser extent, depend for their existence and their funds on government and are therefore expected to respond to national policies and priorities in higher education. Nevertheless, they retain substantial autonomy in terms of their teaching and research and jealously guard their academic freedom, which is largely protected by various acts of Parliament.

Although some universities have a strong local or regional focus, they are national institutions (i.e., they are not subject to any form of local control or regulation, nor are they given funding by any regional, local, or city government). It is currently the exception rather than the rule for U.K. undergraduates studying full-time to attend their hometown university. However, increasing numbers of students are doing so and the expanding number of undergraduates studying part-time almost invariably attend local institutions. Students choose where they wish to study and the university concerned decides whether it wishes to offer applying students a place. There is no restriction placed on a student's choice of university other than the availability of the course desired and the ability of the student to meet the entry requirements for the chosen course of study. For full-time courses, the mechanics of the admissions process are mediated through a national body in a single system known as the Universities and Colleges Admissions Service.

University Degrees

All U.K. universities have degree-awarding powers and exercise these autonomously. A wide variety of professional bodies accredit courses in particular subject areas (e.g., engineering, law, medicine). However, no national agency specifies what should comprise a U.K. degree, and no national body accredits the contents or standards of degrees. Before the 1992 legislation, under which all polytechnics became universities, the Council for National Academic Awards validated courses in those polytechnics without degree-awarding powers, but the council was abolished when the polytechnics became universities.

Bachelor's degrees are generally awarded after three years of study—usually from ages 18 or 19 to 21 or 22—although some subjects, for instance, modern languages and some science subjects, require four years. While still the norm, defining a degree by the number of years of study is becoming less common as systems consisting of a series of separate course modules (followed by an examination) are becoming increasingly prevalent. Further, the notion of "accreditation of prior learning," in which students are given credit for prior studies, or in some cases previous experience, as well as experiments such as a two-year degree, are making it increasingly difficult to characterize U.K. degrees by reference to the time taken to study for them.

Until recently, most U.K. universities required students to reach a specified entry standard, which varied from university to university and, within a university, from course to course. This was usually defined by the achievement of specific grades in two or three A-level subject examinations (i.e., national examinations taken at about age 18 as the final school exam). As other forms of pre-higher education have developed, new routes to postsecondary education have emerged, including a broader system of National Vocational Qualifications, as well as access routes for people without formal qualifications. Nevertheless, most intending full-time students have to pass an "entry hurdle" defined by performance in a national exam before they can begin their undergraduate studies. The major exception to this is the Open University. This is a distance learning university where no entry qualifications are required for undergraduate study.

All U.K. universities also offer degrees at master's and doctorate levels. Both are classified as higher degrees and can usually be earned only by holders of a first degree. Master's degrees are sometimes taken directly after a first degree, but more often follow a period of work experience. A doctorate is generally awarded on the basis of supervised, innovative research work carried out over a period of three or four years. Proposals for a new approach to research qualifications involving a one-year master's program followed by Ph.D. studies creating a so-called "one plus three" pattern of study are currently under discussion.

Public Funding Streams

Research. Research is a significant endeavor at many U.K. universities, although less so in most of the ex-polytechnics. Most research is government funded. A recent government White Paper on science and technology, "Realizing Our Potential," defined three categories of research:

- *Basic research*: experimental or theoretical work undertaken primarily to acquire new knowledge of the underlying foundation of phenomena and observable facts, without any particular application or use in view.

- *Strategic research*: applied research in a subject area that has not yet advanced to the stage where eventual applications can be clearly specified.

- *Applied research*: work undertaken to acquire new knowledge which is directed toward practical aims or objectives.

Universities perform research in all three categories, but it is the government's intention that applied research should be funded privately.

The substantial public funding for research is funneled through two main channels, forming a so-called "dual support system." The three Funding Councils (for England, Scotland, and Wales), established to administer government funds for higher education, generally are the first source of public funding for research. Total funding for research via these Funding Councils in 1993–1994 was £923.8m (U.S. $1385.71M). This element of funding is provided as a block and is intended to support most of the basic infrastructure costs of research: staff, premises, and equipment. It is also intended to cover the substantial fixed costs of training research students.

The second main source of public funds is from the six Research Councils established by the central government.[1] The total funding to U.K. universities via the Research Councils in 1993–1994 was £438.2m (U.S. $657.30M). The Research Councils promote and support research in their particular fields by providing project grants and studentships in response to specific applications, by supporting large-scale research facilities nationally and internationally, and by supporting research groups and individuals in universities and research institutes. In addition, individual government departments commission specific contract research projects for their own purposes in the same way as do private firms.

Teaching. The public funding of teaching also has two main components which, between them, cover virtually the entire costs of university teaching. The first component is the block allocation made to the university by one of the Funding Councils. This "core" funding assumes a certain baseline of student numbers in different subject categories. It is arranged from one year to the next in such a way as to provide an incentive for universities to reduce their unit teaching costs, and in recent years the government has assumed "efficiency savings" in making its allocation of funds to the Funding Councils—which the councils have then passed on to the universities. Over the past decade or so, the implied unit funding has been reduced (in real terms) by about 35 percent.

---

[1] The White Paper heralded a reorganization of the Research Council into six councils covering the following areas: (1) biotechnology and biological sciences, (2) economic and social sciences, (3) engineering and physical sciences, (4) medicine, (5) natural environment, and (6) particle physics and astronomy. Research in the humanities is covered by the British Academy.

The second main source of public funds for teaching is the fee income that a university receives for each student. This varies according to the subject of the students' study in three broad bands (non-laboratory-based courses, laboratory-based courses, and medicine and veterinary science). Most first-degree students are entitled to have their fees paid from public funds. The exceptions are part-time students and students from outside the United Kingdom. A university's fee income is thus directly related to the number of students it recruits.

For their living costs, students receive maintenance grants, which are means tested on parental income. As the number of students in universities has increased, there has been growing concern about how long the government can continue to provide such support. To help reduce this commitment of public funds, the government introduced a national loan system, which supplements but does not replace the grant. Many see this as the first step toward changing the balance of the financial contribution to higher education between government (on behalf of society and the economy at large) and those persons who benefit from a university education.

Private Funding.   With a few notable exceptions, U.K. universities generate very little revenue from private sources. Most of the private funding is for research contracts and other activities allied to research. In addition, universities generate a small amount of private income through trading and consultancy services and through the organization of conferences and events using university premises. A limited amount of income is secured from the tuition fees of part-time students and, for some universities, fees from non-European Union students. Unlike some U.S. institutions, U.K. universities derive very little funds from alumni and other sources of donations.

However, this is gradually changing, and many universities are now devoting much more time to raising private income than they have in the past. For the system as a whole, these various sources of private income will be of little significance for some time when compared with the income from public sources. Nevertheless, there are a few universities that have succeeded in securing private funds covering about half their total budget.

13.3   INCOME SOURCES

Public Funding of Research

Four major developments in the public funding of research have affected the ways in which universities undertake their research activities. The four are:

- Clarification of the respective roles of the funding bodies. The Funding Councils (through their block grants) are intended to fund the infrastructure costs of research—mainly research staff and premises. The Research Councils are responsible for the additional direct costs of defined research projects and for some of their indirect costs.

- Increasing selectivity by the Funding Councils in the allocation of their research funds to departments in universities which have a proven record of high-quality research (the allocation is done on a subject by subject basis).

- For the resources allocated by the Funding Councils to universities, a clear division between the funds to support research activity and the funds allocated for teaching purposes.

- A requirement that universities account for the use of the research funds allocated by the Funding Councils.

These developments demonstrate an increasing focus on the more selective use of public funds for research and increasing requirements to account for those funds.

Increasing Selectivity in the Allocation of Research Funds.   For many years, institutions were confused about the intended coverage of the Funding Councils' funds for research and those of the Research Councils. Research Council funds are, by definition, allocated selectively. The Funding Council funds were supposed to provide for the "well found research laboratory." (Although these words were used, no definitive definition was ever produced.) In a move toward greater clarity, a substantial part of the Funding Councils' research funds were transferred to the Research Councils in order to fund directly more of the direct and indirect costs of projects; in itself, this is also likely to increase selectivity.

It is not clear why all the Funding Councils' research funds could not have been transferred to the Research Councils. Then project bids would have to be fully costed and funded—the ultimate in selectivity. Of course a small proportion of undirected research funds would still need to be available for research that has not reached a stage where a project could be specified. The reason given for stopping short of a complete shift was that universities would not be able to handle the associated uncertainties, or at least, they were not yet ready to do so. Time will tell whether this full shift will be eventually made.

In the meantime, selectivity is increasing in the allocation of the Funding Councils' research funds, partly because many more institutions are now eligible for research funds (since the abolition of the binary line) but with no more research funds being available. To achieve this objective, the Funding Councils established national quality ratings (by subject) based on an assessment exercise every three (or four) years covering the research activity of each university. The Funding Councils, using peer review, rated the quality of research activity in each department in each university on a five-point scale.

The results were published. Not surprisingly, it was the old universities (which had been historically funded at a much higher level for research) which emerged with the highest ratings. However, the results also indicated subjects with high-quality research in a number of the ex-polytechnics, despite the fact that they had had little funding for research. Some poor research performances were indicated within universities whose overall reputation might have suggested that all their research would be of high quality.

The research funds of the Funding Councils represent approximately one-fourth of the total funds they distribute. The distribution formula for research used by the Funding Council for England consists of three main elements: QR, CR, and Dev R. QR is designed to reflect the volume and the quality of current research in a university and determines the allocation of about 95 percent of the available Funding Council research funds. It draws on the research assessment exercise referred to above. The CR element is directly related to the success of the university in securing contract income from research. Again, it is designed to channel funding to universities with an established track record. Dev R is the element designed to foster the development of new research potential, particularly in the ex-polytechnics and the higher education colleges which have demonstrated potential for high-quality research but have not yet received funding for it.

The research assessment exercise, with its emphasis on rewarding quality in selective areas, has significantly affected university behavior. Success in the ratings results not only in increased research income but also in greater peer prestige (thus serving as a strong motivator for many academic staff). As a result, many universities are now concentrating significant time, effort, and resources on trying to increase their research volume and quality and thus improve their ratings. Some are buying expertise in the form of complete research groups; others are providing incentives to academic staff, including the provision of seed research money; others have changed their internal resource allocation methods to favor active research staff. The majority of universities continue to emphasize successful research as a key criterion in academic promotion.

Many of the new universities, which as polytechnics had limited access to public funding for research, are working particularly vigorously to improve their prospects and have fought hard to secure some Dev R funds in the funding allocation. However, Dev R is a small pot and unless these universities can increase their research funding from other sources, only a handful will succeed in catching up with their older counterparts.

Of course, not all universities will succeed in improving their research rating. Indeed, since the rating is relative and no extra funds will be made available for research overall, the struggle is a zero-sum game, suggesting that for the lower performers, much of the effort to improve their rating will prove to be a waste of time. For some universities it would have been better to concentrate on areas in which they were already strong (e.g., to focus on teaching rather than research even though this may not appeal so readily to the aspirations of their academic staff). Nonetheless, "positioning" behavior continues apace.

As long as the methods of funding research and teaching remain as they are today, it seems likely that differentiation between universities will increase in the future. One of the results is likely to be the emergence of distinct groupings of universities, colloquially known as "R, T, X." These initials refer to different categories of universities which have, or will have, their primary mission as research (R) or as teaching (T) or as mixed (X) institutions. As the British concept of a "university" (despite the success of the polytechnics) is undoubtedly linked to the academic kudos of research, the result may well be a "class" system of universities. Indeed, some British newspapers now publish their own "rankings" of universities, which may prove influential in the future since for the first time they provide readily accessible information on universities. It is unlikely that these will develop into formal rankings such as those in the United States, but nonetheless, they will be powerful influences on public perception.

Increasing Accountability for Research Funds.   In theory, research projects funded by the Research Councils are already subject to reporting requirements. Research groups are expected to report both on the results of what they achieved in their research and on how the grant given to them was deployed to achieve those results. Accountability requirements for Funding Council research money are still evolving. Pressure has been growing for this money to be tracked systematically, and universities are now required to differentiate between the uses they make of teaching and research funds.

In attempting to account separately for teaching and research funds when they are allocated as a single block grant, both philosophical and technical issues arise. There are those who see the whole principle of, and the effort involved in, accounting separately for research funds as intrusive and unnecessary. Such attitudes usually reflect a reluctance to provide greater accountability for the use of public funds. At a more philosophical level, the separation of teaching from research funds can be resisted on the grounds that teaching and research are intrinsically inter-

related, that the separate allocation of, and accounting for, these resources is impossible, and that even attempting to make such a separation
would be harmful to overall academic activity.

Experience elsewhere, including in a number of other European countries, suggests that such objections are overstated. Moreover, it is generally
accepted in the United Kingdom that many of the ex-polytechnics provided
excellent teaching without having a substantial research base. On the
other hand, recent quality assessments of teaching have shown that those
universities that scored well in the research ratings also scored well in the
teaching assessments. Some argue that this reinforces the point that there
should be no attempt to split funds for teaching from those for research at
either the national- or university-level allocation. But it may not be a
coincidence that most universities that have done well both in teaching
and in research are those that have historically been better funded.

At a technical level, accounting separately for the use of teaching and
research funds requires greater sophistication in university and departmental planning, budgeting, and monitoring than had previously been
necessary. The most obvious challenge is how to allocate academic staff
(i.e., faculty) time between teaching and research; academic staff time
accounts for the majority of recurrent costs (typically around 70 to 80
percent). Academics have strongly resisted any form of time and effort
reporting. Increasingly, however, accounting for the use of academic staff
time will be critically important if university managers are to have sufficiently reliable information for planning and managing within their institutions. These management needs are quite separate from the growing
requirements of the Funding Councils for information about the use of
their allocated research funds.

Problems also arise in attempting to attribute support and infrastructure costs separately to teaching and to research (especially accommodation and equipment), although there are proxies that can be used as
approximations. However, the approach needed is much less contentious
than that needed for the allocation of academic staff time.

Whether stimulated by government requirements or not, the successful universities of the future are likely to be those which, for reasons of
good internal management, pay more attention to both the planning and
the monitoring and control of all aspects of their spending. The more
enlightened universities are already using government and Funding
Council requirements as a stimulus to their own management thinking.

Allocation of Public Funds for Teaching

As mentioned earlier, public funding of teaching occurs through two
principal vehicles:

- *Core funding*: resources that are granted in a block to each institution in the form of annual revenue funds.

- *Tuition fees*: which in the case of U.K. residents are also government funded and accompany students automatically once they enroll at a particular institution.

A key issue both for university managers who receive these two income streams and for the public funding agencies that are responsible for them is the effect of the combined funding methods on university behavior and on the nature, range, and quality of higher education that is offered within the universities.

The current funding arrangements are best described as a quasi-market. They represent a compromise between two extremes. At one end of the spectrum would be a model of the marketplace in which all funds would follow the students. For example, students could be given funds directly to purchase their higher education. At the other end of the spectrum would be a pure planning concept in which funding would be provided by government grant to individual universities. The government would thus be acting as the primary "purchaser" and would fix the prices and take as much or as little control of the contents, range, and quality of courses as it chose, depending on the nature of the "contract" it chose to have with each university.

The current methodology strikes a balance between these two extremes and offers a guaranteed block of funds to a university from government (now incorporating a contract to deliver a specified number of students) plus the fee income received for actual students. The assumed number of students for the block grant is determined by reference to a price bidding system in which universities with lower prices are "rewarded" with higher increases in the allocation of student numbers. These combined funds (block grant plus fees) are assumed to meet in aggregate the full costs of the provision made for the funded students. Thus the "price" offered by the Funding Council will represent the lowest "cost" of provision offered by universities. Each university is then usually free to take as many further students as it wishes on a fees-only basis until it exhausts its marginal capacity for expansion without requiring further baseline funding through the block grant.

In theory, the result is a balance of cost control for the government together with encouragement for universities to be entrepreneurial at the margins without expanding too rapidly or lowering the quality of their courses. Experience suggests that this funding approach has helped foster expansion while also driving down university costs. A vital policy issue is the relative balance between the funds provided by fees (as a proxy for a market) and those provided by the Funding Councils (on a planning basis). The proportionate cost of educating a student that the fee

■ 291 ■

element represents has been varied up and down by government to provide signals to universities to increase or reduce their recruitment.

However, there is an important ingredient missing in this approach: There is no agreed (or even explicitly discussed) "specification" of what it is that the universities will provide in exchange for the public funding they receive—beyond "educating" an agreed minimum numbers of students.

There are also specific issues concerned with which variables it is reasonable to take into account for the block grant part of the funds provided by the Funding Councils, although the Funding Council grant does not guide (or even suggest) how much universities should spend subject by subject. The main issues are:

- The extent to which the funding mechanism should accept that different academic disciplines traditionally incur different costs and should therefore be funded accordingly—and how detailed and sophisticated those differences in funding should be;

- Whether the differences in costs between universities for equivalent degree courses can continue to be viewed as historic differences over which universities have no control, or whether the Funding Councils now need more justification for above-average costs before agreeing to fund them;

- Whether there should be payment for results in the block grant (a model being developed for another sector of education rewards colleges at three stages in a student's career: on entry, on "programme," and on exit) and if so, whether the financial pressure to ensure a satisfactory outcome for each student might lead to a lowering of final assessment standards;

- How the funding system can best recognize the growing variety in modes of study so as not to disadvantage students wishing to study or universities planning to provide part-time courses or accelerated learning programs.

Private Income

As has already been noted, the private income of universities, in aggregate, is proportionately small compared with their income from public funds—with a few notable exceptions. However, the proportion of private revenue has been increasing gradually over recent years. Universities have devoted increasing attention to privately funded research and consultancy, to contract teaching, and to the provision of "full-cost" courses.

Seeking to increase the amount of private income has raised both technical and motivational issues which university managers have addressed in a variety of ways. On the technical side, it has become more important for universities to know the full costs of their activities and, in particular, to have reliable methods for the allocation of overhead costs to activities. Despite increasing attention to this area, there are still many universities providing full-cost courses and research at substantially less than the actual full cost. An unrealistic 40 percent overhead addition to direct staff costs remains a popular way of attempting to allow for overhead costs. Some use a more realistic figure of 100 percent, although this is almost certainly still well below the real full cost.

The twin tasks of persuading academic staff to participate in income-generating activities and then of controlling their activities have proven to be a significant challenge for many universities. For some universities, the challenge has been to stimulate any activity at all. Some academic staff consider that they are employed to teach and to undertake research in a publicly funded institution and that it is not their role to generate private income to compensate for what they see as inadequate public funding.

For other universities, the issue has been how to ensure that entrepreneurial work is not excessive and does not impinge on academic activities. Once legitimized, a further issue is how to ensure that the university receives its fair share of the income generated by the work undertaken on university time and using its resources and reputation. A variety of approaches have been used, including income-sharing schemes, university companies, and most significant nationally, the renegotiation of academic contracts for staff. Unless and until accounting for the use of academic staff time is standard, university managers will find it difficult to track, let alone to control, such activites.

As pressure on public funding continues, a new area of potential growth in private income is emerging—*top-up fees*—where students would be charged an additional fee over and above the set level of fee that government is prepared to pay. Thus a university might decide to charge top-up fees where it wished to establish or maintain a course that it felt unable to provide from the available public funds. Alternatively, such additional income could provide a means for expansion or other development that could not be supported from available public funds.

No U.K. university as a whole has yet imposed "top-up fees," although the matter has been debated publicly and one or two individual university departments have introduced them. The concept of charging extra fees cuts across a strong British tradition, but it seems likely that at some point in the future such fees will be introduced, although no doubt some universities will continue to resist introducing them on the grounds of social equity and access. Perhaps a more powerful restraint on the introduction of top-up fees will be the extent to which they would place a university in a less competitive position as far as student recruitment is concerned. However, the reputation of some universities in particular subject areas may enable them to charge top-up fees without damaging their recruitment chances.

If top-up fees do become prevalent, this may result in students from lower socioeconomic groups being inhibited from entering higher education. In turn, this may lead to a widening of the purpose and nature of the current system of student loans (so far covering only students' maintenance) and thus lessen the immediate financial effect on students of the liability for such fees, although students from lower socioeconomic groups are often reluctant to take on loans. Such a development would erode a key principle that has underpinned post–World War II U.K. higher education: It should be available to all those who are qualified and able to benefit from it. This has been one of the primary arguments against top-up fees.

Whatever method universities choose for increasing private income, there can be little doubt that they will need to concentrate more vigorously on identifying and optimizing sources of private income. There is ongoing political pressure to control public spending and little evidence that higher education would receive special attention even within a less constrained public spending regime. Private income may therefore become the key to maintaining the level and range of activities to which individual universities aspire.

For some universities there could be an additional, less tangible but perhaps equally powerful motivation to increase private income. Those most successful in doing so could ultimately change the nature of their relationship with government. In principle, at least, the greater the private income a university raises, the greater its freedom from future government influences.

Increasing reliance on private funding is not risk free. Private funding sources can dry up and markets can change. Universities will need to make clear-sighted decisions about the optimum balance between the public and private funding they want and are able to sustain. For some universities, this is likely to involve difficult choices about priorities. The universities that are addressing such decisions now are those most likely to be successful at the turn of the century. For some universities, this may mean abandoning aspirations to be significant in research. For others, it may mean identifying new teaching niches. For all, it will mean reviewing internal organization and management, particularly the management of resources, to provide maximum flexibility.

13.4 MANAGEMENT CHANGES

Pressure on universities to improve the management of their resources over the next decade is likely to continue. Many universities have already recognized this. Not as many have actively sought to address the issues and change their management practices. A national study in the mid-1980s, the Jarratt Review, provided guidelines on university management. Implementation of the study's recommendations has been very patchy, but the importance of good management has been thrust unexpectedly upon some universities. Although no university has yet gone bankrupt, several have had severe financial shocks. As the financial pressures increase, not least as a result of continuing calls for more output for less input, such shocks are likely to continue to occur.

Levers for Change

The Funding Councils ask each university routinely to provide a strategic plan. The councils have also completed national investigations about how universities can use resources more efficiently. One of the most radical of these investigations examined possible changes to the academic calendar, for example, staggering terms (or semesters) so that the physical resources of the university would be used throughout the year. This review also considered the possibility of more intensive attendance by students, which would open the way for two-year degrees.

Perhaps more significant than any specific initiative, the Funding Councils can bring about change in university behavior by adjusting their funding methodologies. Thus it would be possible, and not surprising, if through the Funding Councils, the government provided incentives and penalties to stimulate fundamental changes in areas such as modularization. (Modular courses typically provide students with a menu of modules—each lasting one term and followed by an exam—from which to choose, in contrast with the traditional integrated degree, which takes place over three years and has a largely prescribed curriculum.)

The government has also brought about management change directly (i.e., not through the Funding Councils). For example, the government encouraged the introduction of performance-related pay in universities by holding back an element of public funding contingent on the introduction of such pay schemes. Similarly, the government was keen to see the system of tenure abolished and eventually did so through an Act of Parliament, partly because universities were reluctant to make this change voluntarily. All new academic staff are now appointed on nontenured contracts, although most existing tenured staff remain as such until they leave or retire.

Financial Management

Universities have responded to the pressures for greater efficiency in a wide variety of ways. For many, the first reaction to the decrease of public funds was to make a series of cuts in funding across their entire range of activities; this was termed *equality of misery*. As the squeeze on public funding continued, many universities moved away from this approach. Either they had cut as much as they could, or more fundamentally, they decided to adopt less crude methods of planning.

A number of universities are adopting a more rigorous and thought-ful approach to planning and budgeting. This involves moving away from the historic approach, in which the costs of plans were not actively considered, and toward an approach in which decisions are made about the relative importance of different activities in light of overall objectives and of their relative costs. Operational plans are then drawn up through a planning and budgeting process. The old universities were encouraged to adopt this approach by the Jarratt Review, a key recommendation of which was to strengthen strategic and operational planning through an increase in the responsibilities of individuals and a reduction in the role and number of committees.

Although an approach using some form of activity based budgeting is still relatively rare in U.K. universities, the majority have developed financial monitoring and control arrangements. A decade ago, even the largest universities set budgets and then monitored and controlled expenditures almost entirely from the center. Many universities have now introduced a system of "devolved budgeting" in which faculties, or in some cases departments and research units, have been given devolved responsibility both for planning their own future with associated budgets and for financial monitoring and control. The center provides a reserve check. The principle, borne out in practice, is that those closest to the action are best able to make resource decisions and control their own expenditures.

On the whole, devolved budgeting and financial control have worked well. However, there have been some notable exceptions, where universities have failed to realize that flows of timely management information to the center are essential in a devolved system—and found out too late that their overall expenditures were out of control.

Increasing Individuals' Responsibilities

The moves toward more individual accountability have led some universities to review their management arrangements and their committee structures. For example, rather than electing deans of faculties and heads of departments (often on a three- or five-year basis), it is now more common for such posts to be appointed. Similarly, some universities are changing senior-level responsibilities to be more clearly executive. They are also questioning whether it is possible for the most senior academic managers to continue to undertake their management duties on a part-time basis, as has been the case to date in many universities.

Some universities have also streamlined their committee systems. Many still have a plethora of committees. Senior, costly staff are engaged in many hours of debate, sometimes not reaching a decision—or, in some cases, without even a clear purpose. In some universities, committees are regarded as a way of maintaining collegiality in decision making, and any attempt to reduce the number of committees is seen as a threat to this fundamental aspect of university life. In others, arguably the more enlightened, there is a growing recognition that good planning, combined with participative management styles and underpinned by clear systems of responsibility and accountability, can adequately maintain and enhance a sense of university community—while also being more efficient. But of course, to manage a university in this way requires capable and experienced managers and leaders, and an academic career is rarely a successful breeding ground for the skills required.

More Professional Administration

There has been a trend toward greater professionalism in nonacademic administration and management in universities. Senior management teams are now likely to include the finance director or planning manager (both of whom would typically not be academics). Many senior teams, particularly in the more management-oriented universities, also include a human resource director. Universities are also beginning to pay salaries to their senior administrative staff which are competitive with those of the outside market and have even attracted senior staff from outside education.

Universities are slowly introducing management approaches, which have thus far been more familiar in private companies than in universities. We mentioned devolved budgeting and activity-based management above. Other approaches include internal charging, for example, through the levying of accommodation charges to departments. There is also an increasing use of external contractors in place of internal university labor forces. Such items may include property maintenance, and cleaning and catering services. Some are also considering contracting out white-collar activities (e.g., in finance and personnel). This trend is likely to increase over the next few years.

Stimulated by government, there has also been a general move in the United Kingdom to "market test" public services. Many parts of government administration are now required by law to test how well they compare on quality and efficiency grounds with equivalent private-sector providers by putting the service out to competitive tender (but allowing an "in-house" bid). The legislation does not currently apply to universities, but the general philosophy could transfer and there may be expectations that it will do so.

13.5 TEACHING QUALITY AND STANDARDS

External Examiner System

Each university sets and marks its own exams, and some form of exam board then awards students their degree (and the level of achievement: first, second, or third class). In an attempt to secure some consistency between universities, each university appoints—from other universities—"external" examiners who usually scrutinize a sample of students' completed scripts and take part in some form of oral examination (e.g., for borderline cases). These external examiners then give their view on the standards achieved by the students, but by reference to the curriculum (and achievement levels) set by the university itself.

There has been considerable concern about the efficacy and even validity of the external examiner system for a number of years. Various attempts have been made to improve it, for example, through the development of codes of conduct aimed at ensuring the independence and rigor of the process. The fact that the system continues to be under review suggests that universities have not yet satisfied themselves (let alone outside observers) that the external examiner system is a sufficient check even on the comparative standards of degrees.

Funding Council Approach to Quality Assessment

The government has explicitly acknowledged the importance of having some form of "quality watch" in universities. The research assessment exercise described above is a major check on quality of research activities by the Funding Councils; it is undertaken through peer review. The Research Councils also use peer group assessment for each research grant application. For teaching, the government has required the Funding Councils to undertake assessments of quality and has empowered them to link funding for teaching to assessed quality. The process designed by the Funding Councils assesses (again through peer review) the quality of provision against the aims, objectives, and standards devised by the universities themselves. Thus the Funding Councils are able to measure the quality with which universities deliver what they set out to deliver.

Higher Education Quality Council: Quality Audit

The Funding Council quality assessment is not the only national mechanism for examining the quality of teaching. In the same legislation that required the Funding Councils to undertake quality assessment, the government also required the establishment of a separate Higher Education Quality Council (HEQC). This is effectively the universities' self-regulating body, in that it belongs to the Committee of Vice-Chancellors and Principals. It is chaired by a vice-chancellor, it is financed by university subscriptions, and its committees consist predominantly, although not exclusively, of academics from universities. Its main purpose is to audit quality control in each university. Periodically, the HEQC reviews the systems by which each university sets, monitors, and adjusts the quality of its courses. HEQC does not review the aims, objectives, or content of courses; it accepts those set by the university.

Both HEQC's quality audit check and the Funding Councils' quality assessment process create considerable work for the universities, many of which complain about the burden of visits and the paperwork required by having two separate approaches. Not surprisingly, there are calls that there should be just one organization involved in reviewing quality, but there is no consensus as to which it should be. There is a fundamental point at stake.

If the entire responsibility for quality were to pass to the Funding Councils, this would be viewed as an increase in government involvement. Some universities would see it as a fundamental threat to their jealously guarded autonomy, despite the fact that in the past, there was a national body (CNAA) that examined such matters for all the polytechnics and colleges.

If the entire responsibility for quality were to pass to the universities' own organization (HEQC), the government would want to assure itself that the universities could regulate themselves effectively. The reluctance of universities to provide any information on quality designed to help inform funding decisions is unlikely to reassure the government that universities could undertake the task of taking sole responsibility for overall quality.

Standards and Specifications

Recently, the following question has arisen in the United Kingdom: How does the purchaser, the government, or the customer (student or employer) know whether a degree from one institution is equivalent to that awarded by another institution? Neither of the two quality control processes is charged with providing a direct answer to this fundamental question. It is one thing to say that there is a need to set standards for a degree; it is much more difficult to produce specifications. What comprises a degree may be so difficult to define that the idea of seeking consensus on it may be an impossible task. It might be more practical to attempt to develop minimum specifications (i.e., threshold standards that all degrees must satisfy), although there will always be universities that exceed such minimums.

In any funding methodology, a "specification" of what it is that is being purchased for what price is normally a basic element of the purchaser/provider transaction. In the United Kingdom, government provides £3823.8M (U.S. $5735.70M) (1993–1994 figures) for the purchase of higher education annually. Yet it makes this purchase with little or no explicit specification of what it is intending to purchase nor of the cost it is prepared to pay. Of course, government does exercise high-level policy guidance which influences what universities provide, although usually only by reference to the current provision. For example, the government might request the universities to produce more science graduates or to give more emphasis to transferable skills. But at the level of the degree, there is relatively little attempt to search for a view about what it is that should be provided; indeed, it could be argued that the continuing government squeeze on price without any such specification indicates an absence of concern about specification.

To date, in accordance with the long-standing tradition of autonomous and self-regulating universities, there has been a broad national consensus about what comprises a degree, and thus about what should and can be provided by universities for the "prices" on offer through the Funding Councils. The universities themselves decide on the nature of the courses they will offer. They also decide what resources they will devote to deliver the curriculum they design. In principle, as long as this broad consensus continues and the universities prove themselves to be responsible and reliable self-regulators (i.e., producing results acceptable to the public funders), this consensus approach to specification is adequate and requires no intervention.

In practice, the continuation of a consensus arrangement appears unlikely, especially in light of continuing pressure to increase the numbers of students participating in higher education while lowering unit costs. In this climate there are increasing signs that specifications are, in fact, being changed by universities and that the national consensus about what comprises a degree may be breaking down, even if universities are not yet prepared to recognize this in public.

The recent past has seen a range of changes in specification. In efforts to reduce their unit costs, universities have, for example, reduced staff/student ratios, reduced tutorial and seminar opportunities, increased class sizes, reduced library opening hours, changed laboratory access, and franchised courses to institutions with lower costs. Some of these developments are appropriate new approaches to teaching and learning. Others are purely cost-cutting exercises that do affect the specification of the degree.

Some of these changes have undoubtedly resulted in increased efficiency with no qualitative change in the courses offered or in student results. But at some point the continuing downward pressures on price and thus costs are likely to reduce the specification itself. Some would argue that this has occurred already.

Implicitly at least, the government has recognized this danger and begun to address it via the quality mechanisms outlined above. However, it was noted that this assessment of quality is made against the individual university's own aims and objectives and against its own degree specifications.

Thus, although there is no nationally agreed minimum specification for degrees, it is likely that some of the universities with low costs would be close to one as a result of working to lower standards. Of course, this may also have been combined with higher efficiency. In an environment in which there is competition for core as well as for marginal funding, there is the further danger that the actions taken to lower costs by one university will put pressure on others to match the lower costs by reducing their specifications.

Such pressures may produce a downward spiral of costs and specifications, with the possible result that the Funding Councils will be inadvertently funding courses that do not produce the standard of output that the government expects. There is thus a strong theoretical argument that government, either through the Funding Councils or through some other agency, should, as the major purchaser of higher education, begin to specify, however broadly, what it expects the standard of a degree to be.

Such a development has already happened in the United Kingdom in school-level education (i.e., ages 5 to 16) for which there is now a National Curriculum specifying by law a minimum core of what should be taught in schools. In post-16 vocational education, there are also specifications in terms of defined National Vocational Qualifications, in which standards for different levels of vocational competence are set. It is only higher education that has no such specification (except in those areas in which professional bodies operate), merely the self-regulating consensus to which we referred earlier.

The first steps toward a specification may already be under way. The Higher Education Quality Council has recently been given the task of examining the comparability of U.K. degrees. It is not yet clear how it will do this. However, if HEQC as the "voice of the universities" is able to develop comparability measures and to start to develop threshold indicators and, most important, to get these accepted by the universities as a whole, this could be a major step toward some form of specification.

With specification in place, the government could be more certain that its funding was supporting degrees of an adequate standard. In turn, the universities could better make the link between specification and costs (and incidentally, improve their case for additional public funding). The customers of higher education, be they government, industry, or individual students could then have a reasonable measure of assurance that their "purchase" is a good one.

13.6 CONCLUSIONS

The last 10 years have seen major changes in U.K. higher education, mainly as a result of government policy. An overall consequence of those changes has been a requirement of greater accountability by universities for their use of public funds. This is not a situation with which many universities feel comfortable. However, as the sector is largely dependent on public funding, their ability to resist such developments is severely constrained.

The challenge for universities over the next 10 years, both individually and collectively, will be to ensure that they take the initiative in determining the shape and future direction of higher education. To be able to do this, universities will need to be able to demonstrate to government that they are capable of responding in the three key areas of:

- Effective management of, and accountability for, public resources

- Responsiveness to changing national economic needs and the needs of a changing student population

- Defining and maintaining standards and quality of the education that they provide

There are encouraging signs that the challenge is being taken up by universities. Much remains to be done and a successful outcome will depend on the ability and willingness of university managers to tackle this agenda.

CHAPTER FOURTEEN

Assessing Outcomes:
The SPRE Initiative

WILLIAM S. REED

Wellesley College

14.1 **Introduction**

14.2 **Regulatory Climate Behind the 1992 Reauthorization Act**

Decline in Public Trust

Default Rates in Federal Student Aid Programs

An Overwhelmed Department of Education

Disillusionment with the Accreditation Process

Legislative Response to Public Discontent

14.3 **Linkage Between Title IV Student Aid Programs and Governmental Control**

Grove City College Case

Civil Rights Restoration Act of 1987

14.4 **Triad of Federal Government, Accrediting Agencies, and State Entities**

HEA '92

National Policy Board

Accreditation Agencies' Role in Reviewing SPREs

State Postsecondary Review Entities

First Triggered Institutions

SPRE Standards Development Process

The Fourteen Standards

Massachusetts Standards Development Process

The Writing of Standard 14: Student Outcomes

Concerns of the Education Community

14.5 **Factors Behind the Pressure for Increased Documentation on Student Learning Outcomes**

Regulatory and Accreditation Pressures

Growth in Consumerism

Quality Movement in Management

Debate over Performance Measurement

14.6 **Predictions of the Long-Term Effect of HEA '92 on Higher Education**

Challenge to Maintain Institutional Independence Will Intensify

The Quality Movement Will Change the Way Institutions Are Managed and Evaluated

Governing Boards Will Devote
More Attention to
Monitoring Institutional
Performance

The SPRE Program Will Be
Transformed in Three Ways

Accreditation Reviews Will Be
More Substantive

Institutional Research Will
Grow in Importance

14.7 **Steps Institutions Can Take to
Meet the Challenges to
Their Independence**

Turn the Issue of Institutional
Accountability into an
Opportunity

Support the Role of
Independent Accrediting
Agencies

Be Vigilant

14.1   INTRODUCTION

The passage of the 1992 Reauthorization of the Higher Education Act
(HEA '92) sent shock waves through the higher education community. At
issue was the federal government's role in setting performance standards
for Title IV institutions, virtually every accredited school in the country
that participates in federal student aid programs.[1] Headlines in the *Boston
Globe* and the *Chronicle of Higher Education* read: "Colleges feel loss of
control under new law"[2] and "A threat to autonomy: critics say U.S.
accrediting rules would undermine college independence."[3]

Education leaders accused the Department of Education (DOE) of
going too far, of using the student aid program as a means of seizing
control over higher education and the accrediting process. The Department of Education said it was merely carrying out the congressional
mandate to eliminate fraud and abuse in student loan programs. The
simmering tension that has long characterized the relationship between
the DOE and the higher education community rose to a full boil. The level
of tension was high because the stakes were so high. Nannerl Overholser
Keohane, president of Duke University, wrote to Secretary of Education
Richard Riley, asserting that the proposed regulation "threatens the very
heart of what has made American higher education uniquely successful."[4]

In this chapter we discuss the fundamental issues raised by the 1992
Reauthorization of Higher Education Act and the implications for those

[1] Title IV programs include the Pell Grant Program, Perkins Loan Program, College
Work-Study Program, Supplemental Education Opportunity Grant Program,
Stafford Loan Program, and Supplemental Loans to Students Program.
[2] *The Boston Globe*, November 20, 1993.
[3] *The Chronicle of Higher Education*, December 1, 1993.
[4] From letter from Nannerl Keohane to Secretary of Education Richard Riley dated
October 25, 1993.

who control, set the standards, assess the quality, and are accountable for institutions of higher education in the United States.

14.2   REGULATORY CLIMATE BEHIND THE 1992 REAUTHORIZATION ACT

Decline in Public Trust

The fact that HEA '92 fundamentally changed oversight responsibility for the quality of higher education should not have come as a surprise. The stage was set by a decline in the public's confidence in higher education. In recent years, the media has regularly run stories about the shortcomings of higher education. Among the topics commonly covered were highly publicized reports about the misuse of federal student loans, boosts in tuition costs that seemed unreasonable, faculty who teach too little, intercollegiate athletic programs totally out of balance with the academic experience, graduates who are not well educated, elite institutions accused of cheating the government, and graduates who cannot get a meaningful job commensurate with their education. There was a growing public suspicion that the higher education industry was incapable of self-regulation. Colleges and universities seemed to have too much entitlement and too little public accountability.

Beleaguered college officials chafed at the negative slant given to the reporting. Where were the stories about the lives transformed, of the opportunity given to so many students through financial aid, of the rigors of the tenure process, of the difficulty of trying to maintain morale in a period of salary freezes and budget cuts, of the positive economic impact of colleges and universities on local economies, of teaching students who come ill-prepared for college-level work, and of the 350,000 foreign students who come to this country each year to study because the U.S. system is considered the best in the world?

The imbalance in reporting may help to explain the change in the public's attitude toward higher education, but the basic cause seems to be the anxiety that families face when considering how they can afford to send their children to college. At the same time, parents and guardians question whether the education their children will receive will be worth the financial sacrifice. The influence of a skeptical and resentful public is powerful. These concerns become part of the political agenda and legislative reforms often follow.

The issues of access, affordability, and accountability for quality that led to a restructuring of the health care industry are similar to the issues that now confront higher education. Whether higher education will have to undergo the drastic changes facing health care remains to be seen. Alan

Guskin, chancellor of the Antioch University System, succinctly summed up these issues:

> People are beginning to make comparisons between the economics of higher education and the health care system. And the comparisons are surprising: costs that rise relentlessly; the unwillingness of providers to deal directly with the core delivery system; governance structures that rest decision-making power about costs in the hands of professionals whose personal interests are compromised by reducing costs; belief systems that increase in quality always require increase in expenditures; and a decentralized system that is heavily underwritten by federal dollars, but that allows federal policy makers little direct capability to reduce costs. These are not small issues. The frustrations, even anger, may produce new expression in a host of recent federal and state "accountability" initiatives—SPREs, report cards, faculty workload legislation—or questioning the public value delivered by higher education.[5]

Default Rates in Federal Student Aid Programs

Congressional concern and the public outcry over the rate of student defaults on student loan programs are understandable. Significant sums of money are involved. In the last five years the Department of Education issued $13.8 billion a year in loans and lost $2.7 billion annually to defaults. Robert Atwell, president of the American Council on Education, called the student default rate "an intolerable embarrassment."[6]

Default rates vary significantly among types of postsecondary institutions. In 1991, the most recent year figures were published, Department of Education records show average default rates ranging from 5.7 percent for private four-year colleges to 35.9 percent for trade schools (Exhibit 14–1).

The *New York Times* began a three-part series with the headline "Billions for schools are lost in fraud, waste, and abuse."[7] Reporter Michael Winerip wrote: "For several years, the federal government has been losing $3 billion to $4 billion annually to waste, fraud, and loan defaults in its higher education student aid programs. That is more than 10% of the Education Department's annual budget of $29 billion—enough to finance the nation's entire Headstart Program."[8]

---

[5] Alan Guskin, "Reducing student cost and enhancing student learning," *Change*, July–August 1994.
[6] The *New York Times*, February 2, 1994.
[7] Ibid.
[8] Ibid.

Exhibit 14–1
DEFAULT RATES FOR POSTSECONDARY INSTITUTIONS

Type	Total Institutions	Borrowers Defaulted	Default Rate (%)
Public 4-year college	645	44,220	8.5
Public 2-year college	1,431	31,391	14.7
Private 4-year college	1,510	31,447	5.7
Private 2-year college	850	7,904	15.5
Trade schools	3,756	287,999	35.9
Foreign	456	188	4.5
Unclassified[a]	31	632	20.2
Total	8,719	403,781	17.5

[a] Schools that do not have a "type of institution" designation and no longer participate in the student loan program
Source: U.S. Department of Education as reported in The New York Times, August 10, 1994.

An Overwhelmed Department of Education

Overseeing federal student aid programs is a monumental task. It requires a large and highly trained staff, a sophisticated computer system, and resources to adapt to changing program requirements and new regulations. Historically, the Department of Education has had none of these elements in place. In the second part of his The New York Times student aid series, Winerip wrote of the Department of Education:

> . . . During the Reagan and Bush administrations it was hit harder than any other Cabinet-level department, losing 33 percent of its work force.
>
> A 1993 General Accounting Office audit of the department reads like a social worker's report on an abandoned child, or in this case, an abandoned department. It is an "impaired" department, says the G.A.O. report, that "suffers from management neglect," "negative self-image," and has become "a dumping ground for staff and equipment that other agencies did not want.[9]

Responding to congressional concern over the department's ineffectiveness in dealing with fraud and abuse, the beleaguered Department of Education staff seized the opportunity provided by HEA '92 to improve its image and standing. The writing of aggressive and expansive implementation regulations soon followed.

[9] Michael Winerip, The New York Times, February 3, 1994.

Disillusionment with the Accreditation Process

The accreditation process is founded on a voluntary, peer review system designed to assure the quality and integrity of higher education institutions. It has been in existence for over a century. There are six regional associations which comprise nine accrediting commissions. In addition to the regional associations, which accredit institutions of higher education, there are several national accrediting bodies that accredit proprietary schools and Bible colleges. There are also a variety of specialized or professional accrediting agencies that accredit individual programs of study. The accrediting associations generally follow similar review practices, but specific policies and standards may differ from one region to another. The absence of national standards and the fact that few, if any, institutions have lost their accreditation through this voluntary, peer review system led the Department of Education and other federal policymakers to question the efficacy of the system. They concluded that the current accreditation process was neither effective in assuring educational quality nor in protecting the taxpayer from fraudulent use of federal student aid.

Legislative Response to Public Discontent

The decline in the public's trust of higher education, the growing default rates in student loans, the Department of Education's management failures, and the disillusionment with the accreditation process all contributed to the 1992 Reauthorization Act that was designed to eliminate fraud and abuse in federal student aid programs. The Department of Education, seeing an opportunity to increase its oversight of institutions, expanded the intent of the act to give itself, along with the states, a generic oversight of all higher education institutions.

The DOE's aggressive interpretation of the language in the 1992 Reauthorization Act providing federal and state authorities with broad oversight responsibilities of all higher education represented a direct challenge to institutional independence. In an unusual display of bipartisan unity, six U.S. senators (Senators Edward M. Kennedy, Nancy Landon Kassebaum, James M. Jeffords, Claiborne Pell, Harris Wofford, and Christopher J. Dodd) from the Committee on Labor and Human Resources wrote to the Secretary of the Department of Education, warning that the department's proposed Statement of Purpose to the Postsecondary Review Entity (SPRE) was too expansive. "[W]e want to assure that the SPRE regulations place emphasis on the need for a concerted attack on fraud and abuse, rather than on generic oversight of all institutions."[10] The DOE yielded to the pressure from the senators and from

[10] Letter from members of Committee on Labor and Human Resources, March 25, 1994.

higher education associations. The final regulations narrowed the purpose of SPREs to the reduction of fraud and abuse in Title IV programs. Nonetheless, the 1992 act and the implementing regulations significantly increased federal and state influence and power over educational institutions.

14.3 LINKAGE BETWEEN TITLE IV STUDENT AID PROGRAMS AND GOVERNMENTAL CONTROL

The struggle to maintain institutional independence has a long history. Colleges and universities have long been leery of the degree of governmental control that comes with government funding. In 1975, Kingman Brewster, then president of Yale University, warned of the dangers of the loss of institutional independence through the strings attached to federal funding.

> My fear is that there is a growing tendency for the central government to use the spending power to prescribe educational policies. Use of the leverage of the government dollar to accomplish objectives which have nothing to do with the purposes for which the dollar is given has become dangerously fashionable. Institutional diversity, autonomous trusteeship, and faculty self-determination are the essence of the envied vitality of American higher education and its responsiveness to new fields of knowledge. These strengths would be lost if, as a condition of receiving a federal dollar for some purposes, it were to be subject to federal regulations for all purposes.[11]

When William J. Bennett was Secretary of Education during the Reagan administration, he recognized the linkage between Title IV funding and the government's ability to influence college policies. He knew that most institutions are heavily tuition dependent and could not survive without the federal student aid programs. In a speech delivered at Catholic University in Washington, D.C. on November 19, 1986, Bennett was quoted by the *New York Times*:

> Secretary of Education, William J. Bennett, said today that "skyrocketing" costs for higher education would make fundamental reform of the Federal student aid program essential.
>
> Colleges can permit costs to rise, he said, because they feel assured that "where students cannot meet their costs, the Federal Government will help out."

[11] Kingman Brewster, *1974–75 Report of the President*, Yale University, New Haven, Conn.

"Some of our colleges and universities charge what the market will bear," he said. "And lately they have found that it will bear quite a lot indeed. The heart of the matter is that colleges raise costs because they can. And a very important factor in that ability to raise costs has been the availability of Federal student aid in the current form."

"More loan money does not make it easier for families to meet college costs," he said. "Rather, in the end, more loan money makes it easier for colleges to raise college costs."[12]

Responses from members of the higher education community came swiftly. They challenged Bennett's linkage of federally subsidized student aid programs and college cost, arguing that such an analysis was simplistic.

Secretary Bennett was responding, in part, to the public's growing concern about the affordability of higher education. In so doing, he took a shot across the bow of higher education, warning that if colleges did not control their costs, the federal government could exercise a heavy influence through Title IV regulations. Since Secretary Bennett's 1986 speech, the growth in volume of regulations associated with the administration of the student aid programs has been staggering. These regulations have raised important questions about the scope of federal regulatory powers on the management and independence of educational institutions.

Grove City College Case

The struggle to maintain institutional independence while participating in Title IV programs was an issue so important to Grove City College that in 1984 it fought the federal government all the way to the U.S. Supreme Court. The basic question in that case was whether a single student's receipt of federal student aid subjected the institution to federal regulation. Grove City students received Pell Grants directly from the government through the alternate dispersal system. Because the students used their Pell Grants to pay their tuition, HEW (U.S. Department of Health, Education, and Welfare, predecessor to DOE) argued "that if an institution benefits from any program that receives federal financial assistance, then the entire institution and all its programs and activities are subject to regulation."[13] Grove City College argued that it should not have to sign Title IX's Assurance of Compliance (even though it was in compliance) solely because some of its students received federal student aid grants. The Supreme Court ruled that the receipt of federal aid funds did not subject the entire college to all federal regulations but, rather, only the department that received the funds, in this case the financial aid office.

[12] Leslie Maitland Werner, The *New York Times*, November 20, 1986, p. B13.
[13] Plaintiff's brief: Nixon, Hargrave, Devares, and Doyle.

Civil Rights Restoration Act of 1987

Limiting the applicability of federal regulations to the programs that actually receive the federal funds was shortlived. In 1987, language was inserted into the Civil Rights Restoration Act that restored the principle that the receipt of student federal aid funds subjected the entire institution to all federal regulations. "Certain aspects of recent decisions and opinions of the Supreme Court have unduly narrowed or cast doubt upon the broad application of Title IX of the Education Amendments of 1972. . . . Legislative action is necessary to restore the prior consistent and long-standing executive branch interpretation and broad, institution-wide application of those laws as previously administered."[14]

14.4 TRIAD OF FEDERAL GOVERNMENT, ACCREDITING AGENCIES, AND STATE ENTITIES

The responsibility for monitoring the quality of higher education was established in the Higher Education Act of 1965. Congress designated a triad of agencies—the federal government, state educational agencies, and accrediting bodies—the interlocking responsibility for monitoring higher education quality. This triumvirate was, at best, loosely coordinated. Students could use federal funds only if the institution where they were enrolled met the standards established by an accrediting agency recognized by the Secretary of Education and was licensed by the state. The accreditation process became the gatekeeper for institutional access to federal funds. The Department of Education took a laissez-faire approach to determining and monitoring the schools that participated in the federal student aid programs, relying on the independent accreditation process.[15]

HEA '92

Congress redirected the focus of the triad in Part H (Program Integrity Triad) of Title IV of the Higher Education Amendments of 1992 (HEA '92). These amendments specifically defined the responsibility of each part of the triad and, for the first time, put all federal provisions related to the triad into the higher education act. The HEA '92 significantly altered the balance among the triad, limiting the independence of accreditation agencies and increasing the role of the states through the creation of state postsecondary review entities (SPREs). The Secretary of Education assumed overall responsibility for coordinating the gatekeeping roles of the triad.

---

[14] Civil Rights Restoration Act of 1987, Section 20 U.S.C.A., 1688.
[15] Joseph Malik and John Peterson, "Higher Education Act Reauthorization," *AACC Journal*, August–September 1993.

Exhibit 14–2
THE TWELVE STANDARDS REQUIRED BY AN ACCREDITING AGENCY

1. Curricula
2. Faculty
3. Facilities, equipment, and supplies
4. Fiscal and administrative capacity
5. Student support services
6. Recruitment and admissions practices, academic calendars, catalogs, publications, grading, and advertising
7. Program length and tuition and fees in relation to the subject matters taught and the objectives of the degrees offered
8. Measures of program length in clock hours or credential hours
9. Success with respect to student achievement, including, as appropriate, consideration of course completion, state licensing examination, and job placement rates
10. Default rates in the federal student loan programs
11. Record of student complaints received by or available to the agency
12. Compliance with responsibilities under federal student aid programs

Source: Joseph Malik and John Peterson, "Higher Education Act Reauthorization," *AAAC Journal,* August–September 1993.

The HEA '92 had a profound effect on the autonomy of independent accreditation agencies. No longer would they have broad discretionary authority to assess institutional quality. To be recognized by the Secretary of Education, an accrediting agency was required to have 12 standards (Exhibit 14–2).

National Policy Board

Responding to what they regarded as federal intrusion into the accreditation process, the accreditation agencies along with the major higher education associations formed a temporary National Policy Board (NPB) on higher education institutional accreditation. The NPB, which replaced the defunct Council on Postsecondary Accreditation (COPA), sought to win back the public's and the federal policymakers' confidence. The NPB acknowledged the need for basic reform of the higher education accreditation process. Robert Atwell, who served as co-chair of the NPB, said: "[R]eform is needed to let the public know that we are serious about guaranteeing the integrity of our colleges and universities and striving for improvement in the education of students, and for assuring elected officials that taxpayer dollars are being spent wisely and effectively."[16]

[16] Press release, National Policy Board on Higher Education Institutional Accreditation, January 28, 1994.

The improvements the NPB proposed were to create a permanent national organization to oversee higher education accreditation. The organization would establish core standards that would be used by all accrediting associations and would serve as a recognition body for both regional and specialized agencies. The organization would recognize and evaluate accrediting associations, establish common standards of good practice, and undertake research and public relations efforts at the national level focused on improving the accreditation process.[17]

Accreditation Agencies' Role in Reviewing SPREs

Missing from this list of "characteristics" was oversight of the institutions' adherence to federal laws and regulations. An important issue for accreditation agencies has been how to maintain independence if they are used to monitor compliance to federal student loan regulations. The NPB's position was that the accreditation process should focus on educational quality rather than on compliance with federal laws and regulations. On this issue the NPB's January 28, 1994, statement said: "The responsibility for assuring adherence to federal law and regulations belongs to the federal government, not to accrediting agencies. The central purpose of accreditation is to guarantee the quality and integrity of higher education institutions. It is a fundamental error to assign responsibility for overseeing institutional management of federal student aid funds to accrediting agencies. The Higher Education Amendments of 1992 destroyed the essential balance of the triad."[18]

Whether accreditation agencies can maintain their independence while possibly serving as an agent of the state postsecondary review entities is an important issue for higher education. It is far from being resolved.

State Postsecondary Review Entities

The HEA '92 refocusing of the triad greatly expanded the oversight and monitoring role of the states. Each state was required to establish a state postsecondary review entity (SPRE) which would be responsible for setting standards for all Title IV institutions in the state. The standards would provide the basis for reviewing institutions referred to the SPRE by the U.S. Secretary of Education. A referred institution would be required to demonstrate that it satisfied the standards developed by the SPRE. Failure to meet the standards could mean termination from participation in Title IV programs. All Title IV institutions were required to be prepared, after a

[17] Ibid.
[18] Ibid.

Exhibit 14–3
TRIGGERS FOR A SPRE REVIEW

The HEA '92 delineated 11 conditions that could serve as "triggers" for the Department of Education to refer an institution to a SPRE for review.

1. A default rate of 25 percent or higher
2. A default rate of 20 percent or more and either more than two-thirds of students receiving federal student aid or two-thirds or more of education and general expenditures come from federal student aid funds
3. Two-thirds or more of a school's education and general expenditures come from federal student aid funds
4. A limitation/suspension or termination action by the Department of Education against the institution during the last five years
5. A negative audit finding resulting in repayment of more than 5 percent of federal student aid funds
6. A failure to submit audits to the Department of Education in a timely fashion
7. A significant year-to-year fluctuation in federal student aid funds
8. Failure to meet standards of financial responsibility.
9. A change of ownership resulting in a change of control
10. For private institutions only, being in federal student aid less than five years
11. A pattern of student complaints related to the management or conduct of federal student aid programs, or relating to misleading or inappropriate advertising

Source: Title IV, Part H, Subpart 1 of the Higher Education Act of 1965, as amended.

reasonable period, to meet the review standards if "triggered" for a SPRE review (Exhibit 14–3).

First Triggered Institutions

On August 1, 1994, the Department of Education sent overnight letters informing more than 2000 institutions that they had been triggered for a SPRE review. In this initial wave, only five of the 11 criteria were used. The most bureaucratic of the triggers, failure to submit audits in a timely fashion, was the most common reason cited. The higher education associations and the triggered institutions were shocked at the DOE's action, for a number of reasons. Many of the institutions had submitted the audits as required, but the DOE had lost or misfiled them. Institutions were given only 7 days to file an "intent to challenge" and 30 days to submit documentation during a time of year when many administrators were on vacation. In addition, none of the states had approved SPRE standards, nor was a review process in place. This shaky beginning of the implementation of the HEA '92 did nothing to enhance the reputation of the Department of Education in the eyes of the higher education community and only served to raise the apprehension of academe about DOE's motives.

The *New York Times* carried a story on August 9, 1994 which described the confusion over the triggering letters.

> [T]he Department of Education warned 2,000 colleges and universities last week that if they do not get their records in order, their finances since 1988 would be reviewed and their Federal financing would be in jeopardy. But there are problems: the review boards are not in place, the Government's list of possible transgressions is vague, and in many cases administrators were not on campus to receive the warning letters anyway. "It's just a real mess," said an official in the Education Department.[19]

The outrage from the higher education community was predictable because a SPRE review is so costly in terms of data collection and time and it also puts an institution in limbo until it knows whether it will continue to be eligible to receive federal funds. The first wave seemed designed more to establish the authority of the DOE over institutions than to address the issue of fraud and abuse of federal student aid programs.

SPRE Standards Development Process

One of the most significant features of the HEA '92 was the state's responsibility to identify a state entity that would oversee the establishment of a state SPRE. Each SPRE was responsible for developing, in consultation with the postsecondary institutions in the state, the SPRE standards. The SPREs' discretion to develop standards specific to the characteristics of the postsecondary institutions in the state was highly proscribed. The statutory language of HEA '92 specified 14 areas that the SPRE standards had to address. Specific definitions of each standard was left to the states' SPREs but the standards could not require less than current laws and federal regulations mandated. Once written and approved by the state entity, the standards were reviewed by the Department of Education. Technically, the Secretary of Education does not have the authority to approve the standards; rather, the secretary was given the authority to disapprove[20] the standards.

The Fourteen Standards

The 14 standards cover a wide range of activities and areas.[21] They can be broken down into the following broad categories: consumer information,

---

[19] Catherine Manegold, The *New York Times*, August 9, 1994.
[20] The Reauthorization of the Higher Education Act of 1992, Sec. 494c.(d) Review Standards.
[21] Title IV, Part H, Subpart 1 of the Higher Education Act of 1965, as amended.

compliance with safety and health standards, financial and administrative capacity, and the assessment of student outcomes.[22]

The process for developing specific definitions for each of the 14 standards differed from one state to another. The only requirements that the states had to follow were that the standards be developed with broad

---

[22] From the Higher Education Act of 1965, as amended:

   (i) Consumer information.
    (Standards 1,8,12)

     1. The accuracy and availability of catalogs, admissions requirements, course outlines, schedules of tuition and fees, policies regarding course cancellations, and the rules and regulations relating to students.

     8. Availability to students of relevant information, including (a) information relating to market and job availability for students in occupational, professional or vocational programs; and (b) information regarding the relationship of courses to specific standards necessary for state licensure in specific occupations.

    12. The appropriateness of advertising and student recruitment practices.

   (ii) Compliance with safety and health standards.
    (Standard 4)

     4. Compliance by the institution with relevant safety and health standards, such as fire, building and sanitation codes.

   (iii) Financial and administrative capacity.
    (Standards 3, 5, 6, 10, 11, and 13)

     3. Assurance that the institution maintains and enforces standards relating to academic progress and maintains adequate student and other records.

     5. The financial and administrative capacity of the institution and the maintenance of adequate information necessary to determine the financial and administrative capacity of the institution.

     6. For financially at-risk institutions, adequate provisions for the instruction of students and the retention and accessibility of academic and financial records in the event the school closes.

    10. The actions of any owner, shareholder, or person exercising control over the educational institution that may affect eligibility for federal student aid.

    11. The procedures for investigating and resolving student complaints.

    13. A fair and equitable refund policy.

   (iv) The Assessment of student outcomes.
    (Standards 2, 7, 9, 14)

     2. Assurance that the institution can assess a student's ability to successfully complete the course of study for which she/he has applied.

     7. "If the stated objectives . . . are to prepare students for employ-

consultation with the educational community and that they be consistent with current Title IV regulations. The Massachusetts process was typical of many states and provides an insight into the difficulty of developing state standards for a mix of schools that range from Harvard University to barber schools.

Massachusetts Standards Development Process

The governor of Massachusetts appointed the Higher Education Coordinating Committee (HECC) to serve as the state SPRE. The chancellor of higher education appointed a 15-member advisory group, representing the major public, private, and proprietary institutions. The advisory group was comprised of presidents, financial officers, academic deans, financial aid officers, and owners of proprietary schools. Although the advisory group represented a diverse group of Massachusetts institutions, the members shared a concern that the use of SPRE standards as a means of eliminating fraud and abuse in federal programs had the potential to do more harm than good.

The charge to the advisory group was to write the state's standards for the HECC to review and approve. Throughout the process, there was to be regular reporting to the various Title IV constituencies. In addition, there were public hearings held throughout the state to provide direct input to the advisory committee.

The advisory group wanted its standards to consider both the needs of students and the current administrative burdens on educational institutions. The advisory group realized that it could not write the SPRE stan-

22 (continued)   ment," the relationship of the tuition and fees to the remuneration that can "reasonably be expected by students who complete the course or program," and the relation of the courses or programs to providing the student with quality training and useful employment in recognized occupations.

    9. The appropriateness of the number of credit or clock hours required for the completion of programs.

  14. The success of the "program at the institution", including:

     a. graduation or completion rates, taking into account the length of the program and the selectivity of the institution;

     b. withdrawal rates;

     c. with respect to vocational and professional programs, the rates of placement of the institution's graduates in occupations related to their course of study;

     d. where appropriate, the rates at which the institution's graduates pass licensure examinations; and

     e. other student completion goals, including transfer to another institution of higher education, full-time employment, and military service.

dards without first agreeing on a set of principles on which the standards would be formulated.

A particular challenge faced by the advisory group involved the issue of how specific the standards should be. Great specificity would require less judgment and evaluation by the SPRE reviewer. Standards that describe desired outcomes without specifying how the outcomes should be achieved permit more institutional discretion but at the same time require greater judgment and analysis by the reviewer. In the end, the advisory group opted for broad standards to accommodate the diversity of missions and educational programs that characterize the Massachusetts higher education system. It was the advisory group's belief that the SPRE standards should be designed to *inform the SPRE reviewer* rather than provide a simple checklist that would determine the outcome of the review. With this basic understanding, the advisory group crafted the principles that would underlie the standards (Exhibit 14–4).

The advisory group also developed a set of questions that were used to guide the development of each standard.

1. What is the intent of this standard?

2. Are existing standards or regulations already in existence that address the standard?

Exhibit 14–4
PROPOSED PRINCIPLES UNDERLYING MASSACHUSETTS SPRE STANDARDS

1. Any standard must directly inform the review process to determine if an institution is in compliance.
2. Standards should be developed as "baseline" thresholds which provide for different methods of demonstrating compliance with the standard.
3. Standards should be developed from the perspective of both the students and the institution.
4. Standards should be as clear and simple as possible. They should be expressed in terminology already clearly defined in federal and state statutes and regulations.
5. Standards should minimize additional data collection efforts to control administrative costs. Whenever possible, data requirements should rely on information already collected.
6. Where comparable Title IV or other regulations are sufficient to establish a "baseline" for a given standard, the regulation(s) may be applied as the SPRE standard.
7. Any variation in individual standards should be dictated by the differences in mission for the various types or categories of Title IV institutions.
8. When viewed as a whole, the standards should be consistent and complementary.

Source: Proposed Massachusetts State Review Standards Questionnaire, July 1, 1994.

3. What are the data implications of the standard?

4. What are the criteria for compliance?

5. What documentation will be necessary to establish compliance?[23]

Working with an educational consultant, a comprehensive list of all the laws, regulations, accreditation standards, and licensing requirements were compiled for each of the 14 standards. This was a monumental undertaking because eight different entities[24] had rules and regulations for each standard.

As one might expect, the advisory group had less difficulty establishing standards in the areas of consumer information, health and safety, and administration and finance than it did with those requiring the assessment of student outcomes. Attempting to assess student outcomes was breaking new ground. It was extremely difficult to write one standard that would be appropriate for each institution in Massachusetts. The other standards were easier to quantify, and most of the appropriate data were routinely kept by all of the institutions. There were, to be sure, exacting discussions on definitions and the different record-keeping and reporting requirements among the public, private, and proprietary institutions, but in the final analysis, there was enough in common to write standards that applied to all.

The Writing of Standard 14:[25] Student Outcomes

Standard 14 required the establishment of quantitative thresholds for student completion, withdrawal, placement, and licensure-pass rates. On the surface, the establishment of thresholds appeared to be straightforward. In reality, it was extremely complex. Completion rates are highly

---

[23] Proposed Massachusetts State Review Standards Questionnaire, July 1, 1994.
[24] Title IV Regulations of HEA Provisions, Higher Education Coordinating Council, Massachusetts Department of Education; American Student Assistance, New England Association of Schools and Colleges, Accrediting Commission of Career Schools and Colleges of Technology, The Accrediting Council for Independent Colleges and Schools, and National Accrediting Commission of Cosmetology Arts and Sciences.
[25] From the Higher Education Act of 1965, as amended, Standard 14 is:
   14. The success of the "program at the institution," including:
      a. graduation or completion rates, taking into account the length of the program and the selectivity of the institution;
      b. withdrawal rates;
      c. with respect to vocational and professional programs, the rates of placement of the institution's graduates in occupations related to their course of study;

dependent on the level and type of program, the ratio of full-time to part-time students, definition of what constitutes an educational program, the mission and location of the institution, and the condition of the national economy. For example, a highly selective liberal arts college should be expected to have a graduation rate of 80 percent or greater. A community college might well be proud of a graduation rate of 40 percent. To complicate matters even more, some institutions, particularly technical colleges, offer a variety of degree and certificate programs, such as baccalaureate and associate degrees, postsecondary credit hour diplomas and certificates, and postsecondary clock hour diplomas and certificates. The law requires that the institution report *one* completion rate.

How do you calculate *one* rate for a multi-degree-granting institution? Should the institution be required to calculate completion rates according to the award or degree level but then report one overall rate of completion? Or should an institution's calculations be limited to its predominant degree level?

The Massachusetts advisory group decided to rely on the "cohort method" for calculating completion rates as outlined in the Student Right-to-Know section of HEA.[26] Under this methodology, a cohort of full-time, undergraduate degree- or certificate-seeking students who are entering postsecondary education for the first time is established. A student is considered to have completed a program if he or she completes the program within 150 percent of the normal time frame for that program. Because time frames vary by program length, an institution must track students by program to calculate the institutional rate. Each year the data from each of the institution's programs are combined to produce an overall rate of completion. It was this single institutional rate that was to be used for the student completion standard.

Because there were no reliable data on completion rates for Massachusetts, the advisory group had to choose a threshold based on a test of reasonableness that would not be "disapproved" by the U.S. Department of Education. If the threshold was set too low, it would not be considered a standard. It had to be high enough to be seen as a true standard by the public while recognizing that certain institutions, because of their particular mission, might have low completion rates yet meet an important societal need. A completion rate of 50 percent was chosen with the full understanding that many community colleges could not meet that threshold. To protect them from an unattainable standard, two other

[25 (continued)] d. where appropriate, the rates at which the institution's graduates pass licensure examinations; and

e. other student completion goals, including transfer to another institution of higher education, full-time employment, and military service.

[26] CFR Part 568, Student Assistance General Provision, July 10, 1992.

provisions were included to provide them an opportunity to account for the reasons they failed to meet the threshold.

Concerns of the Education Community

The question that must be asked was whether Standard 14 on assessing student outcomes accomplishes anything. It may identify the most egregious offenders and that would be good. But there are less cumbersome ways to accomplish that goal. The formulation of Standard 14 illustrates how difficult it is to develop meaningful outcome-based standards applicable to a variety of institutions. Institutions should know their completion rates. They should know how their graduates do on standardized examinations for admission to professional and graduate schools and on license examinations, and they should know why their students withdraw. It is simply a matter of good management. It is hard to comprehend how a serious educational institution could assess its effectiveness without having answered these basic questions. It is one thing for an institution to establish outcome-based standards to improve its effectiveness and quite another to establish overarching SPRE standards for the purpose of eliminating fraud and abuse.

The problem with the SPRE standards is not that they ask the wrong questions or measure the wrong outcomes. Surely the federal government has the fiduciary responsibility to protect public funds from fraud and abuse. The use of outcome-based standards as a means to eliminate fraud and abuse has a certain logic. If an institution deceives the public, it should be identified. It is both in the public's and higher education's interests to deny such institutions access to public funds. The problem is that the SPRE standards must be broadly based to encompass the wide range of institutions covered under Title IV. They become susceptible to politicization and expansion, with new federal templates requiring tighter standards and more assessing procedures.

The SPRE process has the potential to escalate from measuring basic student achievement outcomes to specifying how curricula should be structured, the number of hours deemed necessary to teach specific courses, and the appropriate pedagogical methods for presenting course material. The laudable goal of eliminating fraud and abuse may have the unintended consequence of eliminating institutional autonomy and with it much of the creativity and experimentation that has characterized the American higher education system.

The SPRE Review Process.   Educational institutions were apprehensive, not only about the standards, but about the state review process itself. An overzealous reviewer could wreak havoc on an institution. Many specific, thoughtful, and realistic concerns were expressed.

Would the state use accrediting bodies to conduct an institution's review, or would another outside agency perform the review? In the former case, couldn't there be a conflict between the accreditation evaluation and a subsequent review process? Would faculty and administrators be expected, and willing, to donate their time to conduct a review using standards developed by the state for the purpose of eliminating fraud?

How would priorities be established for reviewing triggered institutions? Once triggered, how long would an institution have to wait before it was reviewed? Would it have adequate time to collect the germane data?

A state's standards are not necessarily all of equal weight or importance. Some are quite specific, requiring quantitative measurements of student outcomes, for example, while others are relatively straightforward, requiring only the maintenance of good record-keeping practices. Would (and could) an individual reviewer be circumspect in imposing the various standards?

Is there a particular number or set of standards an institution must meet to be considered in compliance? Could the failure to meet any one standard put an institution's financial aid program in jeopardy? Could an institution be summarily closed down?

Would there be a middle ground between being found in full compliance, with no further action required, and being determined ineligible for Title IV funds? If the latter were the case, by what process or means would an institution get out of its probationary status?

Might there be an appreciable deviation among the 50 individual state standards and review procedures? Would institutions with similar missions, but scattered throughout the entire country, be treated in an equal or consistent manner from one state to another, or would some states be considered tough and others easy?

The imposition of a state bureaucracy that would have such considerable control over public and private institutions was not an easy concept for higher education to accept philosophically and certainly was not going to be easy to embrace in practice.

14.5 FACTORS BEHIND THE PRESSURE FOR INCREASED DOCUMENTATION ON STUDENT LEARNING OUTCOMES

The public pressure for more accountability, measurement, and control of higher education has served to advance an important and public debate within the academy on how to define and measure institutional effectiveness and quality. Three external forces—regulatory and accreditation pressures, growth in consumerism, and the quality movement in management—have joined to make institutional assessment an important and compelling new agenda topic for higher education.

14.5 FACTORS BEHIND PRESSURE FOR DOCUMENTATION

Regulatory and Accreditation Pressures

Federal policymakers, responding to the public's pressure for greater institutional accountability, have made the assessment of outcomes an important feature of new federal regulations. As discussed earlier, the passage of HEA '92 realigned the responsibilities within the triad (federal and state governments and independent accreditation agencies) for assuring the quality of higher education. The Department of Education established standards that accreditation agencies must meet to be recognized by the secretary. These standards include qualitative and quantitative assessments of institutional quality and effectiveness. In addition, the DOE's template for the development of SPRE standards requires colleges to be able to assess a variety of student outcomes.

The accreditation agencies have placed renewed emphasis on an institution's responsibility to develop ways to assess its effectiveness. The New England Association of Schools and Colleges (NESC), the accreditation agency for New England, revised its *Standards for Accreditation* emphasizing:

> the importance of affiliated colleges and universities assessing their effectiveness as an improvement mechanism, but also to assure that institutions are able, to the extent possible, to demonstrate the accomplishment of their stated purposes. This is not a departure from the past, but an affirmation and elaboration of the long-held perspective in regional accreditation that an indicator of quality is an institution's capacity to assess its effectiveness and use the results for improvement. In addition, this emphasis reflects the increasing demand for greater accountability.[27]

In its policy statement on institutional effectiveness the NESC stated that "an institution's efforts and ability to assess its effectiveness and use the obtained information for its improvement are important indicators of institutional quality. The NESC, through its evaluative processes, will appraise these quality indicators. Just as assessment is now a pervasive theme throughout the revised standards, so too should it be a theme in all comprehensive self-studies."[28]

Institutions have no choice but to be responsive to the regulatory and accreditation emphasis on these new criteria for accreditation and participation in Title IV funds.

---

[27] New England Association of Schools and Colleges, Inc., Standards for Accreditation, excerpts related to institutional effectiveness, January 22, 1992.
[28] Ibid.

Growth in Consumerism

The movement toward a consumer-oriented society has changed the relationship between educators and students. Students are now recognized as consumers with legal rights to information and to assurances about the quality of education an institution sells. The first significant law that recognized students as consumers was the Educational Rights and Privacy Act of 1977, commonly referred to as the Buckley Amendment. It gave students the right to see their admissions files and letters of recommendation. The same legislation also gave employees the right to see their personnel files. In 1991, the Student Right-to-Know and Campus Security Act was enacted. This act required an institution of higher education to disclose to current students and employees information about completion and graduation rates and campus safety policies and procedures.[29] Similarly, interspersed throughout the SPRE standards, there are requirements to report outcome assessments, to receive and respond to customer complaints, and to provide information designed to protect consumers from fraud.

In short, the consumer movement has raised the level of expectation about information that students, as consumers, can access. As in commercial transactions, students are entitled to essential information so they can make informed judgments about institutions' educational products. Information about quality and cost are vital to the consumer. A basic question institutions are expected to answer is whether and how they measure the quality of their product.

Quality Movement in Management

The effect of the consumer movement can be seen in the transformation of institutions' organization and management. There is a new management orientation that is focused not only in meeting customers' needs and expectations but also on the process by which goods and services are provided. The recent evolution of management theory has moved from management by objectives (MBO), to strategic planning, to quality assurance (QA), to total quality management (TQM), benchmarking, and business process reengineering (BPR). A basic tenet underlying the new management theory is that decision making should be data based and made at the lowest possible level. The emphasis is placed on improving an organization's quality through a restructuring guided by a thorough understanding of the interlinking processes involved in delivering services or producing goods. Continuous quality improvement is the goal of total quality management. Performance measurements, customer feed-

[29] CFR Part 568, Student Assistance General Provisions, July 10, 1992.

back, benchmarking, and value-added analyses are the foundation on which the new management theory is built.[30]

Many colleges and universities are experimenting with these concepts, trying to assess their usefulness in managing a higher education institution. The initial experimentations have concentrated on the finance and business areas as these areas lend themselves readily to the new management approach. A growing number of institutions are engaged in a serious effort to adapt the concept of continuous quality improvement principles to academic programs. The American Association of Higher Education's 1994 conference, Assessment and Quality, featured numerous panel discussions and presentations that reflect the relevance and adaptation of these new management theories to the classroom. A sampling of the topics discussed were: Using Outcomes Data to Improve Student Success, Further Development of and Support for a Faculty-Led Continuous Improvement Model for General Education, Continuous Quality Improvement: Begin with the Facts, Quality Management in Performing Arts Education, and Building a Student-Oriented Assessment Program.[31] The same management techniques that are transforming American industry are solidly integrating into the management of higher education.

Debate over Performance Measurement

The value of assessing student learning outcomes is a highly debated topic. Many educators see little value in it and are skeptical of the quantitative approaches it employs. Harold Enarson, former president of Ohio State University, is attributed to have said: "Quality I know in my bones . . . [using] inputs and outputs is bush league economics. It is zeal for quantification carried to its logical absurdity."[32] Many professors share Enarson's views, claiming that the effects of a college education are "(a) self-evident, (b) ineffable, and/or (c) already measured by grades."[33]

The reason that assessing educational outcomes is controversial is that it is very difficult to do well. It is costly, time consuming, and elusive. It requires highly sophisticated tests, survey instruments, and careful

---

[30] See Edmund Coate, "Implementing total quality management in a university setting," Oregon State University, July 1990, and Sean Rush, "Benchmarking: How Good Is It?" in *Measuring Institutional Performance in Higher Education*, William Massy and Joel Meyerson, eds. (Princeton, New Jersey: Peterson's Guides, 1994).
[31] American Association of Higher Education Conference on Assessment and Quality, 1994, General Session Syllabi.
[32] Roger Peters, "Some snarks are boojums: accountability and the end of higher education," commissioned paper for the AAHE's 9th Annual Conference on Assessment and Quality, June 12–15, 1994.
[33] Ibid.

interpretation of data. Poorly designed questionnaires and overly simplistic interpretation of data can lead to faulty policy decisions. Increasing the difficulty of assessing student learning outcomes is that students come with a variety of backgrounds and experiences that affect how they learn and what they retain. Many faculty believe that outcome assessments may be a truer measure of inputs than outputs. Students' performances are highly influenced by "their own self-discipline, ambition, willingness to learn, work habits, and desire to excel—in short, by the character of the students themselves."[34]

It is hard to find agreement on what to measure and how to judge the quality of the education students receive when there is no agreement on educational goals. For example, should students be tested on specific courses they have taken or on their general education? Should comparative appraisals between institutions concentrate on the student's ability to "think critically, communicate effectively, and solve problems"?[35] Other questions focus on how to measure the quality of the whole educational experience. Does it make sense to measure cognitive ability without also measuring affective (attitudes and values) outcomes? What are the benchmarks and the standards used to measure success or failure? What evidence would indicate whether an institution's educational objects have been attained? Should outcome assessments measure immediate results, or is it more important to know the long-term effect of the education on the student?[36]

Although faculty in many disciplines reject the notion of the validity of outcome assessments, there are a number of success stories. Richard Light, director of the Harvard Assessments Seminars, has worked with the Harvard faculty since 1988 to develop an assessment process that is faculty-owned, process-oriented, and focused on outcomes. The goal of this assessment effort is to influence Harvard's educational policy and improve teaching. It has been successful in introducing a number of important pedagogical changes.

Another example is the Council on Financing Higher Education (COFHE) alumni survey of the class of 1982. COFHE surveyed 7500 alumni from its member colleges and universities. The survey focused on self-reported gains while at college in such areas as writing skills and lifelong learning, alumni satisfaction, and willingness to recommend their alma mater to others. The comparative data contained in this survey

---

[34] George Keller, "Increasing quality on campus," *Change*, May–June 1992.

[35] Goal 5.5, "National higher education goals," NCHEMS Report, *A Preliminary Study of the Feasibility and Utility for National Policy of Instructional "Good Practice" Indicators in Undergraduate Education.*

[36] Robert C. Pace, "Perspectives and problems in student outcomes research," in *Assessing Educational Outcomes*, E. Peter Ewell, ed. September 1985).

have the potential to be extremely instructive in assessing the strengths and weaknesses of the academic programs of the participating institutions.[37]

The debate over defining educational quality and how to measure it will be ongoing. Many faculty and education administrators will challenge the importance and utility of outcome assessments for deeply held epistemological reasons. Regulatory requirements, consumerism, and the new management techniques have made the debate moot. The need to assess outcomes as a way of measuring an institution's performance is now embedded in the accreditation process. As higher education comes under greater scrutiny it will have to take the time and exert the self-discipline to engage seriously in assessment activities.

14.6 PREDICTIONS OF THE LONG-TERM EFFECT OF HEA '92 ON HIGHER EDUCATION

It is particularly difficult to make predictions about the effects of the Higher Education Amendment of 1992 on Higher Education; although HEA '92 was passed by Congress, the details of its implementation are still in process. Predictions are inherently tricky, but more so here because of the uncertainty of the final regulations. Nonetheless, I believe that at least six broad predictions can be made. They are as follows.

Challenge to Maintain Institutional Independence Will Intensify

The public will remain skeptical about the integrity of higher education. For whatever reason, this shift in the public's attitude toward higher education has become the new reality. It will have a profound affect on the governance and management of colleges and universities. Education leaders will have to confront fundamental questions on how to maintain their institutions' independence in an atmosphere that is charged with suspicion and mistrust. Issues of accountability and quality assurance have a momentum that will not easily dissipate. Federal and state policy-makers will increasingly see their roles as defining the goals and setting the standards for higher education. External pressures on the academy to justify the use of public funds will grow as the competition for scarce resources intensifies. Boards of trustees, presidents, senior administrators, and faculty will find themselves devoting more and more time addressing issues of accountability, compliance with external regulations, consumerism, quality assurance and assessment, and affordability. The demand for more public accountability and quality assurance can be

[37] AAHE Assessment and Quality Conference, June 12–15, 1994.

viewed as another crisis to be managed or as an opportunity to win back the public's confidence. It will be both.

The Quality Movement Will Change the Way
Institutions Are Managed and Evaluated

By the year 2000, the new management theories that emphasize defining, measuring, and continuously improving quality will be ingrained in the management of higher education. Higher education will have adapted the quality movement to meet its particular needs. Outside assessors will force institutions to devote substantial resources to developing and perfecting ways of measuring institutional performance.

The measurement of an institution's performance by outside agencies—be they accreditation reviews, SPRE reviews, or the *U.S. News & World Report's* Annual Survey of academic institutions—will focus on qualitative and quantitative data on student learning outcomes. Outside evaluators will concentrate more on generic areas such as critical thinking, communication skills, and problem-solving ability rather than course-specific subject matter. In response to this new assessment emphasis, institutions will be forced to examine the integration and cohesiveness of their curricula, to develop ways of measuring a student's cognitive growth in broad terms, and to assess the effectiveness of the totality of the student's educational experience. Academic advising will take on increased importance and will be used as a means of monitoring a student's progress, based on tests and data, to assure the quality of the student's education.

Governing Boards Will Devote More Attention
to Monitoring Institutional Performance

An institution's accountability to the public and to its consumers ultimately rests with its governing board. Boards which have traditionally viewed their primary responsibility as a fiduciary one will find that they are also held accountable for assuring institutional quality. This new focus on institutional quality will require governing boards to put in place processes for monitoring performance. The pressure to meet externally imposed performance standards to justify the use of public funds and ensure the quality of education will change the way in which boards have traditionally functioned. Less board time will be devoted to operational matters and more time will be devoted to strategic issues. Governing boards will require management to develop strategic plans that address both financial and quality assurance issues. CEOs and senior-level administrators will find boards asking more substantive questions about ways of evaluating the effectiveness of programs, the evidence of institutional quality, and the pace of progress in improving performance at all levels in the institution. Trustees will be less reluctant to ask probing questions in the heretofore sacrosanct area of academic programs.

Effective boards will not attempt to dictate or micromanage the academic program. Rather, they will insist that management will have developed a well-thought-out process of evaluating the effectiveness of the curriculum, the quality of teaching, and the performance of its graduates in the larger world.

The SPRE Program Will Be Transformed in Three Ways

SPRE Standards Will Be Federalized. A basic premise on which the SPRE program was founded was that states could fashion standards, using a federal template, that would be appropriate to the institutions in the state. State standards could differ from one another depending on the specificity of the requirements for adherence to the standards. Just as the accreditation process was criticized for having policies and standards that differed from one state to another, so will the SPRE standards be criticized. Over time, the Secretary of Education will be pressured to impose more uniformity among the states' standards until there is, effectively, a national set of SPRE standards for all 50 states.

The Number and Specificity of Standards Will Increase. Once standards are federalized, they will be more vulnerable to political control. Politicians will find it tempting to write a new national standard in response to a particular problem. The DOE will remain understaffed and stretched to manage the direct lending program. To maintain control of Title IV programs and its influence over higher education, the natural bureaucratic reaction of the DOE will be to write tighter and highly specific standards. The development of standards will be seen as an end in itself rather than as a means to an end.

The SPRE Review Process Will Be Replaced by Outside Audits. Because the SPRE program is costly to run, it will be an easy target for budget cutters. Absent federal funding, states do not have the resources, nor the inclination, to sustain the SPRE program. As a way of saving money and maintaining control, the DOE will phase out the SPRE program and substitute it with annual audits of the standards by the institutions' independent auditors. Institutions will be required to undergo periodic audits of their adherence to the SPRE standards to remain eligible for Title IV funds. Independent auditors will have to submit letters of findings to the DOE, listing an institution's deficiencies in adherence to the standards. The DOE will implement this new review process by augmenting the scope of the current financial aid audit requirements. The new audit scope will have a striking resemblance to the A-133 audit for federally funded research projects.

Accreditation Reviews Will Be More Substantive

Accrediting agencies will continue to be the primary gatekeeper for determining eligibility to participate in Title IV programs. The influence of the Secretary of Education's requirement that accrediting agencies set standards in 12 areas will be substantial. Incorporation of these 12 standards into the accreditation process will place renewed emphasis on institutional self-assessment, on monitoring the institutional effectiveness in meeting its stated mission, and in providing evidence that the institution has a program to assess institutional quality and to provide for continuous quality improvement. These new standards of accreditation will require much more effort on the part of both the institution and the review teams. The end result will be that being "accredited" will be seen as a significant achievement. The new standards should help restore the public's confidence that the accreditation process is an effective gatekeeper to Title IV programs.

It is my belief that accreditation agencies will not have to serve as federal compliance agents for Title IV programs. That function will be assumed by the institutions' independent auditors.

Institutional Research Will Grow in Importance

SPRE standards, accreditation standards, and governing boards' demands for better data on performance measures will place greater importance on the institutional research function. Institutions will become more data dependent for both short-term decision making and long-term planning. The need for a comprehensive outcomes assessment program will lead to the creation of more offices of institutional research. The size and importance of the institutional research function will depend on the institution's mission and the problems it faces.

Institutional research can take many forms. It can offer a centralized location for the gathering and assimilation of data and a place to respond to surveys and questionnaires. It can help policymakers (particularly governing boards) interpret data and its staff can undertake assessments ranging from simple to highly complex longitudinal studies employing sophisticated measuring instruments. A well-trained institutional research staff can help in strategic planning. It can also serve a missionary role by helping to develop an institutional culture of assessment and accountability. In addition, the institutional research staff can identify appropriate peer groups for comparative analysis and work with various data consortia, such as the Higher Education Data Systems (HEDS), to help make basic choices about what to investigate. Without an institutional research group in place, institutions would have difficulty conducting meaningful assessments of their effectiveness.

14.7 STEPS INSTITUTIONS CAN TAKE TO MEET THE CHALLENGES TO THEIR INDEPENDENCE

Turn the Issue of Institutional Accountability into an Opportunity

The demand for institutions to be more accountable to the public can be an opportunity to strengthen self-governance. The debate over who should set standards provides an occasion for institutional self-assessment of values and standards. A careful examination to determine if an institution is fulfilling its mission and is committed to its core values raises important questions. What evidence does the institution have about its performance? Who assumes responsibility for assuring the integrity of the curriculum? Are all important constituencies involved in the decision-making process? How is the institution's assessment of its performance communicated to the general public? Is the public well served by the institution?

An institution that is comfortable with its answers to these questions should be in a good position to deal with externally imposed standards. If an institution has not addressed these questions in a serious way, a SPRE review or the new accreditation standards could be problematical. The key to maintaining independence is maintaining quality.

Support the Role of Independent Accrediting Agencies

The traditional concept that accrediting agencies have oversight responsibility for ensuring the quality of education of the institutions they accredit, through the peer review process, should be preserved. The integrity of the accrediting process requires that independent accrediting agencies remain free from proscriptive government direction. The government may proscribe areas where standards should be developed but should not attempt to dictate the actual content of academic standards for accrediting agencies. The agencies' focus should be on assuring institutional quality, setting standards for accreditation, and through the accreditation process, enhancing an institution's overall performance. Accrediting agencies should not have to assume the responsibility for reviewing institutions that fail to meet SPRE standards.

The restoration of the trust and the integrity in the independent accrediting process will require support and vigilance from the higher education community. One way to accomplish this is to make available an institution's best people to serve on review teams or for critiquing standards. Vigilance should come in monitoring the Department of Education's intrusion into areas that go beyond the intent and language of the Higher Education Act of 1992.

Be Vigilant

HEA '92 provides new opportunities for governmental agencies to impose onerous and intrusive regulations on higher education. The number of regulations that have followed its passage have been nearly impossible to track. Colleges and universities have had to rely on their national and state educational associations to keep them informed of the legislative initiatives. Educational associations cannot influence legislation without sustained help from the higher education community. Trustees of institutions often have important political connections. Institutions should use those connections to help make the case for higher education. In addition, college presidents should meet regularly with their congressional representatives to apprise them of the implications of proposed federal rules and regulations.

The independence of educational institutions has been seriously eroded over the years through federal regulations attached to Title IV funding. The latest and most crucial challenge to institutional autonomy is focused on the controversy over the development of federal standards for all Title IV institutions. Specific federal standards for curricula, faculty, and student services have been proposed. If ultimately adopted, these standards would strike at the very heart of academic institutions. The issues of preserving the independence and integrity of the higher education system are too important for institutional leaders to sit passively on the sidelines.

Greater Accountability in Financial Reporting

ROBERT M. TURNER

Babson College

KENNETH D. WILLIAMS

Coopers & Lybrand L.L.P.

15.1   Introduction
15.2   Historical Context
15.3   SFAC No. 4
15.4   External Financial Reporting
15.5   FASB's Not-for-Profit Agenda
15.6   New Financial Reporting
    Requirements
Statement of Financial Position
Statement of Activities
Statement of Cash Flows
Summary of New Reporting
    Requirements
15.7   Other FASB and AICPA
    Projects
15.8   Service Efforts and
    Accomplishments
5.9   The Future
5.10   Questions to Consider
5.11   Conclusions

15.1   INTRODUCTION

Financial accounting and reporting by not-for-profit organizations have undergone significant changes over the last 25 years. Colleges and universities, as a major sector in the not-for-profit arena, saw significant growth during the 1950s and 1960s, and accompanying this growth came increased reliance on outside resource providers for loans, grants, and other support. Institutional reliance on outside funding sources led to increased financial reporting and accountability to these external resource providers. As a result, colleges and universities in the 1990s are required to provide more information in differing formats to numerous governmental agencies as well as other resource providers, including donors and lenders.

Calls for increased accountability were founded in the changing environment in which colleges and universities operate. Prior to the mid-1970s, financial reporting by these institutions focused primarily on providing feedback to governing boards, management, and resource providers regarding funds received and funds expended. The emphasis was more on internal reporting than reporting to the general public. Subsequent to the mid-1970s, the emphasis shifted to providing information to a number of external users of financial reports.

15.2 HISTORICAL CONTEXT

Until the early 1970s, the most authoritative source for guidance on financial reporting by colleges and universities was *College and University Business Administration* (CUBA), originally published by the National Association of College and University Business Officers (NACUBO) in 1953.[1] In 1973, the American Institute of Certified Public Accountants (AICPA) published the industry audit guide, *Audits of Colleges and Universities*.[2] The objective of the guide was to bring uniformity and full disclosure to the reporting of financial information in college and university financial reports since more institutions were now required to provide audited financial statements.

Each of these guides emphasized the stewardship approach to reporting, characteristic of fund accounting. This reflected the fact that the objective of financial reporting was to assist with monitoring by boards, in the case of private colleges and universities, and by state and local governing bodies, in the case of public institutions. Fund accounting, a set of self-balancing "funds" that provided donors with an historical report on how funds had been used, was the primary vehicle for carrying out this objective. Separate funds allowed colleges and universities to report to donors and governmental agencies that funds had been expended according to the requirements of the gift or the appropriation. What separate funds did not do, however, was provide an overall financial picture of the institution. This made it difficult for external report users to assess the overall financial health of colleges, universities, and other types of not-for-profit organizations.

As the size of the higher education industry grew, from $2.3 billion in expenditures in 1949–1950 to over $135 billion in 1989–1990 and from

[1] NACUBO, *College and University Business Administration* (Washington, D.C.: National Association of College and University Business Officers, 1953).

[2] AICPA, *Audits of Colleges and Universities* (New York: American Institute of Certified Public Accountants, 1973).

enrollments of 2.7 million in 1949–1950 to over 13.5 million in 1989–1990,[3] colleges and universities found themselves facing a number of financial difficulties. Derek Bok, former president of Harvard University, noted in *Beyond the Ivory Tower* that as "society came to rely more and more on the universities, universities in turn grew ever more dependent on society for the money required to support their expanding activity."[4] The result was a "vast and intricate network of relationships" that linked universities to other institutions in the society. No longer was the college or university the "ivory tower" that it had been in the past.

When enrollments began leveling off in the mid-1970s, college and university budgets were squeezed. Since higher education budgets were characterized by a high degree of fixed costs, it was difficult to achieve cost savings as enrollment growth slowed. At the same time, higher education was hit harder than other industries by inflation. Colleges and universities in both the public and private sectors were forced to reckon with higher costs and limited financial resources. As a result, they turned increasingly to outside resource providers for additional funding. Institutions sought more gifts and grants and also turned to the financial markets for debt. Increased reliance on outside funding sources led to a demand, especially from the financial markets, for more information to assess the financial health of these institutions.

One of the first studies of this "new depression"[5] was commissioned by the Carnegie Commission and the Ford Foundation, after college presidents approached the two groups and requested that they look at the downward trend of their campus's fiscal situation. Earl Cheit, the author of the study, listed numerous reasons for the difficulties facing higher education. During the 1960s, the number of young people seeking higher education had risen steadily; post–World War II babies reached college age; the post-*Sputnik* era encouraged increased state and federal spending for research and education; and equal access to education became a theme of the times.[6]

While educational and general expenditures per student rose an average of 8 percent through 1970, for the 41 schools in the study, percent increases in support from state, federal, and private sources began to decline from 1967 onward.[7] Expenditures by colleges and universities had often been determined by the amount of revenue that could be generated

---

[3] *Digest of Education Statistics—1992* (Washington, D.C.: U.S. Department of Education—Office of Educational Research and Improvement, 1992), p. 171.

[4] Derek Bok, *Beyond the Ivory Tower* (Cambridge, MA: Harvard University Press, 1982), p. 7.

[5] Earl F. Cheit, *The New Depression in Higher Education* (New York: McGraw-Hill Book Co., 1971), p. vii.

[6] Ibid., p. vii.

[7] Ibid., p. viii.

and with more support pouring in during the 1960s, colleges and universities continued to grow. Once the support slowed, however, institutions were left with cost structures that could not readily be curbed or turned around. Enrollment demands, inflation, the notion of equal access, and the demand for quality had driven costs up, but suddenly revenue was not keeping pace. Cheit noted that most institutions had neither a budget nor a plan for permanent financing in the event of a downturn.[8] Colleges and universities had begun to rely on outside sources for funding during the 1960s and these institutions had little or no control over the continuance of external funding. However, they had become increasingly dependent on receiving external funds.

The initial response to these financial difficulties was an effort to control institutional costs. The two main areas that allowed for immediate cost reductions and/or cost controls were faculty salaries and deferred maintenance.[9] While these cost-cutting measures may have helped in the short run, they did not offer long-term solutions to the financial crisis. In fact, cost-cutting moves in the early 1970s may have led to higher cost increases in the late 1970s and early 1980s as colleges and universities tried to make up the differences.

One benefit of the new concern for finances was that institutions became more willing to exchange information among themselves about their financial situations.[10] In his second study, Cheit found evidence of improved financial reporting. Institutions were beginning to develop information systems, budgeting systems, and systems for decision making. As resources became more scarce, institutions had to address planning issues and develop strategies. There was a realization that administrators were no longer at the periphery of the academic community, but instead, made critical decisions that affected the very heart of academe. Cheit suggested there would be an increasing effort to measure the outputs, or the outcomes, of higher education. As a result, questions of a financial nature would lead to methods for evaluating the effectiveness and efficiency with which institutions carried out their academic purpose.[11]

As noted, increased costs and the subsequent need to generate additional financial resources from external groups resulted in demands for more accountability from institutions. Similarly, increasing tuition to compensate for decreased revenue from other sources led parents, students, and governmental agencies to question the ability of institutions to manage their resources. Therefore, colleges and universities were called

[8] Ibid., p. 5.
[9] Earl F. Cheit, *The New Depression in Higher Education—Two Years Later* (Berkeley: The Carnegie Commission on Higher Education, 1973), p. 51.
[10] Ibid., p. v.
[11] Ibid., p. 74.

upon to justify tuition increases that were in excess of cost-of-living increases. As a result, institutions began looking at their budget processes from the revenue side (previously, they had focused more on expenditures), targeting goals for maximum increases in tuition, rather than letting it be determined by the sum of projected costs.

Along with the demand for greater accountability by government and consumers of education regarding the cost of postsecondary education, more financial and nonfinancial information was also demanded when institutions entered the bond market. In rating bonds of colleges and universities, Standard & Poor's, for example, developed a model that included such qualitative and quantitative factors as quality of faculty and student body, experience of the management team, selectivity of the institution, geographical location of the institution, and trend information on enrollments, revenues, and expenditures.

To meet the demand for accountability on all fronts, colleges and universities began to publish additional financial reports. Since no standards existed regarding the form or content of these reports, a number of reporting formats and practices developed. Many institutions produced multiple reports aimed at different audiences. Some included complete audited financial statements while others were only summary in nature. Reports might include comparative information on previous year's activities and/or total columns to reflect the overall financial position of the institution.

A research report by Brace et al.,[12] commissioned by the Financial Accounting Standards Board (FASB), found that the purpose of these reports was not stated and that trend information on revenues, expenditures, enrollments, and so on, was often lacking. If trend information was included, there was little documentation regarding how amounts were compiled or computations made. It was noted that if state and federal agencies required certain financial information to assess services, financial viability, and management performance, similar information might prove to be relevant for resource providers.

15.3 SFAC NO. 4

At the same time that demands for more financial information were being made, the FASB took on the task of addressing the objectives of external financial reporting by not-for-profit organizations. Formed in 1973, the FASB developed a conceptual framework that is used by the Board to

[12] Paul K. Brace, Robert Elkin, Daniel D. Robinson, and Harold I. Steinberg, *Reporting of Service Efforts and Accomplishments* (Norwalk, CT: Financial Accounting Standards Board, 1980), pp. 22–30.

guide standard setting for the accounting profession. This conceptual framework applies to for-profit and not-for-profit organizations. Statement of Financial Accounting Concepts (SFAC) No. 4[13] deals with the objectives of financial reporting by not-for-profit organizations, including (generally private) colleges and universities. SFAC No. 4 defines the objectives of general-purpose external financial reporting as providing information that is useful to resource providers and other users about the financial viability as well as service efforts and accomplishments of the organization. [Financial reporting by governmental organizations, including public colleges and universities, is generally governed by the Governmental Accounting Standards Board (GASB).]

The FASB's view of financial reporting by not-for-profit organizations is similar to its view of financial reporting by the for-profit sector. According to SFAC No. 4, the key objective of general-purpose external financial reporting is to provide information for decision making by the primary users of the reports. In the case of for-profit organizations, the primary users are investors and creditors. In the case of not-for-profit organizations, the primary users are more numerous and have more diverse information needs. Per the FASB, users of not-for-profit reports include:

- *Resource providers*: including those directly compensated for providing resources (lenders, suppliers, and employees) and those not compensated (members, contributors, and taxpayers).

- *Constituents*: those who use and benefit from the services of the organization.

- *Governing and oversight bodies*: those responsible for setting policies and for overseeing and appraising managers of nonbusiness organizations. This includes boards of trustees, legislatures, and those with similar responsibilities.

- *Managers*: those responsible for carrying out the policy mandates of the governing bodies.[14]

Each of these user groups may take a different view regarding the information they need, its interpretation, and how best to display it in a financial report. For example, a surplus on the statement of activities (a financial report that will soon be required of not-for-profit organizations) may be viewed positively by one user group (e.g., a bond rating agency)

---

[13] Financial Accounting Standards Board, *Statement of Financial Accounting Concepts No. 4: Objectives of Financial Reporting by Nonbusiness Organizations* (Stamford, CT: Financial Accounting Standards Board, 1980), par. 33.
[14] Ibid., par. 29.

and more negatively by another (e.g., families concerned with increased tuition costs).

According to SFAC No. 4, the FASB also emphasized that the focus was on financial reporting, not just financial statements. There is a difference. Financial reporting includes not only the financial statements but also the quantitative and qualitative information that enhances the financial information found in the statements.[15] Therefore, the trend is toward a form of financial reporting that "tells a story" about an institution rather than just reporting on past events. It is important that the management of the institution as well as the board carefully determine the particular story or message they want to convey to the users of the report. The form and content of the report should be directed toward this objective.

The information contained in the financial report should emphasize both quantitative and qualitative information. Since the focus of financial reporting is to provide information for decision making, by definition this implies that the information must be predictive. It should assist the user in making better decisions about the future allocation of resources to institutions.

Financial reporting is no longer focused on reporting on past events. The information must be relevant as well as reliable. The FASB in SFAC No. 2[16] emphasized the importance of the balance between relevance and reliability. To be relevant, information must have predictive value, feedback value, and be timely. Reliability includes verifiability, representational faithfulness, and neutrality. In the past, emphasis would have been placed more on reliability. Now the focus must be on both relevance and reliability.

15.4 EXTERNAL FINANCIAL REPORTING

In a user-needs study—the users included experts from public accounting firms, preparers of reports, financial institutions, bond rating agencies, accreditation agencies, and state agencies—on external financial reporting by colleges and universities,[17] the following information was identified as important to the majority of these user groups:

- Reports that provide users with comparative statements for the current and previous years that can be used to assess operating results as well as the present financial position of the institution

[15] Ibid., par. 11.

[16] Financial Accounting Standards Board, *Statement of Financial Accounting Concepts No. 2: Qualitative Characteristics of Accounting Information* (Stamford, CT: Financial Accounting Standards Board, 1980), par. 33.

[17] Robert M. Turner, An Examination of External Financial Reporting by Colleges and Universities (Unpublished Dissertation, Boston University, 1992), p. 132.

- A statement of financial position (balance sheet) that shows a consolidated financial picture of the institution

- A statement of cash flows (instead of a statement of changes in fund balances), providing better distinction between operating cash flows and other capital funds flow

- A performance measure (i.e., a "bottom line")

- Information on revenue sources and their stability

- Expense information—functional and/or natural expenses distinct from capital expenditures

- Supplemental disclosures on students, faculty, enrollments, level of experience and quality of management, and better measures of service efforts and accomplishments—These supplemental disclosures were requested to enhance the financial information provided

- More discussion of liquidity, financial flexibility, and financial viability

The Turner study also showed how the field of financial reporting by colleges and universities was evolving. Some participants were still using the terms *expenses* and *expenditures* interchangeably, reflecting an accrual-based view of accounting (when using the term *expenses*) versus a fund accounting approach (when using the term *expenditures*). Others had only begun to think about the cash flow statement as an integral part of financial reporting by not-for-profit organizations since that was not a required statement at that time.

Finally, the inclusion of qualitative institutional information was supported by financial institutions, foundations, and accrediting groups. Again, this focuses on the importance of financial reporting, not just financial statements. As institutions become more complex and financial statements include more estimates, the notes to the financial statements are more integral to the financial report. They serve to enhance the financial statements and give users a clearer picture of the overall financial condition of the organization.

Since financial accounting and reporting are directed to external users, whether in the for-profit or not-for-profit arena, the information contained in these reports should address the decision-making needs of users of the reports. SFAC No. 4 requires that financial reporting by nonbusiness organizations provide information useful to present and potential resource providers and other users in:

- Making rational decisions about the allocation of resources to these organizations

- Assessing the services that an organization provides and its ability to continue to provide those services

- Assessing how managers have discharged their stewardship responsibilities, both effectively and efficiently

- Analyzing economic resources, obligations, net resources, and changes in them, including a consolidated view of the organization and a basis for measuring performance

- Evaluating an organization's service efforts and accomplishments (i.e., its measures of effectiveness and efficiency)[18]

The GASB also addressed the objectives of general-purpose external financial reporting by state and local governmental entities in its Concepts Statement No. 1.[19] (As noted, public colleges and universities generally fall under the jurisdiction of the GASB.) The GASB identified three user groups of financial reports: the citizenry, legislative and oversight bodies, and investors and creditors. The GASB noted that financial reporting "is used in making economic, social, and political decisions and in assessing accountability primarily by: (a) Comparing actual financial results with the legally adopted budget, (b) Assessing financial condition and results of operations, (c) Assisting in determining compliance with finance-related laws, rules, and regulations, (d) Assisting in evaluating efficiency and effectiveness."[20]

Although there are some differences between financial reporting by public and private colleges and universities, both the FASB and the GASB have emphasized the importance of focusing on the users of financial reports and their information needs. They have emphasized the need to be able to measure results of operations, to assess the financial condition of institutions, and to have a means of assessing the effectiveness and efficiency with which institutions carry out their stated mission. While public and private institutions may be governed by different standard-setting bodies, there is still considerable overlap regarding the objectives of the financial reports issued by private and public colleges and universities.

---

[18] Financial Accounting Standards Board, *Statement of Financial Accounting Concepts No. 4: Objectives of Financial Reporting by Nonbusiness Organizations* (Stamford, CT: Financial Accounting Standards Board, 1980), pars. 35–54.
[19] Governmental Accounting Standards Board, *Concepts Statement No. 1 of the Governmental Accounting Standards Board: Objectives of Financial Reporting* (Stamford, CT: Governmental Accounting Standards Board, 1987), par. 32.
[20] Ibid., par. 32.

15.5 FASB'S NOT-FOR-PROFIT AGENDA

Subsequent to the issuance of SFAC No. 4, the FASB outlined five issues it would consider in the area of not-for-profit financial reporting: depreciation, financial statement display, contributions, consolidation policies, and accounting for investments. Why is the FASB addressing these issues? Its objective is to make financial reporting by not-for-profit organizations more comparable to that of for-profit financial reporting, emphasizing the many areas of similarity between these organizations. According to SFAC No. 4, "The need to consider the objectives of general purpose external financial reporting by nonbusiness organizations generally is recognized. An increasing number of public officials and private citizens are questioning the relevance and reliability of financial accounting and reporting by nonbusiness organizations. That concern has been reflected in legislative initiatives and well-publicized allegations of serious deficiencies in the financial reporting of various types of nonbusiness organizations."[21] In addition to the five issues listed above, as financial display becomes more clearly defined, it is the FASB's intent to address the issue of service efforts and accomplishments.

The FASB has already addressed depreciation. In 1987, the FASB issued Statement of Financial Accounting Standards (SFAS) No. 93.[22] This pronouncement required that private not-for-profit organizations depreciate assets in the same manner as for-profit organizations. Up until this time, depreciation was not required of all segments in the not-for-profit sector. The effect of this FASB pronouncement was to move not-for-profit external financial reporting closer to full accrual-based reporting. Although there are still disagreements about how depreciation should be measured, most would agree that there is a cost associated with using up an organization's resources. Accounting for depreciation attempts to measure this cost. Accrual-based accounting has as its underlying premise that all costs be matched against revenues to better measure the performance of an organization.

In the Turner study on user needs, the majority of respondents favored a method of depreciation that would more closely capture de-

---

[21] Financial Accounting Standards Board, *Statement of Financial Accounting Concepts No. 4: Objectives of Financial Reporting by Nonbusiness Organizations* (Stamford, CT: Financial Accounting Standards Board, 1980), par. 59.

[22] Financial Accounting Standards Board, *Statement of Financial Accounting Standards No. 93: Recognition of Depreciation by Not-for-Profit Organizations* (Stamford, CT: Financial Accounting Standards Board, 1987).

ferred maintenance or the cost of replacing fixed assets. Since deferred maintenance is a major concern for colleges and universities, replacement cost depreciation (i.e., basing depreciation on the cost of replacing the asset rather than on its historical cost) would permit institutions to capture this cost. SFAS No. 93, however, requires institutions to use historical costs to calculate depreciation.

In 1993, the FASB issued SFAS Nos. 116[23] and 117.[24] These pronouncements are effective for financial statements issued for fiscal years beginning after December 15, 1994; organizations with less than $1 million in total assets and less than $1 million in annual expenses have a one-year delay for implementation. SFAS Nos. 116 and 117 represent major changes in the way not-for-profit organizations report contributions and in the way they report their financial results to the general public. Rather than the internal focus of the past, these pronouncements direct not-for-profit organizations to focus on the information needs of the users of their financial reports and the decisions that are made by these users. Thus these FASB pronouncements implement the conceptual objectives of SFAC No. 4.

SFAS Nos. 116 and 117 are based on the definition of three classes of net assets found in SFAC No. 6.[25] Net assets are similar to "stockholders equity" found in for-profit financial reporting. The three classes of net assets are unrestricted, temporarily restricted, and permanently restricted. The major distinction among the three classes is the degree of control that an organization has over the assets.

Unrestricted implies that the organization has complete control over the use of these assets, and therefore the assets can be used to meet its general obligations and its operating needs. *Temporarily restricted* net assets are assets that the organization must use for a specific purpose and are therefore not available for discretionary use. *Permanently restricted* net assets are assets that must be retained by the organization indefinitely. Therefore, these assets are not available for meeting the current obligations of the organization, although the income from these assets may be available for current use depending on the stipulation of the donor. The terms *temporarily restricted* and *permanently restricted* net assets relate only

---

[23] Financial Accounting Standards Board, *Statement of Financial Accounting Standards No. 116: Accounting for Contributions Received and Contributions Made* (Stamford, CT: Financial Accounting Standards Board, 1993).
[24] Financial Accounting Standards Board, *Statement of Financial Accounting Standards No. 117: Financial Statements of Not-for-Profit Organizations* (Stamford, CT: Financial Accounting Standards Board, 1993).
[25] Financial Accounting Standards Board, *Statement of Financial Accounting Concepts No. 6: Elements of Financial Statements* (Stamford, CT: Financial Accounting Standards Board, 1985).

to donor restrictions on the use of resources, not to organizationally imposed restrictions.[26]

The FASB's pronouncement on contributions[27] requires recognition of contributions as revenue in the year in which the contribution is received, including multiyear and unconditional promises to give (i.e., pledges). This is a change from past reporting practices since most organizations recognized pledges only when the pledge had been received. The FASB took the position that pledges met the criteria for revenue recognition as well as the definition of an asset. Therefore, promises to give should be included as revenue and as an asset in the financial statements of the organization in the year the pledge is made.

15.6 NEW FINANCIAL REPORTING REQUIREMENTS

The new financial reporting requirements will result in major changes in the way not-for-profit organizations, including colleges and universities, display their financial results. The FASB felt that change was necessary since a number of different formats had developed over time for each type of not-for-profit industry group. The new statements required by this pronouncement are meant to bring more consistency and comparability to the financial reports of not-for-profit organizations and to enhance their understandability.

SFAS No. 117[28] is concerned only with financial statement display, not with recognition and measurement issues. It defines three statements to be included in general-purpose external financial reports: a statement of activities, a statement of financial position, and a statement of cash flows. These statements more closely resemble those found in the for-profit sector. The statement must focus on the organization as a whole rather than the self-balancing funds characteristic of past reporting.

Historically, like other types of not-for-profit organizations, colleges and universities displayed multiple funds in their financial statements. With the issuance of SFAS No. 117, they will be required to display information on the three classes of net assets. This does not preclude the use of fund accounting, but it does require more aggregated information as well as the display of these three classes of net assets. The main difference among these three classes of net assets relates to donor-

---

[26] Ibid., pars. 92–94.

[27] Financial Accounting Standards Board, *Statement of Financial Accounting Standards No. 116: Accounting for Contributions Received and Contributions Made* (Stamford, CT: Financial Accounting Standards Board, 1993).

[28] Financial Accounting Standards Board, *Statement of Financial Accounting Standards No. 117: Financial Statements of Not-for-Profit Organizations* (Stamford, CT: Financial Accounting Standards Board, 1993).

imposed limitations on the use of temporarily and permanently restricted net assets and therefore limits the financial flexibility of the organization to use these funds at their own discretion. Aside from this distinction, all the net assets could be included in one net asset (equity) account. Combined, these three classes of net assets represent the net worth of the organization.

Statement of Financial Position

The statement of financial position (i.e., the balance sheet) provides users with information about the organization's assets, liabilities, and net assets (similar to equity in for-profit entities.) The statement must focus on the organization as a whole and is meant to provide information about an organization's liquidity and financial flexibility. Previously, the statement of financial position included a set of self-balancing funds and there was no requirement to aggregate all the fund groups into a total column. Without this total column, the aggregate financial position of the organization was not readily apparent.

Due to the degree of flexibility built into SFAS No. 117, the organization can decide how best to display information about its assets, liabilities, and net assets within the statement of financial position. The choice of display format should be based on user needs. Aggregated statements provide an overall view of the financial position of the organization at a point in time and support the pronouncement's emphasis on the organization as a whole and users' ability to determine the financial viability and financial flexibility of the organization. In addition, while comparative information for previous years is not required, if included, it provides the reader with trend information on the organization.

The statement of financial position must also provide information about the liquidity of the organization. According to the FASB, information about cash flows is one of the central objectives of financial reporting. (The inclusion of the cash flow statement as one of the required financial statements highlights the importance that the FASB and users of financial reports place on liquidity and cash flow issues.) Again, the FASB has allowed for a number of options in the way liquidity is displayed in the statement of activities. However, providing a classified statement with subtotals for current assets and current liabilities gives the user information about liquidity in a summary format, within the statement itself, similar to that found in for-profit reporting.

Finally, organizations can decide on the level of detail they provide on the face of the statement or in footnote disclosures. Due to the new requirements of the FASB regarding display and contributions, a major portion of net assets is likely to fall in the unrestricted net assets column. Previously, there would be a separate fund balance for endowment as well as for property, plant and equipment, and so on. Unless restricted by the donor, these fund balances now become part of unrestricted net assets. This will result in a significant change from present reporting formats. Depending on the materiality of the items making up the three classes of net assets, organizations may decide to further break out the balances in each of the three classes on the face of the statement. If only one line item is included on the face of the statement, the term *unrestricted net assets* may imply to the reader that a large surplus is available for use by an organization. It may be more relevant to the reader to disaggregate unrestricted net assets into its major components on the face of the statement itself. Major components could include categories for unrestricted, board-designated long-term investments, and for property, plant, and equipment.

Statement of Activities

The statement of activities is similar to the income statement in the for-profit sector. It provides information on how financial transactions have affected the organization over the previous year. The FASB provided many acceptable examples of this statement in SFAS No. 117. The degree of flexibility allowed with the statement of activities reflects the FASB's view that there are differences among not-for-profit industry groups and that there is not a clearly defined best approach to displaying operating results. As a result, the FASB would like organizations to consider the objectives of the statement of activities and what form the statement should take for their particular needs.

Previously, organizations were required to provide information on inflows and outflows of funds—including revenue sources as well as expenses and capital expenditures—in the statement of changes in fund balances and in the statement of current funds revenues, expenditures, and other changes. These two statements were more concerned with the financial activity of each fund group. As a result, capital expenditures and debt repayment were intermingled with expenses. The new statement of activities is concerned only with revenues, expenses, gains, and losses and as such is a statement of operations, not funds flow. (Information on funds flow is provided in the statement of cash flows.)

The purpose of the statement of activities under the new FASB pronouncement is to provide users with information about the changes in the three classes of net assets as well as to provide information about the organization as a whole.[29] The FASB's overriding objective is to give users the information necessary to evaluate an organization's performance in providing services and carrying out its stewardship responsibilities. With

[29] Ibid., par. 18.

this objective in mind, organizations may choose how best to display the changes in net assets on the statement of activities.

Before a format is chosen for the statement of activities, the objectives identified by the organization should be reviewed along with the central message that is to be conveyed to readers. This approach should govern the choice of a display format. For example, the statement of activities may convey to the reader how the organization is using resources to provide services to its constituents. The statement can provide information on how the organization is providing these services and whether it has been able to operate with its available resources. It may also be formatted to provide results by segment (e.g., by major schools or by major schools and the university-affiliated hospital), especially if budgeting is done in this manner.

Another key decision regarding the statement of activities is whether or not to include a "measure of operations" similar to the "net income" number found in for-profit reporting. A major concern for the organization is not only defining a measure of operations but also determining whether it is possible to distinguish revenue sources that are operational in nature from those that might be considered "nonoperating" or "capital contributions." Questions organizations may want to consider include: Does the decision to develop a measure of operations allow the user of the report to make the distinction between operating and capital transactions across the three classes of net assets? How do users view the temporarily and permanently restricted net assets columns, and how can changes in these two classes of net assets be agreed to the change in unrestricted net assets?

If a decision is made to include a measure of operations in the statement of activities, the organization will have to develop policy guidelines regarding revenues and expenses that would fall above or below the measure of operations. In deciding to include such a measure, the organization will have to determine how a surplus or deficit will be viewed by constituencies internal and external to the organization. Many users of financial statements of not-for-profit organizations may consider a surplus to be a negative rather than a positive factor, implying that the organization had more resources than it needed. Others will consider a deficit to be a negative factor, especially financial institutions and bond rating agencies.

Displaying such a measure may involve educating the organization's various constituencies about its nature and purpose. Some questions that might need to be considered include: What is a reasonable net operating result given the size of the organization? To what use is the surplus put? Is it, for example, added to board-designated long-term investments? Is it available for deferred maintenance or similar needs? Is this obvious either in the statements themselves or in the footnote disclosures? Information on an organization's surplus or deficit is considered important by investors and rating agencies. Investors want to know if an organization is breaking even, adding to endowment, or losing money.

The FASB does require that if a measure of operations is used, it must be clear in the statement itself or in the footnote disclosures how this term is used and the items that are included and/or excluded from the definition. Footnote disclosures on the measure of operations should be clear to allow users to understand the significance of this measure and the effect of the surplus or deficit on the organization.

The key issue for the statement of activities is that it should report on the performance of the organization and provide information to the user on the organization's revenues and expenses as well as trend information on how these revenues and expenses have changed over time. Since the FASB has emphasized the concept of service efforts and accomplishments, the expenses of colleges and universities, for example, will be reported on a functional basis (i.e., research expenses, instructional expenses, etc.) rather than on a natural basis (i.e., salary expenses, utility expenses, etc.). Therefore, expenses are allocated to program and support services so that users can assess the total cost of individual programs and ultimately develop measures to evaluate the effectiveness and efficiency with which these programs are operating.

Organizations should keep the issue of service efforts and accomplishments in mind as they develop the statement of activities. How organizations group expenses by major programs and support functions will affect the users of these statements. This represents another area where comparability among organizations may be lacking in the short run, as not-for-profit industry groups grapple with the new display formats. Ultimately, guidance will come from professional associations, such as the NACUBO and the AICPA, as certain approaches emerge as better methods of financial reporting. The pronouncement's flexibility offers the management and boards of educational institutions the opportunity to formulate policy rather than have it thrust upon them by experimenting with different measures of service efforts and accomplishments.

Statement of Cash Flows

The third statement required by SFAS No. 117 is the cash flow statement. Since this statement has been required in the for-profit sector since the 1988 issuance of SFAS No. 95,[30] SFAS No. 117 on financial statement

[30] Financial Accounting Standards Board, *Statement of Financial Accounting Standards No. 95: Statement of Cash Flows* (Stamford, CT: Financial Accounting Standards Board, 1988).

display simply extended the cash flow requirement to not-for-profit organizations.

The cash flow statement is used to explain the change in cash and cash equivalents from one fiscal year to the next. It focuses on cash flows from operating, investing, and financing activities. Since the statement of activities focuses only on revenues and expenses, the cash flow statement provides readers with information on capital expenditures, borrowing activity, and capital contributions that were formerly found in the statement of changes in fund balances and in the statement of current funds revenues, expenditures, and other changes. The one major difference between the cash flow statement in the for-profit sector and the cash flow statement in the not-for-profit sector is that contributions of fixed assets and endowment income, as well as interest and dividends that are for long-term purposes, are included under cash flows from financing activities in the not-for-profit sector, items that would not be found in the for-profit sector.

The statement of cash flows also highlights the importance of funds flow and liquidity information to financial report users. By separating operating information from funds flow information, users can address the separate issues of operating performance and the cash flows necessary for the continued financial health of the organization. This was not the case with the prior reporting format for not-for-profit organizations.

Summary of New Reporting Requirements

Finally, the three new statements will be accompanied by footnotes and qualitative information that will enhance the information found in the statements themselves. As discussed earlier, the FASB is concerned primarily with financial reporting, not just financial statements, and as such, the statements are made more relevant by the footnote disclosures and qualitative information that enhance the numbers found in the statements.

Since the FASB recognized the major changes in reporting that this pronouncement involved, they provided for some flexibility in how information could be displayed within each statement. It was their intent that display would evolve over time within each type of not-for-profit industry group. This flexibility allows not-for-profit industry groups, including colleges and universities, to consider the message they want to convey in these reports and how best to present this information. The next few years are therefore important ones for institutions and it is critical that management and board members be actively involved in the discussions so that industry practices evolve in a constructive and informed manner.

SFAS No. 117 is not just a technical standard. It has major policy implications for institutions. It will result in changes to the information systems of institutions and it requires analysis and decision making at the board and executive levels. Since the focus is now on the external users of the reports, the emphasis will be on comparability across the not-for-profit industry as well as within its sectors, such as the college and university sector. Financial reporting includes quantitative *and* qualitative information about the college or university. In the Turner user needs study, external users wanted information on applications, enrollments, the selectivity of the institution, and the quality of the student body, since such information represented a surrogate for demand that drives tuition revenue.[31] This information is already being requested by a number of user groups, including bond rating agencies, financial institutions, and other resource providers. The issue for the future will be the degree to which this type of information becomes a part of external financial reporting.

While the GASB has not completed its project on display, they are in the process of reviewing various approaches to financial statement display that address the objectives outlined in their Concepts Statement No. 1.[32] While the GASB recognized differences in the objectives of business-type activities versus governmental-type activities, it has stressed the importance of accountability and information important to financial report users. This again includes measuring service efforts and accomplishments as an indicator of the effectiveness and efficiency of these organizations.

All three of the models included in a GASB's Invitation to Comment[33] call for changes to the present reporting format, including presentation of fund information in an aggregated format. This agrees with the FASB approach of viewing not-for-profit organizations in an aggregated manner. Since the GASB is interested in a reporting model that will encompass the needs of governmental agencies as well as other users, it has also emphasized budgetary information and a comparison of budget to actual results. Moreover, the GASB has highlighted the need for disaggregated information in addition to the aggregated information requested by the FASB.

15.7 OTHER FASB AND AICPA PROJECTS

The FASB has begun two more projects in the not-for-profit arena: consolidations and reporting on investments. The former project is concerned with the level of consolidation necessary given the multiple activities in

[31] Turner, pp. 125–130.

[32] Governmental Accounting Standards Board, *Concepts Statement No. 1 of the Governmental Accounting Standards Board: Objectives of Financial Reporting* (Stamford, CT: Governmental Accounting Standards Board, 1987).

[33] Governmental Accounting Standards Board, *Invitation to Comment: College and University Financial Reporting Model* (Stamford, CT: Governmental Accounting Standards Board, 1994).

which a not-for-profit organization may be involved. (In the interim, the AICPA has issued a Statement of Position that provides guidance on accounting by not-for-profit organizations for related entities.) The FASB's investment project is looking at recognition and measurement issues relating to investments, including recognition of unrealized gains/losses in the statement of activities and display of the fair value of investments in the statement of financial position.

Recently, the AICPA has also issued a Statement of Position that clearly defines the applicability of pronouncements by the FASB, as well as its predecessors (the Committee on Accounting Procedure and the Accounting Principles Board) to not-for-profit organizations. Unless a pronouncement specifically excludes not-for-profit organizations, or by its nature (if it dealt with earnings per share, for example), it is evident that it would not apply, pronouncements are considered applicable to not-for-profit organizations.

15.8 SERVICE EFFORTS AND ACCOMPLISHMENTS

In addition to the issues of financial statement display, the GASB and the FASB have both indicated that measuring service efforts and accomplishments is an important component of financial reporting. In 1994, the GASB published Concepts Statement No. 2. The GASB has defined three categories of service efforts and accomplishments (SEA), including:

1. *Measures of service efforts.* "Efforts are the amount of financial and nonfinancial resources (in terms of money, material, and so forth) that are applied to a service." These efforts include financial information, such as salaries, and nonfinancial information, such as the number of personnel.

2. *Measures of accomplishments.* "Accomplishment measures report what was provided and achieved with the resources used. There are two types of measures of accomplishments—outputs and outcomes. Outputs measure the quantity of services provided; outcomes measure the results of providing those outputs." Examples of output measures might include the number of students graduating in a given year. Outcome measures could include employer satisfaction with graduates and the success of graduates in applying to professional schools.

3. *Measures that relate efforts to accomplishments.* These can include efficiency measures that relate efforts to outputs of services (i.e.,

resources used or cost per unit of output), as well as cost-outcome measures that look at efforts in relation to outcomes.[34]

According to the GASB, the objective of SEA reporting "is to provide more complete information about a governmental entity's performance than can be provided by the operating statement, balance sheet, and budgetary comparison statements and schedules to assist users in assessing the economy, efficiency, and effectiveness of services provided."[35] Therefore, measures of service efforts and accomplishments should enhance the information found in the financial statements and provide the user with information on the efficiency and effectiveness with which the organization carries out its stated mission.

The FASB will also be addressing the issue of service efforts and accomplishments in the future. SFAC No. 4 discusses the importance of service efforts and accomplishments because: "(a) the accomplishments of nonbusiness organizations generally cannot be measured in terms of sales, profit, or return on investment; (b) resource providers often are not in a position to have direct knowledge of the goods or services provided when they also are not users or beneficiaries of those goods and services."[36]

The FASB views service efforts and accomplishments as a "surrogate" for net income found in the for-profit sector. It is an attempt to measure the effectiveness and efficiency with which a not-for-profit organization carries out its services. While service efforts and accomplishments are not completely defined now, higher education needs to direct more attention to them. Such measures have already been developed by a number of different outside concerns, including the ratings of colleges and universities by various media. Although we might disagree with these ratings, they have become a reality. Also, bond rating agencies include both qualitative and quantitative information in their analysis of a college's or university's ability to carry debt. Management and boards would be better served by being part of the process of defining these measures rather than having them dictated by outside groups.

SFAC No. 4 addresses service efforts and accomplishments, noting:

> Financial reporting should provide information about the service efforts of a nonbusiness organization. Information about service efforts should focus on how the organization's resources (inputs, such as money, personnel, and

---

[34] Governmental Accounting Standards Board, *Concepts Statement No. 2 of the Governmental Accounting Standards Board: Service Efforts and Accomplishments Reporting* (Stamford, CT: Governmental Accounting Standards Board, 1994), par. 50.
[35] Ibid., par. 55.
[36] Financial Accounting Standards Board, *Statement of Financial Accounting Concepts No. 4: Objectives of Financial Reporting by Nonbusiness Organizations* (Stamford, CT: Financial Accounting Standards Board, 1980), par. 51.

materials) are used in providing different programs or services. Techniques for measuring the cost of significant programs or services are well developed and this information normally should be included in financial statements.

Ideally, financial reporting also should provide information about the service accomplishments of a nonbusiness organization. Information about service accomplishments in terms of goods or services produced (outputs) and of program results may enhance significantly the value of information provided about service efforts. However, the ability to measure service accomplishments, particularly program results, is generally undeveloped. At present, such measures may not satisfy the qualitative characteristics of accounting information identified in Concepts Statement 2. Research should be conducted to determine if measures of service accomplishments with the requisite characteristics of relevance, reliability, comparability, verifiability, and neutrality can be developed. If such measures are developed, they should be included in financial reports. In the absence of measures suitable for financial reporting, information about service accomplishments may be furnished by manager's explanations and sources other than financial reporting.[37]

In summary, present reporting requirements now emphasize a user approach to external financial reporting that focuses on an institution as a whole and allows users to make decisions about the allocation of resources to the institution. The FASB's new financial reporting requirements allow for a period of "experimentation" with different reporting formats so that both preparers and users can assess which approaches best meet the objectives of these reports. This period of evolution is an important one and the form that these statements take will ultimately influence the future development of measures of service efforts and accomplishments.

15.9 THE FUTURE

The next 10 years will be important ones for higher education as institutions grapple with the issue of accountability. Higher education has been attacked on a number of fronts for failing to control costs, increasing tuition without regard to students and families' ability to pay, alleged misuse of government funds, and so on. The accountability issue is crucial in the area of financial reporting as users demand more information that is relevant, understandable, and comparable. No longer will financial reports be simply historical in perspective, reporting only on past results in a stewardship manner. The financial report of the future

[37] Ibid., pars. 52–53.

will provide users with a comprehensive picture of the organization and with the information needed for decision making.

The management teams of colleges and universities, together with members of their boards, must look beyond their particular institutions and address the needs of the major users of their financial reports and the message they hope to convey in them. With the implementation of new display formats by the FASB and comparable work on the horizon by the GASB, colleges, universities, and the people who govern them are in a unique position to influence the form and content of financial reports and to be leaders in the development of measures of service efforts and accomplishments that will provide users with a critical analysis of their performance. Financial information important to all users of financial reports should be included, as well as qualitative information that will convey information about program results. The standard-setting bodies have provided a window of opportunity to not-for-profit organizations to take the lead in this regard. It is important that this opportunity not be lost.

15.10   QUESTIONS TO CONSIDER[38]

Consequently, the management and boards of colleges and universities must ask themselves the following questions as they prepare the financial reports of the future. The answers to these questions should result in reports that provide a comprehensive view of the institution and "tell the story" of that institution to the key constituency groups.

1.   *Who are the primary users of the information contained in our financial statements and the accompanying notes: Are our statements addressed to governing boards, financial institutions, investors, bond rating agencies, government agencies (federal, state, and local), resource providers (foundations, corporations, and individual donors), students and families, faculty, staff, recipients of the organization's services, and/or others?* In the past, institutions issued different versions of what might be called a "financial report" to their various constituencies. Evaluating the key users and their decision-making needs will allow colleges and universities to reduce the number of reports issued and produce ones with key objectives in mind. The focus should be on the minimum level of disclosure that should be available to all users of these reports.

[38] Adapted from *Financial Reporting and Contributions: A Decision Making Guide to FASB Nos. 116 and 117* by Professor Robert Turner at Babson College and the Coopers & Lybrand team of Kenneth Williams, Robert Forrester, Jack McCarthy, and Sandra Johnson, Coopers & Lybrand, 1994.

2. *What is the message that we would like to convey in our report? Do the statements convey relevant and reliable information about our institution in terms of financial viability, financial flexibility, liquidity, cash flows, and service efforts?* While the FASB has permitted flexibility in the new display pronouncement, its objective is that institutions use this flexibility to enhance the information provided to readers about financial viability, financial flexibility, liquidity, cash flows, and service efforts and accomplishments. Therefore, management must consider how best to display this information not only in the statements themselves but also in the accompanying footnote disclosures and supplemental information.

3. *How do we demonstrate financial flexibility, liquidity, and service efforts to external user groups?* Each of the three new statements should be designed to contribute information about financial flexibility, liquidity, and service efforts to external user groups. The statement of financial position, along with related notes, should allow users "to assess: (a) the organization's ability to continue to provide services, and (b) the organization's liquidity, financial flexibility, ability to meet obligations, and needs for external financing."[39] Liquidity is generally defined as indicating an asset's or liability's nearness to cash. The statement of financial position should be sequenced and/or classified in a manner that allows readers to answer these questions. Financial flexibility is an indication of an organization's ability to respond to changes in its economic circumstances; information on the stability of revenue sources and debt levels is an important part of this analysis. For example, how much financial flexibility does an institution have if there is a downturn in research funds or in applications, the enrollment factor that drives tuition revenue?

The statement of activities focuses on the effect of transactions on the three classes of net assets and how the institution is using those resources to provide services.[40] External users look to this statement for information on whether an institution has been able to operate with its available resources.

Finally, the statement of cash flows provides users, such as investment bankers (Exhibit 15–1), with information about an institution's operating cash flows, as well as its investing and financing activities. It allows the user to assess the institution's ability to continue to generate the funds necessary for carrying out its services.

4. *In the case of all three statements, are there disclosures, key ratios, or other summary financial information that would enhance the financial information found in our statements? What financial evaluations, credit analyses, and so on,*

[39] Financial Accounting Standards Board, *Statement of Financial Accounting Standards No. 117: Financial Statements of Not-for-Profit Organizations* (Stamford, CT: Financial Accounting Standards Board, 1993), par. 9.
[40] Ibid., par. 17.

Exhibit 15–1
JOHN AUGUSTINE, SENIOR VICE PRESIDENT, LEHMAN BROTHERS

The intended audience for corporate financial statements is primarily the equity or debt holder. Consequently, the primary purpose of the corporate financial statement is to provide a snapshot in time of a particular company's financial flexibility and liquidity for investors. College and university financial statements, on the other hand, serve a much broader audience: trustees, legislators, donors, faculty, and staff as well as investors, so the scope of financial disclosure is often broader.

A central element to financial market analysis of colleges and universities is an institution's financial flexibility to pay debt holders on time. This requires liquidity. Perhaps one way to proceed under SFAS No. 117 is to increase the use of footnotes as part of the cash flow requirement since liquidity is so important to debt holders. These footnotes could also highlight issues of relevance to bond holders.

---

are presently being used by financial institutions and/or bond rating agencies, and how will these analyses be affected by the changing reporting requirements? The accountability question is most acute in the case of financial markets. With the change in reporting formats, models for financial analyses will change and footnote disclosures will be much more important than before. Bond rating agencies such as Standard & Poor's will still be concerned with assessing revenue diversity, operating results, leverage, and liquidity, as well as assessing the information behind the numbers presented in the financial statements (Exhibit 15–2).

5. *As financial reporting requirements change, can we streamline our information systems to meet reporting requirements both internal and external to the institution? Are there ways to tie our external reporting requirements to other reports that must be prepared for participation in various federal or state programs? Can the information contained in our financial statements be tied to the budgetary reporting requirements of our institution?* After reviewing their systems, colleges and universities may find they can tie together the objectives of some or all of their information needs to avoid producing multiple reports for different constituencies. By developing better measures of efforts and accomplishments, institutions may be able to streamline their information systems.

6. *Does the institution have a management information system capable of providing the information required to meet the new reporting requirements?* In the short term, institutions will have to decide what changes will be necessary in their information systems to allow them to produce the new financial statements as well as capture information from the development office that will be needed to meet the requirements of the pronouncement on contributions. Many institutions are unsure at this time whether or not to

Exhibit 15–2
LISA DANZIG, DIRECTOR, STANDARD & POOR'S

S&P uses the financial statements of colleges and universities to help assess creditworthiness for the purpose of assigning long-term bond ratings. While financial operations are an important part of the analysis, our review also encompasses demand, management, governance, debt structure, and debt history.

For example, when reduced to essentials, our financial review of a higher education institution is concerned primarily with its revenue and expenditure base and financial reserves. The new reporting standards will dramatically change how we assess colleges and universities. For example, we will need to consider how best to:

- Calculate what portion of unrestricted net assets is truly available to cover items such as debt service, unforeseen expenditures, and revenue fluctuations.
- Determine an institution's operating results.
- Measure debt burden.
- Measure revenue diversity (i.e., tuition dependency for colleges and universities).

---

retain their fund accounting systems or to convert to an entirely new system based more on the corporate model.

These decisions must be made in light of internal and external reporting needs and should be based on good business practices. Since substantial time and money may be necessary to carry out information technology changes, careful thought and consideration must be given to these decisions. As part of this process, it is important that colleges and universities share information, since comparability will be an important outcome of this evolution in financial reporting.

7. *Should the institution display a "measure of operations"?* The decision to display such a measure must be made in light of user needs, including investment bankers such as Morgan Stanley (Exhibit 15–3), and whether such a measure presents the message the institution wants to convey.

8. *What measures of service efforts and accomplishments best capture the performance of the institution?* While the issue of service efforts and accomplishments is not presently on the agenda of the FASB, the GASB has already issued its concept statement on this issue. Regardless of requirements from standard-setting bodies regarding such measures, colleges and universities are already under evaluation by a number of outside interest groups, from the Department of Education (see Chapter 14) to news journals, each of which is designing its own measures of performance evaluation.

Often in the not-for-profit sector, any mention of "management" terms or of linking financial information to program results is met with

---

Exhibit 15–3
PATRICK J. HENNIGAN, VICE PRESIDENT, MORGAN STANLEY GROUP, INC.

Developing a "bottom line measure of operations" is always somewhat controversial for colleges and universities yet it is essential for external users of financial information. Investors are interested in how well the institution is managing its resources and how much available revenue is being generated after expenses to pay debt service. Is the institution recording a net surplus or net deficit at year-end before making voluntary transfers? Under the new format, the bottom line may be overstated. Also, it may be difficult to determine the proportion of cash and cash equivalents available. For institutions of higher education, the bottom line measure should include all educational and general as well as auxiliary operations.

---

great suspicion if not outright attack. Measuring outcomes in education is viewed as too subjective. However, regardless of how these measures may be viewed by faculty or management, higher education is a multi-billion-dollar industry with scarce resources and numerous constituencies clamoring for such measures.

The next few years will be characterized by experimentation with the new reporting formats by both private and public colleges and universities. This experimentation will lead to increased comparability as "best practices" emerge and as professional associations begin to narrow the options available for reporting. Once the financial statements come into clearer focus, measures will develop that will capture such objectives as financial flexibility, liquidity, and solvency on the financial side and linkages will be made to service efforts and accomplishments to evaluate institutional performance more easily.

The development of such measures should find their genesis with management and boards of colleges and universities. The FASB has directed initial attention to this throughout their pronouncements affecting not-for-profit organizations, and the GASB has done the same. While difficult to capture, measures of service efforts and accomplishments provide relevant information to the users of financial reports and bring life to the numbers themselves. It carries the analysis beyond simply a review of inputs and outputs. Outputs are quantifiable measures such as faculty/student ratios, number of volumes in the library, size of the physical plant, number of graduates, and so on. This information provides the reader with measures of the "efforts" of the institution.

Important to the future of financial reporting will be the development of measures of "accomplishments," those outcome assessments that will address the objectives of efficiency and effectiveness. The GASB and FASB have defined these in general terms, but it will be up to colleges and universities to bring them into focus for their industry group. Other groups, such as financial institutions and bond rating agencies, are already doing this for their own purposes. All affected parties at the college or university must be part of the process of the development of service efforts and accomplishment measures.

(See also Chapter 14 where the federal government's initiatives to develop outcome measures for institutions receiving Title IV funds is discussed. SPREs are an outcome of the federal government's demands for greater accountability by colleges and universities; in this regard, they are similar to the FASB's and GASB's initiatives to develop assessment measures for not-for-profit organizations, including colleges and universities.)

9. *What level of aggregation and disaggregation will be important to users of financial reports?* As colleges and universities have grown in size, the need to segment divisions and departments within the institution has increased to better plan and control activities. Responsibility for managing various institutional segments may now reside in different schools, departments, divisions, and so on. Segmentation could be on the basis of programs (e.g., education, health care, and research). Often, budgets are linked to institutional segments. Whether defined as programs or departments, if the institution manages at these levels, financial reporting should capture this level of responsibility. How much of this information is disaggregated and included in the financial report of the institution will depend on its size as well as the diversity of its programs and objectives. There is always a concern with "information overload," and this must be kept in mind when deciding on the level of disaggregation that is included in financial reports.

10. *How do we measure the cost of providing educational services?* With the implementation of depreciation reporting by the FASB, college and university financial reporting, at least in the private sector, is closer to full accrual-based accounting that is the norm in for-profit financial reporting. Prior to the FASB's depreciation pronouncement, institutions could more readily ignore certain costs when matching revenues and expenses and appear to be on sounder financial footing. Deferred maintenance became a major problem for the higher education industry, and the recording of depreciation is one step toward trying to capture this cost in the financial statements. Although there may still be a debate about how best to measure this cost, at least it is now recognized as part of the cost of providing educational services.

Developing better measures of full cost accounting, at least as a management tool but also for discussions with board members and faculty, will continue to be emphasized. Full-cost accounting will also provide a basis for matching costs with revenues as institutions look at the total cost of providing various programs and services. This refinement will also allow for increased comparability across institutions as well as opportunities for benchmarking to evaluate how effectively the institution is delivering services.

11. *How will the new financial reporting requirements affect the budgeting process at our institution?* The GASB included discussions about the importance of budgeted information as part of financial reporting in an Invitation to Comment.[41] Financial institutions look at budgeted information as a means of measuring how well an institution's actual results compare to its budgeted numbers. Since previous budgets were based on fund accounting, which may have included both operating expenses and capital expenditures for equipment, institutions will need to decide how the budget process will relate to the new statement formats. Will budgets be considered an internal management tool as they are in the for-profit arena, or will they be seen as an integral part of financial reporting by colleges and universities? Institutions will have to decide if they want to retain fund accounting as a basis for budgeting or shift to a different budget approach incorporating operating information separate from other funds flow.

12. *How much "reeducation" will be necessary to allow the various constituencies to read and interpret financial information contained in the new reports?* Fund accounting has been a different, often foreign language which needed to be interpreted for boards, financial markets, and other user groups. The FASB believes that the same language should apply to all organizations, whether for-profit or not-for-profit, since in many cases, they are competing for the same resources. However, during this transition period, all users will have to change the way they evaluate financial results of not-for-profit organizations, including colleges and universities. Until "best practices" emerge from industry groups, footnote disclosures will be an even more important part of the financial report. Preparers will have to provide sufficient narrative to allow users to adapt to these changes.

15.11 CONCLUSIONS

This is an exciting and challenging time for those involved in managing and governing colleges and universities. While the next 10 years will bring major changes in the way institutions are evaluated, the standard setting bodies have provided the not-for-profit industry with the opportunity to play a major role in how methods of accountability and evaluation develop. Those institutions that actively play a role in this process will be able to develop meaningful systems of reporting that not only enhance

---

[41] Governmental Accounting Standards Board, *Invitation to Comment: College and University Financial Reporting Model* (Stamford, CT: Governmental Accounting Standards Board, 1994).

their external financial reports, but also those internal reports that are critical to carrying out their managerial and governing responsibilities successfully.

Throughout the process, it is important that all parties be involved in determining the form and content of the financial report as well as in developing measures of service efforts and accomplishments. These issues will affect colleges and universities well into the next century, and management and boards must be an integral part of the changing ways in which institutions present their financial results. By providing input to this process, those closest to the mission of our institutions of higher learning can better define the outcome measures that will be used to evaluate their performance. It is a critical time for all involved in financial reporting and for those concerned with the future financial viability of colleges and universities.

The Question of Tax Exemption

KAYE B. FERRITER
JANET M. BUEHLER

Coopers & Lybrand L.L.P.

16.1 Introduction
16.2 Increased Scrutiny
16.3 Theoretical Basis for
       Exemption
16.4 Current Environment
16.5 990 Revision
       Disclosures on Form 990
16.6 The Coordinated Examination
       Program

16.7 Congressional Oversight
       Intermediate Sanctions
16.8 Compensation
16.9 Financing New Facilities
16.10 Property Taxes
16.11 Technology Transfer
16.12 Conclusions

16.1 INTRODUCTION

Tax-exempt status gives colleges and universities a significant economic advantage. The first and most obvious advantage is that institutions do not have to pay federal income taxes or other state and local taxes on income related to their tax-exempt purpose. At the current rate of 35 percent, federal income taxes alone would command a third of the institutional budget after expenditures. Exempt status also allows colleges and universities to finance their facilities using tax-exempt bonds. Another advantage of tax-exempt status is that it allows colleges and universities to accept donations—often a significant part of an institution's budget—which are tax deductible for the donor. Without this feature, donors would not be as generous with their gifts.

Although the tax-exempt status of colleges and universities has not changed (and there is no indication that it will, especially in the short term), threats are on the horizon. Property tax bases are eroding in U.S. cities and towns. States are looking to raise tax revenues. At the federal level, budgetary constraints are forcing explorations for new sources of tax revenue.

At the same time, traditional institutional revenue sources are not growing as fast as expenditures. As a result, colleges and universities are looking for new sources of revenue, such as joint research ventures with private business, leasing land to private or government enterprises, and developing businesses on campuses. In so doing, they are more apt to come into conflict with local businesses, and subsequently, complaints arise from the local business community about unfair competition.

Why are colleges and universities exempt from taxes in the first place? There is actually no compelling reason for their exempt status other than they exist to provide a public service—education. Education is good public policy. However, if it becomes so expensive that only the wealthy can attend, the public benefit of higher education is diminished.

Under current law, colleges and universities will not lose their tax-exempt status. The less accessible education becomes, however, the greater the pressure on Congress and other bodies to encroach on the tax-exempt status of institutions. The thesis of this chapter is that it behooves institutions not necessarily to change their activities but to become increasingly sensitive about the effect of their activities on the public. The tax-exempt status of higher education arose to promote the public good, and this underlying premise should not be taken lightly.

16.2 INCREASED SCRUTINY

Over the past several years, colleges and universities faced increased scrutiny from both the public and various federal and state regulatory authorities. Public and regulatory scrutiny has taken many forms. The Internal Revenue Service has stepped up its enforcement activities at colleges and universities through its implementation of the Coordinated Examination Program (CEP). The Service's Form 990, "Return of an Organization Exempt from Income Tax," has been modified significantly. Increased scrutiny of tax-exempt organizations has also come from state and local taxing authorities, particularly relating to payroll and property tax payments.

Increased scrutiny of tax-exempt organizations has also come from Congress. Needing to find additional sources of revenue to cut the federal budget deficit, and further spurred by the public sentiment that tax-exempt organizations may be abusing their tax-exempt status and competing unfairly with small business, Congress has held hearings over the past several years to examine these issues and design solutions. Many transactions by tax-exempt organizations (in addition to unrelated business activities) have been examined, including compensation arrangements, fund-raising events, lobbying expenditures, and transactions with employees and insiders. Potential solutions to these problems, including sanctions, continue to be raised and debated in Congress.

16.3 THEORETICAL BASIS FOR EXEMPTION

To more fully understand the current environment, it is useful to examine briefly the history of granting exempt status to certain organizations. Internal Revenue Code (IRC) Section 501(a) provides for an exemption from tax for organizations described in IRC Section 501(c). Among those organizations described under IRC 501(c)(3) are those "organized and operated exclusively for religious, charitable, scientific, testing for public safety, literary or educations purposes . . . ."[1]

A college or university in the "traditional" sense would clearly meet the definition of an educational institution under the Internal Revenue Code (IRC). To qualify for tax-exempt status, a college or university must, like all other 501(c)(3) organizations, also meet other requirements. Namely, the organization may not (1) have part of its net earnings inure to the benefit of an individual; (2) engage in a substantial amount of lobbying activities which include carrying on propaganda or attempting to influence legislation[2]; or (3) participate in or intervene in any political campaign on behalf of a candidate for public office.

In addition to the statutory requirements for exemption, there may be additional requirements, beyond the express language of the IRC Section 501(c) and regulations. Perhaps the most notable example of nonstatutory requirements is that of a nondiscriminatory racial policy.[3] Thus, for a college or university to receive and retain its tax-exempt status, it must be organized and operated for educational purposes, and its activities must not be contrary to public policy.

[1] Organizations that are organized and operated exclusively for educational purposes can be engaged in a wide variety of activities. Regulations Section 1.501(c)(3)-1(d)(3)(i) describes education as "the instruction or training of the individual for the purpose of improving or developing his capabilities; or the instruction of the public on subjects useful to the individual and beneficial to the community." Example (1) of Section 1.5011(c)(3)-1(d)(ii) provides an example of what would constitute an "educational" organization, by describing as educational "an organization, such as a primary or secondary school, a college, or professional or trade school, which has a regularly scheduled curriculum, a regular faculty, and a regularly enrolled body of students in attendance at a place where the educational activities are regularly convened."

[2] Except as provided in IRS Section 501(h).

[3] Per Revenue Ruling 71-447, 1971-2 C.B. 230.

Now that we have addressed how a college or university needs to be organized and operated to be tax-exempt, we must address the more basic question of why a college or university [or other 501(c)(3) organization] is exempt from income taxes. As indicated in Revenue Ruling 71-447 supra, and the Supreme Court case *Bob Jones University* 461 U.S. 574 (1983), the underlying reason for exemption for "charitable" organizations is that they further a public policy goal. The government is willing to forgo tax revenue that it would otherwise be entitled to collect, since the organization is performing a function that the government deems worthwhile, or a function that if it were not performed by the organization would probably be performed by the government. Thus the tax-exempt status enjoyed by a charity can be broadly viewed as an economic trade-off between the government and the organization. The benefits of tax-exempt status are retained as long as the organization operates in a manner that furthers the public policy underlying its basis for exemption as set forth in the Internal Revenue Code, the Regulations, and in the common-law "charity" concepts.

16.4 CURRENT ENVIRONMENT

For many years, colleges and universities faced little or no scrutiny from taxing authorities. Institutions of higher learning enjoyed their tax-exempt status with few reporting requirements. Form 990, which must be filed by private colleges and universities, is an information return that demanded few disclosures about whether the activities in which an institution was engaged could jeopardize its exempt status.

Historically, when colleges or universities have undergone IRS audits, the payroll tax area was typically the focus. This is one area in which reporting and other compliance requirements for tax-exempt organizations are similar to for-profit entities, and therefore similar interest and penalties may be applied by the IRS.

Both state and private colleges and universities are required to file Form 990-T to report their unrelated business income. Unrelated business income is taxed at the normal corporate rates. Few institutions, however, have reported substantial amounts of unrelated business taxable income.

The environment in which all tax-exempt organizations are operating has changed dramatically over the past several years. Once overlooked by the IRS, not-for-profit organizations are now under intense focus. There are many factors responsible for this changing attitude toward tax-exempt entities. Perhaps the most significant underlying factor is the perception that tax-exempt organizations are not always operating in a manner consistent with the purpose for which the exemption was granted. When these organizations' actions are inconsistent with public policy, fairness dictates that they should be treated the same as taxable corporations. Further, as pressure on the federal budget increases, there is continued pressure on Congress and state governments to find additional sources of revenue. Perceived abuses of the tax-exempt status by an organization, particularly when private individuals are benefiting or when tax-exempts are competing directly with taxable entities, has fueled pressure on Congress to stop these abuses and "level the playing field".

Colleges and universities are trying to raise more revenue to cover their operating shortfalls to try to keep a college education within the reach of as many students as possible. This has prompted some to become more "entrepreneurial" and engage in new revenue-raising activities, some of which may compete directly with local area businesses. This type of competition can lead to bitter feelings between the college or university and its surrounding neighbors and raise concerns over the extension of the tax exemption or the lack of enforcement of the UBIT rules over these activities.

Highly publicized cases of public charity executives receiving what may appear to be excessive compensation, including lavish "perks," is another factor that focuses attention on tax-exempt organizations. Once perceived as "doers of the public good," charities are now examined more critically. Again, abuses, whether perceived or real, have caused many to rethink the rationale of tax-exempt status, at least as it extends to those charities that use public funds to benefit "insiders," or where they compete directly or indirectly with taxable entities.

The heightened scrutiny from the public and from various governmental agencies, most notably the IRS, has manifested itself in many ways. Discussed below are the most significant examples for colleges and universities.

16.5 990 REVISION

Form 990 is an information return filed by public charities. Because detailed information was not required in the past, this document failed to present accurately how an organization was operating in the public interest. It also presented little information about the types of activities that organizations engaged in and how those activities were conducted. Few of these returns were audited by the IRS or returned if they were incomplete.

According to the August 2, 1993 written statement of Richard Blumenthal, Attorney General of the State of Connecticut, which he prepared for the Committee on Ways and Means Subcommittee on Oversight, "Three years ago my office conducted a study that revealed that two-thirds of the 990's filed in Connecticut contained one or more arithmetic errors. The extent to which these errors were intentional or the result of carelessness is unknown but nonetheless astonishing."

The IRS, in response to both congressional and public perception that organizations may be abusing their exempt status while also looking for potential new sources of tax revenue, has significantly increased the level of detail required on Form 990. As a result, Form 990 compliance has become more burdensome. This is particularly true in areas receiving significant media attention, such as compensation of officers, directors, trustees, and key employees; revenue sources; transactions with "insiders;" and lobbying expenditures.

Disclosures on Form 990

Part V of Form 990 requires disclosure of compensation paid to officers, directors, trustees, and key employees. In the past, many organizations only disclosed compensation reflected on Form W-2 because the instructions to Form 990 were vague. Since Form 990 is open to public inspection, many organizations were sensitive about disclosing the amount of compensation paid to their executives.

The IRS has revisited Form 990's instructions regarding compensation disclosure requirements to provide a more accurate view of compensation packages for officers, directors, trustees, and key employees and has made it clear that all forms of compensation to such persons must be disclosed in Part V of Form 990. The instructions now specifically require any fringe benefits (taxable or nontaxable) to be disclosed. For example, disclosure of contributions to benefits plans and qualified and non-qualified deferred compensation arrangements made by the organization on behalf of its officers, directors, trustees, and key employees is required. Also mandated is disclosure of nontaxable fringe benefits received, such as tuition remission for children, employer-provided lodging, account allowances, and other allowances.

In addition, Schedule A to Form 990, which must be filed by private colleges and universities and other organizations that are exempt under 501(c)(3), requires similar disclosure of compensation paid to the organization's five highest-paid employees. The purpose of these changes is to provide the IRS and the public with a more accurate picture of the compensation paid to those who control the organization.

Schedule A, Part III, also requires a tax-exempt entity to disclose any transactions it has with "insiders." These transactions include (1) the sale or exchange of property, (2) the lending of money, and (3) the furnishing of goods or services. The underlying question is: Are insiders benefiting at the expense of the organization?

In addition, Form 990 requires the organization to provide detailed information about its lobbying activities. Public policy dictates that tax-exempt organizations not engage in significant amounts of lobbying.

The single biggest change to the Form 990 in recent years has been the addition of Parts VII and VIII. In response to complaints by the small business community about the activities of tax-exempt organizations, the House Oversight Subcommittee of the Committee on Ways and Means held hearings on the unrelated business activities of tax-exempt organizations. Many people believed that these hearings would result in changes in the unrelated business income rules. However, no consensus was reached about what those changes should be. Further, the IRS lacked detailed information with which to make revenue estimates about the effect of changes in the rules.

Part VII was introduced to Form 990 as an attempt to accumulate information so that at some time in the future, revenue estimation would be possible. Part VII requires that all revenue sources be listed in detail. This revenue must then be categorized into either (1) unrelated; (2) that which is excluded from UBI by IRC Sections 512, 513 or 514; and (3) that which is related to the performance of the organization's exempt function. For revenue related to an organization's exempt function, an explanation must be given on Part VIII about how this revenue has contributed importantly to the accomplishment of the organization's exempt purpose.

Thus the changes in Form 990 and Schedule A are designed to provide the IRS and the public with a better picture of an exempt organization's activities and specifically to highlight problem areas that were given little attention in the past.

16.6 THE COORDINATED EXAMINATION PROGRAM

The heightened scrutiny received by tax-exempt organizations, especially colleges and universities, is also evidenced by the IRS's increased audit activity. The public perception has been that colleges and universities are hiding behind their tax-exempt status to engage in competition with for-profit businesses. After congressional hearings, the IRS was pressured to institute better reporting and audit procedures.

In response, the IRS developed examination guidelines to institute the Coordinated Exam Program (CEP) for colleges and universities. Announcement 93-2 contained the proposed audit guidelines for colleges and universities. On August 25, 1994 the IRS issued Announcement 94-112, the final audit exam guidelines. The aim of the CEP program is to determine if and to what extent colleges and universities are acting inconsistently with their exempt status. Traditional IRS audits of tax-exempt organizations focused only on specific areas such as payroll or unrelated business income. Under the CEP, agents who are experts in various areas are brought in to audit all aspects of the institution at once. (This type of audit has been conducted at large for-profit corporations for many years.)

Sixteen colleges and universities were selected for the first round of CEP audits. The IRS is developing their CEP audit program by auditing these colleges and universities. The IRS will then use what is learned to perform smaller-scale "target" audits of other institutions. The IRS has indicated that as part of the CEP, they will examine issues such as private inurement[4] and private benefit,[5] excess compensation, payroll reporting, impermissible use of tax-exempt funds, and pension plan compliance. Never before have colleges and universities undergone such rigorous IRS audits.

16.7 CONGRESSIONAL OVERSIGHT

Congressional scrutiny of tax-exempt organizations has increased along with IRS and public scrutiny. The Subcommittee on Oversight of the House Ways and Means Committee has held hearings over the past six years regarding the activities of tax-exempt entities.

Early hearings focused on unrelated business income tax issues. More recent hearings have focused on the broader issue of whether tax-exempt organizations are operating in a manner consistent with their tax-exempt status. Concerns raised in these hearings include private inurement and benefit, compensation and fund-raising practices, and competition with small business. Questions were also raised about how to increase compliance by tax-exempt entities and how to sanction those who fail to "get in line." The IRS has been reluctant to revoke an organization's exempt status in all but the most egregious cases. In part, their reluctance is based on the recognition that despite some abuses, most tax-exempt organizations do provide a community benefit. Revoking their exemption could do more harm than good. Revocation has been the only "weapon" the IRS has to enforce compliance, but for good reason, its use has been extremely limited.

---

[4] Per General Counsel Memorandum 38459, inurement "is likely to arise where the financial benefit represents a transfer of the organization's financial resources to an individual solely by virtue of the individual's relationship with the organization, and without regard to accomplishing exempt purposes."

[5] According to General Counsel Memorandum 38459, "An organization which serves a private interest other than incidentally is not entitled to exemption as an organization described in section 501(c)(3). . . . The determination of whether private benefit is merely incidental to overall public interest will turn on the nature of the activity under consideration and the manner by which the public benefit will be derived." This quote helps to define the concept of private benefit.

Intermediate Sanctions

Congress has explored other means through which tax-exempt organizations can be brought into compliance. Intermediate sanctions are the proposed solution that has received the most attention recently.

Intermediate sanctions would allow for the imposition of penalties short of revocation of tax-exempt status. Early discussions regarding intermediate sanctions focused on whether they should be imposed on an organization or on individuals. The rationale for imposing sanctions on the organization is similar to that for imposing tax liabilities on for-profit corporations. The institution is the reporting entity and individual employees and directors act as representatives of the institution. On the other hand, the rationale for imposing the sanction on the individual trustee or employee is that a tax-exempt organization is a public charity and that the public should not suffer as a result of individuals' actions. It appears that the decision will be to place the sanction on the individual, not the organization. This decision is likely to influence who will be willing to be employed by a tax-exempt organization or to serve on its board of trustees.

Proposals introduced in Congress in 1994 called for intermediate sanctions in the form of penalty excise taxes. These excise taxes would be imposed on the individuals benefiting from a prohibited transaction as well as certain persons in the organization who knowingly approved of the transaction. As proposed, the taxes would not be levied on the organization itself. Rather, a penalty excise tax would be imposed on transactions in which an "insider" (someone with a special relationship to the organization) benefits directly or indirectly from this relationship. Examples of some of the arrangements intermediate sanctions are supposed to discourage are unreasonable compensation, improper revenue-sharing arrangements with insiders, and other non-fair-market-value transactions between an organization and an insider.

The intermediate sanctions would be a two-tier excise tax system. The first-tier tax would be imposed on the insider benefiting from the prohibited transaction and managers in the organization who knowingly participated in the transaction. If the prohibited transaction is not corrected, the second-tier tax would then be imposed on the insider in an amount in excess of the benefit received (e.g., 200 percent). A second-tier tax (e.g., 50 percent) may also be imposed on a manager in the organization who refuses to agree to correct the transaction. Given the need for sanctions short of renovation of exempt status, it is likely that intermediate sanctions in some form will be enacted. While these sanctions are targeted primarily to address current problem areas, they may be broadened by Treasury regulations and IRS rulings in the future to address other concerns.

Congress adjourned in 1994 without enacting intermediate sanction legislation. Although intermediate sanctions may be viewed as new taxes and therefore contrary to the pledge in the Republican's "Contract with America," it is likely these proposals will be reintroduced.

The heightened scrutiny by the IRS, Congress, and the public at large of tax-exempt organizations coupled with the possibility of intermediate sanctions may make it difficult for tax-exempt organizations to continue to operate as they have in the past. An organization must be aware of these issues and, if necessary, modify its behavior in light of them. Failure to do so may result in the imposition of penalties on the organization's management and/or its insiders, and, perhaps more important, lead to negative publicity that could severely hinder the ability of the organization to raise funds to carry out its exempt purposes.

16.8 COMPENSATION

Organizations can take measures to help avoid any impropriety as well as the appearance of improprieties. This is particularly true in the area of private inurement as it relates to "unreasonable" compensation.

It is more likely that payments made to or on behalf of a person as compensation that are not disclosed will be questioned as "unreasonable," and possibly be viewed as impermissible private inurement. Current intermediate sanctions proposals define impermissible private inurement as the payment of personal expenses which are not included in the person's wages. Under such proposals, if compensation is not reported on the person's W-2 form, it will be subject to a penalty excise tax even if the person's overall compensation is deemed to be "reasonable."

In the college and university environment, private inurement may occur when key employees are in a position to unduly influence their own compensation. In his opening remarks at hearings held on August 2, 1993 before the Subcommittee on Oversight of the House Ways and Means Committee, Representative J. J. Pickle made the following remark: "Another charity paid $200,000 for its executive director's wedding reception and tropical island honeymoon. The charity also plunked down $90,000 as a down payment for the director's home, and had enough left over to pay for his trip to a health spa." Pickle was referring to a situation in which an executive director took advantage of his position with the organization to reimburse himself for substantial personal expenses. What Pickle's remarks do not address is whether the executive director's compensation package, when looked at in its entirety, was reasonable. Presumably, it was not.

Determining what level of compensation is reasonable has been the subject of much debate for both taxable and tax-exempt organizations.

From time to time, the IRS has become concerned about excessive compensation, but it has been a difficult area for them to monitor. Defining what is reasonable compensation is highly subjective and depends on particular facts and circumstances. Although setting an appropriate compensation level is not an exact science, an institution can take measures to develop a set of policies and procedures to determine appropriate compensation for its senior administrators and professors.

First, an institution should develop its own set of performance-based criteria against which it measures performance. Performance against budgeted objectives, capital campaign results, and meeting strategic objectives are items that could be included in the criteria. Second, a formal performance review process should be established to evaluate current performance against the criteria.

Third, the institution should obtain salary information from comparable institutions. The criteria for comparability are flexible but may include such factors as endowment, student enrollment, the size of the budget, level of research funding, and location (i.e., urban, rural, geographic region). While it is important to review compensation levels at comparable institutions, it is also important to interpret the information and use it to make prudent decisions. It is not difficult to justify an average or below-average compensation package. However, will that package be sufficient to attract and retain top personnel? If not, a higher compensation package must be justified.

Finally, a formal process to establish and approve executive compensation at the board level should exist. Such a process may include full board approval of compensation committee recommendations of executive compensation plans prior to their implementation, detailed presentations to the board of how the approved plan is to be implemented and the cumulative effect on the institution of proposed actions, performance measures or criteria used in setting executive compensation levels, comparisons with peer institutions, and full documentation in the minutes of the board's approval.

16.9 FINANCING NEW FACILITIES

The cost of constructing and maintaining campus facilities has increased dramatically. Colleges and universities faced with budget cutbacks are trying to find innovative ways to utilize their facilities more fully in order to cost-justify them. Such new uses for facilities as professional sports, entertainment events, and research activities can call into question the tax-exempt status of the bonds used to finance the facilities.

For tax-exempt bonds to retain their exempt status, certain compliance guidelines must be met. The Tax Reform Act of 1986 imposed a strict limitation on the amount of permissible private use of facilities financed with the proceeds of tax-exempt bonds.[6] Use of proceeds for nonexempt purposes in excess of 5 percent can result in loss of tax exemption for the entire bond issue. For example, a violation of the private-use limitation would occur in a $100 million tax-exempt bond issue if more than $5 million went to finance a building that was used entirely for nonexempt purposes, such as a restaurant operated by a for-profit outsider.

A less obvious but more likely example might involve a multimillion-dollar bond issue used to construct a multipurpose facility. If it were found that private use of the facility, such as for concerts run by outsiders, was more than 5 percent of the total use (and if the IRS successfully challenged the use of the bond proceeds), the bond would lose its tax-exempt status. The interest income on the bond would also become taxable to the bondholders. In addition, significant legal and financial costs for the institution would result.

To control costs, many colleges and universities outsource various activities, including food services and bookstores. If these activities are conducted in facilities financed with tax-exempt bonds, it is important that the agreements with the outside vendors be structured as qualified management agreements so that they will not result in private use. The IRS has issued a Revenue Procedure that outlines the safe harbor criteria for a qualified management contract.[7]

Use of a tax-exempt-financed facility pursuant to a management contract that does not meet all the criteria in Revenue Procedure 93-19 could be considered private use. When structuring a management agreement, careful attention needs to be paid to this Revenue Procedure, which contains detailed requirements. (In December 1994, proposed regulations were issued which, if enacted, would loosen some of the requirements of Revenue Procedure 93-19.)

It is critical that institutions consider what they will use tax-exempt-financed facilities for at the time that tax-exempt debt is issued and to

[6] For bonds issued prior to August 17, 1986, the private-use limitation is 25 percent. For bonds issued to colleges and universities after August 17, 1986, the limit on the use of proceeds for private purposes is generally 5 percent. If bond offering expenses (up to 2 percent of the bond) are paid from bond proceeds, the limit may be as low as 3 percent.

[7] In general, Revenue Procedure 93-19 states that use of a tax-exempt-financed facility pursuant to a management contract will *not* be treated as private use if (1) the term of the contract is no longer than five years, *including* renewal options; (2) the 501(c)(3) organization has the option to cancel the contract at the end of three years (with or without cause); (3) compensation of the manager under the contract is not based (in whole or in part) on a share of the net profits; and (4) at least 50 percent of the annual compensation of the manager under contract is based on a fixed fee.

continue to monitor activities conducted in these facilities after financing. Even when no private activities were contemplated at the time of the bond issue, the eventual use of a facility can vary significantly from its original intended use. If the eventual use of the facility is nonexempt, the bond issue can be disqualified.

To avoid this potentially disastrous result or a challenge by the IRS in this area, detailed records need to be kept to support the fact that 95 percent or more of the use of the facility is for exempt purposes. All use for other than the organization's exempt purposes should be recorded. The institution needs to track revenues received, how long the building was used for a nonexempt purpose, and how much of the building was used for a nonexempt purpose.

In Announcement 93-92, the IRS unveiled its exempt bond compliance program, which is designed to coordinate all enforcement activities relating to tax-exempt bonds under the IRS National Office. Similar to the drastic methods available to the IRS for curing violations of an organization's exempt status, the result of excess private use of tax-exempt-bond-financed facilities is to recharacterize the bond as taxable. This would cause a hardship to innocent bondholders. Recognizing that an innocent party would pay the price of impermissible use, subsequent IRS guidance has indicated that in carrying out its exempt bond compliance program, the IRS will use closing agreements. These closing agreements may be structured so that the bond user, not the bondholder, will be penalized. However, the IRS noted that in cases of deliberate misuse, the bondholders themselves will be required to pay the tax on the interest received. Such a result could be very financially damaging and publicly embarrassing for an institution.

16.10 PROPERTY TAXES

Colleges and universities are generally exempt from real property taxes, at least to the extent that real property is used to further their exempt educational purpose. In recognition of the services that are available to them from the surrounding community, most colleges and universities make "payments in lieu of taxes." As the IRS's scrutiny of colleges' and universities' unrelated activities for tax and tax-exempt-financing purposes increases, it is likely that local communities will seek to "adjust" the exemption. For example, the local community may try to assess property tax on a multipurpose facility for the portion of unrelated use, especially when there is a perception that the payment in lieu of taxes by a college or university is inadequate.

The institution can take steps to justify their real property tax exemption. In addition to properly documenting the nonrelated use of its facilities, the institution should document the amount of benefit the use of its facilities and its personnel provides to the local community. Using auditoriums and classrooms for community groups or for lectures given by faculty and visitors that are open to the public, or opening athletic facilities to surrounding high schools and other groups should be documented. In addition, the institution may try to quantify the economic benefits, such as additional jobs, it brings to the community. By documenting in detail the community benefit provided by an institution, it can help prevent the perception that it is not paying its fair share of taxes.

16.11 TECHNOLOGY TRANSFER

Colleges and universities are often the incubators of new technology. New technology may be developed, particularly in engineering and medical schools, through normal university activities or with funds provided by government agencies and private industry.

One way to leverage a university's resources and to increase its revenues is to license and commercialize technology that has been developed under the institutional umbrella. As a result of this kind of activity, new relationships among the institution, its faculty members, and private industry have developed. For example, faculty members have formed their own for-profit corporations to exploit the technology developed at the institution. By promoting business incubators, universities have created an avenue for faculty members and small business people to develop and exploit new technology. In some cases, private industry has partnered with the universities or faculty members. These arrangements must be planned carefully to avoid private excess compensation and to minimize unrelated business income.

Traditionally, when faculty members have developed technology as part of their employment, they share in the proceeds of its commercialization. The patent is usually obtained in the institution's name. The technology may be licensed to third parties for a royalty payment, and faculty members subsequently receive a piece of the royalty stream. This has become an industry practice and such arrangements have not been closely scrutinized by the IRS. However, given the increased focus on all compensation agreements, royalty arrangements are likely to be reviewed more closely in the future.

When the university enters into a transaction with a faculty member, it is critical that the pricing be at arm's length. It is imperative to transfer technology and other assets from the university to the faculty member or a faculty-owned corporation at fair market value. Independent third-party appraisals should be obtained. Otherwise, the institution is open to charges of private inurement. When faculty members receive additional compensation for their role in technology development based on their services as an employee, care needs to be taken to assure that the additional compensation is not viewed as excessive.

When technology is developed outside the institution, payments to the institution for the use of its research facilities or personnel can become an issue. Although private inurement is statutorily prohibited, a limited amount of private benefit is allowable. Private benefit becomes a problem when the benefit received by an outside individual or group is disproportionate in relation to the level of investment or effort. An example occurs when outside entities use university's facilities or personnel at below-market rates. The facts and circumstances of each of these arrangements is subject to scrutiny by the IRS.

Another tax issue to be reviewed when engaging in transactions related to technology is whether any of the payments received by the institution result in unrelated business income. Revenue from the leasing of personal property is deemed unrelated business income.

16.12 CONCLUSIONS

The pressure on institutions to document community benefit will increase over time. Many families believe today that a private college education is not attainable due to its high cost. For many private institutions, available scholarship funds are limited and may be declining. To combat the perception that private institutions will be only for the elite (which would be contrary to granting exempt status to organizations that further the private good), colleges will need to document the benefits they provide to their communities. With health-care reform in turmoil, hospitals are currently under increased pressure to document community benefit. If a health-care reform passes in the future, they will be required to do so to maintain their exempt status. While similar proposals have not been raised for higher education, we would expect that in the future, public policy would dictate that similar requirements be met by colleges and universities.

While a radical departure in operations is not suggested, it is important that institutions take a close look at their activities. Although looking for new and creative uses of revenue is to be encouraged, institutions need to be sensitive to the effect of their actions in the community and need to position themselves proactively as contributors to society's well-being.

PART SIX

Epilogue

Chapter Seventeen
Creating a Vision for the Future

Creating a Vision
for the Future

GEORGE KELLER

Former Chair of the Higher Education Management Program
University of Pennsylvania

17.1 Introduction   17.4 The Components of Vision
17.2 The Trouble with Vision   17.5 Fallacies About Vision
17.3 The Pressures for More Vision   17.6 The Vision Imperative

17.1 INTRODUCTION

If any educational group intends to reinvent its university or college it will need to have some idea of what the newly invented institution might look like. It is not sufficient to move away from existing problems, inefficiencies, and outmoded structures and programs. Toward what new directions should the group move? The changes will require a vision of what the renovated university or college could or should become.

The need for vision seems so obvious. Individually we have visions of becoming firemen, great violinists, major league pitchers, fashion models, famous authors, competent doctors or nurses, or owners of our own store or business. We labor to make ourselves more physically fit or financially shrewd; we struggle to have a happy family life or a merry circle of friends. Collectively we often work to make the town we live in one of the loveliest and best run, to have our college be the friendliest and best teaching institution in the region, or to see that the United States is a land of opportunity and freedom for all citizens, as Martin Luther King, Jr. did so magnificently. Nearly all humans carry a dream in their pockets, a vision of what could be one day in the future.

Somehow through evolution, mysteriously, human beings have been provided with two kinds of vision. One is the animal recognition of material objects and movements with our eyes. The other is the ability to see with our minds, to imagine a new political condition, an ideal vegetable garden, a novel law school program. We can look back in time as we do with reflection, regret, or reevaluation; and we can look forward to conceive of a larger or smaller institution, a different organizational structure, a more strategic mode of operating in the decade ahead, or a new kind of international society linked by electronics and clever software. As one essayist recently wrote:

> Our bodies demonstrate, albeit silently, that we are more than just a complex version of our animal ancestors to which a little dab of rationality has been added; and conversely that we are also more than an enlarged brain, a consciousness somehow grafted onto or trapped within a blind mechanism that knows only survival. The human form as a whole impresses on us its inner powers of thought (or awareness and action.) Mind and hand, gait and gaze, breath and tongue, foot and mouth—all are isomorphically part of a single package, suffused with the presence of intelligence.[1]

The history of U.S. higher education is replete with stories of persons who imagined, who saw ahead in their minds a new kind of college or university: Charles William Eliot and Nicholas Murray Butler, who transformed urban colleges for gentlemen into great universities at Harvard and Columbia; Emma Hart Willard, who envisioned young women studying as undergraduates as young men did; the Holy Cross fathers, who imagined a Catholic university in the wilds of northern Indiana at South Bend; president Wallace Sterling and Provost Fred Terman, who envisioned a post-World War II Harvard-like university at Stanford for people on the West Coast; U.S. Congressman Justin Morrill of Vermont, who imagined and fought for a new kind of public college in every state "to promote the liberal and practical education of the industrial classes"— the land-grant college; and Frank Aydelotte who envisioned an Oxford-like college in Swarthmore, Pennsylvania. As I said, the need for vision seems obvious, and natural. Human beings are imaginative, envisioning creatures. Civilizations, and colleges and universities, are built and maintained and improved by people who have created a vision about a kind of life or institution different from the one that exists.

17.2 THE TROUBLE WITH VISION

Yet in the 1990s there is a growing cynicism about vision. When IBM's new chairman, Louis Gerstner, was questioned at a press conference

---

[1] Leon Kass, *The Hungry Soul: Eating and the Perfecting of Our Nature* (New York: Free Press, 1994), pp. 75–76.

about how he intended to halt the decline of the corporation, he responded: "There have been a lot of questions as to whether I'm going to deliver a vision for IBM. I would like to say that the last thing IBM needs right now is a vision. What it needs is very tough-minded . . . strategies for each of its businesses." And Robert Eaton, the new chairman of the Chrysler Corporation, told the *Wall Street Journal*, "Internally we don't use the word vision. I believe in quantifiable short-term results—things we can all relate to, as opposed to some esoteric thing no one can quantify." Billionaire William Gates, chairman of Microsoft Corporation, has sneered, "Being a visionary is trivial."

In higher education, a similar, growing disdain for vision can be heard. The new mood was perhaps best expressed in Richard Chait's opinion article in the September 22, 1993 *Chronicle of Higher Education*. In his view, "The 'vision thing' has been elevated nearly to the level of religion in higher education"; but Chait contends that "the virtues of vision have been exaggerated. The concept should be enshrined in the pantheon of panaceas that already includes management by objectives, zero-based budgeting, quality-control circles, and TQM." Chait believes that "these are not the times for heady visions," and he argues for an Adam Smith-like *laissez-faire* approach by campus administrators:

> For all the emphasis placed upon vision, observers of higher education would be hard pressed to cite more than a dozen or two colleges . . . that have been successfully "reinvented . . . ." More often institutional priorities and opportunities emerge from individual and departmental initiatives . . . .
>
> Freed of the obligation to craft a compelling and comprehensive vision college presidents can concentrate on crucial, if mundane, tasks like controlling costs, increasing productivity, diversifying their work forces, assessing quality and streamlining operations . . . .
>
> Few professors are disposed to be guided, let alone summoned, by the North Star of a presidential vision. . . . Presidents may do better to nip at the heels of the laggards, to contain the strays to the extent possible, and wait importantly, to nudge the entire herd along.[2]

Richard Chait is a member of the higher education faculty at the University of Maryland's School of Education, along with Robert Birnbaum and Frank Schmitlein. Chait and his colleagues at Maryland have been leaders in the higher education studies field in deriding attempts to improve leadership, strategic planning, quality of service enhancement, and vision in academe. Adhering to the incrementalism of political

[2] Richard Chait, "Colleges should not be blinded by vision," *Chronicle of Higher Education*, September 22, 1993, pp. B1, B2.

scientist Charles Lindblom, who wrote that "Patching up an old system is the most rational way to change it, for the patch constitutes about as big a change as one can comprehend at a time,"[3] the Maryland school of skeptics believes in the beneficent "hidden hand" of multifold and scattered initiatives, chiefly by the faculty.

In this the Maryland scholars reflect the views of dozens of college and university presidents I have met who feel they are able to be little more than highly paid janitors and dignified spokespersons, and who are convinced that passive, unobtrusive administration of the semi-anarchic status quo is the only "realistic" course. They also concur with the view of Clark Kerr and others who argue that the new power of federal grant agencies, state commissioners of higher education, scholar-entrepreneurs in their midst, the courts, special-interest racial, gender, and ethnic groups, and accrediting bodies prevents academic executives from having a vision of their own for their institutions. In the words of Clark Kerr during his 1963 Godkin lectures at Harvard: "There is a 'kind of lawlessness,' in any large university . . . and the task is to keep this lawlessness within reasonable bounds. . . . The president becomes the central mediator . . . among groups and institutions moving at different rates of speed and sometimes different directions. . . . He has no new and bold 'vision of the end.' He is driven more by necessity than by voices in the air."[4]

This Ronald Reagan-like perspective on modern academic leadership is, I think, a salutary caution, particularly against the sometimes hyperbolic claims for "reinventing" the university and those academic management texts which assume that campus deans and presidents have the charisma and power of England's Henry IV. To "reinvent" is to make over completely, or to reestablish in a very different form an already established institution. This is not very likely to happen. Universities are among the oldest, most conservative and adaptive organizations in Western civilization.[5]

But the caretaker view of college leadership—administration without vision, patching up and nipping at the heels of the professorial laggards—has become a perilous one to advocate at the end of the twentieth century. It is also flawed in its analysis and suppositions. For one thing, not having a vision is a kind of vision. To imagine that a college will

---

[3] Robert Dahl and Charles Lindblom, *Politics, Economics, and Welfare* (Chicago: University of Chicago Press, 1976), p. 86.

[4] Clark Kerr, *The Uses of the University* (Cambridge, Mass.: Harvard University Press, 1963), pp. 35, 37.

[5] It is instructive to read medieval historian Charles Homer Haskins' *The Rise of Universities* (Ithaca, N.Y.: Cornell University Press, 1957).

remain pretty much the same over the next 15 to 20 years in the face of radical changes in demography, technology, and finances is an apparition—and a decision about the future—as much as a vision to double in size or to become more multicultural.

For another thing, if an institution has no vision, other persons or outside agencies may force a new mission, usually a more restricted or specialized one, on the institution. For a third item, a concentration on the basics—"good, solid blocking and tackling," as IBM's Louis Gerstner puts it—is quite appropriate for an organization that is badly run and in trouble because of ineptitude and neglect, and lack of vision. The first priority for poorly run colleges, after all, is to get their house in order. TQM, well done, has been a considerable help to some colleges in this situation. But if a university is functioning fairly well, the priority becomes: What should it do in the future to maintain its position and excellence? Or to move to a slightly higher level of quality?

There are larger reasons for vision in higher education, however.

17.3 THE PRESSURES FOR MORE VISION

It is not an historical accident that the calls for greater attention to the future began in the late 1960s and reached an almost nagging emphasis in the 1970s and 1980s. Herman Kahn and Daniel Bell (who invented the term *postindustrial society*) in 1967, Michael Young in 1968, and Peter Drucker in 1969 were prominent among those who pointed out that North America and Western Europe were at the edge of major social, technological, demographic, and economic changes.[6] After the 1965 amendments to the Immigration and Nationality Act, the United States began admitting more immigrants (including 150,000 to 300,000 illegal entries) each year than all the rest of the developed world combined, ushering in a new period of multiculturalism. The personal computer was introduced. The traditional two-parent family began disintegrating. Since the family has long been the coeducator of children, the change has meant new problems for the schools and cities. Out-of-wedlock births have increased rapidly, to the point where 30 percent of all babies in the United States are now born in that way. Adult education has become a giant, growing addition to the customary youth education for many colleges and univer-

[6] Herman Kahn and Anthony Weiner, *The Year 2000: A Framework for Speculation* (New York: Collier Macmillan, 1967); Daniel Bell, "Notes on the post-industrial society," *Public Interest*, No. 6, 1967, pp. 24–35, No. 7, 1967, pp. 102–118; Michael Young, ed., *Forecasting and the Social Sciences* (London: Heinemann, 1968); Peter Drucker, *The Age of Discontinuity* (New York: Harper & Row, 1969).

sities. And the United States faces new financial pressures from Japan and other countries abroad and from escalating expenses for crime prevention and prisons, pollution, pensions for the elderly, and health care from inside the nation. In short, the environment has become very turbulent, and educators are increasingly being asked to respond to the radical changes and "reinvent" their structures and services for the new environment.

A second source of pressure for greater vision is from those who believe that the increasing decentralization and fragmentation of universities and many colleges demands something to hold the institution together—what two business professors have called "superordinate goals." These are "significant meanings or guiding concepts that an organization imbues in its members."[7] In effect, a vision of where the institution is going seems necessary to bind together the loose coupling of many campus parts.

As colleges grew larger, and as numerous universities (and some community colleges) expanded to 25,000 to 40,000 students in the 1970s, educational leaders pushed decisions out of the president's and academic vice president's office to the schools, departments, and divisions. This frequently resulted in quasi-independent medical, business, or law schools, or departments of physics or economics, or maintenance or student affairs divisions. The question thus becomes: How can a university decentralize and at the same time have a coordinated effort? As two scholars put it: "How can people in the far reaches of these flatter organizations know where it is heading? The development of a shared organizational vision represents a response to this problem."[8]

There are other pressures to create a vision too. Colleges and universities have long lead times. Change at most campuses is remarkably slow, with lengthy debates over the processes, details, and educational policies. New facilities often have to be planned for five to eight years in advance. And students are preparing for work in society 10 to 20 years from the present. A vision that imagines the institution 10 years hence therefore is an enormous help. Also, arriving at a desirable vision for the institution's future circumvents some of the fierce discussion about the details of the present situation and immediate reallocations. A vision enables academics to think seriously about the purposes, priorities, and distinctiveness of their college or university without threats to current positions and arrangements.

---

[7] Richard Tanner Pascale and Anthony Athos, *The Art of Japanese Management* (New York: Warner Books, 1982), p. 125.
[8] James Collins and Jerry Porras, "Organizational vision and visionary organizations," *California Management Review*, Vol. 34, Fall 1991, p. 1.

Then too, Henry Mintzberg, a leading Canadian scholar of planning, has argued that strategic planning is largely instrumental. It provides reasonable priorities and detailed steps after the leaders have formulated a vision. To him, "planning does not promote significant change in the organization so much as deal with it when it is introduced by other means," and "a plan as vision—expressed in imagery, or metaphorically—may prove a greater incentive to action than a plan that is formally detailed, simply because it is more attractive and less constraining."[9] A vision with some emotional content is often more likely to spur action toward a rearranged college than a well-conceived, quantified strategy; and a vision gives faculty members a greater freedom to invent.

17.4 THE COMPONENTS OF VISION

Vision is not the same as a mission statement, which is almost always a bland stew of platitudes, past achievements, beliefs, and vague goals. Vision is a combination of gut values and a tangible goal.

The gut values need to be ones that are part of the college's tradition and to which at least a large minority of people on campus already subscribe. If the values articulated in a vision are too idealistic or vague, the vision will be treated cynically. For example, a fine, historic liberal arts college might say: "Our college will continue to educate a small number of very able undergraduates for the highest positions in society through intense and scholarly study with exceptional scholar-teachers." Or, a major, large state university might advocate something like benefactor Ezra Cornell did when he established Cornell University: "I would found an institution where any person can find instruction in any study," thus giving equal value to poultry science, forestry, and labor relations and to history, literature, and science. But if a college proclaims that it will be a place giving supreme importance to the cultivation of every individual's personal and intellectual growth—as half of America's colleges do in their catalogs—when the faculty union, the director of athletics, or the dean of students has other priorities, the values are a fanciful bromide rather than an expression of gut values. L. L. Bean, the Maine clothing and camping merchant, said in 1947: "Sell good merchandise at a reasonable price, and treat your customers as you would your friends, and the business will take care of itself." These were Bean's gut values.

But it is not enough to express one's deepest values in the vision statement. The vision must also have a tangible outcome. It should be an inspiring picture of a different future, something that seems slightly out of reach but achievable if enough people work on it, as when President

[9] Henry Mintzberg, *The Rise and Fall of Strategic Planning* (New York: Free Press, 1994), pp. 292–293.

John Kennedy proclaimed in 1961 as a vision, "before this decade is out, of landing a man on the moon and returning him safely to earth."

The tangible outcome is tricky. It should not be too definite and detailed, yet vivid enough to allow persons to imagine a new and better set of conditions and services and to strive toward their fulfillment. For instance, in 1909 Henry Ford said his vision was "to democratize the automobile." The statement did not suggest the Model T but made it clear that Ford would concentrate on low-cost cars, not Cadillac-like vehicles. The vision implied a target audience and the kind of automobile with which the company would seek preeminence.

There are two kinds of tangible outcomes. One is that of setting a clear, unambiguous target. Here are some fictional examples of targeting:

- "Within the next 20 years we will become the equal of Harvard for West Coast youth and adults."

- "We will become widely known as the best managed and financially open private college in our region."

- "The college will in the next 10 years be the finest teaching institution among state colleges in our state."

- "Our state university will be smaller, more focused, and regarded as one of the top 10 or 12 public universities in the nation."

The other kind of tangible outcome is that of institutional transformation, of picturing a slightly "reinvented" institution to meet the emerging realities of the next decades. Again, some fictional examples:

- "The university will have more blacks, Latinos, and Asians among its students and faculty, and reorient its curriculum and scholarship to be more international and multicultural."

- "Our university will employ the newest technology for teaching, financial planning and controls, and linkages with other academic, cultural, and scientific entities."

- "Recognizing the increase in state and community colleges, this historic state university will enlarge its graduate education, research, and leadership in professional education, admitting fewer undergraduates and chiefly those of demonstrated scholarly interests."

17.5 FALLACIES ABOUT VISION

One of the most common errors that critics of vision make is that vision requires a charismatic or exceptionally clairvoyant president. This is patently untrue. Department chairpersons have sometimes created extraordinary collections of scholars in their departments. I have often been told that a "visionary" financial officer has kept some institution's eyes on long-term financial strength rather than short-term expenditures. Three times in my travels I have encountered extraordinary directors of buildings and grounds who take unusual pride in their work and staff and have a vision of what the campus grounds and horticulture will look like in the next decade.

Another error is that visionaries are dreamers, ambitious utopians who can't and won't pay attention to costs, details, and current problems. They lack realism, with realism usually defined as accommodation to the status quo and small, incremental changes at the edges. The fact is that good visions emerge from an unusual attention to the myriad workings of the institution, not from a neglect of such attention. And even small changes can't be carried out effectively unless one has a vision of the direction toward which the changes should be made. Some of the most acerbic critics of "vision" usually have an implicit vision of their own about where the college or university should be going. Yet there is a small but growing band of higher education scholars who seem resigned to drift, semianarchy, and lack of fiscal priorities or controls as the only satisfactory way of administering a varied, rambunctious, and quarrelsome collection of specialized scholars. To them, a vision seems a confining rather than a bonding agent which provides purpose and distinctiveness to an institution competing with numerous others of the 3600 colleges and universities in the United States.

However, there are several key ingredients that those educators who would develop and promote a vision must possess. One is a sense of history, of what works and doesn't in social organizations and during times of change. Another is a willingness to understand the public's view as well as the parochial campus interests. Peter Drucker once expressed it this way: "[The visionary leader] has to establish himself as a spokesman for the interest of society in producing, in performing, in achieving. . . . He has to become the proponent, the educator, the advocate. The manager, in other words, will have to learn to create the 'issues.'"[10] The vision of an education leader should connect the private interests of the professors and staff to the public urgencies of society in the years ahead.

Educators also need to sharpen their imaginative thinking. Faculty members are passionately devoted to "critical thinking" but they say very little about *creative* thinking, which in our time has become essential. Our colleges and universities, as well as our other institutions, lack sufficient

[10] Peter Drucker, *Managing in Turbulent Times* (New York: Harper & Row, 1980), p. 218.

powers of social invention. No one ever did this better than Alexis de Tocqueville, when he observed Americans, identified the central features of young America, and constructed a pattern for likely future developments for this country.[11] In recent years more educators have become adept at analyzing the thrusts and novel features of society and have begun to create visions and strategic plans to implement the visions.[12]

17.6 THE VISION IMPERATIVE

In a remarkable new book, Antonio Damasio, one of the world's leading neuroscientists, has provided scientific evidence of "Descartes' error," the notion that there is an area of the brain that is capable of pure, objective thought.[13] Damasio and others have demonstrated in the past decade that every part of the brain is tied to emotion and to physical movements. People are creatures of their genetic material, their environmental conditioning, and their emotions.

Visions have emotional power. They help us organize our knowledge and supply hope, passion, and direction. They help give meaning to our lives. Visions speak to our entire selves rather than just to dry-as-felt goals or quantitative objectives.

If colleges and universities are to reform their structures, finances, and services, they will have to possess some vision of how they will do so, and why. The vision for any institution should combine its tradition, culture, and core values with the emerging conditions in society and the public's expectations about higher education's role and behavior in the new environment.

The vision may take root in one of a university's colleges that is led by a farsighted dean. It can originate with department or division chairs or with a courageous vice president. It can be forced by a strong, forward-looking board of trustees if the president and faculty drag their feet. Whatever its source, each college and university should design a vision for itself. David Riesman once wrote, "there has always been room for innovation and fresh starts in American higher education, even if this freedom, which rested partly on expanding enrollments and funds, is more circumscribed now. What is really lacking is strong and visionary academic leadership."[14]

---

[11] Alexis de Tocqueville, *Democracy in America* (New York: Oxford University Press, 1947).

[12] George Keller, *Academic Strategy* (Baltimore: Johns Hopkins University Press, 1983).

[13] Antonio Damasio, *Descartes' Error: Emotion, Reason, and the Human Brain* (New York: G. P. Putnam's Sons, 1994).

[14] Quoted in Keller, p. 164.

Index

Access:
aid and affordability, 37–38
price versus, 31–32
United Kingdom, 280
Accountability:
administrative restructuring, implementation program, 93–94
board effectiveness, 65
change and, 38–40, 51, 77
executive evaluation and, 44–45
financial reporting, 333–361. *See also*
Financial reporting
information technology, 256–260
United Kingdom, 281, 289–290
Accounting procedures, enrollment
income, gross versus net income,
153–154. *See also* Financial
reporting
Accreditation, 308, 313, 323, 330, 331
Acheson, Dean, 22
Action, change and, 17
Activities statement, 346–348
Administration. *See also* Leadership;
Management; Presidents
business case for change in, 104–105
inefficiency in, 101–104
information technology, 251–275. *See
also* Information technology
revenue and, 133–134
Administrative assistant. *See* Process
navigator
Administrative restructuring/reengineering, 79–100
approach to, 82–83
business case for, 104–105
business model agreement, 96–99
categorization and prioritization, 81–82
context establishment, 83–84
corporate experience, 106–107
guidelines for, 99–100

higher education applicability, 107–108
implementation program, 90–96
accountability measures, 93–94
communications network, 94
generally, 90
governance, organization, and staffing, 92–93
human resource factors, 94–95
key resources, 95–96
prioritization, sequencing, and goals, 90–91
process treatments, methods, and work plans, 91–92
training and technology transfer, 92
methodology, 81
opportunity identification and prioritization, 84–90
baseline analysis, 85–88
business case preparation, 90
long-term enhancements, 88–90
performance assessment, 84–85
quick wins, 88
strategic questions, 85
overview of, 79–80, 105
process of, 108–116
evaluating and fixing processes, 109–111
generally, 108–109
process map, 111–116
Stanford University School of Medicine experience, 116–125
fragmentation implications, 120–122
generally, 116–117
organizational construct, 122–125
perceptions, 118, 120
process map, 117–118, 119
United Kingdom, 294–298. *See also*
United Kingdom
Affordability, change strategies, factors in, 37–38
AGB Reports, 26

INDEX

Alpert, Daniel, 50
Alumni, revenue resources, 138–139
Analytical dimension, board effectiveness, 62
Anderson, Richard E., 50–51
Annenberg, Walter, 150
Arbitrage pricing theory, 182
Asset protection/enhancement, trustee role, 60–61
Association of American Universities, 12
Atwell, Robert, 312
Audits:
  trustee role, 60–61
  United Kingdom, 298–299
Augustine, John, 356
Aydelotte, Frank, 382

Background process, 82, 110
Baseline analysis, administrative restructuring, opportunity identification and prioritization, 85–88
Bell, Daniel, 385
Benefits. See Compensation and benefits
Benezet, Louis T., 67
Bennett, William J., 309, 310
Biggs, Barton, 202
Birnbaum, Robert, 55, 56, 65, 66
Black colleges, history of, 7
Blumenthal, Richard, 367
Bok, Derek, 335
Bonds, financial markets, 185–207. See also Financial markets
Boston College, 7
Boulding, Kenneth, 26
Bowen, Howard R., 51
Boyer, Ernest, 36
Brace, Paul K., 337
Brewster, Kingman, 309
Brown College (Rhode Island College), 5
Budget pressures. See Financial pressure
Buildings and grounds. See Facilities management
Bureaucracy, corporate values and, 106–107
Bush, George, 307
Business case preparation, administrative restructuring, 90
Business model, agreement on, 96–99
Business process engineering, information technology and, 253
Butler, Nicholas Murray, 382

California, 25
  spending priorities in, 27, 28
  tax reform in, 30

Cameron, Kim S., 51, 52, 53, 67, 69, 70, 71, 72, 73, 74
Campus population, revenue resources, 139–140
Capital:
  facilities management, 232–233, 235
  financial markets, 185–207. See also Financial markets
Capital asset pricing model, investment theory, endowment management, 182
Capital assets, facilities management, 238–241, 246–247
Capital structure strategy, endowment management, 176–177
Career counseling, administrative restructuring, implementation program, 95
Carlin, George, 26
Cash flow statement, 348–349
Categorization, administrative restructuring, 81–82
Catholic Church, education and, 7
Centralization. See also Decentralization
  leadership and, 76
  organizational models, 54–56
Central specialist, administrative inefficiency and, 103–104
Chaffee, Ellen E., 67, 69
Chait, Richard P., 50, 57, 61, 62, 63, 383
Champy, James, 106, 111
Change, 13–17
  administrative restructuring, 79–100. See also Administrative restructuring/reengineering
  business case for, 104–105
  challenge of, 22–23
  in corporate values, 106–107
  higher education and, 13–17
  historical context of, 23–27
  information technology, 262
  leadership and, 16–17, 70–75
  maxims of, 75–78
  mechanisms of, 15–16
  overview of, 13–14
  pace of, 14–15, 52–53
  types of, 50–53
Change strategies:
  factors in, 35–42
    aid and affordability, 37–38
    generally, 35–36
    leverage and constraint mechanisms, 36–37
    public accountability, 38–40

technology use, 40–42
value and reward system, 36
leadership-management questions,
42–47
controversial issues, 45–47
executive evaluation and accountabil-
ity, 44–45
executive search and reward, 42–44
generally, 42
Cheit, Earl, 335, 336
Churchill, Winston, 48
Civilization, education and, 5–6
Civil Rights Restoration Act of 1987, 311
Civil War (U.S.), 23
Clark, Burton R., 55
Classical curriculum, historical perspective
on, 7
Cleary, Robert E., 61
Cohen, Michael, 66
Columbia College (King's College), 5
Commitment, generation of, leadership
role, 73–74
Communications. *See also*
Telecommunications
administrative restructuring, implementation program, 94
change and, 17
information technology, 251–275. *See
also* Information technology
Community colleges, history of, 7
Comparative ratios, as benchmarks, financial markets, 196–197
Compensation and benefits, 213–215
internal and individual pay equity, 223
labor market studies, 217–218
performance appraisals and merit pay,
223–224
salary structures, 218–220
salary surveys, 218
tax exemption, 372–373
theoretical versus practical considerations, 220–222
Computer:
facilities management, 245–246
information technology and, 255. *See
also* Information technology
Consolidation, financial reporting,
350–351
Construction. *See* Facilities management
Consumer expectations, information technology, 260–263
Consumerism, student outcomes, SPRE
initiative, 324

Context establishment, administrative
restructuring, 83–84
Conversion, facilities management,
239–240
Coordinated Examination Program,
369–370
Cornell, Ezra, 7, 387
Cornell University, 8
Corporate boards, change and, 57–58
Corporate values:
change in, 106–107
executive search and reward, 42–43
public accountability, change strategy
factor, 39–40
Costs:
cutting of, 148–149
increases in, 147–148

Damasio, Antonio, 390
Danzig, Lisa, 357
Dartmouth College, 5
Database management. *See* Information
technology
Davenport, Thomas H., 259
Debt:
capital structure strategy, endowment
management, 176–177
management of, financial markets,
185–207. *See also* Financial markets
Debt capacity assessment, financial mar-
kets, 194–196
Decentralization. *See also* Centralization
information technology, 252
leadership and, 74, 76
organizational models, 54–56
Default rates, financial markets, 197–198
Deferred compensation plans, 225–226
Deferred maintenance, facilities manage-
ment, 236–237
Demb, Ada, 58
Democracy, education and, 6
Demographics:
change and, 51
financial markets, future prospects, 201
information technology, 256–257
Discount minimization, revenue, 154–156
Discrimination, human resource develop-
ment, 226–227
Division of labor, hierarchy and, 109
Dodd, Christopher J., 308
Dodd, David, 179
Drew University, 22
Drucker, Peter, 14, 385, 389

Eaton, Robert, 383
Eccles, Robert G., 259
Economic factors. *See* Financial pressure
Education, religion and, 5
Educational dimension, board effectiveness, 62
Educational Rights and Privacy Act of 1977 (Buckley Amendment), 324
Effectiveness:
  efficiency compared, 50
  in leadership, 66–68
Efficiency, effectiveness compared, 50
Eliot, Charles William, 382
Employment practices, human resource development, 226–227
Employment prospects, higher education and, 33
Empowerment, information technology, 270
Enarson, Harold, 325
Endowment(s):
  revenue, 150
  summary of, listed, 173
  types and uses of, 171–172, 177–179
Endowment management, 169–184
  capital structure strategy, 176–177
  endowment types and uses, 171–172
  future trends, 183–184
  historical perspective on, 170–171
  investment policy, 183
  investment theory, 179–182
  overview of, 169–170
  spending and accumulation policies, 172–176
Equity, human resource development, 226–227
European Union, government subsidy in, 280. *See also* United Kingdom
Evaluation. *See* Performance appraisal
Executive evaluation and accountability, leadership-management questions, 44–45
Executive search and reward, leadership-management questions, 42–44
Expenditures, higher education, current status of, 33–35

Facilities management, 229–250
  capital asset productivity improvement, 238–241
  critical issues in, 232–233
  future management, 248–250

future projects prospectus, 242–248
historical context of, 230–232
new facilities, 241–242
overview of, 229–230
preservation and, 233–235
renewal, 236–238
tax exemption, 373–375
Faculty:
  administrative inefficiency and, 102
  change role of, 76
  information technology, 260–263
  leverage and constraint mechanisms, change strategy factor, 36–37
Federal government. *See* Government
Fees. *See* Tuition and fees
Financial Accounting Standards Board (FASB), 342–344. *See also* Financial reporting
Financial aid. *See also* Student loans
  change strategies, factors in, 37–38
  decline in, 148
Financial management model. *See* Business model
Financial markets, 185–207
  comparative ratios as benchmarks, 196–197
  credit quality issue, 194
  current situation, described, 190–194
  debt capacity assessment, 194–196
  default rates, 197–198
  future prospects, 201–204
    demographics, 201
    global restructuring, 201–204
  historical context, 186–190
  opportunities and challenges in, 206–207
  overview of, 185–186
  risk management, 205–206
  yield curve, 198–201
Financial position statement, 345–346
Financial pressure:
  change and, 50, 52
  facilities management, 232–233
  higher education and, 9–10, 30–31
  information technology and, 253–256
  United Kingdom, 295–296
Financial reporting, 333–361. *See also* Accounting procedures
  considerations in, 354–360
  external reporting, 339–341
  Financial Accounting Standards Board (FASB) agenda, 342–344
  future trends, 353–354

historical context, 334–337
new requirements, 344–350
  activities statement, 346–348
  cash flow statement, 348–349
  consolidation, 350–351
  financial position statement, 345–346
  generally, 344–345
  investment reporting, 351
  summarized, 349–350
overview of, 333–334
service efforts and accomplishments,
  351–353
SFAC No. 4, 337–339
Financial resources. *See also* Revenue
presidents and, 67
variety in, 54
Fincher, Cameron, 65, 67, 68, 69
Focus group, Stanford University School
  of Medicine experience, 118, 120
Ford, Henry, 388
Foreign students, revenue, 149
Foundations, philanthropic giving, 152,
  164
Fragmentation, implications of, administrative restructuring/reengineering,
  120–122
Frances, Carol, 64
Fund-raising:
  higher education, current status of, 32
  legal corporations for, 134
  limits of, 151–152
  president role, 66, 67
  revenue, 150–151
  trustee role, 60

Gade, Marian L., 65
Gallagher, John, 11
Gates, William, 383
Gee, E. Gordon, 4, 14
Germanic model, 24, 25
Gerstner, Louis, 382–383
GI Bill, 24, 25
Glade, Marian L., 69
Globalization:
  change and, 51
  financial markets, future prospects,
    201–204
  United Kingdom, 281
Goals, administrative restructuring,
  implementation program, 90–91
Good, Mary, 47
Governance, administrative restructuring,
  implementation program, 92–93

Governing boards, 57–65. *See also* Trustees
composition of, 58–59
corporate boards, 57–58
effectiveness of, 62–65
evolution of, 57
functioning of, 61–62
growth of influence of, 57
in higher education, 58
trustee roles, 59–62
Government regulation:
  facilities management, 247
  health care system, 15
  SPRE initiative, 303–332. *See also* SPRE
    initiative
  student aid linkage, 309–311
  student outcomes, 323
  United Kingdom, 280
Government subsidy:
  cost-effectiveness of, 164
  education and, 24, 54
  government regulation linkage, SPRE
    initiative, 309–311
  reductions in, 27, 104, 130–131, 148,
    155
  replacement of, 131–132
  student loan defaults, SPRE initiative,
    306–307
  United Kingdom, 280, 283. *See also*
    United Kingdom
Graham, Benjamin, 179
Great Depression, 27
Gross versus net income, enrollment
  income, 152–154
Grove City College, 310
Guskin, Alan, 305–306

Hammer, Michael, 106, 111, 254
Hansen, W. Lee, 50
Harvard College, 5, 6, 23
Health care system, change and, 15
Hearn, James C., 74
Hennigan, Patrick J., 358
Heydinger, Richard B., 53, 70
Hierarchy:
  corporate values and, 106–107
  division of labor and, 109
  information technology, 263–268
  job evaluation, human resource devel-
    opment, 215–217
Higher education:
  access to, 24
  challenges facing, 3–5, 8–13
  change and, 13–17. *See also* Change

Higher education (*continued*)
current status of, 27–35
expenditures, 33–35
general revenue restrictions, 30–31
price versus access, 31–32
public opinion, 29–30
public-private partnerships and fund-raising, 32
spending reductions on, 27–29
enrollment statistics, 8, 335
historical perspective on, 5–8, 53–54
organizational models in, 54–56
in United Kingdom, 279–302. *See also* United Kingdom
Higher Education Amendments of 1992, 311–312
Historic preservation, facilities management and, 233–234, 247–248
Holland, Thomas P., 62, 63
Hopkins, Johns, 7
Human resources, 209–227
administrative restructuring, implementation program, 94–95
compensation and benefits, 213–215
equity and employment, 226–227
internal and individual pay equity, 223
job evaluation, 215–217
labor market studies, 217–218
overview of, 210
performance appraisals and merit pay, 223–224
planning benefits, 210–212
planning model, 212–213
salary structures, 218–220
salary surveys, 218
tax considerations, 224–226
theoretical versus practical considerations, 220–222
Hutchins, Robert, 50

Identity process:
administrative restructuring/reengineering, 110, 113
categorization, administrative restructuring, 81–82
Immigration, education and, 7
Implementation, of change, leadership role, 74–75, 77
Implementation program, administrative restructuring, 90–96
accountability measures, 93–94
communications network, 94
generally, 90
governance, organization, and staffing, 92–93
human resource factors, 94–95
key resources, 95–96
prioritization, sequencing, and goals, 90–91
process treatments, methods, and work plans, 91–92
training and technology transfer, 92
Incentives, value and reward system, change strategy factor, 36
Independent institutions. *See* Private institutions
Industrialization, education and, 7
Information requirements, board effectiveness, 64
Information resources, revenue from, 135–136
Information technology, 251–275
accountability and reporting requirements, 256–260
consumer expectations, 260–263
financial pressures and, 253–256
future trends, 271–275
hierarchies, 263–268
overview of, 252
support systems, 268–271
Infrastructure. *See* Facilities management
Ingram, Richard T., 64
Institutional advancement, trustee role, 59–60
Institutional integrity, trustee role, 61
Intellectual property, revenue, information resources, 135–136
Interest rates:
risk management, financial markets, 205
yield curve, financial markets, 198–201
International students. *See* Foreign students
Interpersonal dimension, board effectiveness, 62
Investment:
administrative restructuring/reengineering, 109–110
information technology, 257
long-term enhancements, administrative restructuring, 90
social policy and, 178–179
theory of, endowment management, 179–182
Investment income:
endowments, 150, 169–184. *See also* Endowment management
market volatility, 175

Investments, reporting of, 351
Ivy League, 8

Jefferson, Thomas, 231
Jeffords, James M., 308
Job evaluation, human resource development, 215–217
Johns Hopkins University, 24
Johnson, Sandra, 64
Just-in-time delivery, information technology, 260

Kahn, Herman, 385
Kassebaum, Nancy L., 308
Katz, Joseph, 67
Kauffman, Joseph, 44
Kean, Thomas, 22, 42
Kearns, Doris Goodwin, 24
Keller, George, 16
Kennedy, Edward M., 308
Kennedy, John F., 388
Kerr, Clark, 29, 35, 42, 43, 50, 57, 58, 63, 65, 69, 260, 384
King's College (Columbia College), 5
Knapp, Ellen M., 81

Labor market studies, human resource development, 217–218
Land and facilities, revenue resources, 140–141. See also Facilities management
Land grant colleges:
  history of, 23
  leadership-management questions, 46
Leadership, 65–75. See also Administration; Management; Presidents
  change, 16–17, 75–76
    commitment generation, 73–74
    implementation of, 74–75, 77
    overcoming resistance to, 72–73
    readiness for, 71–72
    vision articulation, 73
  conceptions in, 66
  effectiveness in, 66–68
  role of, 65–66
  theories of, 68–69
  transformational leadership, 70
  vision and, 382. See also Vision
Leadership-management questions:
  controversial issues, 45–47
  executive evaluation and accountability, 44–45
  executive search and reward, 42–44

Learning outcomes. See Student learning outcomes
Legal corporations, for revenue, 134
Leverage and constraint mechanisms, change strategy factor, 36–37
Licensing, revenue, information resources, 135–136
Lindblom, Charles, 384
Long-term enhancements, administrative restructuring, opportunity identification and prioritization, 88–90
Lorsch, Jay W., 58

Machiavelli, N., 38
MacIver, Elizabeth, 58
Magnusson, Frances W., 67
Maintenance. See Facilities management
Management. See also Administration; Leadership; Presidents
  change role of, 77
  resource allocation and, 26–27
  SPRE initiative, 327–331
Mandated process:
  administrative restructuring/reengineering, 110
  categorization, administrative restructuring, 82
March, James, 66
Markets, revenue and, 149–150
Market volatility:
  endowment management, 175
  risk management, financial markets, 205
Massachusetts SPRE initiative, 317–319. See also SPRE initiative
Massy, William F., 16, 51, 55
McPherson, Michael S., 51, 55, 56
Mean-variance principle, investment theory, endowment management, 182
Meyerson, Joel W., 50–51, 64
Mills, D. Quinn, 106
Mintzberg, Henry, 66, 387
Modernization, facilities management, 243
Morrill, Justin, 382
Morrill Land Grant Act, 7, 23, 25, 231
Munitz, Barry, 15–16

National Policy Board, 312–313
Negroponte, Nicholas, 270
Net versus gross income, enrollment income, 152–154
Neubauer, F. Friedrich, 58

New Jersey College (Princeton University), 5
Notre Dame University, 7

Oedel, Laura P., 55, 56
Operating budget, endowment management, 174–175
Opportunity identification, administrative restructuring, 84–90
O'Reilly, B., 67
Organizational boundaries, change and, 77–78
Organizational culture:
  board effectiveness, 62
  change resistance and, 72
Organizational structure:
  administrative restructuring, implementation program, 92–93
  administrative restructuring/reengineering, 122–125
  information technology, 252. See also Information technology
  models
    in higher education, 54–56
    leadership and, 69
    stasis in, 101–102
Outcomes. See Student learning outcomes
Outsourcing, information technology and, 255. See also Information technology
Overholser, Keohane, 304

Patents, revenue, information resources, 135–136
Pell, Claiborne, 308
Performance appraisal:
  administrative restructuring, 84–85
  board effectiveness, 64
  measurement, SPRE initiative, student outcomes, 325–327
  merit pay and, human resource development, 223–224
Perrow, Charles, 56
Peterson, Marvin W., 52
Pfeffer, Jeffrey, 56
Philanthropic giving:
  corporate, 151–152, 164
  increase in, 131
  revenues, 150–151
  tax reform and, 104
Pinchot, Elizabeth, 107
Pinchot, Gifford, 107
Planning. See also Vision
  board effectiveness, 63, 64

facilities management and, 235
human resource development
  benefits of, 210–212
  model for, 212–213
  president role, 66
  revenue and, 134–135
Political factors:
  board effectiveness, 63
  change resistance and, 72
  education and, 6
  information technology, 256–260
  president role, 66
Porter, Randall, 55, 56
Preservation, facilities management and, 233–235
Presidents. See also Administration; Leadership; Management
  board relationship with, 61
  conceptions of, 66
  effectiveness and, 67
  vision and, 382. See also Vision
Prestige ladder, value and reward system, change strategy factor, 36
Price, access versus, higher education, current status of, 31–32
Princeton University (New Jersey College), 5
Prioritization:
  administrative restructuring, 81–82
  facilities management, 237
  implementation program, 90–91
Priority process:
  administrative restructuring/reengineering, 110
  categorization, administrative restructuring, 82
Private institutions. See also Public institutions
  financial aid increases at, 148
  financial markets, 190, 193
  governing boards of, 59, 63
  numbers of, 129, 147, 148
  organizational models, 56
Process. See Administrative restructuring/reengineering
Process analysis, administrative restructuring, opportunity identification and prioritization, 87
Process map:
  administrative restructuring/reengineering, 111–116
  Stanford University School of Medicine, 117–118, 119

Process navigator, administrative inefficiency and, 102–103
Productivity:
change and, 51
of faculty, leverage and constraint
mechanisms, change strategy factor, 36–37
information technology and, 253, 254.
See also Information technology
technology, change strategy factor,
40–42
Property taxes, tax exemption, 375–376
Proposition 13, tax reform and, 30
Prudent man rule, investment theory,
endowment management, 181
Prusak, Laurence, 259
Public accountability. See Accountability
Public institutions. See also Private
institutions
enrollments in, 129–130
financial markets, 190, 191, 193–194
governing boards of, 59, 63
organizational models, 56
Public opinion:
change and, 50
current status of, 29–30
higher education and, 8–9
SPRE initiative, 305–306
Public-private partnerships, higher education, current status of, 32

Quality movement, SPRE initiative, 324,
328. See also Total Quality Management (TQM)
Queen's College (Rutgers College), 5, 8
Quick wins, administrative restructuring,
opportunity identification and prioritization, 88

Reagan, Ronald, 307, 309, 384
Real estate, revenue resources, 140–141
Reauthorization of the Higher Education
Act of 1992, 304. See also SPRE
initiative
Recruitment:
facilities management, 242
foreign students, revenue, 149
of paying students, enrollment income,
157–161
Redeployment pool, administrative
restructuring, implementation program, 95
Regulation. See Government regulation

Reisman, David, 33
Religion, education and, 5, 6, 7, 54
Rensselaer, Stephen Van, 7
Reporting requirements, information technology, 256–260. See also Financial
reporting
Research:
SPRE initiative, 330–331
United Kingdom, 284–285, 286–290
Resource allocation, management and,
26–27
Restructuring. See Administrative restruc-
turing/reengineering
Revenue. See also Financial resources
administration role in, 133–134
alumni resources, 138–139
campus population resources, 139–140
cost cutting and, 148–149
decline in, 130–133, 147–148
discount minimization, 154–156
endowments, 150
enrollment income
gross versus net income, 152–154
optimization of net, 156–157
recruitment of paying students,
157–161
retaining students, 161
expansion of current sources, 141–144
foreign students, 149
fund-raising, 150–151
limits of, 151–152
future prospects, 161–165
information resources, 135–136
land and facilities, 140–141
legal corporations for, 134
markets and, 149–150
planning and, 134–135
programs generating, 133
teaching resources, 136–138
tuition and fees dependent, 150
Revolutionary War, education and, 6
Rhode Island College (Brown College), 5
Riesman, David, 390
Riley, Richard, 304
Risk, long-term enhancements, administrative restructuring, 89
Risk management, financial markets,
205–206
Roche, David, 202
Roman Catholic Church, education and, 7
Roosevelt, Franklin D., 24, 25, 32
Rosenzweig, Robert M., 12
Rowan, Henry, 150

Rudolph, Frederick, 5, 6, 7–8, 54
Rutgers College (Queen's College), 5, 8

Salancik, Gerald R., 56
Salaries. See Compensation and benefits
Schick, Allen, 74
Schmidt, Roland, 46
Science:
  education and, 7
  research universities and, 25
Sequencing, administrative restructuring,
    implementation program, 90–91
Service efforts and accomplishments,
    financial reporting, 351–353
Severance package, administrative restruc-
    turing, implementation program, 95
Sick buildings, facilities management, 247
Simsek, Hasan, 53, 70
Smith, Adam, 109, 383
Social factors:
  higher education and, 10, 13, 16
  public expectation and, 34–35
Social policy, investment and, 178–179
Space program, research universities and, 25
SPRE initiative, 303–332
  accreditation agencies, 313
  concerns about, 321–322
  fourteen standards, 315–317
  government regulation/government aid
    linkage, 309–311
  Higher Education Amendments of 1992,
    311–312
  independence and, 331–332
  Massachusetts experience, 317–319
  National Policy Board, 312–313
  overview of, 303–305
  postsecondary review entities, 313–314
  predictions of long-term effects of,
    327–331
  regulatory climate, 305–309
    accreditation process, 308
    Department of Education (DOE), 307
    legislative response, 308–309
    public opinion, 305–306
    student loan defaults, 306–307
  standards development process, 315
  student outcomes, 319–327
    consumerism, 324
    performance measurement debate,
      325–327
    quality movement, 324–325
    regulatory and accreditation pressure,
      323
  triggered institutions, 314–315
Sputnik, 24

Staffing, administrative restructuring,
    implementation program, 92–93
Stampen, Jacob O., 50
Stanford University School of Medicine
    experience, 116–125
  fragmentation implications, 120–122
  generally, 116–117
  organizational construct, 122–125
  perceptions, 118, 120
  process map, 117–118, 119
Statement of activities, 346–348
Statement of cash flows, 348–349
Statement of financial position, 345–346
Sterling, Wallace, 382
Strategic alliances, change and, 77–78
Strategic dimension. See Planning
Structural/managerial analysis, adminis-
    trative restructuring, opportunity
    identification and prioritization, 86
Student aid. See Financial aid
Student learning outcomes, SPRE initia-
    tive, 319–327. See also SPRE
    initiative
Student loans. See also Financial aid
  defaults
    Department of Education, 307
    SPRE initiative, 306–307
    Grove City College case, 310
Student recruitment. See Recruitment
Student Right-to-Know and Campus
    Security Act of 1991, 324

Tactical asset allocation models, invest-
    ment theory, endowment manage-
    ment, 182
Tax considerations, human resource
    development, 224–226
Tax exemption, 363–377
  compensation, 372–373
  congressional oversight, 370–372
  Coordinated Examination Program,
    369–370
  current environment, 366–367
  Form 900 revision, 367–369
  new facility financing, 373–375
  overview of, 363–364
  property taxes, 375–376
  scrutiny of, increased, 364–365
  technology transfer, 376–377
  theoretical basis for, 365–366
Tax reform:
  financial markets, 187
  higher education, current status of,
    30–31
  philanthropic giving and, 104

Tax Reform Act of 1986, 187, 373
Tax-sheltered annuity, 224–225
Taylor, Barbara E., 61, 62, 63
Technology:
  change and, 40–42, 51, 76
  change resistance and, 72
  facilities management, 244–245
  human resource development, benefits
    of, 210–211
  information technology, 251–275. See
    also Information technology
Technology analysis, administrative
    restructuring, opportunity identi-
    fication and prioritization, 87–88
Technology transfer:
  administrative restructuring, implemen-
    tation program, 92
  tax exemption, 376–377
Telecommunications:
  facilities management, 245
  financial markets, future prospects,
    201–204
Terman, Fred, 382
Tichy, Noel M., 72
Tocqueville, Alexis de, 390
Tolbert, Pamela S., 53
Total Quality Management (TQM):
  administrative restructuring, 91, 105,
    117, 121, 122. See also Administra-
    tive restructuring/reengineering
  higher education and, 34, 71
  information technology and, 253, 261,
    263
  student outcomes, SPRE initiative, 324
  vision and, 383
Tracking systems, administrative restruc-
    turing/reengineering, 108
Training:
  administrative restructuring, implemen-
    tation program, 92
  human resource development, benefits
    of, 211–212
Transformational leadership, described, 70
Trustees. See also Governing boards
  executive search and reward, 42
  roles of, governing boards, 59–62
Tuition and fees:
  increases in, 9, 10, 11, 104, 131, 132, 155
  revenue dependency on, 150

Ulrich, David O., 51, 52, 53, 67, 69, 70,
    71, 72, 73, 74
United Kingdom, 279–302
  degrees awarded in, 283–284
  higher education in, 15

historical context, 281–282
income sources, 286–294
  private, 292–294
  research, 286–290
  teaching, 290–292
management changes, 294–298
  financial management, 295–296
  generally, 294–295
  government and, 295
  individual responsibility, 296–297
  professionalism, 297–298
overview of, 279–280
private funding, 286
public funding, 283–286
  generally, 283
  research, 284–285
  teaching, 285–286
teaching quality and standards, 298–302
U.S. Department of Education, 307
U.S. Supreme Court, 310, 311
University movement, 24
University of Pennsylvania, 23
U.S. News & World Report, 8–9

Value and reward system, change strat-
    egy factor, 36
Vision, 381–390. See also Planning
  articulation of, leadership role, 73
  components of, 387–388
  fallacies about, 388–390
  imperative of, 390
  need for, 381–382
  pressures for, 385–387
  problem of, 382–385

Wages. See Compensation and benefits
Waterman, R. H., 74
Whetten, David A., 67
Willard, Emma Hart, 382
William and Mary College, 5, 6, 8
Wingspread Group, findings of, 10, 11, 12
Winston, Gordon C., 51, 55, 56
Wofford, Harris, 308
Women's colleges, history of, 7
World War II, 24
Wright, Andrea R., 9n8

Yale College, 5, 6
Yield curve, financial markets, 198–201
Young, Michael, 385

Zammuto, Raymond F., 52
Zemsky, Robert, 16, 55, 56
Zuboff, Shoshana, 270